Clark Public Library
303 Westfield Ave.
Clark, NJ 07066
(732)388-5999

NEW JERSEY COUNCIL
FOR THE HUMANITIES

A SECESSION CRISIS ENIGMA

A SECESSION CRISIS ENIGMA

Daniel W. Crofts

WILLIAM HENRY HURLBERT AND
"THE DIARY OF A PUBLIC MAN"

LOUISIANA STATE UNIVERSITY PRESS

BATON ROUGE

Published by Louisiana State University Press
Copyright © 2010 by Louisiana State University Press
All rights reserved
Manufactured in the United States of America
FIRST PRINTING

DESIGNER: Amanda McDonald Scallan
TYPEFACES: Minion, text; Rosewood Fill, display
TYPESETTER: J. Jarrett Engineering, Inc.
PRINTER AND BINDER: Thomson-Shore, Inc.

Parts of this book first appeared as "A Fresh Look at 'The Diary of a Public Man,'" *Civil War History* 55 (December 2009): 442–68.

Library of Congress Cataloging-in-Publication Data
Crofts, Daniel W.
    A secession crisis enigma : William Henry Hurlbert and "The diary of a public man" / Daniel W. Crofts.
        p. cm.
    Includes index.
    ISBN 978-0-8071-3591-4 (cloth : alk. paper) 1. Diary of a public man. 2. Hurlbert, William Henry, 1827–1895.
3. Secession—United States—History—Sources. 4. Fort Sumter (Charleston, S.C.)—Siege, 1861—Sources.
5. United States—Politics and government—1857–1861—Sources. 6. United States—Politics and government—
1861–1865—Sources. 7. Lincoln, Abraham, 1809–1865. 8. Diaries—Authorship—Case studies. 9. United States—
Historiography—Miscellanea. 10. United States—History—Errors, inventions, etc. I. Title.
    E440.5.C94 2010
    973.7'31—dc22

                                                                                                    2009035582

The paper in this book meets the guidelines for permanence and durability of the Committee on Production Guidelines for Book Longevity of the Council on Library Resources.♾

For John P. Karras and
Thomas T. Allsen

CONTENTS

Illustrations follow page 152.

PREVIEW

In 1879 the *North American Review* published "The Diary of a Public Man" in four separate monthly installments. The Diary's entries were dated eighteen years earlier, between December 28, 1860, and March 15, 1861, the desperate weeks just before the start of the Civil War. Although the *NAR*'s editor concealed the diarist's identity and deleted the names of some persons mentioned in the text, the Diary appeared to offer verbatim accounts of behind-the-scenes discussions at the very highest levels during the greatest crisis the country had yet faced. Its pithy quotations attributed to the key principals—Stephen A. Douglas, William H. Seward, Charles Sumner, and especially Abraham Lincoln—have become part of the folklore of American historical writing.[1]

This book will untangle the Diary's heretofore hidden history. To anticipate, the document was a memoir rather than a genuine diary. It was composed after the fact, not in 1861. And the diarist was a fictional construct—no such person ever existed. The Diary nonetheless was rooted in reality. Plenty of its inside information meets the historical test. The person who created the Diary—and who thereby posed what Jacques Barzun and Henry F. Graff called the "most gigantic" problem of uncertain authorship in American historical writing—proves to have been a New York newspaperman, William Henry Hurlbert. His name will not be familiar—hardly anyone today ever has heard of this eccentric nineteenth-century genius. Sic transit gloria mundi. Acclaimed at his height as "the most brilliant talent of the New York press" and "the only artist among American journalists," Hurlbert once commanded attention.[2]

Hurlbert's memoir-cum-diary cannot be dismissed as an antiquarian curi-

1. "The Diary of a Public Man: Unpublished Passages of the Secret History of the American Civil War," *North American Review* 129 (Aug. 1879): 125–40; (Sept. 1879): 259–73; (Oct. 1879): 375–88; (Nov. 1879): 484–96.

2. Jacques Barzun and Henry F. Graff, *The Modern Researcher* (4th ed.; San Diego: Harcourt Brace Jovanovich, 1985), 135–42, quotations on 135–36; Eugene Benson, "W. H. Hurlbut," *The Galaxy* (Jan. 1869): 30–34.

osity, and a faked one at that. It illuminates a uniquely perplexing interval of political breakdown, when the participants themselves hardly understood what was happening. And it offers several striking glimpses of the central player in the drama. Strictly speaking, the three alleged meetings between Lincoln and the diarist never happened—keep in mind that there was no diarist. But the diarist didn't simply imagine what he recounted. Instead, he must have had ways to find out about confidential conversations involving the incoming president— and other luminaries.

Most of the episodes mentioned in the Diary took place immediately before and after Inauguration Day—March 4, 1861. In late February and March peace hung by a thread. Seven states in the Deep South claimed to have become an independent nation, the Confederate States of America, and had begun to form a separate government. Lincoln could not accept secession. He specified in his inaugural address that the Union remained both "perpetual" and "unbroken."[3] Yet he hesitated to challenge the Confederacy with armed force. Anyone who attempts to understand what was going through the new president's mind as he took office is bound to be attracted to "The Diary of a Public Man." Lincoln expressed himself in a "quaint and rather forcible way," often using a homely expression or telling a little story to make a point. The diarist judged him "crafty and sensible" and suspected that he was "more troubled by the outlook than he thought it discreet to show." At the inaugural ceremonies, Lincoln appeared "pale and very nervous." Three days later the diarist was "struck and pained by the haggard, worn look of his face." The new president's responsibilities plainly weighed on him.[4]

"The Diary of a Public Man" cuts against the grain of modern preconceptions. Lincoln has assumed such mythic proportions that the story of his life often is transformed into hagiography. Even though he once insisted that he had not controlled events, but rather that events had "controlled me," his more zealous celebrants rarely accept this striking instance of presidential modesty.[5] They not only acclaim Lincoln's uniquely strong capabilities and his gift for responding effectively to challenges—and who would disagree?—but also cele-

---

3. Roy P. Basler, ed., *The Collected Works of Abraham Lincoln* (9 vols.; New Brunswick: Rutgers Univ. Press, 1953–55), 4:264–65.

4. These quotations are from the Diary. See the appendix, 231–32, 254, 262.

5. Lincoln to Albert G. Hodges, April 4, 1864, in Basler, *Collected Works of Lincoln*, 7:281–83.

brate his almost superhuman prescience. Their Lincoln knew in advance that he was destined to rebuild the Union and abolish slavery. He had his eyes fixed on distant goals.[6]

The Diary returns us to the troubled winter and spring of 1860–61. This interval was not a time when the prescient Lincoln was much in evidence. His efforts to fill the two military slots in his cabinet show that he hardly anticipated a violent outcome to the political crisis. To reassure the South of his peaceful intentions, he offered the post of secretary of the navy to John A. Gilmer, a North Carolina congressman. For two months the job was his for the taking. But Gilmer finally declined it—less confident than Lincoln that the peace would hold—and once the war started he sided reluctantly with the Confederacy.[7] The consolation prize in the cabinet was secretary of war. It went by default to Pennsylvania senator Simon Cameron, widely regarded as corrupt or incompetent—or both. He needed to be appeased because he had been passed over for the more consequential Treasury portfolio. Before the year was out, he was exiled to Russia.[8]

Lincoln's words in early 1861 were consistent with his deeds. His inaugural address appealed for "a peaceful solution of the national troubles, and the restoration of fraternal sympathies and affections." He promised to accept a constitutional amendment protecting slavery in the states where it then was legal. In historian David M. Potter's view, Lincoln "groped and blundered" as he began to realize that the seceding states were in earnest. Potter cautioned against the familiar but misleading image of Lincoln as "a man following the well-marked path of destiny to abolish slavery." Instead, Potter wisely observed, Lincoln was "reluctant to become an Emancipator"—and "the conflict which immortalized him was a conflict which he had believed he could avert."[9]

6. I have in mind especially Doris Kearns Goodwin, *Team of Rivals: The Political Genius of Abraham Lincoln* (New York: Simon & Schuster, 2005), which has attracted a wide readership and exercised a quite extraordinary political influence. See also Harold Holzer, *Lincoln President-Elect: Abraham Lincoln and the Great Secession Winter, 1860–1861* (New York: Simon & Schuster, 2008).

7. Daniel W. Crofts, *Reluctant Confederates: Upper South Unionists in the Secession Crisis* (Chapel Hill: Univ. of North Carolina Press, 1989), 34–36, 221–29, 245–47.

8. William E. Baringer, *A House Dividing: Lincoln as President-Elect* (Springfield, Ill.: Abraham Lincoln Association, 1945), 124–36, 155–89, 318–21.

9. Basler, *Collected Works of Lincoln,* 4:266, 270; David M. Potter, *Lincoln and His Party in the Secession Crisis* (New Haven: Yale Univ. Press, 1942), 315. This book was reprinted in 1962 by Yale

The time may be right to give the Diary a fresh look. In recent years scholars have used unconventional sources to provide insights into Lincoln's personality and career. A revolution in Lincoln scholarship has been spearheaded by historian Douglas L. Wilson, who breathed life into oral testimony collected after Lincoln's death by his law partner, William Herndon. On the face of it, recollections gathered decades later from those who knew Lincoln when they were young would appear suspect. But Wilson's sensible approach to using such evidence now is generally accepted.[10] Somewhat similarly, historian Don E. Fehrenbacher capped his distinguished career by assessing thousands of examples of alleged Lincoln hearsay. Taking into account the vagaries of such evidence, Fehrenbacher devised a system that attempted to rate the plausibility of words attributed by others to Lincoln.[11]

Historian Michael Burlingame's recent encyclopedic two-volume biography of Lincoln explicitly builds on the foundations erected by Wilson and Fehrenbacher. During two decades of research and writing, Burlingame also unearthed and published rich veins of material written by Lincoln's two observant young secretaries, John G. Nicolay and John Hay.[12] His labors have afforded Burlingame "a nose for what 'smells' authentically Lincolnian." He thereby concurs with Wilson in rehabilitating the materials collected by Herndon. And Burlingame goes even further than Fehrenbacher by placing quotation marks around recollected words of Lincoln's that appear reliable. Even though such language

University Press with a new preface by Potter, and in 1995 by Louisiana State University Press with both Potter's 1962 preface and a new preface that I wrote.

10. Douglas L. Wilson and Rodney O. Davis, eds., *Herndon's Informants: Letters, Interviews, and Statements about Abraham Lincoln* (Urbana: Univ. of Illinois Press, 1998); Douglas L. Wilson, *Lincoln Before Washington: New Perspectives on the Illinois Years* (Urbana: Univ. of Illinois Press, 1997); Douglas L. Wilson, *Honor's Voice: The Transformation of Abraham Lincoln* (New York: Knopf, 1998).

11. Don E. Fehrenbacher and Virginia Fehrenbacher, eds., *Recollected Words of Abraham Lincoln* (Stanford: Stanford Univ. Press, 1996).

12. Michael Burlingame, ed., *An Oral History of Abraham Lincoln: John G. Nicolay's Interviews and Essays* (Carbondale: Southern Illinois Univ. Press, 1996); Michael Burlingame and John R. Turner Ettlinger, eds., *Inside Lincoln's White House: The Complete Civil War Diary of John Hay* (Carbondale: Southern Illinois Univ. Press, 1997); Michael Burlingame, ed., *Lincoln's Journalist: John Hay's Anonymous Writings for the Press, 1860–1864* (Carbondale: Southern Illinois Univ. Press, 1998); Michael Burlingame, ed., *With Lincoln in the White House: Letters, Memoranda, and Other Writings of John G. Nicolay, 1860–1865* (Carbondale: Southern Illinois Univ. Press, 2000).

"may not be strictly accurate," Burlingame decided, it conveys the flavor of Lincoln's "direct discourse."[13]

Neither Wilson nor Fehrenbacher nor Burlingame uses "The Diary of a Public Man." Why they did not will become apparent in the pages that follow. Though once almost universally quoted, the Diary has certain suspicious aspects that have raised yellow flags. Upon hearing that I was studying the Diary, one archivist quipped that he thought the Public Man had been "buried with a stake through his heart." But I think the Diary has been scuttled prematurely. In the 1940s, just as professional opinion was about to turn against the Diary, David Potter insisted that it had substance, even if its will-o'-the-wisp author remained inscrutable. Potter recognized that it must have been written by someone "who possessed an authoritative personal knowledge of affairs at the time of secession." Time and again, its accuracy had been corroborated. These insights from the most profound and original scholar of the crisis that led to war ought not be disregarded lightly.[14]

Here is what the reader may expect in the pages that follow. First I shall frame "The Diary of a Public Man" more fully, and show why it long was considered part of the historical canon. Next, I shall explain why the alleged diary fell from favor—but how it has managed to live on in the writings of many modern scholars. Then I shall address the core question of authorship—how the Diary came to be attributed to someone who had a hand in it but who didn't do the writing, and why we now must conclude that William Henry Hurlbert wielded the deftly concealed pen.

Then I shall assess the other core question regarding the Diary—authenticity. What results is a paradoxical verdict. The Diary was created from scratch by a person who could not have been a legitimate diarist. Yet the materials he worked with prove to have been so genuine that the Diary has to be taken seriously despite its seeming disqualifications. The diarist wrote confidently about many matters that were secret at the time the Diary appeared.

Perforce this book also must examine Hurlbert's life and career. I shall attempt to explain how this audacious impostor masterminded the successful

13. Michael Burlingame, *Abraham Lincoln: A Life* (2 vols.; Baltimore: Johns Hopkins Univ. Press, 2008), 2:839–41.

14. David M. Potter, review of *The Diary of a Public Man, and a Page of Political Correspondence, Stanton to Buchanan*, ed. F. Lauriston Bullard, in *Journal of Southern History* 13 (Feb. 1947): 118–19.

ruse. And I shall puzzle through his possible motives for undertaking such an improbable and risky venture. Finally, I shall return to matters briefly touched in this preview—how the Diary impinges on Civil War–era historiography.

You might start by reading "The Diary of a Public Man." It appears as an appendix to this book. You will find that the Diary reads well. Its author had a knack for putting words onto paper. By reading the Diary, you also may better assess what I have written about it.

1

DECIPHERING "THE DIARY OF A PUBLIC MAN"

From its first paragraph to its last, "The Diary of a Public Man" recounts the twists and turns as two successive presidents, the repudiated James Buchanan and the untested Abraham Lincoln, attempted to figure out what to do about Fort Sumter. This besieged federal fortress was (and is) located on an artificial island at the mouth of Charleston Harbor, South Carolina. Tourists standing today at the Battery can see Sumter, low on the horizon and about four miles distant. They also can venture out for a visit on convenient excursion boats.

On the night of December 26, 1860, Major Robert Anderson secretly transported his small contingent of U.S. soldiers across the water to Sumter from Fort Moultrie. His discretionary authority allowed him to move if he suspected that he might be attacked. Secessionist hotheads had started behaving menacingly near Moultrie, which lacked any fortifications to deter them. Sumter, a mile offshore from Moultrie, appeared to offer a more defensible refuge. By averting hostilities, Anderson tried to buy time. He knew that the situation in Charleston Harbor had the potential to trigger civil war. He hoped that neither Buchanan nor Lincoln wished to rush into that cataclysm.[1]

The first Diary entry, dated December 28, 1860, detailed a long conversation with James L. Orr, a commissioner from South Carolina, which had proclaimed its independence from the Union just the week before. A former Speaker of the U.S. House of Representatives, Orr wanted Buchanan to countermand Anderson, whose actions were being trumpeted throughout the South as evidence that the federal government intended "to coerce South Carolina." Were the country to plunge "into a horrible civil strife," Orr predicted, a divided North would face a united South. Orr impressed the diarist as "honestly trying to make the best of what he felt to be a wretched business, and that at heart he was as good a Union man as anybody in Connecticut or New York."[2]

---

1. W. A. Swanberg, *First Blood: The Story of Fort Sumter* (New York: Charles Scribner's Sons, 1957), 34–108; Maury Klein, *Days of Defiance* (New York: Random House, 1997), 151–7.

2. Quotations in this paragraph are from the Diary, pp. 219, 221 herein. Subsequent page references will be given parenthetically in the text.

The diarist also was close to Senator Judah P. Benjamin of Louisiana, one of the most respected Deep South leaders, whom he considered "able and clear-headed" and blessed with "a rare and lucid intelligence" (225, 237). Benjamin initially defended secession as a gambit. It would show "the conservative masses of the Northern people" that they must accept a radical revision of the Constitution (225). But Benjamin's "silvery but truly satanic speech" in early February, as he resigned his Senate seat, convinced the diarist that secession had set in motion disruptive forces that had the potential to trigger a civil war (232). The diarist sadly concluded that Benjamin had allowed himself to be manipulated by those who were "not to be compared with him intellectually" (225).

The same diarist who was in direct touch with leading Southerners and disinclined to assign them full blame for the crisis also knew their polar opposite, Charles Sumner, the Republican senator from Massachusetts and a living symbol of Northern contempt for the slave system and its defenders. Although the diarist "never affected an admiration" for Sumner (246), the latter allegedly sought him out in hopes of using his presumed influence with Lincoln. The diarist discovered that Lincoln likewise found Sumner overbearing: "I have never had much to do with bishops down where we live," the diarist quoted the president-elect as saying, "but do you know, Sumner is just my idea of a bishop" (240).

Stephen A. Douglas of Illinois, the leading Northern Democrat who narrowly defeated Lincoln in 1858 to retain his Senate seat but then lost to him in the 1860 presidential election, shared the diarist's hope that Lincoln would preserve the peace. "A collision and civil war will be fatal to his Administration and to him," Douglas exclaimed, "and he knows it—he knows it" (222). According to the diarist, Lincoln was receptive to overtures from Douglas. Lincoln wanted to keep Northern Democrats "close to the Administration on the naked Union issue" (231). Nothing better symbolized the rapport between the two long-time Illinois rivals than an incident reported by the diarist on Inauguration Day. As Lincoln prepared to speak, he scarcely could find room for his hat on the "miserable little rickety table" that had been provided for the occasion. Douglas reached forward, "took it with a smile and held it during the delivery of the address." This spontaneous gesture "was a trifling act, but a symbolical one, and not to be forgotten, and it attracted much attention all around me" (254).

The diarist and Douglas both pinned their hopes for a peaceful settlement on William Henry Seward, who emerged as Lincoln's secretary of state after having lost the Republican presidential nomination in 1860. Although his long public career as governor and senator from New York earned him a somewhat undeserved reputation for stigmatizing the South, Seward attempted during the secession winter to find a middle ground that would preserve the peace and hold the Union together. He became, in the eyes of the diarist, "the one man in whose ability and moderation the conservative people at the North have most confidence" (244). During the early days of Lincoln's presidency, Seward appeared to gain the upper hand. He dispatched a messenger to Richmond, the diarist noted, to assure antisecession leaders in the Virginia Convention that the new administration would not risk war by trying to hold Sumter. He received word back that "the quiet evacuation of Fort Sumter" would enable "Union men" to control Virginia (270, 266). The last diary entry on March 15, 1861, anticipated that a federal withdrawal from Sumter soon would occur.

The Diary conveys a strong sense of on-the-spot immediacy, reinforced by the diarist's excellent ear. He wrote as if he were seated next to the principals and holding an audio recorder. Consider his accounts of conversations with Douglas, Sumner, and Seward.

Douglas, whose large head, broad shoulders, and powerful torso were mounted incongruously on stubby legs—hence his nickname, the "Little Giant"—characteristically spoke in a forceful, direct, pugnacious manner, which the diarist captured perfectly. He quoted Douglas as saying, just after his rival reached Washington, that Lincoln "has not yet got out of Springfield, sir": "He has Springfield people with him. He has his wife with him. He does not know that he is President-elect of the United States, sir. He does not see that the shadow he casts is any bigger now than it was last year. It will not take him long to find it out when he has got established in the White House. But he has not found it out yet" (234).[3]

The diarist reported that Sumner was much more exercised about the possibility of "a corrupt conspiracy to preserve the Union" than he was about the danger of war. He cared only that the Republican Party and the Lincoln administration act "supremely in the interests of freedom" (249). This too captured both the outlook of the Massachusetts senator and his way of expressing himself.[4] All today would agree that slavery disgraced the United States in the eyes of the world, and that Sumner's revulsion at the slave system placed him on high moral ground. But by disdaining all effort to maintain a Union in which slavery

3. Robert W. Johannsen, *Stephen A. Douglas* (New York: Oxford Univ. Press, 1973), 498–99, 659–60.

4. David Donald, *Charles Sumner and the Coming of the Civil War* (New York: Alfred A. Knopf, 1960), 365–88.

was legal in almost half the states, the tall, austere, self-righteous senator exasperated most of his colleagues.

The diarist observed Seward's "lively, almost . . . boisterous" optimism during the agonies of the secession winter without fully understanding what lay behind it (264). In fact Seward was as troubled as anyone, indeed more troubled—because he recognized sooner than most Republicans the gravity of the crisis. But the New Yorker was a master of pretense. Trapped between intransigent Southerners who had set in motion forces they no longer could control and intransigent Northerners who saw no reason to concede anything, Seward dissembled. He deliberately adopted a jaunty façade—"chipper as a lark," cheerfully swearing that "everything was going on admirably," and predicting that the crisis soon would pass. When the diarist reported on March 12 that reassuring news from Virginia had put Seward "in unusually good spirits, even for him," the Diary caught one of the few moments when the New Yorker's cheerful countenance may have been genuine (270). Having "whipped Mason and Hunter in their own state," Seward is reported elsewhere to have said, he dared to hope that he could also "crush out Davis and Toombs"—if the people in the Deep South would "rebel against their leaders."[5]

Even the casual reader will find the Diary accessible and the narrative lively. When Douglas "launched out into a kind of tirade on Mr. Buchanan's duplicity and cowardice," the diarist "tried to check the torrent" but succeeded only "in pouring oil on the flames" (222). The diarist excoriated Maryland secessionists for sending word to Francis P. Blair, the prominent former Jacksonian Democrat turned Republican, that "a tree had been picked out for him in the woods." Such threats from Blair's "amiable neighbors" would only boomerang: "Much as I dislike the Blairs, and dread their influence on the new Administration,"

5. Frederic Bancroft, *The Life of William H. Seward* (2 vols.; New York: Harper and Brothers, 1899–1900), 2:109–110; Daniel W. Crofts, *Reluctant Confederates: Upper South Unionists in the Secession Crisis* (Chapel Hill: Univ. of North Carolina Press, 1989), 216–20, 240, 244; Henry Adams to Charles Francis Adams, Jr., Dec. 9, 1860, Jan. 26, 1861, in J. C. Levenson et al., eds., *The Letters of Henry Adams* (3 vols.; Cambridge: Belknap Press of Harvard University Press, 1982), 1:204–5, 225. Virginia's two U.S. senators, James M. Mason and Robert M. T. Hunter, stood high among the power elite of Southern Democrats in Congress. But both had risked their power, perhaps fatally, by siding with their state's secessionist minority in January and February 1861. Jefferson Davis of Mississippi and Robert Toombs of Georgia, one a Democrat and the other a former Whig, gave the Deep South a one-two punch in the Senate. The two had resigned their seats in time to become, respectively, the president and the secretary of state of the just-formed Confederacy.

the diarist fumed, the carrying out of this "atrocious threat" would have the likely effect of making Blair's son, Montgomery Blair, "the next President of the United States" (257).

The diarist's secondhand account of an interview on March 2 between Lincoln and some of Seward's "New York men," who did not want Salmon P. Chase appointed to the cabinet, depicts the visitors listening "quite agog with suppressed expectations" as the president-elect appeared to be bending in their direction and gave "the company time to drink in all he had said." But Lincoln then deftly punctured their balloon, announcing that if he had to revise his preferred cabinet roster, then Seward rather than Chase would go. At that juncture, the diarist's informant "told me you could have knocked him or any man in the room down with a feather" (244–45). The diarist thus had an uncommon ability to grasp the essence of a situation. His account is punctuated with embedded quotations that convey immediacy.[6]

Occasionally, the Diary's daily entries record only a single significant conversation or episode. More often, however, the diarist summarizes conversations with several persons, and he frequently includes his own reactions, opinions, or observations. He reports encountering people on the street, staying out late, receiving mail, and being "called out by a card" from a visitor (257). At points the diarist almost talks to himself—he heard a story "so characteristic of all the persons so concerned in it that I must jot it down" (236). The Diary therefore reads like a diary. Even if the diarist had a facile pen—and this one certainly did—a diary needs to read as if it were indeed written at the end of a day. Some evidences of haste are apparent, exactly as one might expect.[7] These various characteristics all convey the impression that the Diary is genuine.

Over three decades ago I first read "The Diary of a Public Man." At the time, I was laying the groundwork for a book about three key Upper South states—

6. Chase, who was both principled and ambitious, frightened those who hoped to defuse the crisis. The former Ohio governor was regarded as someone who would try to stymie Seward's Union-saving schemes.

7. For example, words in close proximity often are repeated. On pages 243–44 there are five duplications of "worse" or "worst," on pages 261–62 there are three duplications of "great" or "greatly," on page 264 there are three duplications of "folly," and on pages 268–69 there are three duplications of "entirely." In many instances words are used twice on the same page and even in the same paragraph; for example, the duplication on pages 235–36 of "assertion" and on pages 263–64 of the words "disturbed" and "uncouth."

Virginia, North Carolina, and Tennessee—as their citizens wrestled with the awful dilemma posed by the action of the Lower South. Large popular majorities in all three states rejected secession and hoped instead for peaceful restoration of the Union. Leading moderates in Virginia, North Carolina, and Tennessee, knowing that war would reverse the Union advantage in their states and fearing that the Upper South would likely bear the brunt of any fighting, attempted to mediate between the Deep South and the federal government. Upper South Unionists judged that Lincoln's election had thrown the Deep South into an ill-considered panic, and they hoped for a sober second thought. They insisted that war would transform North-South estrangement into permanent hatred and destroy any chance for reunion.[8]

I was both intrigued and baffled by the Diary. The author plainly knew a great deal about what was going on behind closed doors in Washington, D.C. He accurately depicted the anxieties of those who feared war. He also shared the widespread (and incorrect) assumption as of mid-March that Lincoln had decided against trying to hold Sumter. But who was the diarist? And was the Diary what it appeared to be, or could it somehow have been concocted after the fact? I knew that questions about the Diary's authenticity had been raised and that the identity of its anonymous author remained elusive. Accordingly, I decided against using it as a source for the book that I then was writing.

More recently, however, I decided to give the Diary a closer look, to see whether its mysteries could be unlocked. Having watched the United States go to war in Iraq in 2003 with its eyes closed, I was reminded that nothing is more unpredictable than the outcome of armed conflict. Rarely do wars conform to some sort of advance script. At no point in American history was the choice between peace and war more difficult than in early 1861. Would war reunite the United States? Or would it permanently divide North and South, and perhaps shatter the republic into irreconcilable fragments? Nobody knew. Of course, we do know today, as we have since 1865, that war ultimately brought Southern independence to an abrupt end, albeit at a high price in blood and treasure. We know, too, that war ended American slavery. With hindsight, reunion and abolition together appear to justify the war's high costs.

I found that from the Diary's first publication in 1879 until the late 1940s, most historians considered it authentic. They kept trying to identify the author,

---

8. Crofts, *Reluctant Confederates*.

thereby continuing a chase that began the moment it first appeared, and they were frustrated by their inability to pinpoint anyone. Leading scholars of the late nineteenth and early twentieth centuries such as James Ford Rhodes, Frederic Bancroft, and Allen Johnson each made use of it. Rhodes and Bancroft corresponded with each other about the diarist's possible identity. "I hope that we can yet solve this mystery," Bancroft wrote to Rhodes in 1896, "for, I do not believe the diary was bogus."[9]

Their successors continued to wrestle with the mystery. In 1927 James G. Randall, who would become the premier Lincoln scholar of his generation, thought he had identified the diarist. Some of the material in the Diary can be read to suggest that the author was a U.S. senator. By the process of elimination, Randall concluded that the diarist had to be Vermont's Jacob Collamer. Randall was reassured to learn that another historian, Irving S. Kull, had reached the same conclusion independently. Randall drafted an essay identifying Collamer, which was accepted for publication in the *American Historical Review.* He assumed that the Diary was genuine and that its contents "had not been tampered with." He shared Kull's view that it had "every ring of genuineness." But Randall's evidence was circumstantial, and he still worried that the Diary somehow might be a forgery. Then another scholar studying the Diary, Frank Maloy Anderson, sent Randall a devastating letter challenging his case for Collamer. In the end, Randall decided against publishing the essay. A decade later he cautioned that the Diary's author remained unidentified, and that its authenticity was unproven. He reiterated his reservations in his subsequent history of Lincoln's presidency.[10]

Despite Randall's misgivings, the other giants in the profession in the 1930s and 1940s—most notably David Potter, Allan Nevins, and Roy Franklin Nichols—continued to use the Diary. Of the three, Potter best explained why he chose to credit the mysterious document. The Diary was published before "the

9. Frederic Bancroft to James Ford Rhodes, Aug. 19, 1896, James Ford Rhodes Papers, Massachusetts Historical Society.

10. James G. Randall to J. Franklin Jameson, Nov. 2, Dec. 22, 1927, Jameson to Randall, June 3, Nov. 7, 1927, Irving S. Kull to Randall, Feb. 1, 11, 1928, Randall to Frank Maloy Anderson, Jan. 15, 1928, Anderson to Randall, Mar. 7, 1928, Randall's typescript essay sent to Kull and Anderson in January 1928, in James G. Randall Papers, University of Illinois Archives, University of Illinois at Urbana-Champaign; James G. Randall, "Has the Lincoln Theme Been Exhausted?" *American Historical Review* 41 (1936): 277–79; James G. Randall, *Lincoln the President: Springfield to Gettysburg* (2 vols.; New York: Dodd, Mead & Co., 1945), 1:295.

great flood of Civil War memoirs and histories which began in the 1880's," Potter observed. This "ceaseless flow" had repeatedly corroborated the Diary's accuracy and apparent reliability. But the Diary remained for Potter a "paradoxical" enigma, because nobody had been able to "unmask the diarist." He quipped that historians always quoted the Public Man's "lively passages," even when they questioned his existence.[11]

The Diary thus remained part of the historical domain. It was published as a book in 1946 by F. Lauriston Bullard, with a foreword by Carl Sandburg, the much-admired interpreter of Lincoln. Both acknowledged the problems that troubled Randall, but each leaned toward seeing the Diary as real. If "by any possibility" the diarist "invented the lines and fabricated the speeches he put within quotation marks," Sandburg observed, "he must be credited not only with an extraordinary fertile imagination but an even more extraordinary familiarity with the American language of that day." Bullard likewise knew that all efforts to identify the diarist had failed, but he held out hope that the Diary would ultimately be judged "an authentic contemporaneous report." Should it somehow prove to be a "fake," then the person who wrote it had committed "an—almost—perfect crime."[12]

In 1948, Frank Maloy Anderson published *The Mystery of "A Public Man": A Historical Detective Story.*[13] Anderson, a tall, spare, blue-eyed, silver-haired Midwesterner who had done graduate work at Harvard and spent most of his teaching career at Dartmouth, was part of the pioneering generation of professionally trained historians.[14] Twenty years before he had dispatched the torpedo that caused Randall to withdraw his article. Anderson's book posed the two key questions regarding this remarkable document—Who was this diarist? And was the Diary genuine? Anderson's conclusions were buttressed by decades of his-

11. David M. Potter, review of *The Diary of a Public Man, and a Page of Political Correspondence, Stanton to Buchanan,* ed. F. Lauriston Bullard, in *Journal of Southern History* 13 (Feb. 1947): 118–19; David M. Potter, *Lincoln and His Party in the Secession Crisis* (New Haven: Yale Univ. Press, 1942, 1962), 385.

12. F. Lauriston Bullard, ed., *The Diary of a Public Man, and a Page of Political Correspondence, Stanton to Buchanan* (New Brunswick: Rutgers Univ. Press, 1946), quotations on vii–viii, 23.

13. Frank Maloy Anderson, *The Mystery of "A Public Man": A Historical Detective Story* (Minneapolis: Univ. of Minnesota Press, 1948).

14. *The Dartmouth,* Oct. 1, 1940, May 25, 1941, copies in Frank Maloy Anderson Papers, Box 1, Library of Congress.

torical detective work. After his death, all his research materials were deposited at the Library of Congress, so that one may examine the evidence and his assessment of it.

Anderson decided that the diarist was Samuel Ward (1814–1884). Born to wealth and prominence in New York City, Ward was a gifted mathematician and linguist who completed his undergraduate work at Columbia at the age of seventeen. He then studied for four years in France and Germany and earned one of the first Ph.D. degrees bestowed on an American. While in Europe he became friends with Henry Wadsworth Longfellow, who stirred Ward's aspirations to write literature and poetry. The Harvard chapter of Phi Beta Kappa soon affirmed his intellectual accomplishments by electing him a member. His father insisted, however, that Ward commit to the family banking business of Prime, Ward, and King. A series of misfortunes followed. His first wife, Emily Astor, a granddaughter of John Jacob Astor, died young in 1841. When Ward remarried two years later, the disapproving Astor family took custody of his daughter. His second wife, a New Orleans belle named Medora Grymes, "the greatest beauty of the South, perhaps of the whole country," absconded to Europe with their two young sons in the late 1840s after Ward suffered catastrophic financial reverses. Escaping the wreckage of his personal and business life and hoping to repair his fortunes, Ward headed to California at the height of the gold rush and stayed for a number of years. During the late 1850s he circulated between New York, Washington, Europe, and Latin America. By the end of the decade he had laid the foundations for his emergence after the war as a successful Washington insider, the "King of the Lobby." Ward loved to entertain and converse. The way to gain men's support, he once revealed, "was to tickle their palates." The goodwill he accumulated was deftly hoarded. "Many a Congressman received a dainty little note just before a vote was taken: 'Be good. This is my little lamb. Sam Ward.'"[15]

Anderson explained that he fixed upon Ward by specifying a number of key characteristics the diarist must possess, and by finding that Ward matched the criteria far better than anyone else. Although a New Yorker or well acquainted with prominent New Yorkers, the author must have lived in Washington during the secession winter. He must have been someone with wide business experience. He also must have had "considerable knowledge [of] and interest in poli-

15. Anderson, *Mystery,* 146–55; *New York Commercial Advertiser,* May 19, 1884; *New York Tribune,* May 25, 1884.

tics," but not strong partisan affiliations. On the key issue of the day, the diarist must have "distrusted and feared the influence of extremists on both sides of the crisis" and had "a manifest preference for moderate men." In particular, he needed to be someone "who was upon at least fairly intimate terms with Seward, for whom he had a qualified admiration, and with Douglas, for whom his admiration was in every respect deep and sincere."[16]

Anderson also satisfied himself that several persons mentioned in the Diary whose identities were concealed by dashes or initials were part of Ward's circle of friends or acquaintances. Thus "Mr. B——," the lawyer for a prominent New York City merchant, William H. Aspinwall, must have been Samuel L. M. Barlow, who will be discussed in chapter 5. Another "Mr. B——," who edited a newspaper and had confidential relations with President James Buchanan, was William M. Browne of the *Washington Constitution*. "Cousin V——," who observed Lincoln at the opera in New York City, probably was Valentine Mott Francis.[17]

Anderson discovered that Ward had been situated so as to learn a great deal about the secret history of the secession winter. He lived next door to Seward in a rented home at 258 F Street. Ward took advantage of this close proximity by cultivating Seward and by passing juicy bits of hearsay along to him. Seward in turn used Ward's quarters to confer privately with persons such as "Senator ——." As had David Potter, Anderson showed why the senator had to be California Democrat William M. Gwin, who was on friendly terms with key secessionists.[18] Plainly, Ward knew much about the secession crisis and had ties to persons mentioned in the Diary. Anderson therefore concluded that Ward must be the author.

Although satisfied that he had finally identified the elusive diarist, Anderson warned that the Diary itself was a clever concoction rather than an actual document:

> It is not a genuine diary actually kept in 1860–1861. It is, on the contrary, in part genuine and in part fictitious. It includes as a core a genuine diary,

16. Anderson, *Mystery*, 140–44; see also 145, 157–61.

17. Ibid., 162–66.

18. Ibid., 166–67; Potter, *Lincoln and His Party*, 269–70, 342–44; Bancroft, *Life of William Seward*, 2:543–45; Evan J. Coleman, "Gwin and Seward—A Secret Chapter in Ante-Bellum History," *Overland Monthly*, 2nd ser., 18 (Nov. 1891): 465–71; Lately Thomas (Robert V. P. Steele), *Sam Ward: "King of the Lobby"* (Boston: Houghton Mifflin, 1965), 241–53.

probably rather meager, actually kept by Sam Ward at Washington during the Secession Winter of 1860–1861. Attached to this genuine core there is a large amount of embellishment added at a later date. This added increment is in part recollection and in part pure invention. The genuine core, the recollection, and the invention have all been skillfully blended with a polished literary style.

Consequently, Anderson specified that the Diary "ought not to be regarded as a reliable source in any of its details" and it "ought not to be regarded as history." Its only redeeming value lay in the "substantially accurate" impression it conveyed of the "confusion and uncertainty" that enveloped Washington during the secession winter.[19]

Anderson originally had thought the Diary was genuine. He spent many years searching for an actual diarist. But he came to suspect that the document was too good to be true. Close study convinced him that many of the Diary's alleged interviews with the key principals—most especially with Lincoln—were imaginary. Would Lincoln really have discussed such a sensitive matter as the composition of his cabinet with the diarist, or was this "a clever ruse to create an impression that the Diarist was a man of considerable importance"? Nor could Anderson find any persuasive corroboration for the story of Douglas holding Lincoln's hat. Anderson also discounted some of the Public Man's interviews with Seward and Douglas.[20]

Anderson's warnings about the Diary have proven influential. But his identification of Ward as the diarist raised doubts. David Potter, who once had made considerable use of the Diary, agreed that some of its episodes must have been concocted. "If I were writing now," Potter admitted, "I would not use it as a source." But Potter never warmed to the idea that Ward wrote the Diary—that remained "a much controverted question." Robin Winks echoed Potter.[21] Roy N. Lokken specifically challenged Anderson's attribution of the diary to Ward. He suggested that it could just as well have been composed by someone who "moved in the

---

19. Anderson, *Mystery*, 169, 178.

20. Ibid., 68–123, quotation on 84.

21. David M. Potter, review of *The Mystery of "A Public Man,"* by Frank Maloy Anderson, in *Mississippi Valley Historical Review* 36 (Sept. 1949): 324–25; Potter, *Lincoln and His Party*, preface to the 1962 edition, xxxvi; Robin Winks, ed., *The Historian as Detective: Essays on Evidence* (New York: Harper and Row, 1968), 232–33.

same circles" as Ward.[22] Lately Thomas (Robert V. P. Steele) published a biography of Ward in 1965. He stated in a postscript that "Professor Anderson's ingenious supposition" about the diarist's identity was unwarranted. Ward would have enjoyed "perpetrating a brilliant hoax," and he may have had some hand in it, Thomas observed, but he did not think Ward composed the Diary.[23] Kathryn Jacob, who has just published a book about Ward's career as a lobbyist, offers her opinion that Ward was not the author of the Diary because the writing "seems so clearly not his style."[24]

Even though historians since 1948 (including this one) have been trained to beware of the Diary, they find it hard to resist the temptation. For example, Edwin M. Stanton's biographers, Benjamin P. Thomas and Harold M. Hyman, noted that Stanton startled the diarist on February 25 when he bitterly denounced Lincoln as a "low, cunning clown" (235).[25] In the first volume of his biography of Charles Sumner, David Donald accepted Anderson's view that the Diary was "a semi-fictional production," which "ought not be regarded as a reliable source." Fewer than twenty pages later, however, Donald relied on the diarist for insights into an encounter between Lincoln and Sumner on February 23, and for Lincoln's characterization of Sumner as a bishop. Donald's biography of Lincoln also echoes the diarist in having Lincoln shock some of Seward's friends on March 2 by threatening to drop the New Yorker from the cabinet, and in having Douglas hold Lincoln's hat at the inauguration.[26] Robert W. Johannsen, the biographer of Stephen A. Douglas, adopted a compromise position. He acknowledged that "considerable doubt has been cast on the authenticity of the Public

22. Roy N. Lokken, "Has the Mystery of 'A Public Man' Been Solved?" *Mississippi Valley Historical Review* 40 (Dec. 1953): 438–39. Lokken's own research base in the sources was not deep enough to enable him to build on his insightful suggestion.

23. Thomas, *Sam Ward*, 501. Thomas also remained uncertain whether the Diary was or was not a hoax.

24. Kathryn Jacob to Daniel W. Crofts, e-mail message, Aug. 15, 2004; Kathryn Allamong Jacob, *King of the Lobby: The Life and Times of Sam Ward, Man-About-Washington in the Gilded Age* (Baltimore: Johns Hopkins Univ. Press, 2009).

25. Benjamin P. Thomas and Harold M. Hyman, *Stanton: The Life and Times of Lincoln's Secretary of War* (New York: Knopf, 1962), 116. Thomas and Hyman mention the Anderson book in a footnote, though without elaboration.

26. Donald, *Charles Sumner and the Coming of the Civil War*, 365–66, 383; David Herbert Donald, *Lincoln* (New York: Simon & Schuster, 1995), 282–83; cf. the Diary, pp. 239–40, 244–46, 254 herein.

Man's observations," but he decided to use them "wherever corroborative evidence is available." On that basis, he credited the Diary's account of a private meeting between Lincoln and Douglas on February 27, at which Douglas implored the president-elect to "recommend the instant calling of a national convention." He too had Douglas hold Lincoln's hat.[27] Quite recently, Doris Kearns Goodwin's sprawling epic on Lincoln's cabinet enlists the Diary to describe the way that Lincoln challenged Seward's loyalists on March 2, to show that there were sharpshooters posted atop buildings on Pennsylvania Avenue as Lincoln's carriage proceeded to the Capitol before the inauguration ceremonies, and to have Douglas hold Lincoln's hat.[28]

Abraham Lincoln, the Civil War, and the crisis that triggered the conflict all continue to fascinate specialists and the wider reading public. Historians know they should not use "The Diary of a Public Man" but many keep using it. In their influential reference work *The Modern Researcher,* Jacques Barzun and Henry F. Graff salute Frank Maloy Anderson for his "undeviating pursuit of truth" and his "tireless and single-minded" efforts to identify a diarist, but they conclude that the author remains mysterious.[29] Surely the time has come to subject the Diary to fresh scrutiny. Can the enigma be deciphered? Let the inquiry begin.

27. Robert W. Johannsen, *Stephen A. Douglas* (New York: Oxford Univ. Press, 1973), 841–43, 962–63n3, 963n5; cf. the Diary, 241, 254 herein.

28. Doris Kearns Goodwin, *Team of Rivals: The Political Genius of Abraham Lincoln* (New York: Simon & Schuster, 2005), 317, 327–28, 809–10; cf. the Diary, 244–46, 253–54 herein. Goodwin appears unaware of the controversies relating to the Diary. The presence of "riflemen" and "sharpshooters" on the roofs of buildings "along the route of the procession" is corroborated in the *New York Herald,* Mar. 5, 1861, and the *New York Tribune,* Mar. 5, 1861.

29. Jacques Barzun and Henry F. Graff, *The Modern Researcher* (4th ed.; San Diego: Harcourt Brace Jovanovich, 1985), 135–42, quotations on 135–36.

2

PROVING WHO WROTE THE DIARY

Frank Maloy Anderson did not conclude that Sam Ward wrote "The Diary of a Public Man" until he had been studying the matter for many years. If the Diary was genuine, its author must have been in Washington, D.C., on the date of each of its entries—except February 20, when the diarist needed to have been in New York City. After considering a variety of possibilities, Anderson became especially interested in Amos Kendall, once a member of Andrew Jackson's Kitchen Cabinet, who had become by the 1850s a wealthy agent for Samuel F. B. Morse and the fast-growing telegraph industry. Anderson laboriously checked hotel registers, train schedules, and daily newspaper entries that identified just-arrived guests at major hotels. Using this technique, he eventually discovered that Kendall, on several different occasions, could not have been in the right place at the right time.[1] At this juncture, probably around 1926, Anderson began to doubt the Diary's validity. Notwithstanding "pen portraits seldom more strikingly drawn," it conveyed a "studied vagueness." Its author had taken pains to conceal his identity and offered little that could be corroborated.[2]

As Anderson commenced the search for a fabricator, he first considered Henry Wikoff, a cosmopolitan bon vivant whose checkered transatlantic career combined journalism, womanizing, and intrigue. Having persuaded himself that "Wikoff might well have been the man" who produced the Diary, Anderson delivered a paper at the 1928 meeting of the American Historical Association in Indianapolis to share his suspicions with fellow historians.[3] But Anderson never found any conclusive evidence pinning responsibility on Wikoff, so he kept an open mind. William Henry Hurlbert, whom Anderson initially "knew little about," briefly attracted his attention. Like Wikoff, Hurlbert lived in the fast

---

1. Frank Maloy Anderson, *The Mystery of "A Public Man": A Historical Detective Story* (Minneapolis: Univ. of Minnesota Press, 1948), 17, 28, 48–67.

2. Ibid., 13, 68–76, 140–44, quotations on 13, 73, 140.

3. Ibid., 126–29, quotation on 126; Michael Burlingame, *Abraham Lincoln: A Life* (2 vols.; Baltimore: Johns Hopkins Univ. Press, 2008), 2:273–76.

lane and had a talent for writing. But Anderson ultimately decided that neither Wikoff nor Hurlbert could have concocted a "bogus diary" from scratch. The task would have been too daunting. The diarist needed to be someone who lived in Washington in early 1861 and who had enjoyed opportunities to find out what was happening at the highest levels.[4] Then Anderson's attention was drawn—in a moment of serendipity—to Ward, a close friend of Hurlbert's. Anderson's epiphany occurred in 1930 as he attempted to learn more about Hurlbert. From that point forward, Anderson was convinced that he had identified the diarist. His line of reasoning is summarized in the previous chapter, as is the basis for his conclusion that the Diary was not what it appeared to be.[5] Anderson ceased to consider other possibilities and started to build the case for Ward, which finally appeared in his 1948 book.

Anderson's sleuthing deserves high marks, but his conclusions must now be modified. Careful scrutiny of Anderson's papers and a variety of other sources shows that Sam Ward was not the author of the Diary, even though he undoubtedly had something to do with it. The alleged diary contains plenty of information that points plainly to Ward. Anderson, however, had little to say about writing style. How does the Diary match up against prose written by Ward? Does it contain patterns of word usage that characterized Ward's writing? Textual analysis tells a different story from the one in Anderson's book.

At the precise time Ward was assisting Seward, he also was busily writing a memoir of his experiences in the California gold fields in 1851–52. This was the most extensive prose venture he ever undertook (he was a frustrated would-be poet). His resources at this time were slender, and he needed the money. Ward's charming and evocative recollections were published in fourteen installments in *Porter's Spirit of the Times*, a New York weekly, starting on January 22, 1861. They concluded abruptly with the issue of April 23, 1861, just as the war began.[6]

4. Anderson, *Mystery*, 126–35, quotations on 130, 134.

5. Ibid., 145–68, quotation on 145. A notation in Box 39 of the Frank Maloy Anderson Papers, Library of Congress, shows that in February 1930 he was trying to track Hurlbert's movements during the secession winter. A year and a half later, however, Anderson was so eager to know more about Sam Ward that he sought an interview with Maud Howe Elliott, Ward's niece. Anderson to Elliott, Aug. 31, 1931, Samuel Ward Papers, Houghton Library, Harvard University.

6. Many years later Ward's columns were assembled as a book: Carvel Collins, ed., *Sam Ward in the Gold Rush* (Stanford: Stanford Univ. Press, 1949). Collins condensed or excised some "digressions" and "wordy passages." The series ended when Ward departed for the seceded states in the company of William H. Russell, the famous correspondent for the *London Times*. Ibid., v, 172, 177.

Internal evidence reveals that Ward wrote the weekly pieces against a dead-line. His fourth installment, in the issue dated February 12, included a nervous aside about "these hours of national excitement and anxiety" and mused briefly about the successor governments that might "arise out of this cataclysm." His eighth installment, which appeared in the March 12 issue, was written "amidst the convulsive throes of the day preceding the Inauguration of President Lincoln, on the Fourth itself, and the day following." Fearful of a collision and con-temptuous of extremists of both parties, Ward observed apprehensively that "Blondin carried a man on stilts across the Niagara chasm; but Mr. Lincoln has to sustain a nation on his shoulders with more turbulent waters foaming at the bottom of a deeper abyss."[7]

For purposes of analysis, therefore, we have an abundance of material that Ward wrote in early 1861. At precisely the time the political crisis was reaching its most acute phase, he was crafting a substantial essay each week on an entirely different subject. Do the gold rush memoir and "The Diary of a Public Man" match up? Do they read as if the same person wrote both?

It should be expected, of course, that the two documents would have dis-similar features. One focuses on elite-level politics. The other is Ward's mem-oir of a time almost a decade earlier when he rusticated for over a year with a memorably diverse group of miners, speculators, Mexicans, and indigenous peoples at an encampment or "rancheria" on the "River of Grace," today's Mer-ced River, which flows down from the high Sierras toward the San Joaquin River and San Francisco Bay. Ward described the challenges of extracting gold ore from hard quartz. Modern readers would find his sympathetic account of "those children of nature whose dusky forms now flit before the eye of memory" of special interest. Members of the Potoyensee tribe had few possessions and lived precariously between "famine and repletion." Having mastered their language in "about a month" and thereby made himself "a favorite with the Indians," the

---

Porter's Spirit of the Times, although published in New York, stayed aloof from the North/South sec-tional crisis and was widely read in the South. Aimed at an audience of privileged outdoorsmen, Porter's attempted to redefine hunting as a sport rather than a source of food. See Nicholas W. Proc-tor, Bathed in Blood: Hunting and Mastery in the Old South (Charlottesville: Univ. Press of Virginia, 2002), 14–16, 20–22.

7. Collins, Sam Ward in the Gold Rush, 54–55, 100. Charles Blondin (Jean François Gravelet), a French tightrope walker, crossed the gorge below Niagara Falls several times between 1855 and 1860.

philologically gifted Ward captured many arresting glimpses of their lives and outlook just as their social order was being overwhelmed by the arrival of outsiders. His memoir should be considered a pioneering contribution to anthropology. Ward sensed that he had stumbled across an endeavor for which he was well suited. "I have mistaken my vocation," he confessed at the time to his sister back in Boston. "I should have been a linguist."[8]

Ward's gold rush memoir is awash with words having "-tion" or "-ion" suffixes. The following occur at least four times each: "admiration," "apprehension," "description," "determination," "exception," "imagination," "portion," "reflection," "satisfaction," and "speculation." When employing a negative adjective, Ward frequently judged things "mournful." His sentences sometimes meandered in a baroque manner. He had a habit of encasing unusual words or phrases within quotation marks and peppering his narrative with Spanish and French expressions. At times Ward alliterated—"audaciously asserted," "chronic continuance," "promising prospects," and "disagreeable demonstrations." Although the memoir occasionally recounted actual conversations, the narrator relied primarily on the past tense.[9]

By contrast, "The Diary of a Public Man" is fast paced and immediate. It was written by someone whose style featured active verbs accompanied by adverbs with an "-ly" suffix ("indignantly refused," "certainly adopt," "trifling designedly," "declined peremptorily," and so on). Several "-ly" words were absolutely central to the diarist's manner of written expression—he used "certainly" on twenty-four occasions, "really" eleven times, "perfectly" nine times, and "entirely" and "finally" eight times each. The diarist had a number of other "-ly" favorites—"apparently," "frankly," "absolutely," "peremptorily," "earnestly," "exactly," "fully," "indescribably," "particularly," and "undoubtedly." Often the diarist preceded the "-ly" adverb with the word "pretty" ("pretty certainly," "pretty clearly," "pretty fully," "pretty nearly," and "pretty plainly," among others). When the diarist encountered something objectionable—and he found much to criticize—he would use words such as "absurd," "folly," "horrible," "wretched," "wild/wilder/wildest," "worse/worst," and "mischief/mischievous." Other sig-

8. Ibid., 62–64, 84, 143, 159–60; Samuel Ward to Julia Ward Howe, Feb. 7, 1852, in Maud Howe Elliott, *Uncle Sam Ward and His Circle* (New York: Macmillan, 1938), 426–32, quotations on 427–29.

9. Ward's "astonishing memory" was remarked on in his obituaries. Lately Thomas (Robert V. P. Steele), *Sam Ward: "King of the Lobby"* (Boston: Houghton Mifflin, 1965), 485; see also Anderson, *Mystery*, 156.

nature words in the Diary include "anxiety/anxious," "ascertain/ascertained," "assure/assured/assurances," "quaint," "scheme," "singular," and "vex/vexations/ vexatious." The Public Man loved words that began with "con-," "dis-," "ex-," "in-," and "un-." And he alliterated—"deeply disturbed," "downright danger," "deplorable display," "excessively enraged," "revising radically," and "virtual vin- dication." The diarist, who supposedly recorded exchanges that took place that same day, far more often provided the words from a conversation than did Ward's California memoir.

The word patterns that Ward used in writing about California do not square with those in "The Diary of a Public Man." Start, for example, with the "-tion" and "-ion" words favored by Ward. Six of the ten do not appear at all in the Diary; three others are used but once, and only "determination" appears more than once in the Diary. Viewed from the opposite angle, many of the Diary's "-ly" words either do not appear at all in the gold rush memoir—"really," "per- fectly," "finally," and "frankly"—or are used only once or twice ("certainly," "en- tirely," and "apparently"). Hardly any of the negatives used by the diarist appear in the memoir—Ward encountered no "folly," nothing that was "wild," "hor- rible," "worse/worst," and but single instances each of "mischief" and "wretched- ness." Ward did not precede his infrequent "-ly" adverbs with the word "pretty." The diarist, unlike the memoir writer, found nothing "mournful." Both writ- ers alliterated, and the two had a few overlapping favorites ("anxiety," "particu- larly," "attention," and "determination")—but each otherwise had his own dis- tinct inventory of frequently called upon words.[10] In sum, the differences in word choice far outweigh the similarities. Ample stylistic evidence shows that these two documents had a different author.

If the Diary and the gold rush memoir were not written by the same person, who besides Ward might have been the diarist? The obvious candidate is Ward's close friend, William Henry Hurlbert (1827–1895), the gifted journalist who cov- ered his tracks so well that his role has been unrecognized until now. He has, therefore, long slumbered in obscurity.[11] But in his prime Hurlbert was widely

10. Ward's gold rush memoir is twice the length of the Diary, so if they shared the same author, words characteristic of the Diary should appear twice as often in the memoir. One other curiosity should be noted—two "-ly" words ("occasionally" and "subsequently") appeared five times each in the memoir but never in the Diary.

11. Hurlbert did rate an entry in the *Dictionary of American Biography* (9:424), but not the re- cent *American National Biography*.

known. He became the chief editorial writer for the *New York Times* in 1857, at the age of thirty. This key assignment continued for three years. By the time of the secession winter, however, Hurlbert had parted ways with the *Times*. Hurlbert moved to the *New York World* in 1862, and for seven years starting in 1876 he was its editor-in-chief. At the *World* he brought his forceful, fluid writing style to bear on a wide range of topics—politics, international affairs, history, and literature. His gift for capturing the cadences of human speech and his "rich fund of expression" enabled him to make "the gravest and heaviest" subjects come instantly alive.[12]

Anderson recognized that "the literary style of the Diary has a good deal of the pungency characteristic of almost everything that Hurlbert wrote." He also surmised, as we have seen, that the published Diary had been skillfully blended by someone with "a polished literary style." The only role that Anderson could imagine for Hurlbert, however, was that of a possible collaborator, someone who might have helped to enlarge Ward's "genuine core" that dated to 1861. Hurlbert's "lively imagination" could have "been equal to the task of supplying inventions so plausible that they could pass for historical facts."[13] Anderson was on the right track. He sensed that Hurlbert had applied his skills to the task at hand. He also knew that the finished document held together well. Rather than being episodic and fragmentary, as might be expected of a composite cut and pasted together, it was strikingly coherent. From its first passage to its last, the Diary calls attention to Fort Sumter, the ticking time bomb in Charleston Harbor.

Ironies abound. Anderson stumbled upon Ward only after he had discovered Hurlbert. But having come tantalizingly close to cracking the mystery, Anderson decided that Hurlbert could not have written the Diary. What prevented him from doing so? Anderson realized by 1930 that the Diary was something other than what it appeared to be, but he clung to the idea that it must consist in part of an actual diary written by an actual diarist. That person must have lived in Washington during the secession winter and he also must have occupied a sufficiently privileged perch to collect sensitive hearsay. Anderson discovered, of course, that Ward lived on F Street next door to William H. Seward. And once he hit upon Ward, Anderson marginalized Hurlbert, who spent the winter three hundred miles away in New York City. Anderson could not accept that anyone simply fabricated the entire Diary. He knew that Hurlbert had talent, but he did not quite recognize the man's extraordinary literary versatility.

12. Eugene Benson, "W. H. Hurlbut," *The Galaxy* (Jan. 1869): 30–34.
13. Anderson, *Mystery*, 134–35, 169–70.

Hurlbert's enormous printed output facilitates comparisons. The Diary abounds with striking parallels to his distinctive writing style. His book about a trip to Cuba, published in 1854, made repeated use of key words that appear in the Diary—"wild," "absurd," "wretched," "execrable," "sedulously"—and it included frequent alliteration.[14] His essay for the *Edinburgh Review* in 1856, to be discussed further later in this chapter and in chapters 3 and 4, likewise included a number of the Diary's signature words—"certainly," "singular/singularly," "absurd," "earnest/earnestly."[15] His editorials written for the *New York Times* in 1859 repeatedly anticipate the vocabulary of the Diary. As will be more fully explained in chapter 4, he considered John Brown's raid on Harpers Ferry the work of a lone fanatic—"a wilder and more hopeless project" could not have been imagined. Hurlbert therefore condemned the Southern press for stirring up an "absurd and disgraceful panic" by pretending that many people in the North were "rabid, ultra-Abolitionists." The editorialist leaned on words that appear in the Diary and most of which stand out there—"entirely," "certainly," "perfectly," "apparently," "especially," "sedulously," "earnestly," "clearly," "deplorable," "mischief," "scheme," "wild/ wilder," "absurd," and "assurances." Hurlbert's 1859 editorials were studded with alliteration, a key element of the pungency noted by Anderson—"promiscuous philanthropists," "sarcastic sneers," "reveling ruffians," "fierce fanaticism," "crowning crime," "utterly unfounded," and so on.[16]

As Hurlbert's career unfolded, he continued to write in ways that exhibit stylistic overlap with the Diary. When he escaped from Confederate captivity in August 1862—a topic that will be examined in chapter 8—he described his experiences in a series of seven articles for the *New York Times*. These articles sound like the Diary. Both employ staples of Hurlbert's rhetorical arsenal—"forbear," "ascertained," "wildest," "horrible," "madness," "wretched," "pretensions," "peremptorily"—and both include a great many words that begin with "dis-" and "in-." Hurlbert's 1862 pieces contained characteristic alliteration—"resolute refusal," "slashing speculations," and "dangerous delusion."[17] Writing editorials for the *New York World* in 1868, Hurlbert condemned the "preposter-

14. William H. Hurlbert, *Gan-Eden; or, Pictures of Cuba* (Boston: J. P. Jewett & Co., 1854), 53, 56, 70, 83, 116, 119, 133, 167.

15. William H. Hurlbert, "The Political Crisis in the United States," *Edinburgh Review* 104 (October 1856): 561–97.

16. *New York Times*, Oct. 19, 27, Nov. 2, 3, 4, 5, 14, 17, 21, 23, 25, 26, Dec. 1, 3, 5, 6, 7, 12, 13, 1859.

17. Ibid., Sept. 10, 11, 15, 23, Oct. 4, 11, 20, 30, 1862.

ous proceedings" of impeachment, castigated Republicans for heating "the cauldron of public passions" and acting in "hot and headlong haste," and predicted that their "revolutionary recklessness" would lead to "defeat and disgrace." He characterized as "absurd" the argument that Andrew Johnson had committed an impeachable offense by removing Edwin Stanton from his cabinet.[18] In his 1874 editorials in defense of Henry Ward Beecher, to be discussed in chapter 10, Hurlbert complained that much of the evidence in the "wretched business" was either "mischievous" or "absurd." It was "perfectly plain" that the famous preacher had been "driven half mad" by "moral scavengers" who were "daily darkening" the skies with "new clouds of filth," and who deserved "condign chastisement" for their "wild, irresponsible" accusations.[19] In 1888 Hurlbert published a long account of his travels through Ireland, a key source for chapter 11. Its word usage is strikingly reminiscent of the Diary—"quaint," "mischief," "disagreeable," "absurd," "ascertained," "wildest," "peremptorily," "disquieted," "intimated." Hurlbert's alliterations persisted—"friendly financiers," "rattled rapidly," "exultingly exclaimed," "utterly unlike," and so on.[20]

One additional tool has been used to assess the Diary and identify the mysterious diarist. David Holmes, a professional statistician, has subjected the Diary to stylometric scrutiny. Stylometry, "the statistical analysis of literary style," is based on the assumption that "authors have an unconscious aspect to their style, an aspect which cannot consciously be manipulated but which possesses features which are quantifiable and which may be distinctive."[21]

---

18. *New York World*, Feb. 24, 25, 26, Mar. 2, 1868.

19. Ibid., July 27, Aug. 1, 13, 1874.

20. William Henry Hurlbert, *Ireland under Coercion: The Diary of an American*, 2nd ed. (2 vols.; Edinburgh: David Douglas, 1888).

21. David I. Holmes, "The Evolution of Stylometry in Humanities Scholarship," *Literary and Linguistic Computing* 13 (1998): 111–17, quotations on 111. See also David I. Holmes, Lesley J. Gordon, and Christine Wilson, "A Widow and Her Soldier: Stylometry and the American Civil War," *Literary and Linguistic Computing* 16 (2001): 403–20; David I. Holmes, Michael Robertson, and Roxanna Paez, "Stephen Crane and the *New-York Tribune*: A Case Study in Traditional and Non-Traditional Authorship Attribution," *Computers and the Humanities* 35 (August 2001): 315–31; Matthew L. Jockers, Daniela M. Witten, and Craig S. Criddle, "Reassessing Authorship of the 'Book of Mormon' Using Delta and Nearest Shrunken Centroid Classification," *Literary and Linguistic Computing* 23 (2008): 465–91. Stylometry applies multivariate statistical analyses to discern patterns of word usage—in particular, the fifty or one hundred most frequently employed words in substantial pas-

Repeated assessment of differing segments of the Diary by Holmes and his assistants provide no evidence that it is a composite. Instead, the Diary appears to have been composed by a single person, and in a seamless manner. Anderson too recognized, as already noted, that the Diary had been written in "a polished literary style," but he judged that the author had added a mix of "recollection" and "pure invention" to a "genuine core."[22] Anderson's cut-and-paste theory may have merit, so far as the substance of the Diary is concerned, but stylometry indicates that only one writer put words on paper. There is, therefore, scientific basis for validating the "common sense" impression created by the Diary—its entries all are part of the same literary whole.

Who might the one writer have been? Holmes cast a wide net. In addition to Ward and Hurlbert, he initially assessed a number of other possibilities, most prominently Allen Thorndike Rice, Thurlow Weed, and Henry Adams.[23] He also considered James E. Harvey, James C. Welling, Richard Grant White, and John W. Forney.[24] The evidence promptly eliminated Rice, Weed, Welling, White, and Forney. Holmes then narrowed the analysis to Ward, Adams, Harvey, and

---

sages (preferably three thousand words or more). This technique has been used to investigate "works of doubtful provenance," by comparing samples known to have been written by particular authors with samples in which the author is unknown or in dispute. Passages written by the same person should exhibit comparable frequencies of word usage. Convergent patterns indicate that one person wrote both passages, most likely at about the same time. Stylometry thus is based on evidence that most writing will create a distinctive stylometric signature or fingerprint. Modern electronic analysis can reveal such patterns. Holmes, "The Evolution of Stylometry," 111.

22. Anderson, *Mystery*, 169.

23. Rice, who edited the *North American Review*, will be discussed in chapter 9. Weed, also to be discussed in chapters 6 and 9, was suggested as a possible diarist at the time the Diary first appeared. Speculation about Adams as the diarist—albeit unfounded—may be found in Evelyn Page, "The Diary and the Public Man," *New England Quarterly* 22 (June 1949): 147–72, and in Benjamin M. Price, "That Baffling Diary," *South Atlantic Quarterly* 54 (Jan. 1955): 56–64.

24. Harvey seemed a promising candidate to the historian Frederic Bancroft. See Bancroft to James Ford Rhodes, Aug. 19, 1896, James Ford Rhodes Papers, Massachusetts Historical Society. Bancroft later concluded that Ward wrote the Diary, thereby anticipating Anderson. Charles P. Whittemore to Frank Maloy Anderson, Aug. 6, 1952, Anderson Papers, Box 1. Whittemore's letter to Anderson referred to Frederic Bancroft to E. E. Hale, Feb. 4, 1910, Bancroft Collection, Special Collections, Butler Library, Columbia University. On Harvey, see Daniel W. Crofts, "James E. Harvey and the Secession Crisis," *Pennsylvania Magazine of History and Biography* 103 (Apr. 1979): 177–95. For various reasons, Welling, White, and Forney also appeared to deserve scrutiny.

Hurlbert. The results are clear—stylometric evidence "points very strongly" to Hurlbert as the author of the Diary. Extensive samples were taken from articles he wrote for the *New York Times* in September and October 1862, which described a year he spent in Confederate captivity, and from the account of his travels through Ireland in the late 1880s. These sources each provide a closer stylometric match to the Diary than anything written by any of the other possible authors considered. Because the Ireland book was composed less than a decade after the Diary appeared, and because the two documents had somewhat the same form, their stylometric similarities become especially significant.[25]

Moreover, Holmes found that Ward's gold rush memoir matched poorly with the Diary. Stylometry thus indicates that the Diary and the memoir were not written by the same person—a conclusion that will seem axiomatic to anyone who reads the two documents side by side. In short, stylometry reinforces my more traditional analysis of literary style. Stylistic and stylometric assessments both strongly suggest that Hurlbert did the writing and that Ward did not.[26]

Substance reinforces style. The Diary reflects Hurlbert's distinctive (and unorthodox) view of the great crisis that led to war in 1861. As we shall see in the next chapter, he was the son of a Yankee schoolteacher who had moved south. His outlook was neither Northern nor Southern. Sooner than most Americans, Hurlbert realized that his native South Carolina was on a collision course with New England, where he studied and lived from the mid-1840s to the mid-1850s. Although drawn for a time to the antislavery critique of the South, he had enough affinity with both sides of the sectional conflict to avoid becoming a partisan for either. He sensed that the sides were mutually blind to the potential catastrophe that their antagonism was creating. Hurlbert remained conflicted after the war started. He wanted the Union preserved, but he feared that prolonged fighting would so embitter the two sides as to make reunion impossible. He opposed emancipation on grounds that it would prompt the South to fight longer and harder. When the war finally ended, he favored a rapid restoration of the Southern states to the Union. He never thought the war should have been fought, and he never accepted the idea that it could be justified by its outcome.

25. Hurlbert, *Ireland under Coercion*. See chapter 11.

26. For more details, see David I. Holmes and Daniel W. Crofts, "The Diary of a Public Man: A Case Study in Traditional and Non-Traditional Authorship Attribution," *Literary and Linguistic Computing* (forthcoming).

Moreover, some of the specific contents of the Diary point to Hurlbert rather than Ward. Twice the diarist mentions Josiah Quincy (1772–1864), who had been president of Harvard College during the 1840s when Hurlbert studied there (218, 253). Quincy was a living link between the New England Federalists of the early nineteenth century, who opposed the expansion of slavery, and the New Englanders of the 1850s, who reacted viscerally against the Fugitive Slave Law, the Kansas-Nebraska Act, and the apparent Southern effort to force slavery into "Bleeding Kansas." During the mid-1850s, when Hurlbert's own outlook on public affairs became most pro-Northern, he held the elderly ex-Federalist in high regard. Hurlbert's important 1856 article for the *Edinburgh Review*, "The Political Crisis in the United States," enthusiastically commended Quincy's speech delivered in Boston in June 1856, shortly after the assault on Charles Sumner. Quincy had spoken "fully, fearlessly, and with amazing force," Hurlbert noted:

> He is persuaded that a time has come at last which must thoroughly try the temper of men's souls, and decide the question whether liberty or slavery shall for ever colour the character and the policy of the American people. If the young men of the North shall be inspired with the wisdom, and her old men animated with the fire which distinguishes this address of Mr. Quincy, there need be little fear for the results of the collision which he so plainly anticipates between national principles and sectional passions in the Republic.

Echoing Quincy, Hurlbert argued that the Louisiana Purchase had constituted an ominous step toward transforming "the anti-slavery republic of Washington, Adams, and Hamilton" into a nation "governed by slaveholders." Thanks to the three-fifths clause of the Constitution, the South acquired disproportionate power in the Union and so imposed its "comparatively *aristocratic* character" on the democratic North.[27]

The Public Man referred to others who would have been more familiar to Hurlbert than to Ward. During 1859 and 1860, Stephen A. Douglas enlisted sev-

27. Hurlbert, "Political Crisis," 561, 568–69, 574–76; Robert A. McCaughey, *Josiah Quincy, 1772–1864: The Last Federalist* (Cambridge: Harvard Univ. Press, 1974), 204–13. The two Diary entries mentioning Quincy purportedly involved persons other than the diarist himself, but Hurlbert had to have the antenna to pick up on these references and make them part of the Diary.

eral people to promote his presidential candidacy. Among them was George N. Sanders, a Kentucky native who risked his federal patronage job, as navy agent in New York City, to support the Little Giant. As shall be explained in chapter 4, Hurlbert and Sanders collaborated to make the *New York Times* a Douglas paper, or to persuade editor Henry J. Raymond to sell it to someone who would do so.[28] Following the election, however, the unpredictable Sanders became "a loud and noisy secessionist," thereby earning a dismissive barb in the Diary (239). Far more than Ward, Hurlbert had reason to notice—and to ridicule—Sanders' erratic course.

The diarist had a higher estimate of another insider from the Douglas campaign. John Forsyth, editor of the *Mobile Register*, was among the most outspoken champions of the Little Giant in the Deep South. Douglas ended his campaign in Alabama, so that on Election Day he was with Forsyth in Mobile. That night Forsyth broke the terrible news to Douglas that he had no choice but to support calling a state convention—that the only way to attempt to control the secession movement in Alabama would be to appear to go along with it.[29] Just a few months later, Forsyth was one of three commissioners sent to Washington by the Confederate government. The diarist claimed to have received a letter from him, before his arrival at the capital, "intimating his own earnest wish to secure an amicable adjustment of the separation, which he insists upon as irreparable at least for the present. I shall be very glad to see him, for he is a man of unusual sense, and I do not believe he can have persuaded himself into the practicability of the fantastic schemes represented in this wild confederacy" (257). The Forsyth reference, like the Sanders one, points to Hurlbert rather than Ward. Hurlbert hobnobbed with those who were close to Douglas; Ward did not.

This is not to say that Hurlbert and Douglas were chums. The two surviving letters that Hurlbert wrote to Douglas display a deferential formality, quite

28. Sanders was energetic, enthusiastic—and uncontrollable. Why Douglas wanted him is a mystery. Eight years before, in 1852, Sanders crippled Douglas by using the *United States Democratic Review* to attack his rivals for the Democratic nomination. The ill will generated by Sanders meant that a dark horse, Franklin Pierce, emerged as the convention nominee that year, rather than Douglas. Whatever the reason, Douglas once again turned to Sanders in 1859. Robert W. Johannsen, *Stephen A. Douglas* (New York: Oxford Univ. Press, 1973), 346–47, 360–63, 732, 761, 853–54; George Fort Milton, *The Eve of Conflict: Stephen A. Douglas and the Needless War* (Boston: Houghton Mifflin, 1934), 86–92, 374, 379–85.

29. Milton, *The Eve of Conflict*, 500.

unlike the manner he used with friends.[30] That said, however, Hurlbert plainly had stronger ties to Douglas and to people around Douglas than did Ward. Hurlbert had been a key Douglas supporter in the most important city in the country, and—as we shall see—Hurlbert had tried valiantly, albeit unsuccessfully, to pull one of the top New York newspapers into the Douglas camp. On the whole, Hurlbert was more likely than Ward to have had ways of finding out what Douglas was saying behind closed doors.[31]

A segment of the Diary having to do with Mexico also points to Hurlbert. At first glance, the entry of February 26 appears only to be a colorful tale the diarist heard late one evening while playing whist. An unnamed companion reported learning from Judah Benjamin that Louisiana's former U.S. senator, Pierre Soulé, had traveled surreptitiously to Mexico "to prevent, if possible, the carrying out of the Tehuantepec scheme" (237). What was this about? During the 1850s rival promoters jousted to build better transport across Mesoamerica and thereby improve the long trip to California. The Isthmus of Tehuantepec in southern Mexico, the one real gap in the chain of mountains that stretches from Alaska to Tierra del Fuego, offered unique advantages. The Gadsden Purchase in 1854 allowed the United States to transport mail and goods across the isthmus via a plank road or a railroad. The McLane-Ocampo Treaty of 1859, which Hurlbert repeatedly boosted in the *New York Times,* affirmed and enlarged American transit rights across Tehuantepec. The treaty failed to gain Senate ratification, but the supposed diarist who picked up gossip about such matters was more likely Hurlbert than Ward.[32]

Hurlbert's fingerprints also may be detected in one of the Diary's most strik-

30. Hurlbert to Douglas, Jan. 16, 1860, Mar. 27, 1861, Stephen A. Douglas Papers, University of Chicago.

31. Ward, too, could have picked up information about Douglas because Seward reached out to Douglas during the secession winter, and Ward, as we have seen, knew a great deal about Seward. But Douglas had no reason to share with Seward the glimpses of his cronies that appear in the Diary.

32. Richard N. Sinkin, *The Mexican Reform, 1855–1876: A Study in Liberal Nation Building* (Austin: Univ. of Texas Press, 1979), 154–57; Walter V. Scholes, *Mexican Politics during the Juárez Regime, 1855–1872* (Columbia: Univ. of Missouri Press, 1957), 31–37; Jerome Joseph Niosi, "The McLane Mission to Mexico, 1859–60" (Ph.D. diss., New York University, 1953); David L. Anderson, "Robert Milligan McLane," *American National Biography,* 15:134–36; *New York Times,* July 26, Dec. 21, 1859, Jan. 5, 20, Feb. 15, 1860. Ward, unlike Hurlbert, had lived in California, but only Hurlbert had played a prominent role in the tussle over the McLane-Ocampo Treaty.

ing features—its abrupt ending on March 15, 1861. Frank Maloy Anderson surmised that Ward quit writing a diary when he left Washington for New York City to meet the renowned British journalist William H. Russell, with whom he spent the next several months. This constituted "strong additional reason for believing that Ward must have been the diarist."[33] But here Anderson tried to have it both ways—he wanted the Diary that was not a diary to reflect Ward's movements. Of course Ward's connection to the project is beyond dispute, but there are more powerful reasons why "The Diary of a Public Man" needed to end when it did. By March 15 it was generally assumed that Sumter soon would be relinquished. A few days thereafter, however, doubts and question began to arise. Perhaps the assumed decision had not been made after all? Perhaps the sigh of relief breathed by all who hoped for a peaceful resolution to the crisis was premature?[34] Hurlbert, the dramatic stylist, initiated the Diary with the late-December flurry about Major Robert Anderson's move from Moultrie to Sumter. As we shall examine in chapter 6, Hurlbert ended the Diary at just the point when the Sumter difficulty supposedly had been resolved—so that history might have followed a different course.

In my view, the case for Hurlbert as the diarist rests on multiple foundations. When both stylistic and stylometric analyses are weighed together, and when the Diary's segments that point to Hurlbert are taken into account, the case for Ward as the author of the Diary unravels, and the case for Hurlbert becomes a certainty. Both contributed information that appears in the Diary, but only one did the actual writing. It is either/or—one wrote it and one did not. Ward did not write it. Hurlbert did. I regard the case as closed.

33. Anderson, *Mystery*, 162.

34. Daniel W. Crofts, *Reluctant Confederates: Upper South Unionists in the Secession Crisis* (Chapel Hill: Univ. of North Carolina Press, 1989), 289–90.

3

YOUNG HURLBERT

This chapter and the two that follow will introduce William Henry Hurlbert and trace his career up through the winter of 1860–61. Readers who want to keep the Diary in sharp focus may be puzzled by this biographical tangent. But these next three Hurlbert chapters are no digression. The Diary cannot be understood unless we know more about the mastermind who pulled it together.

To make sense of Hurlbert, one must start with his formative years. We immediately learn why he never could identify comfortably either with the North or the South. Hurlbert was born in 1827 in Charleston, South Carolina. His father, Martin Luther Hurlbut, a Unitarian minister and schoolmaster from Massachusetts, resettled in South Carolina in 1812 and lived there for most of the next two decades.[1] The elder Hurlbut remained a self-conscious Yankee who nonetheless owned slaves. Hurlbert's mother, Margaret Ashburner Morford Hurlbut, his father's second wife, was a native of Princeton, New Jersey. Hurlbert's parents moved to Philadelphia in 1831, where his father established a successful school.[2]

Fragmentary evidence hints that William's childhood was difficult and intense. His father, described by one observer as "a quiet, dignified, and scholarly man," struck others as an oppressive disciplinarian and pedant. Martin Luther Hurlbut played a dual role as William's parent and schoolmaster. The gifted son displayed a knack for rhetoric, foreign languages, and classical literature. One may surmise that he was pushed to excel and subjected to a hard regimen of paternal authority. Perhaps as a consequence, young William needed to prove himself physically. One classmate recalled him as "a fine-looking, burly lad" who

1. William Henry Hurlbert changed the spelling of his family name, apparently on a whim, shortly after he finished college. He became "Hurlbert" rather than "Hurlbut" upon receiving some erroneous "visiting-cards" from a London stationery store and deciding that he preferred "Hurlbert." His own hasty scrawl had been the source of the confusion. *New York World*, Sept. 7, 1895.

2. Jeffrey N. Lash, *A Politician Turned General: The Civil War Career of Stephen Augustus Hurlbut* (Kent, Ohio: Kent State Univ. Press, 2003), 1–10, 25–27.

could "whip any boy in the school," although he was "by no means a bully." At a time when athletic prowess was "beginning to be in vogue," the school hired a tall Yorkshireman to teach boxing, and William became his apt pupil.[3]

Another of young Hurlbert's classmates, Charles Godfrey Leland, a future philologist, used his artistic talent to delight his friends with drawings and sketches—indeed, Leland may well have stimulated the sophisticated appreciation of visual art that Hurlbert demonstrated as an adult. Leland also wrote, however, a disturbing recollection of the "simply intolerable" demands that Martin Luther Hurlbut imposed on his students. Most ominously, Leland recalled that young William was prone "to fits of blind rage" and "reckless behavior." In 1838, one of his friends pointed a supposedly unloaded pistol between William's eyes and pulled the trigger. The ten-year-old William providentially "jerked his head away" but still caught "one shot in the ear." William emerged from childhood an intellectual prodigy who also, in the judgment of Leland, had "a screw loose." It is tempting to speculate that Hurlbert's subsequent decision to change the way he spelled the family name distanced him from a spectacularly overbearing—and possibly even abusive—paterfamilias.[4]

Martin Luther Hurlbut died unexpectedly in January 1843. William and his mother and sisters promptly returned to South Carolina. There the precocious fifteen-year-old came under the influence of his half brother, Stephen Augustus Hurlbut, an aspiring lawyer and politician who was over a decade William's senior. Stephen—who later moved to Illinois, became an ally of Lincoln's, and served as a Union general during the Civil War—was attempting in the early 1840s to carve out a niche in Charleston society. He arranged for William to study for the Unitarian ministry under the tutelage of the Reverend Dr. Samuel A. Gilman, an admiring friend of their father's.[5]

When Hurlbert enrolled at Harvard College in 1845, he had spent his most recent two years in Charleston and was regarded as a Southerner. He earned an undergraduate degree in 1847 and a divinity degree in 1849. He appears to have been the McGeorge Bundy of his generation, a young man of enormous talent, plainly destined for great success. After college, Hurlbert traveled extensively

3. Ibid., 26, 221n48; B. P., "A Reminiscence of the Hurlberts," *New York Times Saturday Literary Review,* July 5, 1902, p. 453.

4. Charles G. Leland, *Memoirs, by Charles Godfrey Leland (Hans Breitman)* (New York: D. Appleton, 1893), 73, 80–81, 233–34.

5. Lash, *A Politician Turned General,* 26.

in Europe. His personal charm, his gifts as a linguist, and his ability of "acquiring knowledge as if by magic" enabled him to pass easily as "a Frenchman in France, an Italian in Italy, [and] a Spaniard in Spanish countries." He served a brief stint as a Unitarian minister in Salem, Massachusetts, where he was said to be "extremely popular and very much admired as a preacher." In 1855, having been elected to the Phi Beta Kappa chapter at Harvard, he read a poem at commencement.[6]

To supplement the known facts about Hurlbert's young life, the historian must also make use of unconventional sources. Three writers who knew Hurlbert—Charles Kingsley, Theodore Winthrop, and Thomas Wentworth Higginson—each used him as the basis for a character in a novel. Their portraits offer many insights into his personality. Published between 1857 and 1869, the three works of creative imagination each provide a distinct angle of vision. Taken together, they suggest that the baffling mix of qualities exhibited by the mature Hurlbert were apparent to discerning observers during the 1850s when the young prodigy first vaulted to attention. At once warmly ingratiating and intellectually brilliant, Hurlbert was at the same time secretive, self-centered, and ultimately self-destructive. It is somehow fitting that actual evidence about him is overshadowed by three fictional portraits.

The most flattering fictional version of Hurlbert, but at the same time the one that probed least deeply, was penned by the English Victorian novelist Charles Kingsley.[7] *Two Years Ago* (1857) has a message—privileged Britons needed to get serious about sanitary reform. The hero, Tom Tunstall, accomplishes more fighting cholera in a village on the Cornish coast than he does fighting the Russians in the Crimea. Tucked into the sprawling tale is a subplot involving an American, who is designated as Stangrave. This young New York businessman, "tall, dark, and handsome," attempts to persuade his friends in England that op-

6. T. C. Evans, "William H. Hurlbert," *New York Times Saturday Literary Review,* June 14, 1902, p. 408; Thomas Wentworth Higginson, *Cheerful Yesterdays* (Boston: Houghton, Mifflin, 1898), 107; *New York World,* Sept. 7, 1895.

7. Hurlbert's friend T. C. Evans reported a general belief that Kingsley had made Hurlbert "the hero of his American episode in *Two Years Ago*" (Evans, "William H. Hurlbert," 408). Thomas Wentworth Higginson categorically identified Hurlbert as the person whom Kingsley had in mind (Higginson, *Cheerful Yesterdays,* 107).

ponents of slavery in the United States cannot act precipitately. Stangrave, who supported Republican candidate John C. Frémont in the recent U.S. presidential election, favors gradual emancipation. By drawing "a *cordon sanitaire* round the tainted States," slavery's opponents would start a process by which slavery eventually would "die a natural death." Stangrave hopes that Republicans will continue to gain strength and win the next election, just three years in the future. ("We require the delay, too, to discover who are our really best men.")[8]

Stangrave's European listeners will have none of it. They insist that the only proper course for the United States is to "free those slaves at once and utterly." This is especially the view of Marie Cordifiamma, a striking Italian beauty with black curls, who spurns the idea that slaves should "be patient, and endure the rice-swamp, the scourge, the slave-market, and shame unspeakable, a few years more."[9]

Stangrave protests. Do his friends realize that they are inviting "disruption of the Union, an invasion of the South by the North; and an internecine war, aggravated by the horrors of a general rising of the slaves, and such scenes as Hayti beheld sixty years ago"? So, too, he sees white Southerners as brothers— "no worse men than I"—who were doing just what he would do "had I been bred up, as they have been, with irresponsible power over the souls and bodies of human beings." He would not take any "rash step" that might "shut out the whole Southern white population from their share of my country's future glory."[10]

Of course Stangrave falls in love with the lovely Marie. She has thrown a spell over him that he cannot resist. Abandoning his "conceited dream of self-culture" and his indolent life of "wandering luxuriously over the world," Stangrave resolves to become "useful" and "beneficent." He overcomes his "typical American" blindness to the awful reality of slavery and dedicates himself to work against it, albeit "as I think best, patiently, moderately, wisely if I can; for a fanatic I cannot be, even for her sake."[11]

8. Charles Kingsley, *Two Years Ago* (London, 1857; New York: Macmillan, 1911), 2. With a platform promising to stop the spread of slavery, the Republican Party first coalesced in 1856 and nominated Frémont for president. He carried the majority of free states, but not enough to win the election.

9. Ibid., 2, 92, 138.

10. Ibid., 3–4, 382.

11. Ibid., 132–34, 380–82.

Stangrave discovers, however, that the object of his affections is not Italian at all but is instead a runaway American quadroon slave, living incognito in England (the hero of the novel, Tom Tunstall, had enabled her to escape). Marie, brokenhearted, knows that "those Northerners, with all their boasts of freedom, shrink from us just as much as our own masters." She assumes that Stangrave, the brilliant cosmopolitan, cared too much about "wealth, luxury, art, brilliant company, admiration" to enter a marriage that would exclude him from high society. "If he had been one of the Abolitionist party, it would have been different; but he has no sympathy with them, good narrow, pious people."[12]

Kingsley thereby created an impasse for which there was no solution, had the novel stayed true to the racially dichotomized reality that prevailed in the United States. Kingsley's interests, however, were British, and he was content to dabble with fragments of American inspiration. The conventions of Victorian melodrama offered him a way out. After a temporary estrangement, Marie and Stangrave reconnect in Germany. He pledges that he will not "fail or falter, till I have won justice for you and for your race, Marie!" She "let him take her hand, pass her arm through his, and lead her away, as one who had a right." She finally realizes that "you can love me—me, the slave; me, the scourged; the scarred—Oh, Stangrave! It is not much—not much really,—only a little mark or two."

"'I will prize them,' he answered, smiling through tears, 'more than all your loveliness. I will see in them God's commandment to me, written not on tables of stone, but on fair, pure, noble flesh.'" As the book concludes, we find that the happy couple, blessed with two children, has decided to remain in England. Kingsley allows Stangrave one last incongruous scene—out hunting foxes. An inquiring reader might wonder what has become of his tearful promise to win justice for Marie and her race.[13]

In many respects Stangrave plainly was Hurlbert. At the time the novel was written, Kingsley and Hurlbert had recently spent time together and were on the friendliest terms. Before Hurlbert returned to the United States in October 1856 to vote in the presidential election, he used Kingsley's home in Hampshire as his mailing address. Several months later he assured the injured Massachusetts senator Charles Sumner that Kingsley would welcome him under his roof

12. Ibid., 139.
13. Ibid., 377, 457, 462, 466.

should he travel to England (Hurlbert also lauded Kingsley's "noble and charming" wife).[14]

Stangrave was a Yankee who worried about his Southern brothers. He wanted a resolution to the dilemma of American slaveholding that allowed white Southerners to maintain their national allegiance. All of this corresponded with reality. Hurlbert was a Yankee-Southern hybrid who knew that slavery was considered a disgrace by many on both sides of the Atlantic. He hoped that enlightened opinion both north and south might coalesce. The well-traveled young American cosmopolitan surely attempted to educate his English hosts about the advantages of political antislavery, as opposed to outright abolitionism. Hurlbert's support for Frémont, most prominently exhibited in his widely discussed 1856 article in the *Edinburgh Review,* is a matter of record.[15]

But Kingsley's Stangrave had imaginary aspects not shared by the real Hurlbert. The real Hurlbert did not aspire to be "useful" or "beneficent." Before long it would become one of his calling cards to lampoon those who did. The real Hurlbert never articulated moral objections to slavery, and he always distanced himself from the abolitionists who did. By the late 1850s, when the North-South sectional conflict threatened to disrupt the Union and trigger a civil war, the real Hurlbert jettisoned his ties to the Republican Party and disavowed even the gradualist program of political antislavery. So, too, the randy bachelor made a most implausible candidate for a "lived happily ever after" Victorian melodrama. Although the real Hurlbert did have a connoisseur's eye for attractive women, he was not about to commit to one in particular, let alone one with a mixed-race background.

What Kingsley created here was a stereotyped American who suited his own purposes. The moral of *Two Years Ago* was that British elites should take more responsibility for promoting public health—that both self-interest and religious obligation pointed in the same direction. As a prop to sustain the main message, Kingsley imagined an American who had experienced a comparable awakening. It reveals something about Hurlbert's amiable manner that Kingsley could see him as someone who shared his own values and could fill an exem-

14. Hurlbert to John Gorham Palfrey, Oct. 3, 1856, Palfrey Family Papers, Houghton Library, Harvard University; Hurlbert to Sumner, Feb. 23, 1857, Charles Sumner Papers, ibid.; Evans, "William H. Hurlbert," 408.

15. William H. Hurlbert, "The Political Crisis in the United States," *Edinburgh Review* 104 (October 1856): 561–97.

plary role in the novel. Even though Hurlbert abandoned the Unitarian ministry and any kind of theistic belief system, his English friend assumed that religious sensibilities gave him a personal commitment to reform, uplift, and social amelioration.

A far less appealing characterization of Hurlbert appeared in a novel written by one of his American contemporaries, Theodore Winthrop. It suggested that the talented and attractive figure depicted by Kingsley had a dark underside and an array of personal qualities that were far from what they might have seemed on first impression.

Winthrop, born in New Haven in 1828 and graduated from Yale in 1848, was, like Hurlbert, among the small group of privileged young Americans who traveled in Europe after college. Upon his return, he found it difficult to settle down into a conventional career. The introspective would-be writer had "a flower-like delicacy" and a "womanly grace of temperament." Ill health also may have contributed to his "sensitive and refined nature." Winthrop soared to posthumous fame in June 1861 when he chanced to become the first elite New Englander killed in Civil War combat.[16]

Winthrop's novel *Cecil Dreeme,* written near the end of his life and published soon after his death, features a character named Densdeth, whom the narrator, Robert Byng, first met on shipboard when returning from Europe.[17] Byng found Densdeth exceptional—"I know no man of such wide scope of information, such knowledge, such wit, such brilliancy." Densdeth's "slight, elegant, active figure," his "slender grace," his "dark handsome face," and his "olive complexion" gave him a "marked Orientalism." Possessed of magnetism and a "distinguished air," Densdeth exerted a "strange fascination" that affected "old

16. George William Curtis, "Biographical Sketch of the Author," in Theodore Winthrop, *Cecil Dreeme* (Boston: Ticknor and Fields, 1862), 5–19. Winthrop also spent several years in Panama, California, and the Pacific Northwest. On his visit to the Washington Territory, see Timothy Egan, *The Good Rain: Across Time and Terrain in the Pacific Northwest* (New York: Knopf, 1990), 8–11. Winthrop's aesthetic sensibilities were stirred by the paintings of his friend Frederic Edwin Church, whose giant canvas *The Heart of the Andes* offered a spectacular new departure in American art. Andrew Wilton and Tim Barringer, *American Sublime: Landscape Painting in the United States, 1820–1880* (London: Tate Publishing, 2002), 28–30.

17. An extensive obituary of Hurlbert in the *New York World,* Sept. 8, 1895, relied upon Winthrop's character, Densdeth, in order to describe young Hurlbert's appearance and manner. Higginson also noted that Densdeth was based on Hurlbert (Higginson, *Cheerful Yesterdays,* 107).

and young" alike. He had a special appeal to young men. Densdeth "attracts me strangely," Byng admitted; "when his eyes are upon me, I feel something stir in my heart." The voyage "would have been a bore without him. I have never met and hardly heard of him before; but we became intimate at once. He has shown me much attention."[18]

It becomes plain, however, that Densdeth is an unprincipled and sinister figure. "He was a keen, hard analyzer of men, utterly skeptical to good motives." All that mattered to him was power and sensuality. His motives were purely selfish. He was engaged to marry the lovely Clara Denman, the daughter of a wealthy New York City merchant. Clara's father had "gained money-power at the cost of moral weight." He and Densdeth were jointly implicated in gigantic financial schemes. Shortly before the marriage was to have taken place, Clara disappeared. Three days later, what was identified as her body washed ashore on a beach "down the bay," an apparent suicide. Rumor had it that the cruel father had tried "to crowd this poor child into a marriage she abhorred." Even worse, it was whispered that Densdeth had compelled Clara's father to make her marry him by shielding the father from crimes that otherwise could have sent him to prison. Byng comes to realize that Densdeth's "smooth cool manner" conceals a "scornful smile," and notes that his "cruel face" is marred by a telltale drooping "black moustache." The "faithless" Densdeth sneers cynically at any mention of altruism or self-sacrifice. Other characters denounce Densdeth as a "demon" and "fiend" who is "evil personified" and "evil to the core."[19]

The theme of ambiguous sexual identity is central to the novel. Byng tries to befriend a struggling young artist, Cecil Dreeme, who had a "gentle voice" and a "singular, refined beauty," and whose paintings had been mistaken for those of a woman. Dreeme's "feminine element" seemed to exclude him from the world of male sociability. At the end of the novel it suddenly is revealed that Dreeme is Clara Denman in disguise! She had not drowned after all. She "unsexed" herself when her father demanded that she marry a man whom she "disliked and distrusted." Rather than "desecrate my womanhood," she rebelled against Densdeth's "corruption of my father's nature and compulsion of me through him."[20]

The novel ends melodramatically. A secondary character murders Densdeth and is himself killed in the struggle. Emma Denman, Clara's sister, who is de-

18. Winthrop, *Cecil Dreeme*, 24–25, 62, 65–66, 72–73, 153, 168, 195, 209.
19. Ibid., 24–25, 68–70, 109, 179, 183–84, 247–48, 264, 304–5, 312, 317, 353.
20. Ibid., 175, 242, 286, 338–39.

picted as a feminine counterpart to Densdeth ("even baser, more cynical and false"), tardily awakens to contemplate her ignominious failure to help Clara when Clara needed her. An accomplice in Densdeth's wicked deeds and unable to erase "the curse of sin," Emma commits suicide. Byng, who once had been entranced by Emma, realizes that he providentially had escaped her "evil," "taint," and "vice." In fact he really had loved Dreeme but had been reluctant to say so. With Dreeme/Clara having revealed him/herself as a virtuous woman who has escaped all taint, Byng finally finds a suitable object for his affections.[21]

In Winthrop's novel, we find a version of Hurlbert that diverges sharply from that created by Kingsley. And yet each writer shared the same point of departure. Both Stangrave and Densdeth are handsome young American cosmopolitans who make excellent first impressions. Indeed, Winthrop revealed even more than Kingsley about his character's intellectual prowess and ability to charm. But while Stangrave was what he appeared to be, Densdeth was not. It would seem that Kingsley failed to probe beneath the surface, whereas Winthrop revealed the "repulsive" figure concealed behind the "attractive" façade.[22]

Densdeth revealed his true nature only after he had returned to the United States. As we shall see in the next chapter, Winthrop's novel paralleled known aspects of Hurlbert's life. Soon after his arrival in New York City, he became the chief editorial writer for Henry J. Raymond's *New York Times*. Whatever youthful idealism he still possessed soon gave way to a more hard-boiled outlook and a more open pursuit of personal advantage. His politics veered to the right. His relationships with women, already a source of scandalous rumor, became even more notorious. In some circles of New York society, he became persona non grata.

Thomas Wentworth Higginson wrote the most revealing of the three novels featuring a version of Hurlbert. Higginson is best remembered as a radical abolitionist who aided John Brown, commanded a black regiment during the Civil War, and, in later years, encouraged the reclusive poet Emily Dickinson. Of greatest importance here, Higginson and Hurlbert were devoted to each other in college. Soon after they first met in 1845, Higginson wrote admiringly to his mother about the young Carolinian, "a true Southerner, the best sort,—slender

21. Ibid., 227–29, 256–73, 275, 281, 355–60.
22. Ibid., 178.

and graceful, dark with raven eyes and hair."[23] The two became inseparable. "I never loved but one male friend with passion," Higginson later recalled of Hurlbert, "and for him my love had no bounds—all that my natural fastidiousness and cautious reserve kept from others I poured out on him; to say that I would have died for him was nothing."[24] Both aspired to the Unitarian ministry, and they remained close for several years. Hurlbert composed hymns for Higginson—one contained many "holy thoughts with which you have constantly mingled."[25] During the 1850s, however, the friendship cooled. Higginson kept in his files an unsent letter to Hurlbert, in which he voiced regret that they had drifted apart ("I still believe in you and out of the depths of my heart I still love you.").[26] Higginson's politics and associations became totally unlike Hurlbert's.

And yet a torch long burned. Shortly after Hurlbert's death in 1895, the aged Higginson reread the letter he had sent to his mother half a century before. Doing so rekindled fond memories of the "young man so handsome in his dark beauty that he seemed like a picturesque Oriental; slender, keen-eyed, raven-haired, he arrested the eye and the heart like some fascinating girl." Higginson, who had met "many gifted men on both sides of the Atlantic," regarded Hurlbert as "unequaled among them all for natural brilliancy" and "the most variously gifted and accomplished man I have ever known." (Had Higginson enlarged his category of gifted people to include Emily Dickinson, one wonders where she might have fit!) Quite aware that Hurlbert subsequently acquired a reputation for being "selfish and unscrupulous" and lacking in "moral principle," the elderly Higginson still marveled at Hurlbert's "constitutional and invariable impulse to attract and charm." He inspired warm affection from "both sexes," and he "certainly had the power not merely of inspiring affection, but of returning it."[27]

Keeping this context in mind, let us turn to Higginson's only novel. *Malbone:*

23. Thomas Wentworth Higginson to Louisa Higginson, Sept. 20, 1845, Thomas Wentworth Higginson Papers, Houghton Library, Harvard University.

24. Tilden G. Edelstein, *Strange Enthusiasm: A Life of Thomas Wentworth Higginson* (New Haven: Yale Univ. Press, 1968), 64.

25. William Henry Hurlbut to Thomas Wentworth Higginson, Sept. 3, 1847, Higginson Papers; Edelstein, *Strange Enthusiasm*, 77.

26. Thomas Wentworth Higginson to William Henry Hurlbut, Oct. 31, 1852, Higginson Papers.

27. Higginson, *Cheerful Yesterdays*, 107–11.

An Oldport Romance was written and published in 1869 but set a decade earlier in the late 1850s. It cannot be judged a great work of literature. It contains, however, a chief character whom readers of this narrative will recognize immediately. But Higginson's fictional Hurlbert, unlike the versions offered by Kingsley and Winthrop, has a perplexing mix of characteristics.[28]

Philip Malbone, a "young prince" with handsome features and "chestnut-brown eyes," was blessed with a "self-poised easy grace." His charm was "recognized by both sexes." Malbone was "a jewel of a listener" whose "sunny temperament" attracted young and old alike. "He liked everybody and everybody liked him," most especially women and children. Alas, this prince was flawed. He could "love a dozen at once" and was notoriously lacking in "constancy." Nonetheless, he had a gift for communicating a genuine ardor to the immediate object of his affections. His earnestness prompted women to convince themselves that his attachment to them was serious, even though he "trifles with others." Malbone enjoyed the chase. In his view, each affair at the time it occurred was a *"grande passion."* "I love to be loved," he explained; "there was always something new and fascinating to explore in a human heart, that is, a woman's." Malbone lived for the moment. Even though "his heart was not deep," he was "never really insincere."[29]

As the novel unfolds, we find that Malbone is engaged to Hope, a "gifted" New England maiden with long, golden blonde hair, a "commanding presence," and a "peculiarly noble carriage." Hope loves Malbone "ardently" and is "blind" to his shortcomings. Her fiancé, just arrived back from Europe, has brought with him Hope's younger half-sister, Emilia. Raised in France by a "charming and unscrupulous woman" who had "lured" Hope's father into a second marriage, Emilia recently had attempted "to elope from boarding-school with a Swiss servant." Happily, Malbone's charms proved ideally suited to persuade Emilia to accompany him back to the United States.[30]

Of course Emilia became infatuated with Malbone. She decided that he would favor her over her half-sister. Malbone, who found that "no lawful passion can ever be so bewildering or ecstatic as an unlawful one," kept Emilia in

28. Higginson later stated that Hurlbert provided the basis for his fictional Malbone. Higginson, *Cheerful Yesterdays,* 107. See also Edelstein, *Strange Enthusiasm,* 312–15.

29. Thomas Wentworth Higginson, *Malbone: An Oldport Romance* (Boston: Fields, Osgood, & Co., 1869), 6–7, 50–52, 240, 53–56, 58, 102–06.

30. Ibid., 24–29, 57–59.

a state of "perpetual excitement." She in turn put him "in the grasp of a passion too strong to be delightful." Even though Malbone succeeds in having Emilia married to a conveniently available widower, their mutual attraction continues. The novel's moment of truth occurs when Hope interrupts a tryst between Malbone and the newly married Emilia. "Fruit and flowers and wine were on the table." Soon afterward, Emilia drowns in a storm. Hope, keeping to herself "the tragic complication which [Emilia's] death alone could have solved," breaks off her engagement to Malbone.[31]

Plainly Higginson echoes Winthrop's *Cecil Dreeme* in a number of intriguing particulars. Neither Malbone nor Densdeth was to be judged by first impressions. Both were recklessly self-centered, and neither took account of the way he hurt others. Both misused their undoubted talents. But Winthrop's Densdeth was willfully malevolent, whereas Higginson's Malbone was an amoral sensualist whose behavior was more thoughtless than ill-spirited. Unlike Winthrop, Higginson refused to depict Malbone/Hurlbert in an entirely negative way. "He was no more capable of unkindness than of constancy; and so strongly did he fix the allegiance of those who loved him, that the women to whom he had caused most anguish would still defend him when accused; would have crossed the continent, if needed, to nurse him in illness, and would have rained rivers of tears on his grave."[32]

Winthrop and Higginson each depicted a man who was immensely attractive to women, and who routinely pursued new conquests. Enough evidence survives to conclude that these fictional qualities were well based in fact. Rumors about Hurlbert's dalliances began when he was young and continued throughout his life. He was reported to have paid for a trip to Europe with money borrowed from a young woman whom he subsequently chose not to marry. He was accused of selling the letters that another woman wrote to him. He raised eyebrows by dedicating his first book, about a trip to Cuba, to "my friend, Mrs. F. W. S., in the name of one whose memory is linked with the sweetest and saddest recollections of my Cuban journey."[33]

31. Ibid., 110–11. 115–17, 133–47, 151, 155, 186–89, 234, 240.

32. Ibid., 54–55.

33. Hurlbert obituary, *New York World*, Sept. 8, 1895. By the 1850s, "notions of sexual liberty" that would not have been articulated before began to appear. New York City was an arena where racy or erotic printed material fueled a "male sporting culture." But pious businessmen, who were appalled

Kate Field, an accomplished journalist ten years Hurlbert's junior, left a candid recollection of his appeal. In 1883 she described "a flirtation she had with Hurlbert years ago"—probably in the late 1850s—when she was "young and exuberant." Having heard that "he was a lady killer," she resolved to teach him that "there was one lady at least who could be bombproof against his charms." She found him "one of the most gifted conversationalists I ever met." Field's account of tantalizing Hurlbert at a masked ball crackles with sensual electricity. Hurlbert "followed me everywhere, and was so devoted to me that at last my friends came to me and told me I must cut away from him—that he was a very dangerous man." She "managed finally to escape from him" and had "not seen him for a long time," but she judged him still to be "what he has always been—a very handsome, fascinating, gifted, accomplished, naughty fellow." Young Kate was described as "very slender" with a "shapely figure," a "wealth of chestnut hair falling in clustering curls," and "luminous blue eyes." Poised, self-confident, and "always conscious of playing a woman's part in a man's world," she "artfully exploited her own decided femininity." Her account strongly suggests that other women found Hurlbert's overtures irresistible.[34]

No contemporary evidence corroborates a suicide or suicides among the women whom Hurlbert trifled with or jilted. In June 1859 the newspapers turned a lurid spotlight on the drowning in New York Harbor of an attractive young actress, Fanny Deane Halsey—an incident that may have inspired Winthrop and perhaps Higginson—but Hurlbert was not involved.[35] Victorian novelists needed drownings, however, because they could neither redeem nor rehabilitate a tainted woman. It was necessary that such a woman recognize the awfulness of her behavior by removing herself from the scene.

---

by widespread vice and prostitution, organized the Young Men's Christian Association (YMCA) to "offer peer pressure of a different sort." Helen Lefkowitz Horowitz, *Rereading Sex: Battles over Sexual Knowledge and Suppression in Nineteenth-Century America* (New York: Knopf, 2002), quotations on 9, 300, 305.

34. *Cincinnati Commercial* in *Brooklyn Daily Eagle*, Sept. 16, 1883; David Baldwin, "Kate Field," in Edward T. James, ed., *Notable American Women, 1607–1950: A Biographical Dictionary* (3 vols.; Cambridge: Harvard Univ. Press, 1971), 1:612–14; *New York Times*, May 31, 1896; Autumn Stanley, "Scribbling Women as Entrepreneurs: Kate Field (1838–96) and Charlotte Smith (1840–1917)," *Business and Economic History*, 2nd ser., 21 (1992): 74–83, quotation on 74n.

35. *New York Times*, June 7, 8, 1859.

Complaints about Hurlbert's salacious behavior show up in the extensive diary kept by George Templeton Strong, a feisty New York City attorney. Strong's diary contains fascinating glimpses of a Mr. Hyde who lurked behind Hurlbert's Dr. Jekyll exterior. In December 1856, Hurlbert called on Strong, ostensibly to discuss ways of creating a more "permanent organization" for the Republican Party. The diarist was on his guard. Although Hurlbert had "a vast social reputation just now" and was widely considered "brilliant and fascinating," Strong suspected him of being "an unprincipled adventurer." Several months later, in March 1857, Strong noted a "great fuss" about Hurlbert's alleged kleptomania—"habitually borrowing other people's raiment without permission." This difficulty was resolved with Hurlbert winning some kind of endorsement of his good character, but other troubles soon arose. Strong's cousin and law partner, Charles E. Strong, was unhappily married to the former Eleanor Fearing. In the summer of 1857 while at Newport, "Charley" Strong discovered in his wife's room a compromising letter from "that treacherous scoundrel," Hurlbert. It was "such a letter as a foolish man would write to his mistress in the first week of concubinage." George Templeton Strong was left with the distasteful task of interviewing the three parties to the triangle, and trying to arrange a reconciliation that would salvage the marriage. After a visit from Hurlbert, Strong "smashed" the glass "from which some water was given this dog."[36]

Winthrop's Densdeth thus reflected a bitter resentment of Hurlbert that had arisen during the late 1850s.[37] Some of New York's proper churchgoing gentry decried this "unprincipled adventurer" and regretted his prominence and influence. For them as for Winthrop, Hurlbert's talents and winning qualities were simply a camouflage. They judged that he had no moral compass, either for personal behavior or for political outlook. It offended them to open the *New York Times* and find his editorial columns staring them in the face. They had reasons for their strictures, but the one-dimensional caricature they promoted was at best an oversimplification. If nothing else, it failed to explain why, in an era

36. Allan Nevins and Milton Halsey Thomas, eds., *The Diary of George Templeton Strong* (4 vols.; New York: Macmillan, 1952), 2:312–13, 327, 350–51. Between March and November of 1858, Hurlbert returned to London to escape the "petty gossip" in New York. *Diary of Strong*, 2:402–3, 422–23; Evans, "William H. Hurlbert," 408.

37. George Templeton Strong regarded Theodore Winthrop as a "good fellow." It appears that he was part of Strong's circle. *Diary of Strong*, 2:350.

when personal reputation weighed heavily, Hurlbert could shrug off the aroma of scandal, maintain his social position, and continue to enjoy the support of Henry J. Raymond, editor of the *Times*.

The three novels, when read together, should pique our curiosity. Someone who plainly possessed extraordinary gifts and a magnetic personality appears to have used his abilities dubiously. Could one so talented and memorable also be so flawed? What might be the source of such contradictory qualities? Could anything he did or said be relied upon? These questions hover around Hurlbert's life. This book will attempt to make sense of him. In so doing, it will seek to explicate that heretofore inscrutable riddle, "The Diary of a Public Man."

4

HURLBERT THE JOURNALIST

The three fictional versions of William Henry Hurlbert variously depicted his attractive qualities or his repellent features or some combination thereof, but they scarcely hinted at his key attribute. The ingratiating charmer/heartless seducer in the novels is no more than part of the story—and, indeed, not even the main part. But for Hurlbert's extraordinarily facile pen, he would deserve to remain forgotten. He is memorable today because of his gift for writing, and, most especially, for one unforgettable exercise of that gift.

Hurlbert first worked as a journalist in the mid-1850s. He wrote for *Putnam's Monthly,* a high-quality magazine that deserved a better fate than its brief run from 1854 to 1857. *Putnam's,* which aspired to reach both a New York and a national audience, included unmistakably antislavery articles among its political selections. Hurlbert also was a drama critic for *The Albion,* an assignment that likely stimulated his interest in the theater.[1] His first book, published in 1854, recounted a visit to Cuba. It was based on a series of articles that first appeared in the antislavery weekly *The National Era.* The poet John Greenleaf Whittier stated that the person "who had written that could write anything he pleased."[2]

Hurlbert's rise to national visibility coincided with the intensified North-South sectional conflict and the rise of the Republican Party. On May 22, 1856, the political crisis in the United States reached new levels of intensity. South Carolina representative Preston Brooks assaulted Massachusetts senator Charles Sumner on the floor of the U.S. Senate—and won plaudits throughout the South. Northerners were appalled. Disagreement was one thing—and many in

---

1. Thomas Bender, *New York Intellect: A History of Intellectual Life in New York City from 1750 to the Beginnings of Our Own Time* (New York: Knopf, 1987), 162–68; T. C. Evans, "William H. Hurlbert," *New York Times Saturday Literary Review,* June 14, 1902, p. 408.

2. William H. Hurlbert, *Gan-Eden; or, Pictures of Cuba* (Boston: J. P. Jewett & Co., 1854); Whittier quoted in Thomas Wentworth Higginson, *Cheerful Yesterdays* (Boston: Houghton, Mifflin, 1898), 111.

the North did disagree with Sumner's heavy-handed criticisms of the South. But beating a man senseless because you disagreed with him suggested that the "slave power" intended to treat white Northerners the same way they treated their slaves. All rights of free speech and free expression—even on the floor of Congress—appeared subject to Southern whim.[3]

Young Hurlbert poured out his reactions to the stricken Massachusetts senator. The "atrocious deed" had "touched and roused every class of Northern society" and had created an intense awareness of "the terrible reality" that "we *must* confront." Sumner, the "firmest enemy of Slavery," now wore "the martyr's crown." He had become the "perpetual representative alike of Northern honor and Northern manhood." Hurlbert looked forward to Sumner's return to the Senate, a site destined to become "as sacred in the annals of freedom as is the arena of the Coliseum in the story of our faith." Hurlbert also ventured an ominous prediction: "The scoundrelly simpleton who struck you fled from the recoil of his weapon, but there will be a fiercer recoil from that blow and a flowing of blood not so easily to be stanched."[4]

Hurlbert, as we have seen, eagerly supported the Republican presidential candidate, John C. Frémont, on a free soil platform that would bar any future increase in slave territory. During a visit to England in the summer of 1856, he prepared the striking essay for the *Edinburgh Review* that surveyed the history of the North/South political rivalry and "attracted extraordinary attention" on both sides of the Atlantic. From close personal contact and acquaintance, he called attention to the way in which "the great religious community of the Northern States" and "the most respectable and energetic classes of Northern society" had become "agitated on the question of Slavery." This was a sentiment he shared, along with the conclusion that Southern recklessness posed a direct threat to national well-being. Yet he recognized too that the rise of political antislavery had exasperated the South. Hurlbert predicted that "matters cannot go on much further in their present path" and warned that a war of "more than ordinary ferocity" could occur.[5]

3. William E. Gienapp, "The Crime against Sumner: The Caning of Charles Sumner and the Rise of the Republican Party," *Civil War History* 25 (Sept. 1979): 218–45.

4. William Henry Hurlbert to Charles Sumner, June 7, 1856, Charles Sumner Papers, Houghton Library, Harvard University.

5. William H. Hurlbert, "The Political Crisis in the United States," *Edinburgh Review* 104 (October 1856): 561–97, quotes on 566, 592, 596; Evans, "William H. Hurlbert," 408.

Soon after his return to the United States in late 1856, Hurlbert began writing for the *New York Times*. He did not have to work his way up through the ranks. Henry J. Raymond started him at the top by giving him responsibility for writing many of the newspaper's editorials. Hurlbert soon displayed "those talents for which he became remarkable"—"quickness of perception, vividness of ideas, [and] brilliancy of style." He was "au courant with the transpiring of events abroad and at home," and his easily recognized writing instantly "attracted attention." Raymond admired Hurlbert. His staff included many capable writers, "but when shall I find any one to write anything like this?" he asked, while pointing to one of Hurlbert's recent editorials.[6] Although James Gordon Bennett's *New York Herald* and Horace Greeley's *New York Tribune* had more readers, the *Times* too had national perspective and commanded notice. Raymond made Hurlbert his right-hand man.

A. Oakey Hall, the mayor of New York City between 1869 and 1873—and himself a writer of some distinction—marveled at Hurlbert's writing skills. Hurlbert had masterful command of language and could compose "on the top of a hat or in a railroad carriage." But he had little need to take notes because "he never forgot anything he ever heard or read." He effortlessly placed current events in historical perspective, thereby giving his editorials gravity and depth. Hurlbert exhibited a "curious amalgamation of industry and idleness," Hall noted. He was "a great postponer" who loved to spend sociable evenings with his cronies and who "needed spur." Once spurred, however, he wrote with "swift dexterity," not even "stopping for a word or phrase." There was "no plod at all about him." Like "the engineer of an express train delayed at a drawbridge who makes up time," Hurlbert raced ahead. Hall recalled that Hurlbert, having arrived at the *Times* offices at midnight after having been "delayed at a theatre or supper party," could compose "in two hours thereafter before the press closing time" an article for which a more methodical journalist might need six hours.[7]

Hall also recounted how young Hurlbert's celebrity with the *Times* contributed to his dominating social presence in New York City in the late 1850s.

6. *New York Herald*, Sept. 7, 1895; *New York World*, Sept. 7, 8, 1895. Those who had worked closely with him at the *World*, particularly former mayor A. Oakey Hall, marked Hurlbert's passing by writing at length about the brilliant eccentric who once had edited the newspaper. These articles, especially when corroborated by other sources, carry special weight. Incisive and multidimensional, they far transcend the usual formulas for obituary writing.

7. *New York World*, Sept. 8, 1895.

Raymond first introduced "Elegant Oakey" and Hurlbert to each other. Hall found Hurlbert a conspicuous exception to the idea that good-looking men rarely exhibited "cleverness and capacity." The "strikingly handsome" bachelor had a high forehead, dark hair, fascinating eyes, and "winning tones of voice, with musical inflections." His carriage was "erect" and "manly," and he also had "perfect taste in dress." Hurlbert was a delightfully sociable conversationalist. He spoke "without gab or repetition of ideas" and displayed an inexhaustible inventory of "sparkling topics and references." Nobody in New York was more "skilled in repartee." Fashionable hostesses vied to include this "right good, jolly fellow" in their parties. He could converse politely with "even the boresome or twaddling shuttle-cock" and could be counted on "to keep the table in a roar of laughter." Whatever Hurlbert's difficulties with the Strong family and some of their friends, he was otherwise "received into the best society of New York." His "elegant presence, charm of manner and fascinating conversational power made him a favored guest, as he had been in a similar circle in London."[8]

When Hurlbert started writing for the *Times,* his views on North-South issues reflected his piece in the *Edinburgh Review* and the opinions he expressed during the Frémont campaign. He reproved his Southern friends for seeing "Northern antagonism to Slavery" simply as a "vituperative, morbid, extravagant, uproarious clamor." Instead, it was a "grave and resolute feeling, born of profound conviction" and shared by "three-fourths of the civilized world." Proslavery extremists who insisted on the right to extend slavery to the territories were "corrupting the vital principles of the Republic, and endangering the stability of the Union." But rather than harp on the immorality of slavery, Hurlbert preferred to discuss political economy. Slavery was undermining Southern prosperity. He therefore chastised the South for denouncing as an abolitionist anyone who dared to mention that "land in Ohio sells at a higher rate than land in Kentucky" or that "cotton-lands deteriorate under Slave-labor."[9]

Hurlbert hoped for peaceful sectional coexistence, but he recognized long before most other analysts that North-South antagonism could have explosive consequences. The North and South, he wrote, either must "understand each other" or "fight." He recommended that both sides acknowledge their stark differences—"our systems of society, our modes of life, are radically and ab-

8. Ibid.; *New York Herald,* Sept. 7, 1895.
9. *New York Times,* May 4, June 2, 23, 1857.

solutely dissimilar." At the same time, he insisted that North and South were not "necessarily and inevitably hostile to one another." A new spirit of "mutual toleration" and "mutual forbearance" might yet prevent their antagonism from spiraling out of control. A "rational conclusion of this imbroglio" remained possible.[10]

But Hurlbert saw that the South needed to accept certain hard truths. The "growing preponderance of the Free States" could not be reversed. For "natural and legitimate" reasons, slavery never would take root in the western territories. Slavery only would go where it was profitable. "And so a Virginia, Kentucky or Tennessee slaveowner will send his slaves to Mississippi and Alabama—if he parts with them at all—rather than to Kansas, Arizona or Nebraska, because they will command a better price." Hurlbert therefore condemned President James Buchanan's efforts to get Kansas admitted to the Union as a slave state. The "Lecompton fraud" was "a miserable blunder" and a "needless, absurd and ruinous mistake." No sensible Democrat in any free state would support it. He lauded those Democrats, led by Stephen A. Douglas, who stood their ground against Buchanan and the Lecompton "swindle."[11]

In early 1858, several years before most other commentators got to the heart of the matter, Hurlbert insisted that the South had to choose between "*submission* to the substantial supremacy of the Free States, or *secession* from the Union." He did not think the South had "anything to apprehend" from the North. Slavery in the states where it already existed would "never be interfered with," unless "its own aggressions should provoke a resentment which will overleap the bounds of justice and the Constitution." Secession, on the other hand, would plunge the slave states "instantly into a gulf of political ruin." Peaceful secession was impossible. Secession instead would bring "all the horrors of a civil war." Slavery, "which now enjoys the protection of the Federal Constitution, would then be exposed to a thousand dangers from which it is now free."[12]

When France and Austria went to war in April 1859, Raymond headed for Europe to cover the big story. His periodic letters, dispatched to the fastest ships, enabled the *Times* to scoop the *Herald* and the *Tribune*. (The first trans-Atlantic telegraph cable, completed in 1858, had gone dead after a month of deterio-

10. Ibid., June 23, 1857.
11. Ibid., Feb. 3, 19, 26, 1858.
12. Ibid., Feb. 3, 1858.

rating service.) Hurlbert was left in charge of the *Times*. From his newly elevated vantage point, he sustained the newspaper's pro-French slant that Raymond already had articulated. Only in alliance with France, the *Times* maintained, could Piedmont-Sardinia challenge Austria's grip on northern Italy and pave the way for Italian unification. Hurlbert eagerly pointed out the failure of his rivals to provide comparable coverage of the war. He also taunted Horace Greeley, the "impracticable" philanthropist and editor of the *Tribune,* for claiming to favor Italian unification while opposing the use of armed force to bring it about. "So long as the liberation of Italy was a distant vision," Hurlbert charged, "the *Tribune* doated upon Italy; it was a theme so prolific of fine phrases, so abundant in taunts for the despots." But with Italy "awakened" and wielding the sword that the French "put into their hands," the *Tribune* was "appalled at the spectacle of a people really trying to free themselves in a blunt, practical way."[13]

His summertime responsibilities led Hurlbert into an unfortunate gaffe that was remembered decades later. He often wrote more than one editorial at a time, and sometimes finished hard against the deadline after a sociable dinner with friends. Friday evening, July 15, 1859, was just such an occasion. The next morning the *Times* published "The Defensive Square of Austrian Italy." It provided a detailed assessment of the geographical position occupied by retreating Austrian forces in northern Italy. Midway through the editorial, Hurlbert described the winding course of the Mincio River, with its "countless elbows"—"and, if we follow up the course of the Mincio we shall find innumerable elbows formed by the sympathy of youth." A few sentences later Hurlbert veered from discussing Italian geography by calling attention to a "foreign fleet suddenly coming up on our question of citizenship."[14]

Hurlbert, overconfident of his promethean abilities, had ordered the typesetters for the *Times* to set up his editorials exactly as he wrote them. In this instance, however, the pages for two different editorials had gotten mixed up, and proofreaders were unable to prevent the debacle. Hurlbert's role soon became known, "and on him the chaff fell as blindingly as the real stuff falls from a bolter in a flour mill." The *Herald* made the "elbows" article an occasion for much hi-

13. Bern Dibner, "Communications," in Melvin Kranzberg and Carroll W. Pursell, Jr., eds., *Technology in Western Civilization* (2 vols.; New York: Oxford Univ. Press, 1967), 1:458–59; Francis Brown, *Raymond of the Times* (New York: W. W. Norton & Co., 1951), 169; *New York Times*, June 1, 3, Aug. 1, 1859.

14. *New York Times*, July 16, 1859.

larity. It marveled, tongue in cheek, at the "geographical wisdom" of the *Times*, which was "too much for our limited capabilities." The mysteriously sympathetic elbows suggested to the *Herald* that the writer had violated Puritanical norms by imbibing "stronger and more unseemly potations than lager bier." The *Times* quickly apologized to its readers for its "extremely ridiculous blunder." It blamed "a confusion of manuscripts, sent up at a late hour on Friday night." A "series of typographical transpositions" had thereby accidentally converted parts of two different articles into "a mere medley of words." When news of Hurlbert's non-sequiturs reached Europe, Raymond was reported to be furious. The editor's admiration for his young editorialist plainly cooled.[15]

The summer of 1859 also proved to be a watershed time for Hurlbert politically. The unrelenting spiral of North-South antagonism convinced him that the entire national political system had run off the tracks. In the absence of "wise statesmen" who sought common ground on which people from both sections might stand, "an army of cunning politicians" had arisen to exploit "the rapid increase of ill-feeling between the North and the South." The growing Southern clamor for federal protection of slavery in the territories—the so-called "slave code"—seemed both ominous and suicidal to Hurlbert. No candidate who supported this position could "carry the vote of a single Free State." So, too, Southerners calling for revival of the African slave trade would "turn every American seaport from Charleston to Galveston into a harbor of pirates"—and yet the respected Alexander Stephens and John Forsyth had added their voices to the clamor. The South, provoked by Northern "self-righteousness," was "flinging itself with fatal fury against the bulwarks of the law, and threatening the public order of the Union." It was also increasing the chances that a Republican would be elected president in 1860, because "on a purely slave question the North must unite."[16]

Hurlbert searched for middle ground between North and South. He was repelled not just by Southern proslavery zealots, who wanted a slave code and the African slave trade, but also by Northern antislavery zealots, some of whom saw restricting slavery from all territories as the first step leading to abolition.

15. *New York World*, Sept. 8, 1895; *New York Herald*, July 17, 1859; *New York Times*, July 18, Aug. 1, 1859; Brown, *Raymond of the Times*, 178–79; Elmer Davis, *History of the New York Times, 1851–1921* (New York: The New York Times, 1921), 44–46.

16. *New York Times*, June 2, July 11, 18, 21, 29, 1859.

Though he had supported Frémont in 1856 as a way of protesting Southern efforts to force slavery into Kansas, Hurlbert judged by 1859 that Kansas was certain to become a free state. Therefore "the Kansas question" had become "obsolete," and "the Slavery issue will not be half as strong at the next election as it was in the last." In the absence of any remaining proslavery threat to any territory, Republicans should transform their "sectional organization" into a "united opposition" that would reach out to moderates both north and south and run against the "disgraceful" record of the Buchanan administration. But he saw little evidence that Republicans would do so. Taking advantage of the South's proslavery vituperation, they expected to win the presidency with Northern votes alone.[17]

By the late summer of 1859, if not before, Hurlbert decided that Stephen A. Douglas was the only presidential candidate who could bridge the growing chasm between North and South. A. D. Banks, a key manager in New York City, reported to Douglas in October that "our friend Hurlbert of the *Times* consults me daily. He is enthusiastically with us." Banks urged Douglas to "thank Mr. Hurlbert for his kindness."[18] Banks, Hurlbert, and George N. Sanders, another Douglas promoter whom we have encountered in chapter 2, attempted to enlist a group of prosperous investors, sympathetic to the Illinois senator, to buy the *Times*. "It is not possible to successfully conduct a Presidential contest such as you have inaugurated [in] these railway and lightning times without a great Press in this great city speaking to the millions every hour of the day throughout the broad land," the media-conscious Sanders warned Douglas. In January 1860, Hurlbert himself pleaded with Douglas to come to New York for a day or two "to have dinner with gentlemen in the city."[19]

Events in late 1859 intensified Hurlbert's allegiance to the "Little Giant." John Brown's audacious raid on Harpers Ferry widened the sectional breach. Between the time of Brown's assault, on October 16, and his execution, on December 2, the precarious middle ground eroded. Growing numbers of people north and south began to see each other through the distorted lenses of sectional stereotypes. Southerners imagined a North that teemed with abolitionists and wel-

17. Ibid., Mar. 29, July 29, Aug. 22, 1859.

18. George Fort Milton, *The Eve of Conflict: Stephen A. Douglas and the Needless War* (Boston: Houghton Mifflin, 1934), 384; A. D. Banks to Douglas, Oct. 19, 29, 1859, Stephen A. Douglas Papers, University of Chicago.

19. George N. Sanders to Douglas, Dec. 20, 1859; Hurlbert to Douglas, Jan. 16, 1860; see also A. D. Banks to Douglas, Nov. 1, 10, 1859, Douglas Papers.

comed armed invasion of the South; Northerners saw a South in which the most reckless and irresponsible extremists had gained the upper hand. The South pointed an accusing finger at the small minority of Northerners who proclaimed Brown a martyr in a holy cause; the North reacted with disbelief to the Southern panic and threats to leave the Union. Day after day between late October and late December, Hurlbert framed the editorial response of the *Times* to the deepening crisis. This interval may well have been the highlight of his long career as a daily journalist. His bisectional origins made him an astute observer and commentator. His frequent contributions make it possible to trace in close detail the evolution of his own thought.

Initially Hurlbert dismissed Brown's attack on Harpers Ferry as "a short-lived affair" of no lasting significance. "It seems to have been the work of a single man" who had been driven insane by the death of his son in Kansas; "a wilder and more hopeless project than that in which he embarked cannot be imagined." Hurlbert confidently assured his readers that there was no reason to blame any political party for Brown's rash acts. The "angry meteor shot athwart the sky" by "mad John Brown" provided, however, a timely warning that "vast possibilities of evil sleep in our angry sectional politics." Americans had traded for years "in the fiercest of internecine passions as composedly as if no mischief could ever come of such light matters to so great a nation as ours." Brown had "dashed this false and foolish confidence in pieces."[20]

John Brown's speech, given just before he was sentenced to death by a Virginia court, made a decided impact on Hurlbert. Notwithstanding all evidence to the contrary, the "brave old fanatic" insisted that he had no intention to incite "rebellion or insurrection." Instead, he claimed that he intended simply to carry off slaves from Virginia to Canada without "snapping a gun." The "enormous and obvious inconsistency" between Brown's actions and words made his speech "a psychological study." It also demonstrated the "extreme unwisdom" of "treating such a man as the agent of a party." Brown's speech placed him "in a class of one." It was "*sui generis*"—the most astonishing defense of "individual passion against organized order" since "mad Lord George Gordon fanned the Protestant fanaticism of London into flame, 80 years ago, and for three days held the metropolis of England at the mercy of a frantic mob."[21]

20. *New York Times*, Oct. 19, 27, 1859.

21. Ibid., Nov. 3, 1859. A repeal of certain proscriptive laws against Roman Catholics triggered a ferocious upheaval in London in June 1780. The Protestant extremist Lord George Gordon was widely blamed for inciting the orgy of mob violence.

Hurlbert grew increasingly astonished by the "frightened frenzy" spreading across Virginia and the South. Richmond newspapers printed "astounding and alarming revelations," falsely creating the impression that Brown enjoyed widespread support across the North. They alleged that the "great mass" of people in the North were "rabid, ultra-Abolitionists" who were delighted by the attack on Harpers Ferry and stood ready to march south to continue Brown's onslaught. The Richmond press and Virginia governor Henry Wise "fostered those insane fears and unreasoning passions," rather than acting responsibly in a manner that might have "calmed and subdued" public anxiety. The "absurd and disgraceful panic" exposed a gnawing Southern insecurity. Having boasted incessantly about the impossibility that slaves could ever "be enticed or goaded into rebellion against their masters," Southerners suddenly acted as if their entire social order stood in imminent peril.[22]

Hurlbert, writing as a Southerner who had long lived in the North, attempted to persuade Southerners that they misunderstood the free states and willfully exaggerated "the perils to which they are exposed." He explained that Northern willingness to tolerate abolitionists did not signify agreement with them. "Toleration is the law of the land in this section of the Union," he noted. "Lynch law,—tar and feathers,—expulsion" were not practiced in the North. "The South does not understand, and therefore misinterprets this forbearance." Southern expectations of continued armed invasion were, in Hurlbert's opinion, "something which any man who can read and write ought to be ashamed to discuss." Northern opponents of slavery typically were "immersed in business and in professions, have wives and houses, and lands." They were "as likely to arm and march on Virginia" as they were to "turn pirates."[23]

How ought Northerners to react? "Must the North," Hurlbert asked, "mimic this madness"? He hoped not. Much as he faulted the South for its outrageous overreaction to the Brown raid, he knew that a counterreaction in the North would only make matters worse. Sectional difficulties should be "controlled, tempered and subordinated to the broad common interests of both sections." The "conservative men at the North" should reach out to "the sanest and soundest leaders of Southern opinion." He continued to hope that the North would allow the South to come to its senses—and recognize that the Brown raid was

22. Ibid., Nov. 4, 14, 17, 21, 23, Dec. 9, 1859.
23. Ibid., Dec. 6, 7, 1859.

"simply the desperate attempt of a misguided fanatic" who had come to see himself as "the Moses of a new exodus."[24]

By early December, Hurlbert saw that conservative sentiment in the South had been silenced. An "irrational and disastrous" tide of public opinion there was "sweeping away all reason and judgment" and making the South "hostile to the preservation of the Union." He kept trying to point out what Southerners refused to understand. "Nine-tenths of the Northern people" gave no countenance whatsoever to Brown's armed assault on the South, and looked with uncomprehending dismay at the uproar in the slave states. But many in the North thought Brown "personally honest and sincere" and credited him with believing that he had been "doing a religious duty in the work which he undertook." And "the public heart always weighs the motives, as well as the acts of men." This widespread Northern tendency to distinguish between Brown's actions and his motives developed in the month between his speech in court and his execution. Respect for Brown's motives resulted, of course, from "the Anti-Slavery feeling of the North." That feeling was widespread and deeply rooted, and there was no way that it could be changed simply to appease Southern sensibilities.[25]

Even though few in the North yet understood the extent of Southern alienation, Hurlbert began to fear the worst. His alarm grew when the highly regarded J. L. M. Curry of Alabama spoke in Congress on December 10. Unlike many from the South, Curry absolved Republicans of any complicity in the Brown raid and acknowledged that most Republicans honestly believed they posed no threat "to the rights and interests of the South." Curry insisted, however, that "the ideas and principles and politics of the Republican Party" would lead inevitably to an increase of "Anti-Slavery agitation and feeling." The election of a Republican president on a sectional platform would be "an assurance of our subjugation." It would deprive the South of "all security in the future"— something to which no Southerner should "submit."[26]

Hurlbert had recently written that "nobody out of a lunatic asylum" contemplated "a settlement of Northern and Southern differences by the sword." He had heaped scorn on the South Carolina legislature's "thoroughly ridiculous" proposal to fortify the long border between the free and slave states—perhaps they would "construct a big wall, like the great wall of China, from Richmond

24. Ibid., Nov. 5, Dec. 5, 1859.
25. Ibid., Dec. 3, 5, 1859.
26. Ibid., Dec. 12, 13, 1859.

to St. Louis, and place Gov. Wise in charge of it"? Curry's speech obliged Hurlbert to reconsider. Even though nobody in the North expected war, he began to see that the South was fast painting itself into a corner from which there might be no other escape but through armed conflict. Southerners would participate in the presidential election, but they would refuse to accept the results if they lost—"they act, in short, like a man who agrees to leave a controversy to arbitration upon condition that judgment be given in his own favor."[27]

The political ramifications of Harpers Ferry never were far from Hurlbert's mind. He suspected that Governor Wise had deliberately "magnified and exaggerated" the Brown raid because he thought it "his stepping-stone to the Presidential nomination." And Wise was not the only one. The balance of power within the Democratic Party appeared to shift toward "Southern Rights"—in other words, a specific guarantee by Congress that slaveholders could take slaves to any federal territory. Hurlbert ridiculed this "dangerous experiment for the Democratic party." He hoped "the Democracy of the North" would refuse to be steamrolled. Allowing the South to dictate the nominee and the platform would cripple the Democratic ticket in the free states. If Democrats were to "yield to Southern ultraism," it would "leave the Southern States at the mercy of the ultraism of the North." In an election that pitted a Republican against a Southern Rights Democrat, the "conservatism of the Free States would no longer have any hold upon either party."[28]

Hurlbert correctly prognosticated that Republicans would downplay all evidence of Southern estrangement from the Union. Even though "innumerable Southern orators and journalists" relentlessly insisted that the election of a Republican president would lead directly to disunion, Republicans intended "to proceed with their regular party nominations as if no such warning had ever been uttered."[29] The only solution to the dangerous dilemma, in his view, lay in keeping the Democratic Party out of the hands of Southern Rights zealots. And the only candidate who could do this was Stephen A. Douglas.

It was once observed that Hurlbert made the *Times* "for months virtually a Douglas paper."[30] There was much truth in this, but the word "virtually" requires emphasis. Hurlbert had to be discreet. To the extent that he could, he gave

27. Ibid., Nov. 26, Dec. 1, 7, 1859.
28. Ibid., Nov. 21, 25, 1859.
29. Ibid., Dec. 22, 1859.
30. Evans, "William H. Hurlbert," 408.

Douglas good press in the *Times*. It applauded his refusal to knuckle under to ultra Southerners and predicted that he would gain three votes in the North for every one he lost in the South. Raymond liked to depict the *Times* as an independent voice rather than "a Republican journal," untrammeled by "mere partisan fealty."[31] In city elections in December 1859, it did not endorse the Republican candidate for mayor, George Opdyke. It threw its support instead to Democrat William Havemeyer, in hopes of stopping former mayor Fernando Wood, who commanded a dissident Democratic faction and was attempting a comeback.[32] On both local and national matters, Hurlbert was given free rein to tangle with Horace Greeley, and he routinely did so. He assailed Greeley's support for Opdyke as an act of narrow partisanship that would divide the anti-Wood vote and risk delivering control of the city to a "vulgar, violent and unscrupulous demagogue." (Indeed, Wood gained a plurality victory.) Both Raymond and Hurlbert likewise were repelled by the *Tribune*'s self-righteous contempt for the South. When the *Tribune* took the position that John Brown desired "not to injure but benefit the South," so that he and his band were "the least sectional of human beings," Hurlbert hit back hard. Language of that sort played into the hands of those who insisted that Republicans "were preparing to wage open war on Slavery."[33]

Raymond kept the *Times* on the fence in the winter and spring of 1860, though privately he favored New York senator William H. Seward, the most prominent Republican of all and the odds-on favorite to win the party's presidential nomination. Raymond agreed to serve as a delegate to the Republican national convention in Chicago, confident that Seward had the inside track. Behind the scenes, however, the Douglas managers continued assiduously to court Raymond. A. D. Banks reported to Douglas on May 11 that "I shall see Raymond and endeavor to get the *Times* to enter at once on the canvass." After Lincoln's surprising nomination, in which Greeley played a conspicuous role, it appeared that Raymond might bolt to Douglas. George Sanders sent an elated message to Douglas from the *Times* office, late in the evening on May 19. Sanders reported that he had just seen

31. *New York Times,* Oct. 15, Aug. 30, 1859, May 26, 1860; Carl F. Krummel, "Henry J. Raymond and the *New York Times* in the Secession Crisis," *New York History* 32 (Oct. 1951): 382.

32. *New York Times,* Nov. 30, Dec. 1, 3, 5, 6, 7, 1859. See also Jerome Mushkat, *Fernando Wood: A Political Biography* (Kent, Ohio: Kent State Univ. Press, 1990), 92–97.

33. *New York Times,* Dec. 10, 12, 1859.

a dispatch from Raymond dated today at Chicago telling Hurlbert not to commit to Lincoln. Hurlbert and all the writers and managers of the *Times* are in ecstasy at the prospect of at last being able to bring out the *Times* squarely for you. I hope Raymond will be at our monster meeting on Tuesday. . . . Lincoln's nomination has fallen still born here. You will beat him in this city from forty to fifty thousand. The Seward men will not pay a dollar (and they have all the money) towards the election.[34]

Hurlbert continued to give favorable editorial coverage to the Little Giant. Douglas stood on high ground, denounced both by "the fanatics of New-England" and by "the secessionists of the Gulf States." Echoing a theme he had sounded since the previous winter, Hurlbert worried that Republicans thoughtlessly dismissed the chances of "any formidable resistance on the part of the South" and refused to see the possibility of "secession or disunion." He warned that "even the most conservative of Southern men" considered Republican blindness "a fatal mistake." By contrast, Douglas would "relieve us from the immediate pressure" of this explosive impasse.[35]

There was smoke but no fire. En route back from Chicago to New York City, Raymond consulted with Seward at the senator's home in upstate New York. Though crestfallen, both grudgingly decided to put the best face they could on the situation and to swallow Lincoln's nomination.[36] Raymond remained a moderate Republican. He conceded that Douglas had many admirable qualities—"quickness of intellect," an "indomitable" self-confidence, and "tenacity of purpose." Raymond also allowed that the Douglas formula for resolving the territorial issue was all but certain to be applied. There was only the most remote possibility that Republicans ever would need to bar slavery from the territories by federal law, because the people in each territory would "decide for themselves whether they will have slavery among them"—and they would never tolerate it.

Raymond nonetheless considered the Douglas candidacy hopeless. The Democratic Party lay in ruins—its Southern Rights wing had bolted the national convention rather than accept anything less than the slave code. In Ray-

34. A. D. Banks to Douglas, May 11, 1860, George N. Sanders to Douglas, May 19, 1860, in Douglas Papers.

35. *New York Times*, May 16, 19, 1860.

36. Ibid., May 24, 26, 1860.

mond's view, Republicans had become "the only compact, responsible and effective political organization" in the country, and "the only party in a position to achieve success, or to use it wisely when it has been won." Republicans stood "midway between the pro-Slavery-ism which has ruled the Federal Government so long, and the Anti-Slavery-ism which would overthrow it altogether." Raymond insisted that Republicans respected "the limitations which the Constitution imposes," and therefore posed no menace whatsoever to slavery in the states where it already existed.[37]

Hurlbert continued with the *Times,* probably unhappily, through the presidential election and into December.[38] His output of editorials slowed to a trickle and was confined to topics other than the all-absorbing presidential contest. Raymond supported Lincoln while Hurlbert favored Douglas. Hurlbert did not share Raymond's confidence that the South would quietly acquiesce in Lincoln's election.

37. Ibid., June 26, 1860.

38. William Henry Hurlbert to Henry Wadsworth Longfellow, Aug. 20, 1860, Henry Wadsworth Longfellow Papers, Houghton Library, Harvard University; *Annual Cyclopedia* (1895), 577; *Philadelphia Press,* Dec. 3, 1860.

5

HURLBERT AND THE SECESSION CRISIS

Sidelined from the *New York Times* following the presidential election, William Henry Hurlbert nevertheless remained well situated to gain an inside perspective on events as the Union unraveled. The *Times* maintained an editorial stance during the secession crisis that opposed the use of force, was ready to offer symbolic concessions to the South, and looked forward to the peaceful restoration of the Union—a position broadly comparable to his own views. Hurlbert could interpret what he read in the *Times,* even after his formal ties to the paper ceased. Moreover, his contacts among *Times* correspondents could add glimpses that had not made it into print. New York senator William H. Seward, a long-time ally of editor Henry J. Raymond, made extraordinary efforts to defuse the crisis, and the *Times* was implicated in Seward's Union-saving schemes.[1]

Hurlbert enjoyed even more exclusive sources of information. A powerful Democratic insider, Samuel L. M. Barlow (1826–1889), afforded him an extraordinary vantage point. Once again, we encounter a person who loomed large in his own lifetime but is forgotten now. To unravel "The Diary of a Public Man," however, we must look closely at Barlow. Yes, this chapter is about Hurlbert, but his ties to Barlow are an essential part of the story.

Self-made and self-effacing, Barlow had risen to the top of the New York legal profession through his quiet ability to reconcile competing interests. He specialized in railroad building and management, for which he raised large sums of European capital. He also promoted Central American transit routes linking the Atlantic and the Pacific, and he financed mining operations in both the American West and Mexico. In the process he became immensely wealthy. Of most importance here, Barlow used his wealth to make himself a key player

---

1. Carl F. Krummel, "Henry J. Raymond and the *New York Times* in the Secession Crisis," *New York History* 32 (Oct. 1951): 377–98; Patrick M. Sowle, "A Reappraisal of Seward's Memorandum of April 1, 1861, to Lincoln," *Journal of Southern History* 33 (May 1967): 234–39; Daniel W. Crofts, *Reluctant Confederates: Upper South Unionists in the Secession Crisis* (Chapel Hill: Univ. of North Carolina Press, 1989), 260, 300–1.

behind the scenes in American politics. He and a small Democratic cabal orchestrated the presidential nomination of James Buchanan in 1856. Three of his key allies, Louisiana senators Judah Benjamin and John Slidell and Delaware senator James Bayard, lived in a house that Barlow rented for them in Washington, D.C.[2]

Barlow saw Hurlbert as the person who could build up a strong Democratic newspaper in New York City. Reports in early December 1860 had it that Hurlbert and two others associated with the *Times* soon would purchase the *New York Daily News*, with Hurlbert to become the editor-in-chief. Barlow was to be their key financial backer. He aspired to challenge the three best-selling newspapers in the city (the *Herald, Times,* and *Tribune*).[3] Nothing came of this, quite likely because the secession tidal wave threatened to engulf the Union. Barlow, the mediator extraordinaire, suddenly faced a stern test of his mediating skills. His papers clearly reveal that he knew as much about the unfolding crisis as anyone in Washington. Within weeks of Lincoln's election he could see the potential for catastrophe, because he knew what was happening both north and south, and he recognized that each section was blind to its counterpart. Barlow wrote candidly to leading Southern members of the Senate, to William M. Browne, editor of the pro-Southern *Washington Constitution,* the administration's official newspaper, and to Buchanan himself. He also crossed party lines to meet and correspond with leading New York businessmen such as Moses Grinnell and Samuel Blatchford—and with newspaper publisher and Republican strategist Thurlow Weed. Nobody was as close to William H. Seward as Weed. The two had been intimate allies for thirty years, as Weed attended to the practical details that made Seward's career possible.[4]

Barlow, worried that disunion might lead to civil war, hoped initially that

2. The voluminous Samuel Latham Mitchill Barlow Papers are housed at the Huntington Library, San Marino, California. These include not only incoming mail but also letterbooks with copies of Barlow's outgoing correspondence. See Albert V. House, "The Samuel Latham Mitchill Barlow Papers in the Huntington Library," *Huntington Library Quarterly* 28 (Aug. 1965): 341–52; Lately Thomas (Robert V. P. Steele), *Sam Ward: "King of the Lobby"* (Boston: Houghton Mifflin, 1965), 228–30. On Buchanan's 1856 nomination and Barlow's ties to the Senate cabal, see Roy Franklin Nichols, *The Disruption of American Democracy* (New York: Macmillan, 1948), 17–32, esp. 29–30.

3. Barlow to William M. Browne, Nov. 26, 1860, Barlow Papers; *Philadelphia Press*, Dec. 3, 1860; *Springfield Republican*, Dec. 6, 1860.

4. Barlow to Benjamin, Dec. 24, 1860, Barlow to Browne, Dec. 31, 1860, Barlow to Samuel F. Butterworth, Dec. 4, 5, 1860, Barlow to Weed, Nov. 30, Dec. 21, 1860, Browne to Barlow, Dec. 10, 18,

"the good sense of most of the Southern States will keep them in the Union." He therefore cautioned his Southern friends to act calmly and ignore "the furious rage of the secessionists." He called attention to growing Northern support for a Union-saving compromise which would, he predicted, leave the Republican Party "broken in pieces" and incapable of hurting the South.[5]

To the horror of Barlow and like-minded Northern Democrats, the situation in the South rapidly spiraled out of control. When Judah Benjamin visited New York in early December, Barlow found the Louisiana senator "very desponding." Suspecting that Republicans would spurn any compromise, Benjamin predicted that "the Union hangs by a thread." Three days later, after Benjamin had returned to Washington, he informed Barlow that "no conceivable circumstances can in my judgment change the naked fact that the Union is dissolved." The "prudent and conservative men" in the South faced the impossible task of trying to stem "the wild torrent of passion which is carrying everything before it," Benjamin wrote. A "revolution" was sweeping the land, "and it can no more be checked by human effort . . . than a prairie fire by a gardener's watering pot." Barlow, who was "almost forced to the conclusion our Southern friends are mad," responded immediately to Benjamin's "fearful" missive. He pointed out that few Northern voters were abolitionists—most were Democrats or moderate Republicans. In almost every Northern state, support for a compromise was widespread. Republicans would have to offer "fair terms" or risk being supplanted by "a great Union party." If the South acted prudently, it could gain the reassurances it deserved. If, however, the South overreacted, Barlow warned, the North could well unite to support the use of force against secession.[6]

As he attempted to reassure Benjamin and other Southerners, Barlow quietly reached out to Seward's alter ego, Weed. In late November and early December, long before others in his party awoke to confront the gravity of the crisis, Weed placed himself out on a limb. He suggested that Republicans compromise the vexing territorial issue. No territory south of 36° 30', the old Missouri Compro-

26, 30, 1860, Barlow Papers; Frederic Bancroft, *The Life of William H. Seward* (2 vols.; New York: Harper and Brothers, 1899–1900), 1:29–35, 38–39, 200–1.

5. Barlow to John Slidell, Nov. 27, 1860, Barlow to Browne, Nov. 19, 23, 1860, Barlow to James Bayard, Nov. 27, 1860, Barlow Papers.

6. Barlow to Henry D. Bacon, Dec. 6, 1860, Judah Benjamin to Barlow, Dec. 9, 1860, Barlow to Benjamin, Dec. 11, 1860, Barlow to Browne, Dec. 8, 1860, Barlow Papers.

mise line, was suitable for plantation slavery, Weed argued. Therefore, Republicans could safely abstain from restricting slavery there. The editor ventured further, suggesting that his party might acknowledge a Southern right to take slaves there.[7] Barlow privately commended Weed's "bold and patriotic stand" in putting urgent national interests ahead of "party organizations." Of course, Barlow knew that Horace Greeley and party ideologues would try to block any compromise. But if Weed and Seward could bring most Republicans to accept restoration of the Missouri line, then "all may be saved."[8]

A combination of miscommunication and wishful thinking prompted Barlow to regard Weed's overture as a turning point. In a "strictly confidential" letter dated December 24, Barlow told Benjamin to share with John Slidell and Jefferson Davis the news that "Thurlow Weed's articles were written at the request of Seward." That was true. Barlow went on, however, to claim that Weed—during a recent trip to Springfield, Illinois—had persuaded Lincoln to support a constitutional amendment protecting the right to hold slaves in territory south of 36° 30'. This key bit of information was doubly erroneous. Weed had suggested to Lincoln that Republicans might reasonably accept restoration of the Missouri Compromise of 1820; after all, their party coalesced to protest the Kansas-Nebraska Act's repeal of the Missouri line. But the Missouri line simply prohibited slavery in territory north of 36° 30'. Although it tacitly allowed slavery in territory south of the line, it offered no "protection" of the sort that Southern Democrats increasingly demanded by the late 1850s. Barlow also mangled the story of how Lincoln treated Weed's overture. The president-elect made it plain that he would not countenance a territorial compromise, and Weed returned home empty-handed. At that juncture, as historian David Potter noted, "the active leadership of the Republican party passed from Seward to Lincoln, and the cause of territorial compromise received a blow from which there was no recovery."[9]

Barlow soon learned that he had gotten it wrong. Seward voted in late December against any territorial compromise that included "protection," thereby leaving Kentucky senator John J. Crittenden, the leading would-be compro-

7. *Albany Evening Journal,* Nov. 24, 30, 1860; Crofts, *Reluctant Confederates,* 217–20.

8. Barlow to Thurlow Weed, Nov. 30, Dec. 21, 1860, Barlow Papers.

9. Barlow to Benjamin, Dec. 24, 1860; Crofts, *Reluctant Confederates,* 198–200, 219–21; David M. Potter, *Lincoln and His Party in the Secession Crisis* (New Haven: Yale Univ. Press, 1942, 1962), 71–74, 165–70, quotation on 170.

miser, in "utter despair." Some Republicans did, however, support turning all territory south of 36° 30' into a single state—New Mexico—and thereby finessing the territorial issue. They also offered a constitutional amendment protecting slavery in the states where it already existed. "Our leaders are mad if they do not accept these terms," Barlow judged. His Southern friends, however, spurned any such "milk and water compromise" that the Republican Party might "fraudulently offer." By the end of December, they insisted that secession and Southern independence were irreversible, and they predicted that most if not all Southern states would leave the Union before Lincoln took office.[10]

Amid these intensifying signs of a hopeless impasse, a spectacular confrontation erupted between the state of South Carolina and the federal government. On December 20, South Carolina declared itself out of the Union. Six days later, as we have seen in chapter 1, Major Robert Anderson moved the small contingent of U.S. soldiers under his command from the indefensible Fort Moultrie, near Charleston, South Carolina, to Fort Sumter, located on a less vulnerable artificial island at the mouth of the harbor. South Carolina immediately dispatched three commissioners to Washington to demand that Buchanan withdraw all federal troops from the state. Suddenly the heretofore-obscure Anderson and the little-known outpost where he repositioned his forces were on every tongue and emblazoned on the front page of every newspaper. President Buchanan and his cabinet had to choose. After several days of "extraordinary suspense," he decided on New Year's Eve to reject South Carolina's demands and to back Anderson.[11]

Barlow's Northern sensibilities were roused. He told his Southern correspondents that he had "never known the *entire people* more unanimous on any question. We are ruined if Anderson is disgraced or if Sumpter is given up." Buchanan's refusal to heed the plea of the South Carolina commissioners "meets the hearty and unanimous approval of every one in the North," Barlow wrote. Judah Benjamin fired back. Would Northern Democrats support Republican efforts to hold the Union together by armed force? Barlow recognized the potential tragedy. He lamented to Buchanan that "we, the Northern Democracy, who hate the Republican doctrines and their authors, will be compelled in the asser-

10. Benjamin to Barlow, Dec. 23, 1860, Browne to Barlow, Dec. 26, 30, 1860, Jan. 4, 1861, Barlow to Browne, Dec. 31, 1860, Barlow Papers.

11. Potter, *Lincoln and His Party*, 253–54, 268; David M. Potter, *The Impending Crisis, 1848–1861* (New York: Harper and Row, 1976), 535–42.

tion of our manhood and to preserve our Government, to fight our Southern friends whom we like and with whom we have no real quarrel."[12]

How close was Hurlbert to Barlow, and how much was he party to the explosive confidences being exchanged within Barlow's elite circle? These questions cannot be answered with finality, but Barlow must have shared a good deal with his would-be editor. As will be recalled, the first segment of "The Diary of a Public Man" focuses on the potentially explosive jousting over Sumter in late December. The following summer, after the war started, Hurlbert talked at length in Richmond with both Judah Benjamin and William M. Browne, the former editor of the *Washington Constitution*. The evidence indicates that Hurlbert already was well acquainted with both, and it is difficult to see how that could have been the case unless through Barlow. Hurlbert identified with the Douglas wing of the party, but Douglas was anathema both to Benjamin and to Browne; only by situating himself in close proximity to Barlow could Hurlbert have been on familiar terms with either. From that privileged position, however, Hurlbert could learn from a distance what was being discussed behind closed doors in Washington, quite aside from contacts he already may have enjoyed from his position at the *Times*.

The Public Man reported having an extensive conversation with Judah Benjamin on January 13. As mentioned in chapter 1, the Louisiana senator then defended secession as a negotiating gambit, designed to make "the conservative masses of the Northern people" amenable to a "final adjustment." The diarist sensed, however, that Benjamin "evidently feels the ground giving way under him" (225–26). Less than a month later, when Benjamin resigned his seat in the Senate and declared secession an irreversible fixed fact, the diarist reported himself "painfully" affected (232). These segments of the Diary almost certainly result from the exchanges between Barlow and Benjamin and from Barlow's apparent readiness to confide in Hurlbert.

Hurlbert's participation at a Union-saving gathering in Albany from January 29 to February 1 provides additional evidence that he collaborated with leading Democrats during the secession winter. He was part of a delegation of New York City conservatives, mostly Democrats, who gathered at a statewide convention to urge Northern concessions. "Civil war will not restore the Union, but will defeat forever its restoration," the convention resolved. What was needed in-

12. Barlow to Browne, Dec. 29, 31, 1860, Benjamin to Barlow, Jan. 8, 1861, Barlow to Buchanan, Dec. 31, 1860, Barlow Papers.

stead was "conciliation and compromise." By allying with "the loyal men in the Border States" to prevent all violence and by supporting "the Crittenden proposition, or some other measure acceptable to the Border States," sensible Northerners might yet reverse the secession clamor in the Lower South and save the Union.[13]

Let us move ahead to mid-March, when Hurlbert and several other like-minded New Yorkers, including Barlow, befriended William H. Russell of the *London Times,* the world's most famous journalist. Russell's vivid coverage of the Crimean War in 1854–55 brought home to the English reading public the hardships suffered by British soldiers and the awfulness of armed combat. Crimea was the first major war to occur since the rise of mass-circulation newspapers, and the *Times* was by far the largest in Britain. Russell's writings in effect created a new profession, that of military correspondent.[14] He was greeted as a celebrity when he arrived in New York City on March 16. His presence showed that the editors of the *Times* thought he might soon have another war to cover. Influential Americans jostled to gain Russell's ear, realizing that he had the power to shape international understanding of the situation here.

It will be remembered that this mid-March juncture was the same point at which the Diary ended. In the days leading up to Russell's arrival, indications from Washington suggested that the new Lincoln administration had decided to remove its soldiers from Fort Sumter. Nothing was yet certain, but those who feared war were guardedly optimistic. The author of the Diary chose to end his narrative at this misleading might-have-been moment.

A few days later, on March 20, Hurlbert hosted a dinner for Russell, designed to expose him to the views of those who hoped for a peaceful resolution of the crisis. Russell recalled that his host was "once a Southern man with such strong anti-slavery convictions, that his expression of them in an English quarterly had secured him the hostility of his own people." More recently, however, this person had "abandoned his connection with one of the New York papers on the Republican side, because he believed that the course of the journal was

13. *New York Tribune,* Jan. 30, Feb. 2, 1861; *New York Times,* Sep. 11, 1862. Crittenden sponsored legislation that recognized and protected the right to hold slaves in territory south of 36° 30'.

14. Alan Hankinson, *Man of Wars: William Howard Russell of "The Times"* (London: Heinemann, 1982), 38–104; Trevor Royle, *Crimea: The Great Crimean War, 1854–1856* (New York: Palgrave Macmillan, 2000), 46–47, 114–15, 178–79, 230, 246–47, 276, 373–74.

dictated by anti-Southern fanaticism."[15] On March 25 Hurlbert and other New York newspapermen put on a brunch that Russell considered "great fun."[16]

Russell found himself overwhelmed by "the chaos of opinions" into which he was "at once plunged" upon arriving in New York. Even during debates in the House of Commons, he had never before encountered such disagreement about "the minutest matters of fact." Though "the question of fighting seems to be eschewed as far as possible," Russell suspected that Americans were sleepwalking into "a bloody & desperate struggle." Russell did find some New Yorkers "hospitable & jolly." To his editor in London, he reported that "our friend Hurlbert" was "a very clever, very agreeable, & very amusing fellow"—but he had "no position here" because "his line as a journalist" had been "cut short by his secession forced or voluntary from the N.Y. Times."[17]

Hurlbert strived to counteract the time that Russell spent with "Republican extremists in this city." He need not have feared. The visitor took an instant dislike to Horace Greeley, editor of the *Tribune,* who articulated "the nastiest form of narrow minded sectarian philanthropy." Years later, Russell wrote a hilarious account of his encounter with the most uncompromising New Yorker of all. Accepting what he understood to be an invitation to breakfast, Russell sat down in Greeley's office and soon found himself listening to a protracted monologue. Greeley "spoke with earnestness . . . now and then reading a passage from a book or pamphlet, occasionally digressing to heave rhetorical bricks against Mr. Buchanan and Southerners whose names I was not familiar with. An hour passed and still he went on. I was hungry, and heard no clink of cups and saucers." For

15. William Howard Russell, *My Diary North and South,* ed. Eugene Berwanger (New York: Alfred A. Knopf, 1988), 35, 37. Berwanger misidentified the unnamed host as Hinton R. Helper. The editor also misidentified one of the guests. "Mr. Barlow" was Samuel L. M. Barlow, not a writer for the *New York Tribune* editorial staff named Francis C. Barlow!

16. Martin Crawford, ed., *William Howard Russell's Civil War: Private Diary and Letters, 1861–1862* (Athens: Univ. of Georgia Press, 1992), 21.

17. Russell also was amazed to learn that Hurlbert once had been "a Methodist preacher & parson"—"Jerusalem! greased snakes Yes Sirree! It's a fact!" William Howard Russell to John T. Delane, Mar. 26, 1861, in Crawford, *Russell's Civil War,* 23–26. Crawford notes that *My Diary North and South,* first published in 1863, was not actually a diary but rather "a narrative reconstruction based upon the correspondent's notebooks and reports" (*Russell's Civil War,* vii). By contrast, *Russell's Civil War* includes Russell's actual diary, interspersed with selections from his private correspondence (viii).

two more hours, Russell sat "and still the flood poured on. Mr. Greeley had forgotten all about breakfast. I had not." Finally Russell begged off, though Greeley insisted that he had "some more important matters to explain" and that he was "only just breaking ground."[18]

Russell departed shortly thereafter for Washington, prompting Hurlbert to write to Stephen A. Douglas, "I have seen a good deal of him [Russell] here and I charged him earnestly to consult with you as to public affairs." He urged Douglas to reach out to Russell and "impress him as you can, particularly with your views of our actual position." The letter, dated March 27, had an ominous undercurrent. Two weeks before, it seemed that the Lincoln administration had decided to pull back from Fort Sumter in order to avert war. Was that still policy? Hurlbert's tone showed his doubts. He ridiculed "the frantic and foolish policy—or better no-policy" of the "shivering" administration. "Whatever the future may hold in store for our unhappy country," Hurlbert nervously concluded, he was proud to have stood with the Illinois senator in 1860.[19]

The available evidence, then, shows that Hurlbert knew a great deal about the politics of the secession winter. Though not in Washington, he kept his ear close to the ground, and he enjoyed Barlow's confidences. Quite possibly, Hurlbert kept a diary or journal at this time. He was between jobs and had no ready outlet for his facile pen. And there was so much to write about—the sky was falling. We know that Hurlbert was a sometimes diarist. In 1874 he reviewed the third volume of John Quincy Adams's *Memoirs,* edited by his son Charles Francis Adams. The *Memoirs* were extracts from the father's prodigious diary. John Quincy Adams's "enormous industry" and methodical regularity impressed Hurlbert. Adams noted in 1816 that his diary had not missed "a single day" in twenty-two years. "Reader!" Hurlbert exclaimed. "If you have ever tried to keep a diary (and who has not?) you will appreciate the tax" that Adams "so unflinchingly paid" to maintain his daily record.[20]

But this is not the whole story. Hurlbert knew someone who could reveal additional insights. That person was Sam Ward, also part of Barlow's circle. In-

18. Hurlbert to Stephen A. Douglas, Mar. 27, 1861, Stephen A. Douglas Papers, University of Chicago; Russell to Delane, Mar. 26, 1861, in Crawford, *Russell's Civil War,* 24; William Howard Russell, "Recollections of the Civil War," *North American Review* 166 (Feb. 1898): 237–38.

19. Hurlbert to Douglas, Mar. 27, 1861, Douglas Papers.

20. *New York World,* Dec. 14, 1874.

deed, Ward and Hurlbert first got to know each other over dinners at Barlow's New York mansion. In mid-1859 Ward became a Washington lobbyist for Barlow, assigned to corral "Congressional elephants" on behalf of some kind of real estate deal. As part of the arrangement, Barlow picked up the cost of Ward's rental quarters in the capital. Ward's work for Barlow initially had more to do with business than with high politics. By the winter of 1860–61, however, the political upheaval had moved center stage, and it commanded everyone's attention.[21]

As has been noted in chapter 1, Frank Maloy Anderson realized that Ward gained behind-the-scenes knowledge of the secession crisis because of his proximity to Seward and California senator William M. Gwin. The building where Ward lived, 258 F Street, next door to Seward's home, was rented for him by Barlow. Ward enabled the two Senate colleagues to confer privately with each other. Could Hurlbert have been privy to what Ward learned? The evidence strongly suggests that he could have. Ward certainly corresponded with Barlow during the secession winter, and Hurlbert appears to have had a sensitive antenna for things that Barlow knew. Moreover, Ward and Hurlbert repeatedly saw each other in March when Russell visited New York.[22]

During Russell's New York visit in March 1861, Hurlbert, Barlow, and Ward worked as a team. Ward's characteristic sociability helped bring the group together. The year before in 1860 while on a summer trip to London, Ward had been introduced to Russell by the English novelist William M. Thackeray. A bond immediately developed. When Russell reached New York City, Ward awaited him, made it his business to squire the British visitor around town, and introduced him to "many friends." The guests who attended Hurlbert's private dinner for Russell on March 20 included both Barlow and Gwin, whose Senate term had just ended. Ward's presence may be inferred—he clung to Russell like glue in New York and then accompanied him down to Washington. Ward reported to Barlow on March 31 that "Russell makes yr [your] 258 his hiding place and dined with us yesterday and the day previous." An astute observer, Hurlbert certainly would have gained insights about Ward's and Gwin's surreptitious dealings no later than the time of Russell's visit to New York City. And

21. Thomas, *Sam Ward*, 228–30, 241, 248–49.

22. Anderson, *Mystery*, 166–67; Thomas, *Sam Ward*, 228–32, 241–43, 248–61.

it seems likely that Hurlbert knew all along information that Ward shared with Barlow.[23]

Shortly after the appearance of Anderson's book in 1948, a graduate student at the University of Washington, Roy N. Lokken, published a rejoinder. He concluded that "Anderson proved neither that the diary was a mass of reminiscence and fiction built up around a skeleton diary kept during the winter of 1860–1861 nor that the diarist was Sam Ward." Although Lokken called attention to weak links in Anderson's line of reasoning, his own research base in the sources was not deep enough to enable him to suggest an alternative explanation of the mysterious document. His essay did, however, contain a key insight. Anderson's ability to identify "such people as Barlow, Gwin, and Browne" in the Diary did not prove that Ward was the diarist, Lokken asserted. It proved only that "the diarist moved in the same circles as Seward, Gwin, Barlow, and other *dramatis personae* of the diary." Lokken was unaware of Hurlbert, but he grasped something essential in suggesting that others shared Ward's opportunities to peer behind closed doors.[24]

23. Ward to Barlow, Mar. 31, 1861, Barlow Papers; Crawford, *Russell's Civil War*, 20, 27–28, 31; Russell, "Recollections of the Civil War," 237; Robert W. Johannsen, *Stephen A. Douglas* (New York: Oxford Univ. Press, 1973), 852–53, 963–64n16; Hankinson, *Man of Wars*, 150, 156; Thomas, *Sam Ward*, 259–63.

24. Roy N. Lokken, "Has the Mystery of 'A Public Man' Been Solved?" *Mississippi Valley Historical Review* 40 (Dec. 1953): 419–40, quotations on 438–39.

6

A FICTION—NOTHING MORE NOR LESS?

The previous three chapters have introduced the surreptitious diarist William Henry Hurlbert and have carried the account of his life up through March 1861. We now have learned enough about him to evaluate his enigmatic handiwork, "The Diary of a Public Man." This chapter and the next will evaluate the Diary. It purports to inform us about highly confidential discussions taking place during the secession winter. To what extent should the Diary be judged a plausible source? Or is it simply an after-the-fact concoction, worthy of attention only because its author successfully concealed his identity and deceived historians for so long?

The Diary contains passages that are imaginary. These were designed to create the illusion that the diarist was an influential Washington resident who had lived in the capital for many years. Thus, the diarist characterized the weather for the inauguration as "one of our disagreeable, clear, windy, Washington spring days" (254). Three days later he sourly disdained the office seekers who were "lounging about the steps of the Treasury Department and the lobbies of the hotels." "In all my long experience of Washington," the diarist huffed, "I have never seen such a swarm of uncouth beings" (263–64). It was true that Abraham Lincoln took his oath of office on a brisk, raw day, and that the city was inundated by those seeking patronage appointments. However, neither Ward nor Hurlbert had "long experience" there. Ward had worked intermittently at the national capital only for the previous two years, and Hurlbert set down roots in New York City after returning from Europe in 1856.

Other fanciful aspects of the Diary come into sharp focus once its true nature is taken into account. As part of the same effort to depict himself as a person of stature, the diarist complained that he had been "besieged" by job seekers, who sought his influence on their behalf. Above all, the diarist asserted that the busiest and most important men in Washington sought him out, extended him confidences, and valued his opinions. As explained in chapter 1, we are led to believe that South Carolina commissioner and former Speaker of the U.S. House of Representatives James Orr came to see the diarist on December 28, and that "he had hardly gone before Mr. Douglas called" (221). On the morning of February 25, Douglas was again on his doorstep. On March 10, Douglas cheerfully agreed to return that evening so that the diarist could meet with another visitor. In their alleged discussions, the diarist and Douglas routinely talked about matters of great sensitivity. On February 25, just after having been visited by Douglas, the diarist encountered Edwin M. Stanton, the U.S. attorney general, who stopped him on the street to chat. Three days later, the recent presidential candidate John Bell encountered the diarist on the stairs of the Willard Hotel and "stepped aside with me a moment" to exchange a bit of wishful thinking about "the conservative tone of Mr. Lincoln's mind" (240). The next day, March 1, that "most discreet of men," Lord Lyons, the British minister, deftly pointed out to the diarist the "seething peril" that was likely to engulf the United States (242–43). On March 3, Charles Sumner unexpectedly approached the diarist and implored him to intercede with Lincoln against appointing Pennsylvania senator Simon Cameron to the cabinet. The diarist rebuffed the Massachusetts senator, on grounds that such "impertinent" meddling would destroy "any good opinion which Mr. Lincoln might have of me" (247). On March 9, at a time when William H. Seward was overwhelmed with vexing responsibilities, the new secretary of state stopped in for "a moment, not long after breakfast," to enlist the diarist to meet with someone "who had a matter to lay before him of great national importance" (266). Three days later, Seward nudged the diarist to offer his opinion on the difficulties Douglas had created for Republicans in the Senate, but the diarist "positively declined" to rise to the bait (271). All these alleged episodes were designed to validate the reality of a nonexistent diarist.

If some information in the Diary was fabricated—and if the entire document is not in fact a diary—then why should anyone pay attention to what the *North American Review* printed in 1879? This was the view of Edward L. Pierce, the first person to connect Hurlbert to the Diary. Pierce, the biographer of Charles Sumner, read a paper to the Massachusetts Historical Society in 1896 that cautioned against reliance on diaries. For a diary to be creditable, Pierce suggested, the "moral and intellectual character of the diarist" should be unquestioned, as should his "opportunities of observation." Moreover, Pierce insisted, "no credit should be given to anonymous diaries." As a case in point, he condemned "The Diary of a Public Man," which flunked all three of Pierce's tests. It had been issued anonymously by someone of dubious "moral and intellectual character." Its likely author, an untrustworthy adventurer "recently deceased"—albeit unidentified—called into question the Diary's "air of probability." Pierce then set out to demolish the Diary's one remaining prop, the author's "opportunities of observation." Dripping with sarcasm, he rejected the idea that the diarist could ever have participated in the conversations he described:

> The diarist makes himself the most remarkable personage of modern times. His counsels and mediation were eagerly sought by men of adverse opinions and positions, and he was admitted by them to the most confidential interviews. Among these were Douglas, Seward, Sumner, the British Minister, and the Confederate chiefs, Orr and Forsyth. He was solicited to assist in making the Cabinet; all the departments were open to him; and Lincoln, as soon as he was in office, though weighted with unexampled burdens, put aside all other duties to receive him and listen to his wisdom. Who could be this marvellous man, so miscellaneous in his affiliations, whose thoughts statesmen yearned to hear in those dread hours? It is easier to suppose that he did not exist than to point him out among the characters of that eventful period.

Pierce had indeed identified the key flaw in the Diary—the alleged diarist had too much entrée to too many important people. No one person could have enjoyed such confidential access to such a wide range of key officials. Having correctly discerned that the diarist was too "marvellous" to be believed, Pierce concluded that "The Diary of a Public Man" was "a fiction—nothing more nor less."[1]

Frank Maloy Anderson wrestled with Pierce's contemptuous dismissal of the Diary. Retracing Anderson's steps, I went to examine Pierce's letters at Harvard University. There, exactly as Anderson states in *The Mystery of "A Public Man,"* the researcher will find evidence that Pierce sent his cautionary words about diaries to an elite group of politicians, historians, university presidents, and newspaper editors. The responses he elicited, neatly tied in a bundle, were for the most part perfunctory, and did not mention the Public Man. Yes, agreed the president of the University of Michigan, James B. Angell, tainted testimony could lead to "falsified history." The last letter in the collection, however, from Horace White of the *New York Evening Post,* was of more interest to me, just as

1. A. W. Stevens, ed., *Addresses and Papers by Edward L. Pierce* (Boston: Roberts Brothers, 1896), 393–97.

it had been for Anderson. White named Hurlbert as the "adventurer recently deceased" and enthusiastically seconded all of Pierce's strictures against him. The Diary was "rubbish"; Hurlbert and Allen Thorndike Rice, editor of the *North American Review*, were "characterless vagabonds"; and nobody should ever have "attached any importance" to their spurious fabrication.[2]

Pierce had spent two decades writing a reverential four-volume life of Sumner, whom he depicted as selfless, principled, and morally superior. Pierce had ample motive to cast aspersions on a source that painted such an unflattering portrait of the Massachusetts senator.[3] "It attributes to Mr. Sumner activity in Cabinet-making," Pierce complained, "a function from which by taste and habit he kept aloof." But Pierce obscured how the contest to shape Lincoln's cabinet had become interconnected with the issue of Southern policy, a matter dearer to Sumner's heart than any other. Sumner's great goal was to block all compromise or concession to slaveholders—he opposed "any offer now, even of a peppercorn." In January and February when his previously close friends, Seward and Charles Francis Adams, appeared ready to "surrender" on matters of "principle," Sumner worked himself into a frenzy of anxiety.[4] Surely adding to Pierce's animus was his knowledge that young Hurlbert once had held the right values. At the height of Northern alarm over the "slave power" between 1854 and 1856, as we have seen, Hurlbert sent cordial letters to Sumner, commending his support for and sacrifices on behalf of the "great cause."[5] In Pierce's eyes, Hurlbert's subsequent political role was that of an arch traitor.

2. Frank Maloy Anderson, *The Mystery of "A Public Man": A Historical Detective Story* (Minneapolis: Univ. of Minnesota Press, 1948), 124–30; James B. Angell to Edward L. Pierce, June 3, 1896, Horace White to Edward L. Pierce, May 30, 1896, Edward L. Pierce Papers, Houghton Library, Harvard University. Anderson initially suspected that Hurlbert must have been the diarist. But it will be recalled that he stumbled across Sam Ward soon after having discovered Hurlbert, and thereafter only could see Hurlbert as someone who might have assisted Ward (Anderson, *Mystery*, 130–35, 170).

3. Edward L. Pierce, *Memoir and Letters of Charles Sumner* (4 vols.; Boston: Roberts Brothers, 1878–93).

4. Stevens, *Addresses and Papers*, 394; David Donald, *Charles Sumner and the Coming of the Civil War* (New York: Alfred A. Knopf, 1960), 365–88, esp. 372–82, quotations on 374, 377; Daniel W. Crofts, *Reluctant Confederates: Upper South Unionists in the Secession Crisis* (Chapel Hill: Univ. of North Carolina Press, 1989), 227–28, 230, 237, 239, quotation on 230.

5. William Henry Hurlbert to Charles Sumner, June 30, 1854, June 7, Aug. 12, Nov. 12, 1856, Charles Sumner Papers, Houghton Library, Harvard University.

While working on his Sumner biography, Pierce had attempted without success to identify the diarist. "I tried all I could to find out who the author was," Pierce explained to historian James Ford Rhodes. Pierce contacted Hiram Barney, among the few persons mentioned in the Diary who was still alive at the time of its publication. Barney, as will be explained in the next chapter, could not recall assisting the diarist or attending a breakfast with Lincoln in New York City on February 20. And Allen Thorndike Rice, who edited the *North American Review*, rebuffed Barney's request to name the diarist. As late as 1894, Pierce did not think "we shall ever know who the author was." Two years later, however, Pierce decided correctly that the Diary had been written by the "adventurer recently deceased." Obituaries at the time of Hurlbert's death, in September 1895, may have brought him to Pierce's attention. Horace White himself may have been the catalyst. The letter that White sent to Pierce in June 1896 reads as if the two already had discussed or corresponded about the connection between Hurlbert and the Diary.[6]

White, too, would have harbored a grudge against Hurlbert. The young White was an Illinois free soiler turned newspaperman, and an unqualified Lincoln admirer. He had reason to resent the way the Public Man depicted Lincoln in February and March 1861—perplexed, uncertain, and hesitant to risk war. Editor-in-chief of the *Chicago Tribune* from 1865 to 1874, White did his utmost to remove Andrew Johnson from office. But Hurlbert's *New York World* championed Lincoln's successor and depicted the effort to unseat him as "revolutionary recklessness." Even though White soon afterward made his own move to the right, he and Hurlbert never occupied common ground. White personified the holier-than-thou "Liberal Republicans" and mugwumps of the 1870s and 1880s; Hurlbert considered mugwumps insufferable prigs. The *New York Evening Post*, which White edited for many years, had no tolerance for those with presumed moral shortcomings.[7]

Anderson weighed the judgment of Pierce and White—that Hurlbert had

---

6. Edward L. Pierce to James Ford Rhodes, July 5, 1894, James Ford Rhodes Papers, Massachusetts Historical Society; Horace White to Edward L. Pierce, May 30, 1896, Pierce Papers; Anderson, *Mystery*, 21, 184n2–4; 229–30 herein.

7. *New York World*, Feb. 26, 1868; Joseph Logsdon, "Horace White," *American National Biography*, 23:218–19; Joseph Logsdon, *Horace White: Nineteenth-Century Liberal* (Westport, Conn.: Greenwood Press, 1971); on mugwumps, William Henry Hurlbert, *Ireland under Coercion: The Diary of an American*, 2nd ed. (2 vols.; Edinburgh: David Douglas, 1888), 2:291.

written an entirely fictitious diary. He decided that the Diary published in 1879 simply could not have been "concocted" from scratch. He thus rejected Pierce's characterization of the Diary as "a fiction—nothing more nor less." But Anderson also let White's identification of the "adventurer" slip through his fingers. Once Hurlbert led him to Ward, Anderson lost interest in Hurlbert.

Anderson concluded that the material published in the *North American Review* in 1879 was neither a genuine diary nor a complete fabrication. He reached this conclusion only after diligently sifting a mountain of evidence. I am confident that he got closer to the heart of the matter than did Pierce. The Diary is not what it appears to be. It was written after the fact by someone who pretended to have written an actual diary. On the other hand, the Diary never could have been created solely as a work of imagination. Much of it is rooted in reality. However fictitious the alleged diarist, the Diary abounds with legitimate information. Hurlbert and Ward were well-connected insiders who each knew a great deal, and both possessed remarkable memories. They also must have gained access to some kind of confidential written records to have produced the material that appeared in the *North American Review.*

The Diary was, therefore, both less and more than what Anderson concluded. The Diary was not a diary. Every word in the *NAR* was written by Hurlbert, probably in 1879. On the other hand, much of the information presented in the Diary stands up well to close scrutiny, as will be explained in this chapter and the next. The genuine material in the Diary, dismissed by Anderson as skeletal and meager, must have been substantial.[8] In short, the Diary confronts the historian with a maddening paradox. It pretends to be a diary but it is not. Yet it contains many things that prove to have been valid. Hurlbert could never have fabricated all of these purported conversations. He may not have fabricated any of them, if by that we mean concocting purely imaginary episodes from scratch. It is quite possible that Hurlbert confined his ingenious narrative to conversations that actually did take place, even though the alleged diarist was a figment of his fertile imagination, and even though neither he nor Ward could have been directly present at most of the interviews narrated in the Diary.

Many episodes mentioned in the Diary must be judged historical. Let us consider several examples. The Diary's initial entry, on December 28, includes the

8. Anderson, *Mystery,* 169.

startling revelation that Seward met surreptitiously with James L. Orr, one of the three commissioners from the self-proclaimed independent state of South Carolina. Orr and his two colleagues wanted President Buchanan to order Major Anderson back from Fort Sumter to Fort Moultrie—or out of South Carolina altogether. According to the diarist, Seward agreed with them, albeit for his own reasons. The commissioners wanted recognition of South Carolina's independence, whereas Seward feared that Anderson's move to Sumter had the potential to spark armed conflict. Orr even intimated that Seward suggested using the influence of a Southern-born Democratic senator who had "great personal weight" with Buchanan and whose term would expire in March (220). "Certainly," historian David Potter has noted, this story needed more than "the unsupported word of an anonymous and unauthenticated diarist" if it is to be believed.

In fact, however, Potter found a "partial corroboration" of Orr's story. Potter discovered that only one member of the Senate had the various characteristics mentioned in the Diary. This was California's William M. Gwin, whom we already have encountered. It will be recalled that Gwin indeed was close to Seward—the two used Sam Ward's home for secret confabs. In a memoir written around 1881 but published a decade later—all after the Diary had appeared—Gwin allowed that he had been "so thoroughly convinced of Mr. Seward's sincerity" in trying to prevent war that he had agreed to use "all the influence" he could muster "on the outgoing administration." Gwin's account is less specific than the Diary, but it is consistent with it. In short, the diarist somehow obtained word about the most delicate sort of intrigue in high places, and then put his account into print before it appeared elsewhere. Afterwards a key principal came close to validating the episode.[9]

Corroborating evidence that Seward might have welcomed a decision to evacuate Sumter may be found in a cryptic letter written by young Henry Adams, who closely observed the New York senator during the secession winter. On the night of December 28 Seward joined the Adams family for dinner. When they offered the conventional Northern view that it would be "most unfortunate" if Major Anderson were to be "disavowed and cashiered," Seward gruffly rejoined that it might be just as well if Sumter were given up. It would make the

9. David M. Potter, *Lincoln and His Party in the Secession Crisis* (New Haven: Yale Univ. Press, 1942, 1962), 268–71; Evan J. Coleman, "Gwin and Seward—A Secret Chapter in Ante-Bellum History," *Overland Monthly* 18 (Nov. 1891): 465–71.

North mad, and that just might prompt Northern Democrats—who constantly were being bullied by the South—to kick back. After having had "their noses sufficiently ground down by South Carolina," they might "get tired and resist." Seward's jaunty and "chipper" demeanor was a deliberate pretense—he dared not share with the Adams clan his fear that a violent confrontation at Sumter might lead to immediate war. But his professed readiness to abandon Sumter, if only in a private conversation among friends, shows that the Northern war spirit rising in late December left Seward grasping for palliatives.[10]

The Public Man not only asserted that Seward assisted the South Carolina commissioners in trying to get Anderson withdrawn from Sumter, but also coupled this astonishing information with an equally startling claim regarding Buchanan's secretary of war, John B. Floyd. December 1860 was not a good month for Floyd, the former governor of Virginia. That month, news broke that friends of his had abused his trust by using War Department contracts to engineer a massive swindle. Buchanan thereupon asked Floyd to resign. But Floyd dragged his feet, out of fear that his resignation would be seen as an admission of his own guilt. His problems were compounded when other news reports accused him of moving weapons to Southern arsenals, where they might be captured by secessionists. A chorus of patriotic condemnation ensued in many Northern newspapers. As of late December when Fort Sumter vaulted to attention, however, Floyd remained in the cabinet. He joined with a delegation of Southern senators in pressing Buchanan to move Anderson from Sumter back to Moultrie. When Buchanan refused to do so, Floyd took advantage of the opportunity to resign in protest—on December 29—ostensibly for principle rather than in disgrace.[11]

The Public Man later heard that Floyd had played a double game. He had given Major Anderson vague discretionary instructions to exercise "sound military judgment." He expected, however, that Anderson would use this discretion

10. Henry Adams to Charles Francis Adams, Jr., Dec. 29, 1860, in J. C. Levenson et al., eds., *The Letters of Henry Adams* (3 vols.; Cambridge: Belknap Press of Harvard University Press, 1982), 1:215. My thanks to Walter Stahr for calling this letter to my attention.

11. James Ford Rhodes, *History of the United States from the Compromise of 1850 to the Final Restoration of Home Rule at the South in 1877* (7 vols.; New York: Macmillan, 1893–1906), 3:236–41; Roy Franklin Nichols, *The Disruption of American Democracy* (New York: Macmillan, 1948), 416–25; W. A. Swanberg, *First Blood: The Story of Fort Sumter* (New York: Charles Scribner's Sons, 1957), 64–69, 85, 89–90; James Elliott Walmsley, "John Buchanan Floyd," *Dictionary of American Biography*, 6:482–83; William G. Shade, "John Buchanan Floyd," *American National Biography*, 8:148–50.

by moving to Sumter. Floyd's purpose, which he was "very careful not to betray to Mr. Buchanan," was to create "a situation which should make an armed explosion inevitable, and should so force Virginia and the border States into secession" (235). This striking nugget appears suspicious. It credits the inept Floyd with more capability for intrigue than he possessed—maneuvering Anderson into Sumter so as to push Virginia into the arms of the Deep South, while at the same time pretending to support Southern demands that Buchanan countermand Anderson for moving to Sumter, and even turning Buchanan's refusal into a fig leaf that allowed him to resign from the cabinet on his own terms. But could someone have floated this tall tale in late February, when the diarist noted the story? Quite possibly so. Floyd plainly supported secession in January and February, immediately after leaving the cabinet, and he boasted that he had deliberately shipped cannons to the South in the hope that they would be captured by secessionists. By late February, Virginia secessionists increasingly came to see an armed clash as the only way to overcome their state's pro-Union outlook. At that juncture some comment made by Floyd himself might have gotten back to Washington, or someone else just might have tried to connect the dots regarding Floyd in the way that the diarist recorded.[12]

Plenty of historical substance also may be found in a Diary segment dated February 8, in which the diarist recounted a "long conversation" with an unidentified informant regarding the recent action of the New York legislature in filling William H. Seward's seat in the U.S. Senate. The speaker depicted Thurlow Weed—Seward's long-time adviser—as the mastermind who had orchestrated the selection of Judge Ira Harris for the post. Asked by a Republican legislator during the balloting "whether he knew Harris personally and thought him safe," Weed allegedly countered: "Do I know him personally? I should rather think I do. I invented him!" Weed was determined to block Horace Greeley, editor of the *New York Tribune*, whom Weed considered sympathetic to "Massachusetts abolitionists" and unwilling to support any conciliatory overtures to antisecession Southerners. The informant complained to the diarist that Weed and Seward had "deliberately slaughtered" the better-known William M. Evarts, al-

---

12. Crofts, *Reluctant Confederates*, 155, 278–79; John B. Floyd to "My dear Sir," Feb. 7, 1861, Burwell Family Papers, University of Virginia; Jean H. Baker, *James Buchanan* (New York: Times Books, 2004), 132.

legedly because they preferred having a "voting Senator" rather than "a strong man in the Senate" (227–28).

Weed, still alive in 1879, was sought out by an enterprising reporter for Hurlbert's *New York World* and asked to comment on the passage in the Diary. Weed readily recalled opposing Greeley because of his "persistent advocacy of the abolition of slavery," which only would have made the South "more determined and more desperate." Evarts, a good Republican but not an antislavery absolutist, seemed a far better choice to Weed. Evarts, however, once had been a conservative Whig who defended the Fugitive Slave Law. This worried many Republican legislators. When the Republican caucus met, a close race developed between Greeley and Evarts. "We found it very difficult" to gain additional support for Evarts, Weed recalled, and it appeared that "it was no use to hold out any longer." Had they persisted, Greeley would have been nominated. After a "short consultation," Weed, Evarts, and Governor Edwin D. Morgan agreed to throw their support to Harris. This move enabled those who opposed Greeley to gain the upper hand. Harris won the caucus endorsement and thereby gained the Senate seat. Weed was not sure whether he ever claimed to have "invented" Harris, but he did allow that he had recruited Harris into politics. Twenty years before, when Seward was governor, he and Weed had sided with aggrieved tenants who owed semifeudal obligations, including perpetual rents, to wealthy landowners in upstate New York. The "anti-rent" issue upset conservative Whigs but brought into the party some fresh new talent such as Harris. Weed absolved Seward, however, of any role in displacing Evarts—indeed, Seward was "very anxious" that Evarts be his successor in the Senate. Seward was far away in Washington when Weed and other Republican managers in Albany decided suddenly to switch to Harris.[13]

Hurlbert himself could well have been the person who made note of Weed's

13. *New York World*, Aug. 10, 1879; Charles W. McCurdy, *The Anti-Rent Era in New York Law and Politics, 1839–1865* (Chapel Hill: Univ. of North Carolina Press, 2001), 156–59; Reeve Huston, *Land and Freedom: Rural Society, Popular Protest, and Party Politics in Antebellum New York* (New York: Oxford Univ. Press, 2000). Weed's version of events dovetails nicely with the accounts in the *New York Times*, Feb. 4, 1861, and the *New York Tribune*, also Feb. 4, 1861. Evarts and Greeley ran closely for a number of ballots in the Republican legislative caucus on Saturday, February 2, with about 40 votes each, while Harris trailed with 20. On the eighth ballot Greeley rose to 47, whereupon the Evarts supporters broke to Harris, who received 49 on the ninth ballot and 60 on the tenth, sufficient to win the party nomination.

spicy retort to the legislator. As we have seen in the last chapter, Hurlbert was in Albany for several days in late January and early February to attend a convention of those who favored a Union-saving compromise. The day after the convention adjourned, the Republican legislative caucus selected the candidate to fill the Senate seat. If Hurlbert lingered—perhaps made curious by the "feverish and intense activity" in the "halls and parlors of the hotels"—he could easily have gathered juicy gossip about the selection process.[14]

The Diary includes extensive segments supposedly penned on February 24 and 25, in which the diarist excoriates Lincoln and whoever might have advised him to slip into Washington unannounced before dawn on Saturday the 23rd. The diarist thought "this wretched smuggling business" had stirred "a most mischievous feeling of contempt for the personal character of Mr. Lincoln himself throughout the country, especially at the South." It was "a most distressing and ill-advised thing," he fumed, and "Mr. Seward feels about it as I do" (234–35). These passages catch precisely the initial response to the episode. Lincoln was widely criticized for choosing to travel secretly to Washington. His caution was thought to ill befit a president-elect. Some lambasted his timidity or even cowardice.

The commentators and the diarist at first were blind to Seward's key role in the "smuggling." But then the *New York Herald* discovered that Seward had made the decision to warn Lincoln of a "diabolical plot" on his life in Baltimore, and had secretly arranged the president-elect's overnight trip to the capital. The *Herald* also reported that Seward and Representative Elihu B. Washburne of Illinois had met Lincoln at the depot. This account appeared in the *Herald* on Sunday, February 24. But most newspapers at the time did not publish on Sunday, so only on Monday morning, February 25, did other newspapers, notably the *New York Tribune,* start to confirm the *Herald'*s account of Lincoln's arrival in Washington. Without so fully emphasizing Seward's role in initiating the secret trip, the *Tribune* article, written on the 24th and published on the 25th, corroborated the *Herald* by stating that Seward and Washburne, "to whom the information had been imparted confidentially, met Mr. Lincoln at the cars yesterday morning." Soon it became common knowledge that Seward himself had

14. *New York Tribune,* Feb. 4, 1861.

decided that potential danger in Baltimore necessitated Lincoln's furtive arrival in Washington.[15]

The diarist's account mirrors perfectly the emergence of the story. On Sunday, February 24, the diarist condemned the decision to bring Lincoln secretly to Washington. He dismissed "the cock-and-bull story of the Italian assassins, which Mr. Seward told me to-day had been communicated to Mr. Lincoln as coming from General Scott; and it was clear to me that Mr. Seward himself did not believe one word of it" (233). The next day, however, Douglas began to set the diarist straight, even while agreeing with him that Lincoln had acted unwisely. Douglas, the diarist wrote, "both startles and shocks me by what he tells me of Mr. Seward's share in it, asserting positively, as of his own knowledge, that at the urgent request of General Scott, Mr. Seward sent his son to Mr. Lincoln at Philadelphia, to impress upon him and his friends the imminent peril they would be in at Baltimore." The news from Douglas—which was correct—caused the diarist to express his "utter surprise" (233–34).[16]

In order to write the Diary entries of February 24 and 25 long after the fact, the diarist must have had detailed 1861 information. The story of Lincoln's arrival at the capital was not static but dynamic. It morphed significantly in the space of a few days. It seems impossible that anyone could remember precise details eighteen years later and get the daily chronology exactly right. The diarist also demonstrated a striking ability to suppress absolutely the many unforgettable things that had happened in the interim. Less than two months later,

15. Ibid., February 25, 1861, which includes a copy of the dispatch written by a correspondent for the *Herald* on February 23. The matter of whether Seward did or did not join Washburne at the train station early on the 23rd is a minor but intriguing point of disagreement, the sort of thing that causes historians to throw up their hands in confused despair. Seward wrote to his wife on the 23rd: "The President-elect arrived *incog.* at six this morning. I met him at the depot." Frederick W. Seward, *Seward at Washington* (2 vols.; New York: Derby and Miller, 1891), 2:511. The articles in the *Tribune* and the *Herald* corroborated Seward's presence. Postwar recollections by Ward Hill Lamon and Elihu B. Washburne alleged, however, that Seward overslept and so greeted Lincoln only when he arrived at Willard's Hotel. Ward H. Lamon, *The Life of Abraham Lincoln* (Boston: James R. Osgood, 1872), 526; Allen Thorndike Rice, ed., *Reminiscences of Abraham Lincoln by Distinguished Men of His Time* (rev. ed.; New York: Harper and Brothers, 1909), 114–15. On the other hand, John G. Nicolay and John Hay, Lincoln's private secretaries and authors of the massive and detailed ten-volume biography of Lincoln, published in 1890 after Lamon and Washburne had written their accounts, place Seward at the depot with Washburne. John G. Nicolay and John Hay, *Abraham Lincoln: A History* (10 vols.; New York: Century Co, 1890), 3:315.

16. The Douglas account precisely summarized what actually occurred.

on April 19, just after the start of the war, the potential for trouble in Baltimore was fully realized. Soldiers from Massachusetts, attempting to pass from one depot to another in Baltimore on their way to Washington, were set upon by a mob. In one of the most sensational moments of the week following the fall of Fort Sumter, at least four soldiers and a number of rioters were killed.[17] Nobody thereafter could deny that this Southern-leaning city might be a dangerous place. Likewise, it would have been hard indeed anytime after April 1865 to dismiss so curtly fears that Lincoln might face danger from an assassination conspiracy.

On March 3, the diarist penned his longest single daily entry, recounting an unpleasant encounter with Sumner and an evening interview with Douglas. It was "late" when he reached home, only to find an "anxious" but unidentified visitor waiting for him. The caller said that he had been enlisted by "one of Mr. Seward's New York men here" to telegraph Jefferson Davis in Montgomery, Alabama. Using this go-between, Seward wanted to assure Davis that Lincoln's inaugural address, to be delivered the next day, "would be conciliatory." The visitor, who was "in a curiously perturbed state of mind," evidently did not appreciate being so directly implicated in sending a message from Seward to the new Confederate president. But the visitor felt beholden to assist the person who had made the request, because "he had known the man very well in Wall Street, and had occasion to avail himself of his services at various times." The diarist, who concluded that his late-night visitor "has been going into stock speculations again," advised him to send the message, which he finally agreed to do (251–53).

This episode commands attention for two reasons. First, it is *about* Sam Ward, rather than written *by* him. Second, it conveys secret information that definitely was *not* part of the public domain in 1879. Only with the posthumous publication of Senator Gwin's recollections in 1891 was it revealed that Ward dispatched a telegraphic assurance to Davis at just this moment, on the eve of Lin-

17. Nelson D. Lankford, *Cry Havoc! The Crooked Road to Civil War, 1861* (New York: Viking Penguin, 2007), 137–54; Frank Towers, "'A Vociferous Army of Howling Wolves': Baltimore's Civil War Riot of April 19, 1861," *Maryland Historian* 23 (Fall/Winter 1992): 1–27; Frank Towers, *The Urban South and the Coming of the Civil War* (Charlottesville: University of Virginia Press, 2004), 166–69; William J. Evitts, *A Matter of Allegiances: Maryland, 1850–1861* (Baltimore: Johns Hopkins Univ. Press, 1974), 175–84.

coln's inauguration, promising that "the policy of the administration would be for peace, and the amicable settlement of all questions between the sections." Plainly Gwin and the Diary provided two versions of the same episode. Gwin, who believed that Ward kept a copy of the original dispatch, parts of which were in Seward's own handwriting, suspected that Seward thereafter felt obligated to treat Ward with deference, a judgment echoed by Ward's biographer. Once the war started, the secretary of state had ample motive to conceal his secret prewar communications with Davis, and that meant making nice to Ward.[18]

Another striking aspect of the Diary is the ability of the diarist to recapture anxieties about the economic effects of secession. Reflecting on his conversations with Orr in late December, the diarist initially persuaded himself that the Deep South was too disunited to establish a separate nation. South Carolina resented "the great cotton-growing Gulf States" that had "sucked so much of her blood" (220). The diarist speculated that secession might be only a bluff or gambit, designed to win Northern concessions. Quite soon, however, he recognized that the architects of Southern independence were making rapid progress and that the economic effects of their actions had to be taken into account. He worried that "a long period of business prostration" might set in "before any adjustment can be reached" (226). Were the South to establish free trade, he cautioned, even if only for six months or a year, it might seriously hurt Northern manufacturing. When members of Congress from the Deep South resigned their seats, and thereby enabled Republicans to increase the tariff, the diarist condemned the "preposterous" result—importers would divert European ships to Southern ports (243). By March it appeared that Confederates were establishing a new nation with no plans to rejoin the old one, and that the Confederate government was attempting to bring economic pressure against both the free states and the Upper South slave states that remained in the Union. The diarist sputtered in-

18. Coleman, "Gwin and Seward," 465–71, quotation on 469; Lately Thomas (Robert V. P. Steele), *Sam Ward: "King of the Lobby"* (Boston: Houghton Mifflin, 1965), 256–58, 290; Potter, *Lincoln and His Party*, 342–44. As in the late December episode already discussed above, Seward and the secessionists sometimes appeared to want the same thing, albeit for entirely different reasons. Seward's priority was to prevent any outbreak of violence. That priority made it appear that he was ready to acquiesce in Confederate independence. But he wasn't—Seward believed that the Upper South would remain in the Union so long as the peace was preserved, and that the secession movement in the Deep South eventually would falter if the Upper South sided with the Union.

dignantly about "the infinite vexations, annoyances, and calamities which this senseless and insufferable explosion of political passions and follies is destined to inflict on the industrious people of this county and of all sections" (258). He also worried about the uncertainty of patent rights in the seceded states, and about the complexities of maintaining mail service as political authority bifurcated.[19]

It seems hardly possible that a diary about the secession winter, concocted long after the fact, would have included at least a dozen references to economic and business conditions unless the diarist were well supplied with detailed contemporary documents in order to refresh his recollection. It might facilitate the task, of course, if the author had studied the economic effects of secession while it was taking place. Hurlbert is known to have done exactly this. He wrote a pamphlet in May 1861 that called attention to what he considered the ruinous financial consequences of disunion. As we shall see in chapter 8, he shared this material with his friend, Robert M. McLane of Baltimore, and he later used it to warn Confederate officials in Richmond against their reckless course.[20]

Hurlbert's acumen regarding business and finance was not shared by Ward. The latter, however sociable and genial, was an economic ignoramus who allowed money to melt through his hands. Of the two, only Hurlbert possessed the Public Man's sensitive economic antennae. The diarist worried about macroeconomic trends and wrote astutely about them. He predicted that disunion would continue to generate economic woe, as had been happening all winter. He did not allow himself to foresee that once the war started in earnest, each side would establish a command economy to fulfill military demands, and that business doldrums would give way to hyperactivity.

On March 10, the diarist expressed dismay at a "great scheme" unfolded to him by an unnamed contact of Seward's. The visitor proposed to bring the South back into the national fold by building "a great railway to the Pacific through the southwestern portions of the country, on the surveys made under the direction of Mr. Davis while he was Secretary of War." The diarist was amazed that such "wild and fantastic propositions" could be advanced "with so much serious-

19. Anderson, *Mystery,* 38–39.

20. Hurlbert to the Honorable Members of the Congress of the Confederate States of America, July 26, 1861, in *The War of the Rebellion: A Compilation of the Official Records of the Union and Confederate Armies,* 70 volumes in 128 (Washington, D.C.: U. S. Government Printing Office, 1880–1901), Series II, vol. 2, pp. 1492–94.

ness and apparent good faith." He considered it a symptom of how, "in times of great national trial and excitement . . . that madness becomes a sort of epidemic" (267). The diarist may well have been correct in seeing the railroad scheme as a hare-brained response to the grave troubles that impended. Our concern here, however, is whether such a plan might have been advanced by would-be peacemakers in March 1861.

The answer to this question is yes. A number of prominent Tennessee Unionists, led by Jeptha Fowlkes from Memphis, spent the secession winter pushing a grandiose plan to combine a federal subsidy with investment from a French and Belgian consortium to breathe life into the Southern Pacific Rail Road Company. Considering their plan a Union-saving measure, they were delighted when Seward mentioned it in a January speech. Fowlkes, a political ally of Tennessee senator Andrew Johnson, was in Washington in early March. He had gone to Richmond by the 10th, but other railroad promoters remained in Washington.[21] Could the diarist have concocted this episode—or dredged it up from memory—eighteen years after the fact? Neither seems likely. The campaign for a southern transcontinental was waged in earnest. The diarist had no need to manufacture or embroider. But without suitable documentation, even the most retentive mind could scarcely have recalled details of this sort, which were about to be washed away in a torrent of blood.

The Diary also calls attention to the then-secret history of Seward's outreach to Virginia's Unionists during the early days of Lincoln's presidency. The diarist noted on March 6 that "a messenger enjoying the direct personal confidence of Mr. Seward" had just headed to Richmond with assurances that the administration would neither reinforce nor attempt to hold Fort Sumter (262). Cheered by reports three days later that "the Union men will control the action of Virginia, and that we shall consequently have no war," the diarist exclaimed, "Heaven grant it!" (266). On March 12, the diarist learned that Seward had received word from George W. Summers, the leader of Union forces in Richmond, that "the quiet evacuation of Fort Sumter" would undermine the "fire-eaters"— and that "the prospect of defeating the secessionists in the Convention brightens all the time" (270). Did these exchanges take place? Here, too, we now know that the diarist had an inside scoop. Although both parties had motive to main-

21. Crofts, *Reluctant Confederates*, 108–9, 236, 266, 285; Jeptha Fowlkes to Andrew Johnson, Mar. 10, 1861, in LeRoy P. Graf and Ralph W. Haskins, eds., *The Papers of Andrew Johnson* (Knoxville: Univ. of Tennessee Press, 1967–), 4:378–80.

tain a veil of secrecy, Seward and the Virginia Unionists were indeed in close communication.[22]

Some kind of whispered confidences between Washington and Richmond took place during the week-plus after the inauguration. Journalist James E. Harvey, a moderate Republican with Southern antecedents, dispatched word to the *Philadelphia North American* on March 10 that "the latest intelligence from Virginia is more encouraging for reasonable measures." The next day the well-informed reporter for the *Baltimore American* surmised that Seward had persuaded his colleagues in the cabinet to abandon Sumter altogether. By thus removing all possibility of an armed clash, the article suggested, Seward hoped to strengthen Southern Unionists. Secession then would "die out if left to itself." Harvey suggested on March 11–12 that Sumter involved "nothing more than a point of honor." Continued federal control over three forts in the Gulf of Mexico assured that relinquishing Sumter could not be misread as acquiescing in Confederate independence.[23] On March 14, the just-retired secretary of war, Joseph Holt, a Kentucky Unionist, told former president James Buchanan that "the indications from the border States are very encouraging." Holt, who also was alleged to have been an "intimate" source for Harvey, was "*well satisfied*" that the new administration's policies would be "pacific and conciliatory." Holt hoped "to learn any morning that Fort Sumter had been evacuated." He felt "more hope of the result now than I have had for the last three months." The revolution would wither, he predicted; "excitement is the ailment on which it feeds, and without this it could scarcely subsist for sixty days."[24]

22. Lankford, *Cry Havoc!* 49–50; Russell McClintock, *Lincoln and the Decision for War: The Northern Response to Secession* (Chapel Hill: Univ. of North Carolina Press, 2008), 215–19; Crofts, *Reluctant Confederates*, 275–76.

23. "Independent," Mar. 10, 1861, in *Philadelphia North American*, Mar. 11, 1861; "Special," Mar. 11, 1861, in *Baltimore American*, Mar. 12, 1861; "Independent," Mar. 11, 12, 1861, in *Philadelphia North American*, Mar. 12, 13, 1861.

24. Joseph Holt to James Buchanan, Mar. 14, 1861, in George Ticknor Curtis, *Life of James Buchanan* (2 vols.; New York: Harper & Brothers, 1883), 2:531–32, and John Bassett Moore, ed., *The Works of James Buchanan* (11 vols.; Philadelphia: J. B. Lippincott Company, 1910), 11:167–68. Edwin Stanton complained that Holt had leaked the information that Harvey published on March 11. Stanton to Buchanan, Mar. 12, 1861, in Moore, *Works of Buchanan,* 11:166. Three other fragments of evidence suggest a close tie between Holt and Harvey: Harvey to Holt, Jan. 9, 1861, and Harvey's column, "Independent," *Philadelphia North American and United States Gazette,* Mar. 10, 1859, Holt Scrapbook, both in the Joseph Holt Papers, Library of Congress; and J. B. Baker to James Buchanan, Jan. 11, 1861, James Buchanan Papers, Historical Society of Pennsylvania. Baker blasted Harvey as

The clandestine Seward-Summers entente came to a head between March 13 and 19. We know that New York congressman John Cochrane arrived in Richmond on the evening of March 13, having been dispatched thither by Seward. Cochrane was "serenaded by a terrific crowd, headed by Smith's band." While he was in Richmond, Joseph Segar, a commissioner from the Union members of the Virginia Convention, went to Washington. Segar was reported to have met with Lincoln and each member of the cabinet. He returned to Richmond on March 18 with "every assurance that the policy of the Administration is peace and conciliation."[25] Meanwhile Cochrane returned to Washington, and on March 19 Seward sent him to meet with Lincoln. Seward specified to Lincoln that Cochrane was someone with whom the president could "talk freely." The congressman had "just received a noble letter from Summers, which was written upon explanations made to him by Mr. Cochrane from me." This "noble letter" does not survive, but a copy does exist of a letter written from Summers to another of Seward's go-betweens, James C. Welling. In this letter, Summers reported that news of Sumter's pending evacuation had "acted like a charm" and given the Unionists "great strength." Summers soon announced to the Virginia Convention that "a pacific policy has been wisely determined on at Washington, and that the troops in Fort Sumter are now or will soon be withdrawn."[26] The prosecession *Richmond Enquirer,* even without hard evidence in hand, smelled a rat—it slammed Summers as "the most intimate and confidential of Mr. Seward's Richmond allies." But Unionists believed they held the upper hand in Virginia. So long as Lincoln's "peaceful and conciliatory policy is not deviated from," one newspaper account explained, "a clear majority of sixty thousand votes will be shown at the Congressional election in May against the Secessionists."[27]

When the Diary was published, the full story of Seward's secret dealings

---

a "bad man" who flattered Holt and gained "an inkling of the orders from the War Department" as soon as they were issued.

25. *Washington National Republican,* Mar. 15, 1861 (telegraphic communication from Richmond, Mar. 13, 1861); "Special," Mar. 17, 1861, in *Baltimore American,* Mar. 18, 1861; *Springfield Republican,* Mar. 18, 1861.

26. Seward to Lincoln, Mar. 19, 1861, Abraham Lincoln Papers, Library of Congress; George W. Summers to James C. Welling, Mar. 19, 1861, *Nation,* Dec. 4, 1879, pp. 383–84; George H. Reese, ed., *Proceedings of the Virginia State Convention of 1861* (4 vols.; Richmond: Virginia State Library), 1:626; Crofts, *Reluctant Confederates,* 275–76.

27. *Richmond Enquirer,* Mar. 15, 1861; "Special," Mar. 19, 1861, in *Baltimore American,* Mar. 20, 1861.

with the Virginia Unionists remained hidden. The diarist knew things that were not yet in the public realm in 1879. Four years before, in 1875, yet another of Seward's go-betweens, Allan Magruder, had written a magazine article about his trip to Richmond as a courier to the Virginia Unionists in early April of 1861. But Seward's furtive contacts with Summers the month before remained murky. Only in response to publication of the Diary did Welling, Seward's March go-between who received the key surviving letter from Summers, decide to go public.[28]

Had Lincoln been aware of Seward's communications with Summers? If the secretary of state did indeed offer the Virginian assurances about the evacuation of Sumter as soon as March 6, he must have worked behind the president's back initially. Seward was playing his hand desperately at this point. Circumstantial evidence indicates that he also leaked news of Major Anderson's plight to Stephen A. Douglas on March 5 or 6, in hope that the Illinois senator would depict the fort as an unwanted albatross that endangered the peace. Douglas indeed grabbed headlines on both March 6 and 7—he announced in the Senate that Lincoln stood for peace, and that Sumter might best be sacrificed because it threatened the peace. On March 9 Lincoln first raised the Sumter issue at a cabinet meeting, but not until March 15 did he solicit written opinions from each cabinet member regarding the wisdom of trying to reprovision the outpost. Abundant evidence shows that Seward persistently tried to remind Lincoln that holding Sumter was incompatible with holding the Upper South. Did Seward ever level with Lincoln about his exchanges with Summers? I believe that the secretary of state revealed to Lincoln no later than March 19 what may have been going on behind the president's back up until that point. I also believe that Seward then sought after-the-fact approval for overtures that he may have made on his own authority, and which he now hoped Lincoln would accept. But the president probably never resigned himself to giving up Sumter, and Seward's last-ditch effort failed to move him. It appears likely that Seward misrepresented Lincoln's intentions all along.[29]

In retrospect, Seward was fast running out of cards. By the end of March, his would-be allies in the Upper South—oblivious to the perilous impasse over

28. Allan B. Magruder, "A Piece of Secret History: President Lincoln and the Virginia Convention of 1861," *Atlantic Monthly* 35 (1875): 438–45; James C. Welling to the Editor, Nov. 21, 1879, *Nation*, Dec. 4, 1879, pp. 383–84.

29. McClintock, *Lincoln and the Decision for War*, 215, 323n68 (the last is a tour de force); Crofts, *Reluctant Confederates*, 273–76.

Sumter that had paralyzed Washington—also began to demand federal with-drawal from Fort Pickens, offshore from Pensacola, Florida, the one federal out-post within the Deep South other than Sumter that remained in federal hands. Until that point it had been possible to say that Pickens could remain a sym-bol of Union authority in the Deep South, even if Sumter were given up. But if both were abandoned, as part of a policy ostensibly aimed at peaceful reunion, the actual result instead might be peaceful separation. Some observers both north and south began to say as much. In my judgment, Lincoln ultimately de-cided to try to hold Sumter rather than risk a continued drift toward peaceful separation.[30]

Let us return to the Diary, which ends during the deceptive mid-March inter-val when conventional wisdom anticipated federal withdrawal from Sumter. The last several entries in the Diary suggested that a national convention had become the logical concomitant to relinquishing the fort. Douglas allegedly claimed that Lincoln wanted all "points of present irritation" removed and popular passions given time to cool. Lincoln then anticipated "a general demand for a National Convention" at which "all the existing differences could be radically treated" (269). Virginia Unionists likewise hoped to take the initiative in calling such a convention, and Seward seemed receptive to the idea. Of course, a national convention might not have resolved matters of basic disagreement. Republicans who supported the idea wanted to buy time and allow a sober second thought to emerge in the South. They were not about to support a territorial compro-mise or to acquiesce in dismembering the Union. But Southern Unionists re-mained adamant that only a mixture of gentle measures and liberal concessions could repair the situation.[31]

At issue here is not the question of whether a national convention could somehow have resolved the secession crisis. It is, instead, the question of whether the Public Man accurately represented discussions about a national convention that were taking place at the highest levels during the weeks immediately before and after Lincoln's inauguration. The Diary earns high marks. From late Feb-ruary to mid-March, the idea came to be seen as a plausible expedient. Some

30. Crofts, *Reluctant Confederates*, 283–95; McClintock, *Lincoln and the Decision for War*, 226–53. Two forts in the Gulf of Mexico, Fort Taylor at Key West and Fort Jefferson at Dry Tortugas, were regarded as naval bases rather than part of a state.

31. Crofts, *Reluctant Confederates*, 250–51.

Upper South Unionists suggested a willingness to go along, so long as an agreement could be reached "to suspend the operation of the laws in the seceding states until the convention should act." Some Republicans likewise indicated their readiness to consider the idea, so long as states in the Deep South "would agree to pay over the revenue, and to commit no violation of the Federal authority." Harvey, the journalist who often appeared to know what was being discussed behind closed doors, judged it the only plan that might prove acceptable north and south "without compromising principle or honor" for either side. "We are in the midst of a revolution," Harvey warned, and "must deal with facts as they exist, and not as we would wish them."[32]

After holding out hope in his inaugural address for "a peaceful solution of the national troubles, and the restoration of fraternal sympathies and affections," Lincoln stated that he would favor holding a national convention to consider revision of the Constitution. Two days after the inauguration, as we have just seen, Douglas insisted that Lincoln's inaugural address was "much more pacific and conciliatory" than he had anticipated, and that he considered it "a peace-offering rather than a war message." His longtime Illinois nemesis announced that Lincoln's stance regarding a national convention meant that he had "sunk the partisan in the patriot."[33] Secessionists saw something far more sinister. They accused Lincoln of plotting to invite the Canadian provinces to participate in a national convention. With the Gulf States honor bound to stand aloof, Lincoln might then cobble together a new Union with "a Black Republican majority" sufficient to abolish slavery in the Upper South.[34] Whatever one's attitude toward it, a national convention loomed as a tangible possibility in March 1861.

The Diary's last paragraph, dated March 15, predicted that "news of the evacuation of Fort Sumter" would "bring out the innermost truth as to the political chart of the new Administration," and that it would "pretty certainly lead to the complete reorganization of our political parties, if indeed it stops there" (271). A loss of party cohesion was exactly what many Republicans feared. An undercurrent of dismay swept through Republican ranks when word went out

32. "Independent," Feb. 21, Mar. 3, 1861, in *Philadelphia North American*, Feb. 22, Mar. 4, 1861.

33. Roy P. Basler, ed., *The Collected Works of Abraham Lincoln* (9 vols.; New Brunswick: Rutgers Univ. Press, 1953–55), 4:262–71, esp. 266, 269–70; *Congressional Globe*, 37th Cong., Special Senate Sess., 1436–39.

34. *Richmond Enquirer*, Mar. 15, 1861.

that Sumter soon would be abandoned. The "ultra wing of the party," especially in New England and the Northwest, registered "stern opposition" to Seward's "peace policy." It accused him of trying to break up the party "as now consti- tuted." Radical Republicans also took umbrage that Douglas apparently had "en- tered into a league with Mr. Lincoln." They worried that the president under- estimated his rival's "treacherous purpose." Republican senators, bewildered when Douglas "assumed to speak" for the administration, attempted to main- tain a "studied silence."[35]

In February and March there was plenty of discussion about the possibility of establishing a new Union Party. Some of its proponents imagined an anti- administration coalition that would bring together all in the North who had op- posed Lincoln, plus enough disaffected Republican moderates and conservatives to tip the balance of power. To these would be added the numerous Southern antisecessionists, who appeared to control the Upper South. But compelling evi- dence suggests that Seward toyed with the idea that Republicans could domi- nate a pro-administration Union Party. In order to build such a party in the South, Republicans needed to "shift from the dead issue of slavery to the live issue of Union." Some hard-line Republican soreheads would be unhappy, but Seward hoped to avoid any actual party split. His most candid Southern ally— North Carolina's John A. Gilmer—prodded him to take the lead so as to make the Republican Party national rather than sectional. Seward played a deceptive game. He talked about a Union Party when it suited his purposes. And he may have wanted it. But he understood as well as anyone the difficulty of persuading mainstream Republicans to risk what they had just gained. We see in the Diary how delicately the beleaguered secretary of state attempted to tiptoe through a gasoline-soaked terrain.[36]

One cannot easily fabricate at a later date a document alleged to have been written earlier. When the document is lengthy and detailed, the task is com-

35. *Philadelphia Press*, Mar. 11, 1861; *Chicago Tribune*, Mar. 12, 1861; *New York Commercial Ad- vertiser*, Mar. 26, 1861; Mart[in?] Howard to Gideon Welles, Mar. 28, 1861, Gideon Welles Papers, Library of Congress.

36. Crofts, *Reluctant Confederates*, 266–72; William S. Thayer to J. C. Bancroft Davis, Feb. 4, 11, 1861, J. C. Bancroft Davis Papers, Library of Congress, in Martin Crawford, ed., "Politicians in Crisis: The Washington Letters of William S. Thayer, December 1860—March 1861," *Civil War History* 27 (Sept. 1981): 239–41.

pounded. "The Diary of a Public Man" filled fifty-eight printed pages in the *North American Review* when it first appeared in 1879. Nobody has better stated than Frank Maloy Anderson how daunting it would have been to breathe life into the Public Man:

> One of the major difficulties encountered by anyone attempting to con-
> coct a fraudulent diary is that at some points he will unconsciously allow
> to slip into his production some knowledge which a genuine diarist writ-
> ing at a given date could not possibly have had. The utmost precaution
> on the part of a talented concoctor can seldom, if ever, escape the pitfall.
> Unconsciously he refers to some event that has not yet happened; or he
> alludes to some state of affairs that has not yet come about; or he employs
> some form of expression that has not yet come into use.

Yet Anderson found no "indubitable instances of such blunders." He did find "two or three places in which it seemed possible that the Diarist had used a form of expression a little ahead of the time at which it came into common use," but none "constituted a perfectly clear case." With these unspecified possible exceptions, Anderson concluded, "the Diary appeared to be entirely free from the kind of error into which the concoctor of a fictitious diary would almost certainly fall."[37]

Hurlbert's work won wide acceptance for seventy years, and his own role has remained hidden for almost twice that long. How could he have pulled off such a feat? Plainly the explanation involves both his outlook and his abilities. As someone who was both Southern and Northern, he was horrified by the drift toward civil war. He continued to hope that peaceful reunion might be brought about by enlightened leadership. He followed closely the news of the secession winter, and he was in a position to know a great deal about discussions behind closed doors. Ward certainly assisted, possibly revealing to him things that Hurlbert had not known at the time. Authentic information, coupled with his unique gifts as a writer, positioned Hurlbert to attempt the Diary. He could never have succeeded in producing such a convincing "diary," however, had he not stuck to the facts.

Sooner or later, most anonymous productions get discovered, especially

37. Anderson, *Mystery*, 134.

those that circulate widely and generate public discussion. A relatively recent example comes to mind. Initially, Joe Klein successfully concealed his responsibility for *Primary Colors*, an anonymous novel about Bill Clinton published in 1995. A number of months later, however, Klein's role was exposed.[38] Those who engage in such risky undertakings need to think ahead about a possible fallback position. The fallback for "The Diary of a Public Man" was anticipated by Allen Thorndike Rice's delphic introduction, in which he vouched for its "general fidelity and accuracy" and stated that its author "was actuated by a single desire to state things as they were, or at least as he had reason at the time to believe that they were." Note carefully—Rice did not state unequivocally that the Diary was genuine. He simply stated that its author had attempted to show how things were in early 1861. If and when the time came to use the fallback position, the Diary needed to rest on valid underpinnings.

38. Anonymous [Joe Klein], *Primary Colors: A Novel of Politics* (New York: Random House, 1995).

7

THE LINCOLN INTERVIEWS

The Public Man's three alleged encounters with Abraham Lincoln are the high-lights of "The Diary of a Public Man." If historical, they provide fascinating in-sights regarding the sixteenth president, just as he took office. The interviews, however, cannot be read at face value. It is unlikely that Hurlbert or Ward ever met Lincoln, even casually. It is impossible that either merited multiple invita-tions to consult with him about sensitive policy matters, such as his cabinet ros-ter or the Fort Sumter dilemma. In addition, the Diary includes some obviously spurious material in which the diarist purports to have been a longtime resi-dent of Washington—so that Lincoln remembered meeting him there in 1848. Frank Maloy Anderson, after carefully dissecting the supposed conversations between the diarist and Lincoln, concluded that none had occurred. Anderson also decided that other "striking Lincoln incidents" reported in the Diary prob-ably were "inventions."[1]

Strictly speaking, Anderson had it right—there was no diarist. But if either Hurlbert or Ward gathered good second- or thirdhand accounts from persons who had met with Lincoln, then the Diary's alleged interviews with him may have validity, even though the diarist was a fictional construct. The diarist ac-knowledges that some of his Lincoln material is indeed secondhand—things that he heard from someone else. Could the alleged firsthand material likewise have been second- or thirdhand? Do these episodes include material that only could have been known to insiders? Are there matters that can be corroborated? The Lincoln segments in the Diary require close scrutiny.

Hurlbert's proximity to Lincoln's entourage, if not to Lincoln himself, may well have been improved by a nepotistic coincidence. Hurlbert's older half-brother, Stephen Augustus Hurlbut (1815–1882), grew up in Charleston, South Carolina, where, it may be recalled, he took young William under wing in 1843. Soon afterward, however, Stephen Hurlbut spent himself into bankruptcy,

1. Frank Maloy Anderson, *The Mystery of "A Public Man": A Historical Detective Story* (Minne-apolis: Univ. of Minnesota Press, 1948), 77–92, 177, quotation on 177.

100 A SECESSION CRISIS ENIGMA

swindled a friend, and thereby undermined his reputation. The two half-brothers appear to have had somewhat complementary qualities: undoubted talent combined with suspected "moral weakness." Like many other Americans who sought a fresh start, Hurlbut headed west. He arrived in Belvidere, Illinois, northwest of Chicago, in 1845. There he married the daughter of a respectable family and rebuilt a successful career in law and politics. A Whig turned Republican, he became part of the Illinois political movement that propelled Lincoln ahead. The presidential candidate wrote a personal note to Hurlbut's wife at the height of the 1860 campaign, to report that her husband had been "making speeches for us" and rendering "very efficient service."[2]

Stephen Hurlbut came east at the time of Lincoln's inauguration, in hopes of landing an appointive office. Although his quest temporarily was thwarted, Lincoln enlisted him on a delicate mission to obtain accurate information about the situation in the South. Knowing that Hurlbut still had family and ties in Charleston—but not realizing that he had left there in disgrace—Lincoln sent him to South Carolina on March 21 for a quiet visit to see whether any pro-Union sentiment persisted.[3] Hurlbut's political stature was sufficiently formidable that he subsequently became a division commander in Ulysses S. Grant's Army of the Tennessee. Might his younger half-brother, known to be a prominent New York journalist, have gained some kind of entrée to Lincoln's inner circle? We do not know, but the question bears on the first purported Lincoln interview in the Diary.

2. Steven E. Woodworth, "Stephen Augustus Hurlbut," *American National Biography*, 11:560–61; Jeffrey N. Lash, *A Politician Turned General: The Civil War Career of Stephen Augustus Hurlbut* (Kent, Ohio: Kent State Univ. Press, 2003), 26–56; Abraham Lincoln to Mrs. Stephen A. Hurlbut, Oct. 29, 1860, in Roy P. Basler, ed., *The Collected Works of Abraham Lincoln* (9 vols.; New Brunswick: Rutgers Univ. Press, 1953–55), 4:134.

3. The Hurlbut mission took place between March 21 and 27, while Lincoln wrestled with the Sumter dilemma. As explained at the end of the last chapter, Lincoln remained unconvinced that the fort should be abandoned. Seward predicted that the secession cause would ebb so long as a collision could be avoided. That advice applied nicely to the Upper South, but Lincoln doubted whether the Lower South would reconsider its commitment to independence. See Lash, *A Politician Turned General*, 56–60; Daniel W. Crofts, *Reluctant Confederates: Upper South Unionists in the Secession Crisis* (Chapel Hill: Univ. of North Carolina Press, 1989), 285–86, 290, 295–96; Richard N. Current, *Lincoln and the First Shot* (Philadelphia: J. B. Lippincott, 1963), 72–74; John G. Nicolay and John Hay, *Abraham Lincoln: A History* (10 vols.; New York: Century Co., 1890), 3:390–92; and Russell McClintock, *Lincoln and the Decision for War: The Northern Response to Secession* (Chapel Hill: Univ. of North Carolina Press, 2008), 218, 227–28.

The Diary entry on February 20 indicates that the diarist had used "Mr. Barney" as a go-between to set up a meeting with Lincoln, as the president-elect's entourage paused in New York City. Hiram Barney was a prominent New York merchant and active Republican, who soon afterward was appointed Collector of the Port of New York, a key patronage post. Edward Pierce asked Barney in 1886 about the identity of the diarist. Barney replied that he neither recalled playing any such role as the Diary attributed to him nor remembered attending a breakfast for Lincoln on February 20 at the home of Moses H. Grinnell, another prominent merchant, where he was placed by the diarist. Pierce, and later Anderson, regarded Barney's denial as a key element in undermining the authenticity of the Diary. It offered one of the few clear instances where a person still alive was identified by the diarist—and that person could not corroborate the Diary.[4]

Barney could not remember serving as a go-between for the diarist because there was no diarist. The evidence also is conclusive that Barney did not attend the breakfast on February 20. His name does not appear on any of the rosters of those present published in the newspapers, and someone of his prominence would not have been overlooked.[5] The breakfast was attended by "some thirty Republicans of the Seward faction," including Seward's alter ego, Thurlow Weed. Grinnell, too, was close to Seward, and had gone with Weed to Chicago in May 1860 to promote Seward's candidacy at the Republican national convention.[6] Grinnell never would have invited Barney, a leader of the rival Chase-Greeley faction, which was then exerting itself to diminish Seward's influence over Lincoln and to block any conciliatory approach toward the South. The Sewardites had their own candidate for collector, Simeon Draper, a prominent broker and active Republican, one of the persons who did attend the breakfast. The diarist wrote that he conversed with Draper later on February 20. Possibly the Diary's

4. A. W. Stevens, ed., *Addresses and Papers by Edward L. Pierce* (Boston: Roberts Brothers, 1896), 396; Anderson, *Mystery,* 78–79.

5. The *New York Times, New York Tribune, New York Herald,* and *New York World,* all Feb. 21, 1861, make no mention of Hiram Barney at the breakfast.

6. William E. Baringer, *A House Dividing: Lincoln as President Elect* (Springfield, Ill.: Abraham Lincoln Association, 1945), 285. On Grinnell's ties to Seward and the bitterness between Seward's supporters and the Chase-Greeley faction of Republicans, see Frederic Bancroft, *The Life of William H. Seward* (2 vols.; New York: Harper and Brothers, 1899–1900), 2:41–43, 532–33; Allan Nevins, *The Emergence of Lincoln* (2 vols.; New York: Charles Scribner's Sons, 1950), 2:248.

version of Lincoln's comments that day may have been based in part upon input from Draper rather than Barney.

The diarist included an unusual amount of hocus-pocus in recounting his contacts with Barney. First of all, he claimed that Barney helped him make an appointment to meet with Lincoln. He also made Barney the vehicle for passing along Lincoln's recollection of meeting the diarist in Washington in 1848. All of this, of course, was purely fictional. Lincoln probably never so much as shook hands with either Ward or Hurlbert, and certainly not in Washington in 1848.[7] It was also ludicrous to think that Barney might have interceded with Lincoln on behalf of someone with such differing views on the key issues of the hour—the cabinet, and Southern policy. In even placing Barney at the breakfast, Hurlbert may have been confused by newspaper reports that located Lincoln in a carriage with someone named Barney, shortly after the breakfast. That person, however, was George Barney, a Tammany Hall Democrat who was part of the city's official escort for the president-elect. The Diary's reference to Hiram Barney was perhaps Hurlbert's most egregious fumble. He may have assumed—incorrectly— that Barney had died.[8]

On the other hand, Hiram Barney did meet with Lincoln on the afternoon of February 20 as did many others who had "political axes to grind."[9] Just what Barney and Lincoln talked about is not known, but it may be inferred. Barney was a leader among the New York "Free Democrats" allied with Salmon P. Chase, who deplored Seward's backing of Pennsylvania senator Simon Cameron for secretary of the treasury. As we have seen, Barney also was angling for the top patronage post in New York City.[10] Barney's purported comments

7. It is faintly possible that Lincoln and Hurlbert crossed paths in Cambridge, Massachusetts, in September 1848, during the Illinois congressman's speaking tour in New England. Lincoln, the loyal Whig, was attempting to minimize the defection of "Conscience Whigs," whose threat to vote for the Free Soil Party endangered the candidacy of Zachary Taylor. The Harvard Divinity School was full of insurgents. Those with venturesome imaginations therefore might find some substance in the otherwise bizarre Diary passage in which Lincoln remembers meeting the Public Man in 1848 in Washington (230), but the latter has blanked the encounter from his memory. Basler, *Collected Works of Lincoln*, 2:1–9.

8. The *New York World*, Feb. 21, 1861, noted that two city officials, "Aldermen Cornell and Barney," escorted Lincoln later in the morning. These were Alderman Charles G. Cornell and Councilman George A. Barney.

9. Ibid., Feb. 21, 1861.

10. Baringer, *A House Dividing*, 173–74, 285. Baringer, probably misled by the diarist, also placed Hiram Barney in a carriage with Lincoln after the breakfast on February 20. A letter from Barney to

that day, as picked up by the diarist, are consistent with known circumstances and reflect what he could have said. Someone with his political predilections would have welcomed word—and could have passed it along to someone else as gossip—that the Grinnell event had been "a failure, nobody at his ease, and Mr. Lincoln least of all." Barney likewise would have been happy to claim that Lincoln had not written "one line" to Seward since inviting him into the cabinet in December. The diarist, aware that Barney had an "intense personal dislike and distrust of Mr. Seward," hoped that Barney was misinformed (he was). The diarist suspected, however, that Barney might be correct, in which case "matters are in no comfortable shape" (229–30).[11]

The alleged "brief and hurried" conversation that same afternoon between the diarist and Lincoln was, strictly speaking, a fabrication. Its substance, however, was entirely plausible. It reflected exactly the sort of political assessment Lincoln might have shared with a trusted insider (although not likely with Barney). As mentioned in chapter 1, Lincoln thought it of "vital importance" to keep Northern Democrats "close to the Administration on the naked Union issue." He hoped they would "vote to hold the Union now, without bothering whether we [that is, Republicans] or the Southern men got things where they are, and we must make it easy for them to do this, because we can't live through the case without them" (231).[12] It cannot be proven that Lincoln said this, of course, but it is difficult to imagine that Hurlbert could have manufactured it. Both the style and the substance of Lincoln's comment ring true. A private letter Lincoln wrote in May 1860 uses comparable phraseology: "This puts the case in the hardest shape for us."[13] Whoever the actual source may have been, the core of this alleged interview is probably historical rather than imaginary.

Let us move ahead. On February 26 the diarist claimed to have met with a Seward supporter in Washington, who suggested that they both go to see Lin-

---

Lincoln, Feb. 27, 1861, Abraham Lincoln Papers, Library of Congress, shows that Barney saw fit to advise Lincoln about cabinet matters. Consistent with his position as a Chase loyalist, he opposed appointment of Henry Winter Davis (the rivalry for a cabinet post between Davis and Montgomery Blair will be covered later in this chapter).

11. Lincoln had written several times to Seward, but Seward had increasing reason to doubt that Lincoln would heed his suggestions about implementing a conciliatory Southern policy.

12. Anderson expressed "a good deal of doubt" about the entire episode (Anderson, *Mystery,* 77–82, quotation on 82).

13. Lincoln to Cyrus M. Allen, May 1, 1860, in Basler, *Collected Works of Lincoln,* 4:46.

coln to discuss cabinet appointments. The diarist "declined peremptorily to call on Mr. Lincoln in the business" (236). He did promise, however, to tell Lincoln what he thought about the cabinet, if Lincoln wanted to discuss the matter when they met face to face. Two days later, on Thursday, February 28, the diarist claimed to have met for half an hour with Lincoln, who then was headquartered at Willard's Hotel in Washington. Allegedly they did talk about whether to appoint some unnamed person to the cabinet. They also talked about whether the city of Washington was vulnerable to secessionist attack. Lincoln showed the diarist an "alarmish" letter from Charles Sumner, who feared for Lincoln's safety (239).

Could all of this have been imagined? Frank Maloy Anderson concluded that the second purported interview between the diarist and Lincoln, on February 28, was likely a "clever invention." Anderson's suspicions were warranted. We can dismiss in advance the possibility that Lincoln ever did consult privately with Hurlbert about cabinet appointments. The more difficult question is the possible validity of the comments the diarist attributed to Lincoln. The president-elect did converse with many others about his cabinet—it was an incessant topic all week. It also is probable that Lincoln would have inquired of knowledgeable persons about the safety of Washington. Startling rumors abounded. We now know that Buchanan's attorney general, Edwin M. Stanton, "as devious a conniver as American public life has produced," played an astonishing double role. Stanton enlisted a trusted intermediary who regularly fed Seward hair-raising tales of "defections, conspiracies, and treasons." Stanton also told Charles Sumner and others that fifth-column secessionists endangered the capital.[14] Anderson did not consider whether a "clever invention" might be based on reliable secondhand accounts of actual conversations that did take place.

Ward especially was well positioned to gather accurate secondhand information about Lincoln during the hectic week before the inauguration. With his next-door proximity to Seward and his fondness for gossip, Ward simply had to keep his ears open. It is known, for example, that Seward arranged a meeting between California senator William M. Gwin and Lincoln soon after Lincoln's arrival in Washington, in order to impress upon the president-elect the need to

14. David M. Potter, *Lincoln and His Party in the Secession Crisis* (New Haven: Yale Univ. Press, 1942, 1962), 258–62, quotation on 259; Benjamin P. Thomas and Harold P. Hyman, *Stanton: The Life and Times of Lincoln's Secretary of War* (New York: Alfred A. Knopf, 1962), 98–114, quotation on 99.

hold out an olive branch to the South. Seward wanted Gwin to corroborate the merits of "looking to peace rather than to war"—and to argue that Seward's appointment to the cabinet would be well received by "the leaders of the Southern movement." "The interview was a long one," Gwin recalled, "and Mr. Lincoln a patient listener."[15]

Between his arrival in Washington on Saturday morning, February 23, and his inauguration on Monday, March 4, Lincoln found himself obliged to wrestle with three interconnected issues: the composition of his cabinet, his forthcoming inaugural address, and the closely intertwined question of how to deal with the disaffected South—half of which claimed to be establishing an independent nation, the other half of which clung uneasily to the Union while warning against any use of force. Congress remained in session, too paralyzed to deal with secession. The so-called Peace Conference, then near the end of its deliberations in Washington, was laboring to devise a Union-saving settlement.[16] Lincoln gave a great deal of attention to the vexing matter of cabinet appointments during his first days in Washington. So, too, he arrived with a hard-line draft of his inaugural address, but he received a desperate plea from Seward on February 24 to modify it or risk losing Virginia and Maryland. The specter of disunion hung over all these matters like a dark cloud.[17] Lincoln consulted widely during this time and made himself available for several discussions with Peace Conference delegates. Could things that he said have leaked out, either to Ward or others? It would be unwise to reject that possibility. Second- and thirdhand accounts of conversations attributed to Lincoln were swirling around Washington that week. The best-informed news reports sketched an accurate picture of the issues at stake. The Diary must be assessed in light of what we now know.

Rivalries for cabinet appointments had ignited a fierce internal conflict within the Republican Party. In December Lincoln had offered Seward the most

15. Evan J. Coleman, "Gwin and Seward—A Secret Chapter in Ante-Bellum History," *Overland Monthly* 18 (Nov. 1891): 468. It will be recalled that Ward gave Seward and Gwin a place to meet surreptitiously.

16. The Peace Conference, or Peace Convention, met in Washington during February. Its supporters hoped that it might provide the catalyst for peaceful reunion, but it failed to attract any delegates from the seceded states and became bogged down in a complicated snarl regarding slavery in the territories. See Crofts, *Reluctant Confederates,* 207–13.

17. Crofts, *Reluctant Confederates,* 245–53; Seward to Lincoln, Feb. 24, 1861, Lincoln Papers.

visible post in the cabinet, secretary of state. Seward tried with only limited success to recommend other appointees. The New Yorker was eager to enlarge the number of those who might favor a conciliatory policy toward the disaffected South. Most of his allies were former Whigs. His pretensions aroused a furious backlash from the Democratic wing of the Republican Party. So-called Free Democrats—some of them former Free Soilers and Liberty Party men—opposed any compromise with the South and sought to limit Seward's influence. In their eyes, the New Yorker threatened to sell out Republican principles, and to empower tainted spoilsmen like Cameron and Thurlow Weed while doing so. At the very least, they wanted Chase to be secretary of the treasury. If possible, they wanted to drive Seward out of the cabinet and win Lincoln to their side. Long before he got to Washington, Lincoln struggled to harmonize the two camps. At stake was not simply the division of cabinet seats but also the ominous question of how to deal with secession. Chase supporters insisted that concessions to the South were both unnecessary and humiliating. They contended that the secession movement would dissipate so long as Lincoln and the Republican Party stood firm. They had no use for Seward's would-be collaborators, the Unionists in the Upper South, who insisted that the crisis was immensely dangerous, and that it could be mitigated only by Republican concessions and forbearance.[18]

The Diary brings this high-stakes vendetta into sharp focus. On Tuesday, February 26, the diarist began to suspect that "Mr. Chase holds the new President more tightly in his hand than Mr. Seward does" (236). Unionists in the Upper South likewise concluded that Chase had Lincoln's ear, and they feared the worst.[19] Four days later, on Saturday, March 2, the infighting between the Seward and Chase camps remained unrelenting. According to one of the diarist's informants, a delegation of Seward's New York supporters called on Lincoln—this was less than forty-eight hours before the inauguration—"to bring matters to a head." They insisted that Seward and Chase could not serve together, and they urged that Lincoln drop Chase:

> Speaking one after another, they all urged the absolutely essential importance of the presence of Mr. Seward in the Cabinet, to secure for it either the support of the North or any hearing at the South; and they all set forth the downright danger to the cause of the Union of putting

18. Crofts, *Reluctant Confederates,* 227–28.
19. Ibid., 246, 252–53.

into the Cabinet a man like Mr. Chase, identified with and supported by men who did not desire to see the Union maintained on its existing and original basis at all, and who would rather take their chances with a Northern republic, extending itself to Canada, than see the Union of our fathers kept up on the principles of our fathers. (244)

At this juncture Lincoln deftly took control of the meeting, the diarist learned. The president-elect explained to his visitors at some length that he hoped to include both Seward and Chase in the cabinet, because each had "great claims" to a top position. If that could not be brought about, however, he revealed that he had devised an alternate roster. As mentioned in chapter 1, his listeners judged that Lincoln was "weakening," and they grew "quite agog with suppressed expectations of carrying their great point." Then Lincoln punctured their balloon—he proposed putting Chase in the Treasury Department and offering the State Department to William F. Dayton of New Jersey. To the astonishment of his listeners, Lincoln explained that "Mr. Seward could go as Minister to England, where his genius would find great scope in keeping Europe straight as to the troubles here, and so on, and so forth, for twenty minutes." The diarist, who claimed to have heard about this discussion only hours after it occurred, concluded that Seward was not to be "the real head of the Administration," even if he remained in the cabinet (244–46). So, too, the episode suggested to the diarist that Lincoln disagreed with Seward's conciliatory policy toward the South.

Could the alleged exchanges on March 2 between Lincoln and the New Yorkers have taken place? Anderson thought not, because he could not find corroboration. He suspected that it was "an invented good story" because such a significant interview "could scarcely have escaped notice." On the other hand, historian Allan Nevins, writing at about the same time as Anderson, concluded that the diarist accurately reported the meeting, and that a delegation of New Yorkers led by Simeon Draper did indeed confer with Lincoln on March 2. Draper, it will be recalled, was the ally of Seward's who had attended the Moses Grinnell breakfast in New York City on February 20 and who was vying with Hiram Barney to be appointed as collector. The diarist reported on February 26 that Draper soon would visit Washington "with several other gentlemen for the purpose of making Mr. Lincoln understand that he must absolutely drop the idea of putting Mr. Chase into the Treasury." In Nevins's judgment, the Diary's account of these proceedings "bears some inner marks of veracity" even though "its authenticity cannot be completely accepted." Nevins's stance closely parallels that of historian Frederic Bancroft, whose biography of Seward had been published a half century before. Bancroft also made explicit use of the Diary when describing the struggle to shape Lincoln's cabinet. Even though uncertainty regarding the Diary's authorship "might seem to exclude it from the field of trustworthy evidence," Bancroft wrote, "its tone, accuracy, and scope" reflected an "intimate" familiarity with Seward. Bancroft credited as genuine the diarist's report of the March 2 encounter. More recently, as also noted in chapter 1, historians David Donald and Doris Kearns Goodwin both have accepted the Diary's account of the meeting.[20]

Some newspaper reporters during the week before the inauguration had an excellent grasp of what was going on behind closed doors. The *New York Herald* described the intense rivalry between Seward and the "extreme" Republicans, who wanted Chase appointed secretary of the treasury. Conciliatory Republicans associated with Seward demanded that Chase be excluded from the cabinet and that the treasury portfolio go either to Cameron or to some other moderate Republican. The conciliators also hoped to reserve a cabinet seat for a non-Republican Southern Unionist—either Tennessee's Emerson Etheridge or North Carolina's John A. Gilmer, both members of the U.S. House. Each had the refusal of an offer, but neither was willing to take it without "positive assurances as to the policy of the administration in reference to Southern matters." When Lincoln then proposed to include the militaristic Montgomery Blair of Maryland as a token Southerner, the Seward wing made a last-minute bid to substitute Congressman Henry Winter Davis, also of Maryland.[21] By the end of the week, it appeared that Chase and Blair had the inside track. A reporter for the *New York Herald* wrote on Saturday, March 2, that "the conservative element was fully aroused, and made a last desperate effort to-day against the appointment of Gov. Chase to a place in Mr. Lincoln's cabinet, but without success." The struggle pitting Blair against Davis also was reported "very close and hotly con-

20. Anderson, *Mystery,* 87, 95–97; Nevins, *Emergence of Lincoln,* 2:453–54; Bancroft, *Life of Seward,* 2:42–44; David Herbert Donald, *Lincoln* (New York: Simon & Schuster, 1995), 282–83; Doris Kearns Goodwin, *Team of Rivals: The Political Genius of Abraham Lincoln* (New York: Simon & Schuster, 2005), 317.

21. Although Davis would emerge during the war as an outspoken radical, in early 1861 he was a leading member of the "Southern Opposition." He and most other Southern Unionists sought peaceful reunion. Blair, by contrast, was an avowed Republican who viewed the crisis in a way that terrified would-be conciliators. Like his father, Francis Preston Blair, Montgomery Blair thought that armed force would bring secessionists to their senses.

tested." By Saturday night, according to the *New York Times,* Lincoln was besieged by antagonistic supporters of Chase and Cameron, and those favoring Blair or Davis. Lincoln, who "listened with sorrow to the uproar around him" and was "very much agitated," finally called a halt to the discussion. He said that he had selected the men he wanted, although their positions were not "definitely assigned," and that the matter was closed. These reports do not specifically corroborate the diarist, but they do show that the Diary accurately conveyed the nature of the discussion taking place. What is more, the sleuthing for the *Times* and the *Herald* provides considerable circumstantial evidence that Lincoln could indeed have told a group of Seward men on March 2 exactly what the diarist recounted.[22]

Finally, just as this study neared completion, historian Russell McClintock noticed additional evidence that substantiates the March 2 interview. Several days later, Seward wrote privately to his wife to explain why he ultimately decided to join Lincoln's "compound Cabinet"—he dared not "go home, or to England" and thereby "leave the country to chance." England? "The Diary of a Public Man" first revealed Lincoln's heretofore-unknown threat to exile Seward to Britain if the New Yorker persisted in resisting cabinet seats for Chase and other hard-liners. Not until over a decade later, however, did Seward's son first publish the corroborative letter in the biography of his father—a letter that goes far toward validating the Diary's version of the March 2 interview.[23]

On February 28, and then again on March 3, the diarist gleaned some remarkably sensitive information, ostensibly from Douglas, about Lincoln's soon-to-be-delivered inaugural address. Hurlbert could hardly have manufactured these

22. *New York Herald,* Feb. 26, 28, Mar. 2, 3, 1861; *New York Times,* Mar. 4, 1861. Keep in mind that few newspapers published on Sundays at this time (the *New York Herald* was an exception). Something that happened on a Saturday therefore was less likely to remain current for Monday editions. Never was this more true than the first weekend of March 1861, when news of great importance was breaking hourly (Lincoln was inaugurated on Monday, March 4). Frank Maloy Anderson did not understand the cabinet tussle; he doubted that Davis would have been supported eagerly by conciliators (Anderson, *Mystery,* 83–84).

23. McClintock, *Lincoln and the Decision for War,* 198, 319–20n24; William H. Seward to Frances Seward, Mar. 8, 1861, in Frederick W. Seward, *Seward at Washington as Senator and Secretary of State* (2 vols.; New York: Derby and Miller, 1891), 2:518. Like me, McClintock steered away from the Diary, on grounds that Anderson had raised unresolved questions about its authenticity. McClintock now is ready to accept that the document may have "significant historical value" because it can be "corroborated by contemporary sources that were not available to an 1879 writer."

alleged conversations, even though he was not the person in whom Douglas confided. On the 28th, the diarist recounted, Douglas divulged that Lincoln had written his inaugural address at Springfield "without consulting anybody." This was true. Douglas also thought Lincoln had not "showed it to Mr. Seward or anybody else since he reached Washington." The diarist feared that "all our hopes of a settlement through the influence of Mr. Seward" were jeopardized if Lincoln indeed had ignored Seward regarding "the first great act of his official life" (241). Lincoln had, in fact, shown the address to Seward and to several others—and as we have seen, the New Yorker recommended that Lincoln recast the speech so as to emphasize his hopes for a peaceful resolution of the crisis. But neither Lincoln nor Seward had shared that information with Douglas.

On March 3, however, the day before the speech was to be delivered, Douglas revealed to the diarist (that is, to Hurlbert's or Ward's source, whomever that may have been) that Lincoln had "intimated" some key information about what he intended to say. Lincoln faced the awful dilemma of maintaining federal authority over all the states, even though most federal property in the Deep South had fallen into the hands of those who claimed to be building a separate nation. Would he attempt to reclaim the Southern forts? Or would he acquiesce in their occupation by secessionist forces? According to Douglas, Lincoln had revised his message since arriving in Washington. He would assert his duty to "hold, occupy, and possess" all federal property and to collect import duties. But he would not attempt to "enforce the strict rights of the Government" in localities where "hostility to the United States" was "great and universal." Douglas and the diarist concluded that "Mr. Seward's counsels must have brought Mr. Lincoln to this stand" (251). Lincoln's olive branch promised to "give the people breathing-time to recover their senses at the South," thereby averting, at least temporarily, the "seething peril" of war (243). It also gave Union Democrats something to "brace themselves against" (251). In other words, just when Lincoln decided to staff his cabinet in a way that was widely interpreted as a victory for the Chase forces, he secretly accepted Seward's advice to tone down his inaugural address.

All of this was remarkably accurate. The particular conversation between Douglas and Lincoln cannot be pinpointed, but the two spoke repeatedly the week before the inauguration. Most of all, the diarist was exactly right to surmise that Seward played a decisive role in persuading Lincoln to modify the inaugural address. We now know that Lincoln ultimately adopted many changes suggested by Seward in the letter written on February 24, and that Lincoln made his revisions just a day or two before he delivered the speech.[24] Seward may have learned on March 2 that Lincoln intended to follow the New Yorker's advice and give the speech a more conciliatory tone. One newspaper report indicated that Lincoln read him the final draft of his inaugural address late that evening, after calling an end to the uproar about the cabinet. The validity of this report is uncertain, but the alleged meeting between Lincoln and Seward late on March 2 would, if true, have provided the basis for some kind of discussion between Seward and Douglas the next day, March 3. In 1879, however, the behind-the-scenes drama regarding the inaugural address was still concealed. The key documents did not emerge in the public realm until a decade later, when John G. Nicolay and John Hay produced their multivolume life of Lincoln. Only with the publication of Lincoln's *Collected Works* in the 1950s, which included densely annotated versions of the original and final drafts of the inaugural address, could one grasp readily the full extent of Seward's influence. Better perhaps than any other part of the Diary, the segment on the preparation of the inaugural address offered by the Public Man has to be considered a source worthy of respectful attention. Its keen insights and its access to extremely confidential material show that the Diary cannot be dismissed as a groundless fabrication.[25]

This brings us to Inauguration Day, March 4. The diarist "listened attentively" for the key words "about which Mr. Douglas had spoken to me" (255). Lincoln did appear to offer a temporary suspension of federal authority in the Deep South—he would "forego, for the time" his "strict legal right" to compel obedience to federal law in disaffected areas "where hostility to the United States" was "so great and so universal" that officeholders could not be appointed. The diarist noticed, however, that Lincoln's olive branch was no more than tentative. When the new president pointed out that he retained authority "to hold, occupy, and possess the property, and places belonging to the government," he "raised his voice" unmistakably, and then "paused for a moment after closing the sen-

---

24. McClintock, *Lincoln and the Decision for War,* 191–99, esp. 197–98.

25. Nicolay and Hay, *Abraham Lincoln: A History,* 3:319–23; Basler, *Collected Works of Lincoln,* 4:249–71; *New York Times,* Mar. 4, 1861. I wrote in 1989 that Lincoln did not revise his inaugural address until early in the morning on March 4, Inauguration Day. Plainly some revision must have occurred at that point—he accepted the constitutional amendment protecting slavery in the states that had passed Congress just hours before. But it strikes me, on reflection, as a near certainty that more substantive revisions did occur a day or two earlier (Crofts, *Reluctant Confederates,* 247, 254–55). McClintock, *Lincoln and the Decision for War,* 197–98, has it right.

tence as if to allow it to be fully taken in and comprehended by his audience." This emphasis "made an uncomfortable impression" on the diarist, and left him unable to share "the encouraging account given me by Mr. Douglas of the spirit and intent of Mr. Lincoln." The diarist therefore remained "in a morbid and uneasy mood during the whole day" (255–56).[26]

The Public Man's version of Inauguration Day always will be best remembered for his account of the way that Lincoln scarcely could find room for his hat on a "miserable little rickety table" as he prepared to deliver his inaugural speech, whereupon Douglas, who had made his way "to the front of the throng directly beside Mr. Lincoln," graciously reached forward, "took it with a smile and held it during the delivery of the address." As we have seen in chapter 1, the diarist judged it "a trifling act, but a symbolical one, and not to be forgotten," and wrote that "it attracted much attention all around me" (254). Yet it did not appear in newspaper accounts of the event printed the next day. Not until March 11, one week later, did the *Cincinnati Commercial* call attention to the alleged hat holding, and then in the form of a secondhand account based on the authority of "one of the Representatives of this State in Congress." Frank Maloy Anderson decided that this famous episode was "almost certainly a myth," based upon one "highly dubious" newspaper item. Even though the story became part of Lincoln folklore after appearing in the Diary in 1879, Anderson thought it telling that none of the many eulogists for Douglas mentioned it in June 1861, after the Illinois senator's sudden and unexpected death. Allan Nevins, however, held the story from the *Cincinnati Commercial* in higher regard than did Anderson. Even though Anderson's book appears to have made Nevins an agnostic on the subject of the Diary as a whole, Nevins read the Cincinnati article to mean that "we may thus accept the incident, at last, as authentic" and concluded that Douglas "did hold Lincoln's hat."[27] Nevins's judgment, as we have seen, is shared by David Donald, Robert W. Johannsen, and Doris Kearns Goodwin, among others.[28]

Contemporary news reports corroborate many aspects of the famous Diary entry about the inauguration ceremonies, which were held on the east front

26. Basler, *Collected Works of Lincoln*, 4:266.

27. Anderson, *Mystery*, 97–112, quotations on 103, 111–12; Allan Nevins, "He Did Hold Lincoln's Hat," *American Heritage* 10 (Feb. 1959): 98–99; Nevins, *Emergence of Lincoln*, 2:458.

28. Donald, *Lincoln*, 282–83; Robert W. Johannsen, *Stephen A. Douglas* (New York: Oxford Univ. Press, 1973), 843–44; Goodwin, *Team of Rivals*, 328.

of the Capitol beneath the unfinished dome. The diarist complained that little thought had been given to arranging things conveniently for the speaker:

> Mr. Lincoln was pale and very nervous, and did not read his address very well, which is not much to be wondered at under the circumstances. His spectacles troubled him, his position was crowded and uncomfortable, and, in short, nothing had been done which ought to have been done to render the performance of this great duty either dignified in its effect or, physically speaking, easy for the President. (254–55)

The *New York Herald* and the *New York Times* concur in having Lincoln first put on a pair of spectacles before reading his inaugural address. He then had to situate the text on a "small table." Somehow he managed to keep the document in place with his cane. Given that Lincoln was a foot taller than many of his contemporaries, this arrangement sounds potentially awkward, just as the diarist suggests—a higher lectern would better have suited his needs. As Lincoln spoke, according to the *Times,* Douglas made repeated approving comments *"sotto voce"*—"Good," "That's so," "No coercion," and "Good again." As soon as Lincoln finished speaking, the aged chief justice, Roger B. Taney, administered the oath of office. Douglas was among the first to shake hands with Lincoln after he had taken the oath. These accounts make no mention of Lincoln's hat, but they do indicate, as photographs confirm, that hats were an obligatory part of proper attire for the occasion. According to the *Times,* spectators removed their hats as Lincoln took the oath of office, and many then tossed them into the air to celebrate. Lincoln must have placed his own hat somewhere when speaking and taking the oath.[29]

A third interview between the diarist and Lincoln allegedly took place at the White House on March 7. The day before, the diarist reported that a visitor had "come directly through from Montgomery, stopping only a day in Charleston on the way, where he saw and had a long conversation with Major Anderson, who is a connection by marriage of his wife, and with whom he has long been on terms of particular good will" (259). The visitor reported that Robert Anderson gave his primary allegiance to Kentucky rather than to the United States,

29. *New York Herald,* Mar. 5, 1861; *New York Times,* Mar. 5, 1861.

and would follow the orders of whatever higher authority Kentucky acknowledged. Even though Kentucky appeared unlikely to leave the Union, the diarist was alarmed to learn of Anderson's "States rights" views and asked the visitor "to go with me and state these facts to Mr. Lincoln" (260). The visitor, though initially "averse to doing this," consented; the diarist wrote a note to the president on the afternoon of March 6; and early the next morning they got back a note specifying the time for an afternoon appointment. At the White House on March 7, the visitor explained to the president what he had learned. Lincoln "received us very kindly," the diarist noted, "but I was struck and pained by the haggard, worn look of his face, which scarcely left it during the time of our visit." It seemed that the information "did not take the President entirely by surprise." Lincoln ruefully allowed that "it will be a bad job for me if Kentucky secedes," and predicted that when Anderson "goes out of Fort Sumter, I shall have to go out of the White House" (262–63).

Frank Maloy Anderson dismissed the alleged third interview as "clearly fictitious." A Union officer at Sumter had kept a roster of persons who visited the beleaguered outpost, and Anderson could find nobody who matched up with the person mentioned in the Diary. Anderson likewise could find no record of visitors to the White House on March 7 that corresponded with the Diary. On the face of it, Anderson surely was correct. Neither Hurlbert nor Ward ventured into the White House on March 7. And the alleged visitor who accompanied the nonexistent diarist could also have been imagined. That, however, is not the end of the story. The Diary entries for March 6 and 7 call attention to issues that are better understood today than in 1879. The dangerous dilemma posed by Fort Sumter, which had moved to the sidelines after mid-January, reasserted itself on March 5, the day after Lincoln's inauguration. That morning, the outgoing secretary of war, Joseph Holt, forwarded to Lincoln a message from Major Anderson, which reported that the Union outpost at Sumter was now so menaced by recently installed South Carolina cannons that it could not be held unless reinforced by at least twenty thousand soldiers. A subsequent dispatch from Major Anderson stated that he was running low on supplies.[30]

The reports from Major Anderson were unexpected. Until then, it had been assumed that Sumter presented no immediate difficulty. Suddenly, however, just as Lincoln took office, he found that he had been handed a bomb with a sputter-

30. Anderson, *Mystery*, 87–92, quotation on 92; Potter, *Lincoln and His Party*, 332–39; Patrick M. Sowle, "The Conciliatory Republicans during the Winter of Secession" (Ph.D. diss., Duke University, 1963), 448–57.

ing fuse. Lincoln feared a backlash in the free states, especially within his own party, if he relinquished Sumter. But his military advisers said that there was no way to relieve the fort. And the conciliators, led by Seward, who hoped above all to prevent any outbreak of hostilities, thought it a "godsend" to move Anderson out of Charleston Harbor.[31] Had someone been able to offer useful information about the situation there, Lincoln would have been eager to learn more. He certainly talked to many insiders about Sumter during the week after his inauguration.

Anxieties about Major Anderson weighed on both the outgoing and incoming presidents. On the evening of Inauguration Day, Buchanan had a final private meeting with the members of his outgoing cabinet. The message from Anderson was so inconsistent with his previous statements that it raised questions both about his reliability and about his allegiances. Could Anderson have lost his nerve—or even become a secessionist? Should his message be believed? There was "a feeling of doubt" about him.[32] Holt, who remained in charge of the War Department for a week after the inauguration, specifically recalled that Lincoln worried about Anderson. One day the president called Holt to the White House and invited him into a private room:

> Looking at me earnestly and with a great deal of feeling, Lincoln inquired:
> "Have you a doubt of Major Anderson's loyalty?"
> "None whatever," I replied.
> My answer seemed to give Mr. Lincoln very much relief.[33]

31. Crofts, *Reluctant Confederates*, 289–97, 355–58; McClintock, *Lincoln and the Decision for War*, 202–9, "godsend" on 208.

32. James Buchanan, memorandum dated Mar. 4–9, 1861, John A. Dix to James Buchanan, Mar. 14, 28, 1861, Joseph Holt to James Buchanan, May 24, 1861, in John Bassett Moore, ed., *The Works of James Buchanan* (11 vols.; Philadelphia: J. B. Lippincott Company, 1910), 11:156, 168–69, 175–76, 195–97.

33. F. A. Burr, interview with Joseph Holt, Aug. 31, 1881, in *Philadelphia Weekly Press*, Sept. 8, 1881; see also Michael Burlingame, ed., *An Oral History of Abraham Lincoln: John G. Nicolay's Interviews and Essays* (Carbondale: Southern Illinois Univ. Press, 1996), 72. Holt's interview with Lincoln may have occurred on March 12, when the president sought him out for a private consultation: Abraham Lincoln to Joseph Holt, Mar. 12, 1861, Joseph Holt Papers, Library of Congress. Until the day before, Holt had continued as secretary of war because his successor had not yet been confirmed. But "as a Southern man" he was not entrusted with "the fullest confidence of the President or his new advisers" (Burr interview with Holt in *Philadelphia Weekly Press*, Sept. 8, 1881).

In fact, Major Anderson was terribly conflicted. Although a loyal soldier who stood ready to obey orders, he dreaded armed conflict. Like others from Kentucky and the Upper South, he considered war the worst thing that could happen. Because he knew that his beleaguered outpost was the site where fighting most likely could erupt, he wanted to be ordered to withdraw. For our purposes here, the core of the March 7 interview appears to have a factual basis. Lincoln indeed was troubled about Anderson. Note also that Holt did not publicize his discussion with Lincoln until 1881. Here, too, the diarist anticipated information that remained secret until after the Diary had been published.

One other aspect of the Diary's alleged third interview with Lincoln deserves mention. He "brightened up for a moment" as the diarist and visitor stood to depart. The president inquired whether "you haven't such a thing as a postmaster in your pocket, have you?" The visitor momentarily "stared at him in astonishment . . . as if he suspected a sudden attack of insanity." But Lincoln then cheerfully explained his quip—"You see it seems to me kind of unnatural that you shouldn't have at least a postmaster in your pocket. Everybody I've seen for days past has had foreign ministers, and collectors, and all kinds, and I thought you couldn't have got in here without having at least a postmaster in your pocket!" (263). A similar tale had been recorded by the diarist on February 28. Lincoln then recounted that one contender for an appointed office had been encouraged to "pick a quarrel" with a rival, and then shoot him. "Mr. Lincoln's melancholy countenance lightened up with a twinkle in his eye," as he reacted to the possibility. "That was not such a bad idea," he observed, "in a slow, meditative sort of way. . . . Of course I'm glad [he] wasn't shot, and that there wasn't any breach of the peace; but—if the custom could be generally introduced, it might lubricate matters in the way of making political appointments!" (239).

These two incidents together provide a sharp reminder of something that would be difficult to recall in 1879. On the verge of an enormous war, the incoming president had to spend much of his time dealing with patronage seekers. As the astonishing events of the next four years unfolded, it would become difficult to remember that many people in early 1861 were blind to the looming cataclysm and focused on other matters. And yet it was true. These incidents also demonstrate Lincoln's penchant for telling humorous stories, a trait that helped him deal with stress. It also afforded him a way of concealing his own opinions. Could Hurlbert have created from scratch the oddball humor that the diarist attributed to Lincoln? Could Hurlbert have imagined Lincoln's use of homely phrases and his reliance on single-syllable words? Neither seems probable.[34]

The Diary makes one last reference to comments allegedly made by Lincoln. On March 11, the diarist noted having had a long conversation with Douglas, who passed along comments on the vexing Sumter issue that he attributed to the new president. As mentioned in the previous chapter, Douglas had spoken in the Senate on March 6 to defend Lincoln's inaugural as a promise to seek "a peaceful solution of our national difficulties." He also hinted that Lincoln would withdraw the troops from Sumter if that appeared the best way to keep the peace. In response to queries the next day, March 7, Douglas made public the as-yet secret bombshell—that Major Anderson regarded Sumter as untenable, and that Lincoln's military advisers considered it impossible to hold the fort. According to the Diary entry of March 11, Lincoln called Douglas in soon after he had addressed the Senate "to assure him that he entirely agreed with all its views, and sympathized with its spirit." Douglas also told the diarist that Lincoln would evacuate Sumter "as soon as possible" (268–69). Frank Maloy Anderson correctly noted that Lincoln had carefully avoided committing himself to any change at Sumter, and we have reviewed in the last chapter the difficulty of linking Lincoln to the withdrawal policy that Douglas and Seward favored. On the face of it, Douglas reported to the diarist something that Lincoln hardly could have said.[35]

But this segment of the Diary does not pretend to offer a firsthand account of Lincoln's words. It reports a conversation between Douglas and the diarist, probably several days after the senator had spoken with the president. Did the diarist record correctly what Douglas stated on March 11? Douglas might have exaggerated what Lincoln had to say—the wish could have been the father of the

34. Better than any secondary source, the incoming Lincoln Papers reveal the mind-numbing extent of patronage matters in early 1861. They are now conveniently available on line: http://lcweb2 .loc.gov/ammem/alhtml/malhome.html. Lincoln's fondness for storytelling is nicely summarized in William E. Gienapp, *Abraham Lincoln and Civil War America: A Biography* (New York: Oxford Univ. Press, 2002), 12–14, 70, 74, 185–86. Lincoln's preference for "strikingly economical" prose that relied on easily understood words and phrases is discussed by Richard Carwardine in *Lincoln: A Life of Purpose and Power* (New York: Knopf, 2006), 264–66.

35. Johannsen, *Douglas*, 846–51; Anderson, *Mystery*, 121–23; McClintock, *Lincoln and the Decision for War*, 207–12.

thought. Douglas, of course, believed Sumter "ought to have been abandoned already" (268). Mail from the Upper South reminded him every day that Unionists there considered war the ultimate disaster. Believing Lincoln "eminently a man of the atmosphere which surrounds him," Douglas attempted to position himself close to the president (234). He had done so most notably on Inauguration Day. During the next week he tried to counter the influence of militaristic Republicans, led by the Blair family, who itched to fight the Confederacy and who warned Lincoln that he would be impeached if he surrendered Sumter. In order to maintain morale among those who agreed with him, Douglas could have put the best face possible on the situation. And by March 11, the day of the Diary entry, Douglas might have been persuaded by convincing news reports that corroborated what he thought or hoped Lincoln had told him. The stakes could not have been higher. Douglas put himself under such "severe pressure" in early 1861 that he would be dead within months.[36]

Frank Maloy Anderson regarded the three alleged interviews between the diarist and Lincoln as fictitious. In a narrow sense his conclusion must stand—there was no diarist, as such. All three interviews, however, appear to contain authentic material. So likewise does the secondhand account of the discussion between Lincoln and the New Yorkers on March 2, the rumors on March 3 about the inaugural address, and the diarist's account of what actually took place the next day during the inauguration ceremonies. The March 11 discussion is consistent with what Douglas wished Lincoln had said, even though it includes a promise to abandon Sumter that Lincoln would not have volunteered. It seems most unlikely that these various episodes could have been imagined in the late 1870s, even by the gifted Hurlbert, without ample foundation in reality.

36. Johannsen, *Douglas*, 848–50, quotation on 850. Antisecessionists in the Upper South sent many letters to Douglas in March 1861 (Stephen A. Douglas Papers, University of Chicago).

8

HURLBERT AND WARD

The first half of this book has focused on "The Diary of a Public Man," identified its surreptitious author, and demonstrated that many of its key segments have factual foundations. Now we shall move ahead in time to situate the Diary amid the events of the 1860s and 1870s, and to examine the circumstances of its appearance in 1879. We already have met Hurlbert and Ward, but in this chapter we shall learn more about them and their ties to each other. Chapter 9 will investigate the role of Allen Thorndike Rice, editor of the *North American Review,* and it will show how he and Hurlbert cooperated to promote and validate the Diary. Additional insights about the Diary may be gleaned from surveying the many other things Hurlbert wrote after 1861, both before and after publication of the Diary—these matters will be found in chapters 10 and 11. Finally, in chapter 12, we must trace Hurlbert's spectacular demise. When the Diary appeared in 1879 he was an honored pillar of New York City society; but little more than a decade later he disappeared into anonymous exile, a fugitive from the law.

William Henry Hurlbert wrote "The Diary of a Public Man," but could not have acted entirely alone. His crony, Sam Ward, was the source for much of the kiss-and-tell specificity in the Diary. Their high regard for each other must be seen as the crucible from which the Diary emerged. Indeed, the Diary is a remarkable legacy to their friendship. Of necessity the two principals covered their footsteps with utmost circumspection. Kudos to Frank Maloy Anderson—he recognized that Hurlbert and Ward were close, he surmised that they may have collaborated to write the Diary, and he came close to unraveling the mystery.

As mentioned in chapter 5, Hurlbert and Ward first encountered each other shortly before the war at the home of Samuel L. M. Barlow, the prominent New York lawyer, railroad promoter, and Democratic Party manager. Years later, Ward reminisced to Barlow about "those happy days in your old house when we were all so full of life and hope and Hurlbert and I made it our nightly tryst."[1] A special attachment between Hurlbert and Ward soon developed, and for the rest of their lives they were regarded as inseparable. Several of their mutual friends—including William H. Russell, William M. Evarts, and Thomas F. Bayard—routinely included felicitations for Hurlbert in letters to Ward.[2] An obituary of Ward's noted that he and Hurlbert "used to understand one another perfectly. They lived in a world of their own, very agreeable and slightly out of the world." The "bald heads of these two gentlemen" were often visible together in Hurlbert's office at the *World*, or after hours at the Manhattan Club and other choice restaurants. Following the "thunderbolt" of Ward's unexpected death in May 1884, a grieving Hurlbert rushed to Italy, where he and one of Ward's nephews buried Ward's remains and ordered a suitable gravestone.[3]

Hurlbert and Ward shared many traits. When young each became a multilingual cosmopolitan, equally at home in Europe and the United States. Each was intellectually precocious and had a retentive memory. Each exuded personal magnetism and charm but died in exile under a legal cloud. Both shared major attributes for the diarist that Anderson specified: each was a politically moderate New Yorker with ties both to New England and the South, each hoped that secession could be reversed and the Union peacefully restored, each was a political insider with entrée to men at the top, each had contacts and friendships that reached across party and sectional lines, and each enjoyed putting words on paper.

However close, Hurlbert and Ward had differing career trajectories. Ward, thirteen years Hurlbert's senior, was born to greater privilege but encountered sharper reversals. His first wife died, his second absconded to Europe, and he was denied contact with his own children. Ward lacked business acumen and at

1. Samuel Ward to S. L. M. Barlow, Mar. 5, 1881, Samuel Latham Mitchill Barlow Papers, Huntington Library, San Marino, California; Lately Thomas (Robert V. P. Steele), *Sam Ward: "King of the Lobby"* (Boston: Houghton Mifflin, 1965), 228–30.

2. William H. Russell to Samuel Ward, Dec. 17, 1878, Jan. 31, 1879, Thomas F. Bayard to Ward, Aug. 12, Sept. 28, 1879, William M. Evarts to Ward, May 10, Aug. 12, 1879, Samuel Ward Papers, New York Public Library. We have seen in chapter 5 that Russell of the *London Times* spent time with Ward and Hurlbert in New York City in March 1861. Bayard, a U.S. senator and presidential candidate, will be introduced in chapter 9. Evarts, the disappointed U.S. Senate aspirant in February 1861, will reemerge to play an important role in chapter 10 in his capacity as U.S. secretary of state.

3. Letter from New York, May 24, 1884, in *Springfield Republican*, May 26, 1884; *New York World*, Sept. 8, 1895; Thomas, *Sam Ward*, 481–83, 490–92; Maud Howe Elliott, *Uncle Sam Ward and His Circle* (New York: Macmillan, 1938), 677–86.

times was close to flat broke. Twice his friendship with wealthy patrons enabled him to replenish his finances. But he frittered away these windfalls through high living, compulsive gift giving, and ill-advised investment schemes. Two years before his death, he was forced to flee the country in order to escape his creditors. Ward's work as a lobbyist involved promoting "good feelings and friendly relations," and he prided himself on bringing dinner guests together "in the best of humor." Ward's sister, Julia Ward Howe, recalled that "he had an unusual power of reconciling people who were at variance with each other." Ward had no ability, however, as a negotiator, and he lacked political judgment. Once the appropriately good mood had been created, "Ward's function ceased, and it was then time to send him away." He wanted recognition as a poet, but his words lacked magic. Time and again, Henry Wadsworth Longfellow struggled to find something polite to say when confronted with Ward's latest effort to craft verse.[4]

Hurlbert, by contrast, enjoyed far more career satisfaction. An elite journalist, he always was secure and well paid, and he had talents that far surpassed Ward's. Louis Jennings, the crack British reporter for the *New York Times* who brought Boss Tweed to his knees, put things in perspective for Ward in 1876. "We are tolerably clever men," Jennings told Ward, but "Hurlbert has the celestial fire" and had been "touched by the immortal flame."[5] While Ward longed to get into print, Hurlbert knew that his editorials and articles would be featured on a daily basis in a leading New York newspaper. Ward had a splendid memory, but he recognized that Hurlbert's "beats mine."[6] A chastened Ward apparently had few if any intimate relationships with women after the failure of his second

4. Thomas, *Sam Ward,* 321–32, 398–400, 435–37, 451–53; *Springfield Republican,* May 26, 1884; Julia Ward Howe, *Reminiscences, 1819–1899* (1899; rpr. New York: New American Library, 1969), 72.

5. Louis L. Jennings to Ward, July 20 [1876], Ward Papers, New York Public Library; Kenneth D. Ackerman, *Boss Tweed: The Rise and Fall of the Corrupt Pol Who Conceived the Soul of Modern New York* (New York: Carroll & Graf, 2005), 93–95, 148, 160–61, 165–71, 351. William M. ("Boss") Tweed will always be remembered as the target of Thomas Nast's scathing cartoons. Tweed masterminded a far-reaching scheme of kickbacks. If you wanted to build something in New York City in the late 1860s or early 1870s, you had to work through Tweed's "Ring."

6. Ward to Maud Howe [Elliott], July 30, 1882, Samuel Ward Papers, Houghton Library, Harvard University. One of Hurlbert's obituaries noted that he exceeded everyone in "retentiveness of memory" (*New York Times,* Sept. 9, 1895). Ward's "astonishing memory" also was remarked on in his obituaries. See Thomas, *Sam Ward,* 485; Frank Maloy Anderson, *The Mystery of "A Public Man": A Historical Detective Story* (Minneapolis: Univ. of Minnesota Press, 1948), 156.

marriage. But Hurlbert continued to seek out new conquests and was "connected with the names of many women."[7]

For more than a year after the outbreak of war in April 1861, Hurlbert and Ward followed separate paths, as each embarked on an impromptu adventure. Somewhat uncharacteristically, Ward's had a happier outcome than Hurlbert's. Ward decided to accompany William H. Russell, the heralded correspondent for the London *Times,* on a tour of the disaffected South. This venture began just days before the first shots of the war were fired at Fort Sumter. Initially Ward may have imagined that he might yet play some kind of mediating role. At the time he headed south—on April 11—he still surmised that the Lincoln administration would avert any immediate challenge to the Confederacy. Of course Ward's prognostications were incorrect. By the time he departed, the Union resupply mission was approaching Charleston. When Ward arrived there on April 13, a furious cannonade was underway and the fort was ablaze. He and Russell thus witnessed directly the surge of Southern national feeling in the ensuing days and weeks as they traveled from South Carolina to Louisiana.[8]

Ward carefully concealed the most extraordinary aspect of his venture. By prearrangement, he regularly dispatched to Secretary of State William H. Seward a series of reports on the situation in the South. He delved into all kinds of sensitive military topics—the numbers of soldiers and quality of armaments at various locations, estimates of the quality of Confederate defenses, and so on. Ward used a pseudonym, "Carlos Lopez," and addressed his letters to Seward's secretary, George Ellis Baker. He hid them amid Russell's outgoing articles. Even with these precautions, Ward was engaged in a dangerous enterprise. Neither Confederate authorities nor the Southern mass public would have hesitated to treat a Union spy severely. And yet the ruse worked. Ward emerged unscathed, and his "Carlos Lopez" letters remain today as part of the Seward Papers at the University of Rochester.[9]

After his return to Union territory, Ward attempted to remain an informal adviser to Seward. A steady stream of his letters reached the secretary of state.

7. *New York World,* Sept. 8, 1895.

8. Ward to Barlow, Apr. 8, 9, 1861, Barlow Papers; Thomas, *Sam Ward,* 265–83.

9. Thomas, *Sam Ward,* 270–81; Margaret Butterfield, "Sam Ward, Alias Carlos Lopez," *University of Rochester Library Bulletin* 12 (Winter 1957): 23–33.

Ward protested the arrest of former senator William M. Gwin, who was suspected of conspiring with Confederate agents to gain control of California.[10] Freely offering his opinions on many sensitive matters, Ward warned that the seizure of the *Trent* in late 1861 might lead to war with England, he cautioned against enlarging Union war aims to include emancipation, and he predicted that the Union gunship *Monitor* could not stand up to its Confederate counterpart, the *Merrimac*. He also hinted that he would welcome a diplomatic appointment. In the end he wore out his welcome. Seward scrawled on the margins of a note written in July 1862: "This letter would be alarming if Mr. Ward had ever been able to write a cheerful one even under the brightest skies." No diplomatic appointment was forthcoming.[11]

Almost as if he were following Ward's footsteps, Hurlbert decided to head south in order to "see for himself" what was going on there. Equally irritated by "the angry and vehement tone of the North" and "the irrationality and extravagance of the Southern feeling," he feared that both sides were blind to the unimaginable spectacle of wholesale bloodletting. In late May, after publishing at his own expense a pamphlet on the "financial aspects of the war," he decided to bring copies to Richmond.[12]

Hurlbert gained access to Confederate lines with the help of an intermediary, Robert M. McLane of Baltimore. It was noted in chapter 2 that Hurlbert provided strong editorial support in the *New York Times* for the ill-fated McLane-Ocampo treaty with Mexico, which nonetheless died in the Senate. Hurlbert and McLane also responded similarly to the crisis of the Union—opposed both to secession and to war, and eager even after April 15 to find some way to repair the situation peacefully. McLane's wife was from Louisiana, and her sister was married to Joseph Johnston, the Confederate general then stationed nearby at

10. See Frederic Bancroft, *The Life of William H. Seward* (2 vols.; New York: Harper and Brothers, 1899–1900), 2:264–66.

11. Ward to Seward, July 22, 1862, William H. Seward Papers, University of Rochester, New York; Thomas, *Sam Ward*, 281–308.

12. T. C. Evans, "William H. Hurlbert," *New York Times*, June 14, 1902, p. 408; William Henry Hurlbert to the Honorable Members of the Congress of the Confederate States of America, Richmond, 26 July 1861, in *The War of the Rebellion: A Compilation of the Official Records of the Union and Confederate Armies*, 70 volumes in 128 (Washington: U.S. Government Printing Office, 1880–1901), Series II, vol. 2 (hereafter *OR*, II:2), pp. 1492–94.

Harpers Ferry. McLane wrote Hurlbert a letter of introduction, and Johnston gave him a pass to Richmond.[13] Hurlbert arrived in Richmond in early June, less than two months after the outbreak of war, eager to talk sense to officials there. In Richmond he conferred with Judah Benjamin, the Confederate attorney general, with whom he was already acquainted, and with Robert Toombs, the Confederate secretary of state.

Hurlbert insisted that he met with Benjamin and Toombs at their invitation. They wanted an influential New York journalist to see firsthand "the entire unanimity of the seceded populations" and the success of the Confederate revolution. But Hurlbert knew that they failed to understand the tidal wave of popular support for the Northern war effort, and the urgent need to avert hostilities. Hurlbert remained hopeful that peaceful reunion somehow might be effected if his hosts would face up to the terrible peril that stared them in the face. Toombs, however, assaulted him with "the loosest and wildest opinions imaginable." The mercurial Georgian boasted that the Confederacy soon would annex Cuba and Central America and win recognition from France. Benjamin's tone was "more measured," but his "anticipations" were comparably "exultant." He "looked confidently for the downfall of the Federal Administration" and expected that the "great central belt of Free States" would "speedily gravitate to the Confederacy." Hurlbert spoke repeatedly with Benjamin but failed to modify his outlook. The attorney general told his visitor "that he had opposed in the Cabinet all measures which implied a continuance of the war beyond September." From what Hurlbert could learn, Jefferson Davis stood alone among the Confederate hierarchy in predicting and preparing for "a long and costly war."[14]

Hurlbert thereupon left Richmond and proceeded to South Carolina, where his married sister lived. While still in Richmond, accusations began to fly that he was a Yankee spy. The clamor increased after he arrived in Charleston. He attempted a dignified departure but was arrested in Atlanta and then taken back to prison in Richmond, where he was incarcerated until November. He remained under house arrest through the winter and during the all-absorbing drama in the spring and early summer of 1862, as General George B. McClellan's Army of the Potomac attempted unsuccessfully to capture the Confederate capital.

In attempting to win his release from captivity, Hurlbert depicted himself

13. Hurlbert to General R. E. Lee, Richmond, June 24, 1861, *OR*, II:2, p. 1490; David L. Anderson, "Robert Milligan McLane," *American National Biography* 15:134–36.

14. *New York Times*, Sept. 11, 1862.

as a friend of the South, and he secured corroboration to this effect both from Benjamin and from William M. Browne, then assistant secretary of state. Reports that may or may not have originated with Hurlbert specified that he was investigating the possibility of starting a newspaper in Charleston. He remained, however, under a cloud of deep distrust. William S. Bassford, the official who escorted him from Atlanta to Richmond, told a newspaper reporter that Hurlbert was "a bitter enemy to the South and her institutions," even though "in person and in manners he has all the appearance of a gentleman." He was "a fine scholar, a man of very superior talents and accomplishments, and of very insinuating address—all of which, taken into consideration, makes him far more dangerous than an ordinary man would be." One Richmond newspaper demanded that Hurlbert "be speedily made to pay the penalty of his numerous crimes by the forfeiture of his worthless existence." The most that his friends could do, apparently, was to secure his transfer from prison to house arrest. His situation had attracted sufficient notoriety that no Confederate official dared rouse popular displeasure by releasing the purported spy. It strengthens the case for Hurlbert's ultimate pro-Union allegiance that the Union underground in Richmond did its best to assist him throughout the ordeal, and facilitated his eventual escape.[15]

Hurlbert's Southern escapade raised eyebrows in the North. Mid-1861 was a time when rumors swirled on both sides about the duplicity of alleged "spies and traitors." Just as Confederate patriots thought they had nabbed "a notorious Abolitionist incendiary," Hurlbert fell under suspicion in the North for having

15. Hurlbert's version of the entire experience appeared in seven lengthy articles in the *New York Times*, Sept. 10, 11, 15, 23, Oct. 4, 11, 20, 30, 1862. Several of his petitions while in captivity may be found in *OR*, II:2, pp. 1490–1501. In a letter to James Lyons, Dec. 16, 1861, Hurlbert claimed that he hoped, before being captured, to aid "the Southern cause," albeit "independently" (*OR*, II:2, pp. 1499–1500).

A great deal of information from additional sources was compiled by Frank Maloy Anderson and may be found in Box 39 of his papers in the Library of Congress. Especially useful are the *Charleston Mercury*, June 27 and July 4, 8, 1861; *Charleston Daily Courier*, June 21, 24, July 3, 31, 1861; *Richmond Dispatch*, June 25, July 9, 1861; *New York Tribune*, Aug. 22, 23, 1862. William S. Bassford is quoted in the *Richmond Dispatch*, July 9, 1861. See also Evans, "William H. Hurlbert," 408.

Hurlbert's support from the Richmond Unionist underground is established in Elizabeth R. Varon, *Southern Lady, Yankee Spy: The True Story of Elizabeth Van Lew, a Union Agent in the Heart of the Confederacy* (New York: Oxford Univ. Press, 2003), 95–96. Professor Varon kindly shared with me two key documents that she unearthed: William Henry Hurlbert to F. J. Cridland, Aug. 14, 1862, and William Henry Hurlbert to Charles Palmer, Aug. 14, 1862, both in the William Fay Papers, Library of Virginia.

shown his true colors and thrown in with Jefferson Davis.[16] None other than Sam Ward gossiped to Seward that Hurlbert had been "on his way South to obtain the privilege of representing overtly or covertly the Richmond *clique* in Mexico," and thereby undermining "the efforts of Mr. Corwin." Ward almost certainly misunderstood Hurlbert's intentions. Just a few days later Ward changed tack and warned Seward that Hurlbert faced real danger. Ward had learned that Hurlbert's captors said they would hang him if he attempted to escape back north, because he possessed "so many plans and secrets of the C.S.A."[17]

Here indeed was a situation filled with irony. Ward was a flagrant Union spy who managed to escape the South undetected. But Hurlbert, who was innocent of any such involvement, was thrown into a Richmond prison. As he rotted there, it was widely suspected in the North that Hurlbert had gone south to cast his lot with the Confederacy. Hurlbert's ambiguous sectional allegiances made him suspect, both north and south. Worst of all, his supposed friend, Ward, initially passed along to Seward reports of Hurlbert's alleged treachery. Fortunately for the future of their relationship, Hurlbert never learned of Ward's rumor mongering.

From prison in Richmond, Hurlbert managed to get a letter to Barlow in New York City, pouring out his tale of woe and hoping for assistance. Their mutual friends—Benjamin and Browne—turned out to be ineffectual "blockheads" and "bullies," unwilling or unable to challenge "the rabble" by releasing a suspected "spy." Hurlbert sourly concluded that "this whole country is really under a reign of Terror." Weeks and then months passed. Finally, after more than a year in captivity, Hurlbert took advantage of the chaotic situation in the Confederate capital following Union general McClellan's abortive invasion and Confederate general Robert E. Lee's decision to head north on the offensive. Accompanied by a young man from upstate New York who had been living in Richmond before the war and who then was compelled to join the Confederate army, Hurlbert figured out a scheme of escape. He and the young man managed to acquire papers that allowed them to pass as participants in the contraband trade then taking place between Baltimore and Richmond. Plainly someone friendly assisted them and gave them money, which they needed to hire boats that slipped

16. *Richmond Dispatch*, June 25, 26, 1861.

17. Ward to Seward, July 15, 20, 1861, Seward Papers. Thomas Corwin of Ohio, a prominent Whig turned Republican and once an outspoken opponent of the Mexican War, had been appointed U.S. minister to Mexico.

them across the Rappahannock and the Potomac. Even in lower Maryland, they remained in danger, because the civilian population in that region was pro-Confederate. After living by their wits for most of a week, Hurlbert and his companion emerged unscathed in Washington, D.C.—and with a story to tell.[18]

Hurlbert amazed his fellow journalist T. C. Evans by showing up unannounced on August 20, 1862, outside the Metropolitan Hotel on Pennsylvania Avenue, just as Evans had "come from my lodgings near by" to get the morning newspapers. The refugee was "in urgent need of rehabilitation." He borrowed some fresh clothing from Evans, who then escorted him to a "famous restaurant" owned by a "colored man" of "much renown." There they "breakfasted in grandiose manner"—Hurlbert "bringing with him the appetite of Homer's heroes acquired in a long season of rather ill-fed captivity." Soon Hurlbert dispatched a celebratory letter to Barlow in New York City. He claimed for himself a version of the motto that Frederick Douglass had made famous—those "who would be free themselves must strike the blow."[19]

Hurlbert's sudden appearance in Washington created a stir. "News from within the rebel lines was hard to get," Evans recalled, and "the budget he brought back was the most copious and various which had reached the capital since the war broke out." Both the prominent and the obscure came to hear the tale of "the eloquent and vivacious fugitive." In addition to reporters from the major newspapers, his visitors included Walt Whitman, Nathaniel Hawthorne, Henry Ward Beecher, and even Charles Sumner. Hurlbert judged that Richmond easily could have been captured during the Seven Days, because Robert E. Lee had sent the bulk of the Confederate army north of the Chickahominy River to attack Union forces, leaving the city "almost unoccupied." This criticism of McClellan's generalship, which anticipated the scathing account by historian Stephen W. Sears, was not something Hurlbert would repeat in the future. He also hinted that he had been assisted by an underground network of pro-Union supporters in Richmond, but he swiftly recanted that statement too, after realizing that he might endanger those who indeed had helped him.[20]

18. Hurlbert to Barlow, July 25, 1861, Barlow Papers; *New York Times*, Oct. 30, 1862.

19. Evans, "William H. Hurlbert," 408; Hurlbert to Barlow, Aug. 22, 1862, Barlow Papers.

20. Evans, "William H. Hurlbert," 408; *New York Tribune*, Aug. 22, 1862 (Washington correspondent, Aug. 21, 1862), Aug. 23, 1862 ("Card from Mr. Hurlbert"); Stephen W. Sears, *To the Gates of Richmond: The Peninsula Campaign* (New York: Ticknor & Fields, 1992), 195, 215–17.

Although Hurlbert had parted company with the *New York Times,* Henry J. Raymond understood that a full account of his adventures would attract readers, and he promptly commissioned a series of articles. Raymond promised that Hurlbert, who had "an unsurpassed brilliancy of style and vigor of diction," would provide "the first glimpse the public has had behind the scenes of the great Secession rebellion."[21] The stories vied for attention, perhaps not so successfully as Raymond had hoped, with the extraordinary events of September and October—the Confederate invasions of Maryland and Kentucky, the bloodiest single day of the war at Antietam, the preliminary Emancipation Proclamation, and the pivotal fall election season.

Hurlbert detailed his experiences in Confederate captivity and warned about the intensity of Southern national feeling. Even if many in the Confederate government fell victim to the "fool's paradise" of overconfidence after their victory at Manassas in July 1861, "the people of the South were preparing the means for that stern and strong uprising which has astounded us all during the present year. They were planting corn in the stead of cotton; they were developing industries which nothing but the war could ever have called into being upon their soil; they were driving a brisk trans-blockade commerce with the West Indies and with Europe; they were learning a lesson of independence and self-confidence which it will be no light task for us to force them to unlearn."[22]

Hurlbert emphasized that ordinary Southerners demonstrated their patriotism with "ferocity" and fanatical intolerance. Northern citizens had been murdered in "cold blood," to the "malignant delight" of local vigilantes: "The explanation of such phenomena as these is not to be sought in the facts of the present alone. They are the outcropping of sentiments which have been long ripening and strengthening in the South, the final outbreak of a profound alienation, which has flowered at last into aversion. For years the South has been learning to hate the North. Through all its ignorant and isolated communities the seeds of distrust and dislike toward the North and Northern men have been sown broadcast." "By slow but sure degrees," Hurlbert continued, the people of the South had been trained "to anticipate the collision which the North refused to suppose possible till its crash was upon us." He did not "attach much importance" to distinguishing between slaveholders and nonslaveholders, because

21. *New York Times,* Sept. 10, 1862.
22. Ibid., Sept. 15, 1862.

"the slaveholder is the ideal of the non-slaveholder" so that "in sympathies and passions the two classes are indeed but one."[23]

The overall message conveyed in Hurlbert's articles was somber. Even though a "tendency to disintegration" would ultimately stir local grievances against the Richmond government, rebel armies were strong and morale was high. A "gleaming array of Southern bayonets" stood ready to challenge Union forces. Hurlbert no longer thought a compromise possible—no middle ground existed, he cautioned, between recognizing Confederate independence and fighting to achieve "absolute subjugation of the South."[24]

Not long after Hurlbert's escape from Richmond, he made contact with Manton Marble, editor of the *New York World*. At just that juncture, S. L. M. Barlow was arranging with Marble to give the paper a needed financial transfusion and to have it become an avowedly Democratic journal. It will be recalled that Barlow had tried two years before to launch a Democratic newspaper in New York City. His largesse created a tailor-made opportunity both for Marble and for Hurlbert. Marble landed the best editorial writer in the business, and Hurlbert got back on his feet after his bizarre hiatus in the South. Thus began more than two decades of profitable association between Hurlbert and the *World*.[25]

Barlow, Marble, and Hurlbert all opposed emancipation. They believed a war waged to end slavery would make the South fight even more desperately. Only conservative Union war aims—to restore the old Union as it was—promised any chance of victory. Hurlbert chafed at what he considered the revolutionary and dictatorial behavior of the Lincoln administration. "I am astonished to see," he wrote to Barlow in late 1863, "how effectively the Republicans have inoculated the general mind with ideas which involve, sooner or later, the acquiescence of the community in any measures that may be adopted against the Democracy."[26]

Ward's political views were comparable. His sister, Julia Ward Howe, sanctified the "fight to make men free" by composing the stirring words to "The

23. Ibid., Sept. 23, 1862.

24. Ibid., Oct. 4, 20, 1862.

25. George T. McJimsey, *Genteel Partisan: Manton Marble, 1834–1917* (Ames, Iowa: Iowa State Univ. Press, 1971), 38–44, 95–96, 178–81; William H. Hurlbert to Manton Marble, Oct. 23, 1862, Manton Marble Papers, Library of Congress.

26. Hurlbert to Barlow, Sept. 7, 1863, Barlow Papers.

Battle Hymn of the Republic," for which the Ward family today is best remembered. Sam Ward, however, considered emancipation a mistake. His emerging business as a lobbyist made it imprudent for him to take the sort of high-profile partisan stance that Hurlbert necessarily assumed, but Ward was a Democrat and part of the circle of like-minded men of affairs who coalesced around the *World*. In 1864, several wealthy New York Democrats—prominent among them Barlow and August Belmont—put up the money to launch the Manhattan Club. Its comfortable quarters at Fifth Avenue and Fifteenth Street soon provided gentlemen who did not share the pro-Republican sensibilities of the Union League Club with a convenient place to gather and socialize.[27]

For twenty years, Hurlbert lived in a sprawling ten-room apartment at 32 Waverly Place, facing Washington Square, immediately adjacent to New York University. His quarters were distinguished by a fine art collection, the highlight of which was a canvas by J. M. W. Turner, *A Vision of Venice*. There was much else—"rich bric-a-brac armor," rare afghans and tapestries, "unique collections of photos," and a reference library that contained volumes in French, Italian, and German, as well as in English. Even though Hurlbert stored a great deal in memory, he also was "an omnivorous devourer of books" who knew where he could "find out all about a given subject."[28]

Hurlbert's bachelor quarters provided a gathering spot for "a small circle of masculine guests," especially his "chosen companions," Sam Ward and William Stuart, the proprietor of the Park Theatre. They would make their presence known by "certain preconcerted calls and whistles which they uttered from the outside"; Hurlbert "would take no chances of being surprised by duns." He also devised a system of mirrors so that he could "keep out creditors and other undesirable visitors." In addition, Hurlbert welcomed "a still choicer circle of the other sex" to his lair. He once casually asked Manton Marble to send him "a couple of pretty picture books" to reward his "clever little janitrix"—she had "never yet turned away a pretty woman from my door or suffered an ugly one to believe me within sixty miles of Washington Square!"[29]

27. Howe, *Reminiscences*, 273–80; *New York Times*, Apr. 11, 1897, p. SM10; McJimsey, *Genteel Partisan*, 77, 82–83.

28. *New York Times*, June 2, 1883; Hurlbert obituary, *New York World*, Sept. 8, 1895; *New York World*, Sept. 9, 1895.

29. *New York World*, Sept. 9, 1895; Hurlbert to Marble, Dec. 24, 1874, Marble Papers; Crosswell Bowen, *The Elegant Oakey* (New York: Oxford Univ. Press, 1956), 199, 234.

The British journalist George Augustus Sala came to the United States in 1863 to cover the raging conflict for the *Daily Telegraph*. He stayed for more than a year. Sala made two "intimate" American friends—Sam Ward and William Henry Hurlbert. When in New York, Sala lodged at the Brevoort House, located on Fifth Avenue at Eighth Street, close to Washington Square. Ward, whose lobbying activities took him endlessly back and forth between Washington and New York, also kept a basement room at the Brevoort House; Hurlbert lived just around the corner. Thirty years afterward, Sala happily recalled the restaurants the three of them patronized and the "stock of rare wines" that Ward kept in one of them. Ward's "conversation was delightful, and his hospitality inexhaustible." Hurlbert apparently made an even greater impression on Sala, who had "rarely known a man so varied in accomplishment." He was "one of the most brilliant conversationalists I ever met with; and he could judge things from an English as well as from an American standpoint." He was a "scholar, a linguist, and traveler, a brilliant writer, a fluent public speaker, with a singularly melodious, yet forcible voice."[30]

In 1864, the *World* promoted the presidential candidacy of the ill-starred George B. McClellan, a particular favorite of moneyed New York conservatives such as Barlow. Hurlbert dutifully wrote a biography of the retired general. But Democrats remained divided between those who would fight to the bitter end and those who would seek a compromise peace. Was the South the real enemy? Or was it the government in Washington that had imposed emancipation and conscription, tampered with the right of habeas corpus, and clamped down on newspapers that did not follow the party line? By September and October growing evidence that the Confederacy was on its last legs revived Lincoln's political fortunes and enabled him to win a narrow victory. This pattern would continue into the postwar era. A clique of elite New Yorkers imposed Democratic nominees on a rank-and-file that was most numerous in the rural Midwest and South, and in the Irish neighborhoods of America's fast-growing cities. It was an oddly heterogeneous coalition. Democratic bids for the presidency might look promising in the spring or summer, but by Election Day they felt short. Hurlbert, the individualistic aesthete, made an implausible tribune of the people.

30. George Augustus Sala, *The Life and Adventures of George Augustus Sala* (2 vols.; New York: Charles Scribner's Sons, 1895), 2:22, 32–34; Thomas, *Sam Ward*, 357.

While Hurlbert and the *World* attempted to resuscitate the war-torn Democratic Party, Ward hit his stride as a lobbyist. For several years after the war he assisted Treasury Secretary Hugh McCulloch, who prodded Congress to retire "greenbacks," an inflationary expedient that the federal government had used to meet wartime expenses. Ward's stock-in-trade was the dinner party. He served "such food as Washington had seldom known," accompanied by fine European wines. He encouraged "the finest table talk" by specifying that all conversations at his events were confidential. His guests—only men were invited—relaxed and enjoyed themselves. No hard sell or arm twisting marred these occasions. Ward judged instead that the good feelings he nurtured could provide future advantages. By 1868, he found himself in the midst of the campaign to save Andrew Johnson's presidency. Ward always let it be known thereafter that he was "prouder" of having helped to fend off Johnson's conviction "than of any other event in my life," though he had to endure an inquiry by a committee of disappointed congressional Radicals, who wanted to know where the pro-Johnson money had come from.[31]

By the late 1860s and early 1870s, Ward and Hurlbert were at the zenith of their powers. While Ward made himself an indispensable Washington fixer, the *World* gained stature and influence. Breezy memos in the papers of Manton Marble suggest that Hurlbert enjoyed his work. "This evening I have written a lot of things, all timely, all 'talky' and all I think not wholly bad if decently printed," Hurlbert once scrawled. Another night he sent over for Marble's scrutiny "a careful article on Mexico" that "flies I think high up out of all reach!" Hurlbert's competitive streak, earlier directed primarily at Horace Greeley and the *Tribune*, found a fresh (and doubtless satisfying) target: "I am writing down at the office and finished a screed on the *Times* which I think will gravel that amiable sheet even more than it has been graveled," he boasted to Marble.[32] Blessed with an editor he liked and a salary that allowed him to live in comfort, Hurlbert was securely ensconced.

So matters stood in 1873 when Archibald Philip Primrose, the young Earl of Rosebery (1847–1929), made the first of several visits to the United States.

31. Thomas, *Sam Ward*, 336–42, 346–54, quotations on 338–39; Kathryn Allamong Jacob, *King of the Lobby: The Life and Times of Sam Ward, Man-About-Washington in the Gilded Age* (Baltimore: Johns Hopkins Univ. Press, 2009).

32. Hurlbert to Marble, "Saturday p.m.," "Monday," "11 p.m.," all in bound volume 91, Marble Papers.

Rosebery—who soon would embark on a political career that briefly made him prime minister in the 1890s—possessed a keen intellect and an oddball sense of humor. He quickly found two kindred spirits in Hurlbert and Ward, his seniors by twenty and thirty years. Together the three constituted the "Mendacious Club," which they called "the most exclusive club in the world, since its membership was limited to themselves." Ward was the "President," Hurlbert the "Member," and Rosebery the "Sycophant."[33] Samples of their banter survive in Ward's papers. When Hurlbert failed to answer a letter of his, Rosebery mentioned to Ward that he was "thinking of sending him two penn'orth of hot burning coals of fire (Christian fashion)." And when Democrats suffered an electoral defeat, Rosebery predicted that Hurlbert was "probably on a diet of chicken broth, with his head shaved." Hurlbert once chastised Ward as an "utter humbug" for failing to come up from Washington to visit his friends in New York—as penance he should serve as an alderman or join a Presbyterian church. Rosebery commended Ward, tongue in cheek, for "having studied in its native wilds that savage and relentless animal, the mother-in-law." Years later Rosebery happily recalled "those cheerful but not inglorious days at the Brevoort House in New York City." His "doggerel salute" to his American chums often has been reprinted. It is set as he was about to depart:

> Alas! my Samuel, when I think
> I stand upon the ocean's brink,
> The time is near, full is my cup,
> The buoyant *Russia's* steam is up
> And I return, an unlicked cub,
> Leaving the great "Mendacious Club";
> Thy tales no more my mind shall fill,
> And Hurlbert's brilliant voice be still! . . .[34]

33. Thomas, *Sam Ward*, 388–91; Elliott, *Uncle Sam Ward and His Circle*, 580–600. See Robert Rhodes James, *Rosebery: A Biography of Archibald Philip, Fifth Earl of Rosebery* (New York: Macmillan, 1963). This volume, though done in cooperation with Rosebery's aging son, offers critical perspective. As shall be explained in chapter 11, the Liberal Party was undermined by the issue of Irish home rule. Rosebery's star ebbed after a brief tenure as prime minister in 1894–95.

34. Hurlbert to Ward, Dec. 27, 1873, Rosebery to Ward, Dec. 1, 1875, Nov. 12, 1881, Ward Papers, New York Public Library; Rosebery to Ward, Nov. 3, 1873, Mar. 8, 1879, in Elliott, *Uncle Sam Ward and His Circle*, 583, 596; Thomas, *Sam Ward*, 390–91.

Amid these pleasures, at some point before the summer of 1879, Hurlbert transformed his and Ward's information about the secession crisis into "The Diary of a Public Man." It could have been done speedily (Hurlbert was a genius), or it could have matured over a longer period of time. Careful sifting of Ward's surviving papers at Harvard and the New York Public Library yields no clues about the Public Man project, nor can anything tangible be found in the papers of friends such as Barlow and Marble. Plainly, absolute silence bound the two conspirators. Could others have shared the secret? This is a subject to which we shall now turn.

9
PROMOTING THE DIARY

We have established that Hurlbert rather than Ward wrote the diary, but that the two shared responsibility for its contents. Now we shall consider whether others may have been involved. We also shall scrutinize a clever campaign to validate the Diary. As we examine these topics, we shall encounter additional evidence that helps to pinpoint Hurlbert as the master conspirator.

To perpetrate his audacious high-wire act, Hurlbert received help from Ward. As we have seen, Ward spent the secession winter in Washington. His proximity to Seward—and to persons enlisted surreptitiously in Seward's Union-saving schemes—gave him an excellent vantage point. Seward had a uniquely wide range of contacts. While doing nothing overt to jeopardize his stature as a leading Republican, he reached out quietly to his old antagonist, Stephen A. Douglas, to Kentucky senator John J. Crittenden, and to Virginia Unionists, chief among them George W. Summers. He stayed in touch with John A. Gilmer of North Carolina, whom he had promoted for a cabinet seat. Thus, Seward knew more than anyone in his party about the situation in the Upper South. He also knew a great deal about the Lower South and the emerging Confederate government there, thanks especially to his furtive conversations with California senator William M. Gwin. As we have seen, Seward even had a clandestine informer in Buchanan's cabinet—Attorney General Edwin M. Stanton.[1] Ward was well positioned to learn Seward's secrets.

I have surmised in chapter 5 that Ward probably revealed most of his inside information to Hurlbert when it was fresh in early 1861, but Ward also must have continued to assist Hurlbert as the latter composed the memoir-cum-diary many years later. Frank Maloy Anderson could not prove that Ward did the writing, but he did point to a variety of persons and episodes that suggested a linkage to Ward. When Maud Howe Elliott, Ward's niece, learned in

---

1. The most striking account of Seward's secession crisis role remains David M. Potter's magisterial classic, *Lincoln and His Party in the Secession Crisis* (New Haven: Yale Univ. Press, 1942, 1962), esp. 249–314.

1931 that Anderson was studying the connection between Ward, Hurlbert, and the mysterious Diary, she surmised that Hurlbert simply had "got hold of a brief diary of Uncle Sam and padded it and published it." Elliott judged correctly that her uncle did not write the Diary (though she failed to convince Anderson). But her suspicion that Hurlbert acted alone seems fanciful. Ward and Hurlbert were too close for one to have worked behind the back of the other, and Hurlbert needed more from Ward than his notes from eighteen years before. A letter written by Ward in August 1879, just as the Diary appeared in print, mentioned that "William Henry is with me every evening."[2] Hurlbert did the writing, but the Diary was, in other respects, a team effort.

Who besides Ward knew what Hurlbert was doing? The list could not have been long. After all, the more people who know a secret, the less likely the secret will keep. We may quickly exclude Rosebery. The young Briton certainly enjoyed his two "mendacious" American pals, but their bonds involved sociability, not substance. Rosebery only glimpsed the United States from a distance. By the late 1870s he was pouring his energies into British politics.

Samuel L. M. Barlow, the prominent New York attorney who had close ties both to Ward and to Hurlbert, made a more plausible coconspirator. In late 1860, as we have seen, Barlow wanted Hurlbert to edit a Democratic newspaper, assuming that the secession crisis somehow could be resolved. At the same time, Barlow received from Ward many insights about the situation in Washington. Indeed, Ward himself did not understand the importance of some of the gossip he passed on to Barlow. On Sunday, March 31, 1861, most notably, Ward wrote Barlow that "Abe" was becoming "heartily sick" of the situation he faced: "On Friday, he confessed to a friend of mine that he was 'in the dumps,' and yesterday Mrs. Lincoln told [William H.] Russell that her husband had 'keeled over with a sick headache' for the first time in years—all on account of the gloom and worry of politics. This I interpret favorably for peace." Ward got it inside out. Lincoln had just come to grips with the awful reality that he must try to hold Sumter, and he realized that his decision likely meant war.[3]

2. Frank Maloy Anderson, *The Mystery of "A Public Man": A Historical Detective Story* (Minneapolis: Univ. of Minnesota Press, 1948), 145–68; "Padella" (Maud Howe Elliott) to "Darling" (Louise Hubert Guyol), Dec. 9, 1931, Samuel Ward Papers, Houghton Library, Harvard University; Ward to Thomas F. Bayard, Aug. 27, 1879, Thomas F. Bayard Papers, Library of Congress.

3. Ward to Barlow, Mar. 31, 1861, Samuel Latham Mitchill Barlow Papers, Huntington Library, San Marino, California; Daniel W. Crofts, *Reluctant Confederates: Upper South Unionists in the Secession Crisis* (Chapel Hill: Univ. of North Carolina Press, 1989), 297; Russell McClintock, *Lincoln*

For more than two decades thereafter, Ward, Hurlbert, and Barlow remained something of a trio. The Barlow Papers contain many letters from both Ward and Hurlbert. As we have just seen, Ward emerged after the war as the "King of the Lobby," with Barlow one of his steady customers. Cryptic messages from Ward attest to various assignments and an ongoing need for resources. "To accomplish such a result will cost some money and dinners," he once explained to Barlow, "not more than I am giving of the latter, but more of the former than I have to spend." Because Barlow disliked dining out, Ward and Hurlbert frequently visited his Madison Avenue mansion. Indeed, Ward always celebrated his birthday there. When Ward, Hurlbert, and Rosebery established the Mendacious Club, they granted Barlow status as a "Perpetual Candidate."[4]

Hurlbert and Barlow frequently corresponded when one or the other was away from New York, and their messages often convey an easy familiarity. The randy bachelor liked to titillate his more sedate friend. From Vienna in 1869 Hurlbert enclosed photographs of "most dreadfully misconducted young ladies." Soon afterwards, he professed to regret passing up the opportunity presented by "a gentleman in Rhodes who proposed to sell his two daughters aged 15 and 13." "They had lovely eyes," Hurlbert continued, "and we might have pulled straws for the choice when they reached New York." Attending the wedding of his ace reporter, Jim Stillson, Hurlbert waxed eloquent to Barlow about the "picturesque" bride, a "spirited girl with hair like Titian's daughter and eyes as dark as those of the princess in the sleeping wood." The Hurlbert-Barlow relationship also had a business dimension. Hurlbert dodged "bands of utter scoundrels" as he confronted the "perils of the Mexican highway" in 1872, when dispatched there on behalf of one of Barlow's investment schemes. Occasionally such ventures generated disagreements about appropriate compensation, providing fragmentary evidence that Barlow and Hurlbert became less chummy in the 1870s. Perhaps, too, the father of an adolescent daughter was no longer comfortable with Hurlbert's tendency to define women as sexual trophies.[5]

On balance, it seems unlikely that the rich and respectable Barlow was party

---

and the Decision for War: The Northern Response to Secession (Chapel Hill: Univ. of North Carolina Press, 2008), 233.

4. Lately Thomas (Robert V. P. Steele), *Sam Ward: "King of the Lobby"* (Boston: Houghton Mifflin, 1965), 341–42, 345, 389.

5. Hurlbert to Barlow, May 12, Oct. 9, Dec. 11, 1869, Mar. 1, 1872, "Sunday" (summer 1873), June 5, 1876, Barlow Papers.

to the Public Man project. Certainly none of the four letters sent from Hurlbert to Barlow in the summer and fall of 1879 breathe a word of it. Likewise, the three brief messages from Ward to Barlow during those same months are perfunctory and routine. Several years later, after they had ceased to be friends, Barlow correctly surmised that Hurlbert was responsible for a different sort of anonymous concoction, to be discussed later in this chapter. But that discovery generated no hint of awareness that the unconventional editor had gone down the same road before.[6]

So far as can be determined, only one other person besides Hurlbert and Ward was implicated in the Public Man conspiracy. That person was Allen Thorndike Rice, who edited the *North American Review*. The Diary appeared in four issues of the *NAR* between August and November of 1879, only two years after he became its editor. Rice was talented, cosmopolitan, wealthy, and young. Born in 1851, he was a generation Hurlbert's junior. Rice moved the *NAR* offices from Boston to New York, where he transformed a staid quarterly into a popular and widely read monthly. He solicited contributions from a wide variety of prominent persons. Articles on politics, public affairs, science, and recent history became staples of his new regime.[7]

Would Rice have risked the success of his magazine by publishing material that could have been exposed as spurious? On the face of it, this seems unlikely. Frank Maloy Anderson called attention to the obvious—the danger of getting caught perpetrating a hoax on his readers "would have restrained him from personal participation in a fraudulent transaction." On the other hand, Rice must have known what he was doing. Anderson recognized that the two masterminds, Hurlbert and Ward, "were upon intimate terms" with Rice at the time the Diary appeared. Anderson therefore decided that Rice "may have assisted in the process to some extent."[8] Hurlbert and Ward were inveterate risk-takers. Hurlbert's personal affairs routinely bordered on the scandalous. Ward lost several fortunes in his lifetime. Rice may well have been attracted by the unconventional derring-do of the two veteran connivers.

Rice wrote an introduction to the first published installment of the Diary.

6. Hurlbert to Barlow, June 20, July 28, Aug. 29, Oct. 27, 1879, Ward to Barlow, May 20, June 19, Sept. 5, 1879, Barlow Papers; Barlow to Bayard, Jan. 4, 1886, Bayard Papers.

7. Mark G. Schmeller, "Charles Allen Thorndike Rice," *American National Biography* 18:405–6.

8. Anderson, *Mystery*, 135–39, quotations on 139, 170–71.

Though "not permitted to make public the whole of this diary," he was able to publish "a series of extracts" that shed light on the "dark and troubled times" just before the start of the Civil War. He explained that his own "editorial supervision" had been confined to "formulating under proper and expressive headings the incidents and events referred to in the extracts" and in omitting the names of most persons mentioned who were still living. He offered his "firm conviction that the author of it [the Diary] was actuated by a single desire to state things as they were, or at least as he had reason at the time to believe that they were." Rice confidently asserted that "those who are most familiar with the true and exciting times covered by this diary will be the most competent judges of the general fidelity and accuracy of this picture of them" (217).[9]

In Anderson's judgment, which I find persuasive, Rice's introduction was deliberately opaque. It did not verify that Rice had seen an actual manuscript. Although it implied that a more extensive unpublished diary did exist, it "did not give any explicit certification that the Diary was a genuine diary." It did not explain why the published version consisted of extracts, covering only twenty-one of the seventy-eight days between December 28 and March 15. Its justification for omitting names seemed lame. Rice's assurances about the diarist's motives— "to state things as they were, or at least as he had reason at the time to believe that they were"—struck Anderson as weasel words. He concluded that Rice's introduction looked like "a studied attempt to conceal information to which readers of the Diary were entitled." As noted at the end of chapter 6, Rice's circuitous language about "general fidelity and accuracy" looked like "an attempt to lay the foundation for an editorial retreat if the real character of the Diary were discovered."[10]

For the rest of his life—he died far too young in 1889—Rice deflected all overtures to reveal more about the sensational document. He never commented on the widespread speculation in 1879 about the diarist's identity. He rejected inquiries from historians to name the diarist. His single effort to defend the Diary's legitimacy occurred in August 1879—significantly, in Hurlbert's *New York World*. There Rice responded to criticisms of a segment, dated February 8, 1861, that contained a secondhand account of Seward's comments at a gathering

9. It is possible that Hurlbert himself, rather than Rice, wrote the introduction that accompanied the first installment of the Diary. If so, however, the prose was more toned down and constrained than his usual. For the purposes of this discussion, we shall assume Rice was the author.

10. Anderson, *Mystery*, 171–74, quotations on 173–74.

in Richmond, Virginia. Hugh Hastings of the *New York Commercial Advertiser* pointed out that Seward had not visited Richmond then or at any time during the secession winter; the diarist was, therefore, an "impostor" who "could not be relied on." Rice countered by noting correctly that the Diary entry did not refer to something that had occurred in 1861, but rather to a visit in the 1840s, for which he produced two corroborating documents. Rice thereby affirmed "the good faith of the diarist." Anderson judged Rice's comment a warning shot "intended not only to silence one critic but to discourage other possible critics."[11] Could Rice have published such a message—and in the *World*, of all places— without knowing how the alleged Diary originated? I do not think so.

In various other ways, too, Hurlbert's *New York World* promoted the Diary as the *NAR* released it serially in the summer and fall of 1879. "The author knew as much as anybody not himself a conspicuous actor in the scenes he describes could well have learned," the *World* breezily assured its readers in late July, when the first issue appeared. Who might this author have been? The *World* casually waived the question aside—"The diary contains clues enough to his own identity if anybody takes the trouble to trace them." Instead, it was of "more public interest" to discover that neither Buchanan nor Lincoln had any "fixed policy," and that until the firing on Fort Sumter "the political course of the National Government was nothing but a drift." Even though the Diary shed "new light on several things and persons," its insights were "not at all out of character with what is publicly known of the men concerned."[12]

A month later with the arrival of the second installment, the *World* blandly noted that other newspapers were trying to identify the diarist. The *Chicago Tribune*, for example, suggested several possible authors, among them Vermont senator Jacob Collamer, "assuming that the diary is in fact what it purports to be." The *Tribune*, however, confessed to reservations. Was the Diary "the production of a public man" (such as Collamer) "who has passed away, and whose entries were made at the date stated"? Or was it the "*ex post facto* recollections of someone yet living" that had been "revised and improved"?[13] Soon the *New*

11. Ibid., 21, 171–72; *New York World*, Aug. 16, 1879.

12. *New York World*, July 18, 1879.

13. *Chicago Tribune*, Aug. 23, 24, 26, 1879, quotation on Aug. 26; see also *Springfield Republican*, Aug. 21, 30, 1879. The *Tribune* anticipated historian James G. Randall, as noted in chapter 1.

York Times raised even more pointed suspicions. The Diary did not "read at all like that which a man would write down at the time," the *Times* observed, "but proceeds with the judicial gravity of a document drawn up long after the events described."[14]

The *World* deftly sidestepped the guessing game about the identity of the diarist and the suspicions that the Diary might not be a diary. Instead, the *World* simply observed that the author, "whoever he may have been," was evidently on "familiar terms" with the most prominent national officials just as the country was enveloped by "the sad and terrible drama" of civil war. The diarist must also have been "a man of strong conservative impulses and sympathies." The *World,* which continued to find the Diary "racy" and "full of good things," emphasized its value and reliability. It captured "the flying rumors of each successive day." The diarist's vivid account showed the "excitement and confusion" of the secession winter, the outcome of which was "enshrouded in doubt and anxiety." The diarist's "good faith and general accuracy"—echoing Rice!—were "as remarkable as they are interesting."[15]

The *World* called attention to two "confirmations by coincidence." Rice's recently published account of Seward's visit to Richmond in 1846 resolved one disputed point. The *World* also considered the Diary corroborated by S. W. Crawford, one of the few surviving officers stationed at Fort Sumter in the winter of 1860–61. Crawford disputed James L. Orr's allegation, in the first installment of the Diary, that Major Anderson had moved to Sumter from Fort Moultrie at the behest of two or three of his younger officers, who had "gotten themselves into hot water on shore." Crawford insisted, instead, that Anderson had made his decision "alone, without consultation with any one." The *World* triumphantly called attention to an entry in the Diary's second installment, dated February 26, 1861, which "happens to coincide exactly" with Crawford's account.[16]

14. *New York Times,* Sept. 29, 1879.

15. *New York World,* Aug. 24, 26, 1879.

16. Ibid., Aug. 24, 26, 1879. The February 26 entry reported hearing from an unnamed source that Anderson had been given discretionary authority by "the President himself" to move his forces to Sumter. The Diary's fourth installment (March 6 entry), published two months later, affirmed that "Major Anderson transferred his garrison to Fort Sumter from Fort Moultrie of his own motion, on discretionary instructions received last winter from the War Department" (259). See 219–20, 235–36 herein.

Yet another way in which the *World* went out of its way to validate the Diary has already been discussed in chapter 6. In August 1879, amid the first stir about the *NAR*'s mysterious document, a reporter for the *World* sought out the elderly Thurlow Weed, who was depicted in the Diary as the mastermind behind the selection of a new U.S. senator from New York State in early 1861. The interview with Weed effectively corroborated this segment of the Diary. Hurlbert—who himself probably heard and recorded the tales about Weed attributed to the Public Man—had reason to expect that Weed's testimony would prove helpful.[17]

The *World* found much to commend in the final two segments of the Diary, which appeared in September and October. The third segment threw "a magnesium light on the intestine quarrels of the Republican leaders" at the time of Lincoln's inauguration. It also revealed the "curious fact" about Douglas holding Lincoln's hat—"so far as we know" the diarist was the first to record this telling detail! A month later, the *World* heralded the final installment of the Diary, "which has come to be regularly and eagerly looked for and is always interesting." It proceeded to summarize its contents—the careworn Lincoln, besieged by office seekers as he confronted the worst predicament any incoming president had ever faced; Douglas, eager to claim that Lincoln intended to evacuate Fort Sumter "as soon as possible"; and Seward, "almost in a boisterous mood," confident that secession's momentum would soon be reversed and the crisis peacefully surmounted.[18]

Allen Thorndike Rice orchestrated a clever reinforcement for the Diary that appeared in the November 1879 issue of the *NAR*, along with the Diary's final installment. There the editor presented his readers with eight letters written to former president James Buchanan by Edwin M. Stanton between March and July of 1861. Stanton, who had been appointed attorney general by Buchanan in December 1860, later became Lincoln's secretary of war. These letters are unmistakably genuine—indeed, the originals are today part of the Buchanan Papers at the Historical Society of Pennsylvania. They were published verbatim with no editing or obscuring of names. As with the first installment of the Diary,

17. *New York World*, Aug. 10, 1879; 227–28 herein.
18. *New York World*, Sept. 21, Oct. 19, 1879; 264, 268 herein.

Rice preceded the Stanton-Buchanan letters with an introductory comment. He noted specifically that "these letters of Mr. Stanton bear directly upon the very grave and momentous events treated in the extracts which we give in the present number from the contemporaneous 'Diary of a Public Man.'" Both the letters and the Diary "illuminate one of the most trying and important epochs of our own history," the editor continued, and "the corroborative value of the letters to the diary and the diary to the letters will be evident."[19] The newspaper commentary generated by publication of the November 1879 issue of the *NAR* devoted at least as much attention to the Stanton letters as to the Diary's final installment.

Stanton remained in Washington after Lincoln's inauguration, whereas Buchanan moved back to his farm, Wheatland, outside Lancaster, Pennsylvania. On March 14, Stanton reported that "there is no doubt of Sumter being evacuated; report says the order has gone, but I consider that doubtful." Unlike the diarist, Stanton opposed relinquishing the fort that Buchanan had managed to hold; he feared the beginning of the end for the Union and the "first steps toward a strictly Northern non-slaveholding confederacy." Three weeks later, on April 3, Stanton scoffed at rumors that "there will be an effort to reinforce Fort Sumter"—he did not "believe a word of it." Six fateful weeks thereafter, on May 19, as volunteers on both sides swarmed to enlist, Stanton looked back in retrospect. "I have no doubt," he told Buchanan, that Seward "*believed* that Sumter would be evacuated, as he stated it would be. But the war party overruled him with Lincoln."[20]

Stanton's letters to Buchanan afforded readers a peek at the private correspondence between two heavyweights just as the country teetered on the brink of war. These letters would have grabbed attention whenever they were published. Rice chose to disclose them, however, so that they reinforced his magazine's blockbuster, "The Diary of a Public Man." It was apparent by October that the first installments of the Diary had withstood initial scrutiny. Newspapers and the wider reading public continued to speculate about the diarist's identity, but doubts about the Diary's validity never gained wide currency. Rice further

19. "A Page of Political Correspondence: Unpublished Letters of Mr. Stanton to Mr. Buchanan," *North American Review* 129 (Nov. 1879): 473–83, quotations on 473. Buchanan had died in 1868; Stanton, one year later.

20. Stanton to Buchanan, Mar. 14, Apr. 3, May 19, 1861, ibid., 474–75, 478.

inoculated Hurlbert's production from suspicion by juxtaposing the Stanton-Buchanan letters and the Diary's final installment. The *NAR's* editor thereby accomplished what might be called authenticity by association.[21]

Frank Maloy Anderson decided that Rice refused to identify the author of the Diary because he did not wish to embarrass Sam Ward. The diarist had "given rather free rein to his propensity to pour ridicule upon persons of whom he disapproved," and he took special satisfaction in exposing any action "savoring of pretense, pomposity, or hypocrisy." His portraits of Charles Sumner were biting. Such frankness, if revealed, would have grieved both Ward's sister, Julia Ward Howe, and his close friend, Henry Wadsworth Longfellow. Ward thus had motive to keep his role "a profound secret," and Rice respected the arrangement.[22] More persuasively, Anderson pointed out that the Diary appeared to have been written by a "man of prominence." Ward hardly matched that description, either

21. It is not apparent how Rice obtained the letters. The editor explained simply that he had received them "from a distinguished gentleman" who did not wish to be identified. Could this have been the eminent George Ticknor Curtis, whose two-volume *Life of James Buchanan* was published several years later? I think not. Curtis undertook this project a year later, in the summer of 1880, when Buchanan's executors and nearest surviving relatives enlisted him and gave him custody of the enormous cache of Buchanan's private correspondence. Curtis subsequently took umbrage at several conversations reported in the Diary, and complained that the editor of the *NAR* refused to disclose to him the name of the diarist. George Ticknor Curtis, *Life of James Buchanan* (2 vols.; New York: Harper & Brothers, 1883), 1:iii, vi; 2:391–95, 506; Anderson, *Mystery,* 21, 184n2–3. S. L. M. Barlow was friends with Curtis and consulted with him during the research and writing of Buchanan's life. See John Updike, *Buchanan Dying: A Play* (1974; rpr. Mechanicsburg, PA: Stackpole Books, 2000), 186–87. But in 1879 Curtis was not yet working on Buchanan, and Barlow almost certainly was in the dark about the Diary.

We are left with a mystery. Either Rice or Hurlbert somehow discovered copies of the Stanton-Buchanan letters. But careful scrutiny of the James Buchanan Papers at the Historical Society of Pennsylvania provides no clue how this occurred. Buchanan's heirs had made previous efforts to enlist other biographers before they reached an agreement with Curtis. One may surmise that someone who already had copies of the Stanton-Buchanan letters read the initial segments of the Diary and realized that Rice might offer a good price for them.

22. Anderson, *Mystery,* 176–77. Modern scholarship, far more sensitive to matters of sexuality and gender than the work of Anderson's era, provides new ways of understanding how Julia Ward Howe might have seen Sumner. Gary Williams's brilliant book, *Hungry Heart: The Literary Emergence of Julia Ward Howe* (Amherst: Univ. of Massachusetts Press, 1999), establishes that Sumner was an "ongoing rival" for her husband's affections. She told Samuel Gridley Howe that "Sumner

in 1861 or in 1879, and his reputation as a lobbyist—a "none too respectable game"—would have reflected poorly on the Diary. Revealing his identity also would have subjected the Diary to closer scrutiny, especially those few passages that referred to persons still alive, and it would have increased the chance that its "real character" might have been exposed.[23]

Rice's tenacious silence becomes easier to understand once we recognize that Hurlbert was the diarist. For starters, Hurlbert spent the secession winter in New York City, not Washington. Moreover, Hurlbert's reputation among many upscale and genteel readers of the NAR was anything but good. At best they would have looked askance at him as a Democratic hatchet man, someone who had squandered his remarkable talents in an unworthy manner. His "radical defect," in the estimation of Eugene Benson—who wrote an incisive biographical sketch of Hurlbert in 1869—was his absence of "political principles." Lacking "moral indignation," Hurlbert had ignored and belittled "the great moral and political" issue of the era, the struggle to secure "exact and equal justice to all men."[24] Others would have judged Hurlbert even more harshly. As mentioned in chapter 8, he was suspected of having gone south in June 1861 not as a self-styled peacemaker who remained loyal to the United States, but rather as a would-be Confederate recruit.[25] It will be recalled that the novelist Theodore Winthrop depicted Hurlbert as a sinister bohemian or adventurer, and that diarist George Templeton Strong hated the man who had seduced his cousin's wife.[26] Because

---

ought to have been a woman & you to have married her." The emotionally starved wife certainly did admire Sumner the principled politician, but the "triangulated relationship" always soured her appreciation of Sumner the person. Like the diarist, she found Sumner humorless and insensitive. See esp. 6, 42–43, 55, 61. "I little thought when I first knew Mr. Sumner," she recalled, "that his most intimate friend was destined to become my companion for life." Julia Ward Howe, *Reminiscences, 1819–1899* [1899; rpr. New York: New American Library, 1969], 168–82, quotation on 171).

23. Anderson, *Mystery,* 175–76.

24. Eugene Benson, "W. H. Hurlbut," *The Galaxy* (Jan. 1869): 30–34.

25. Carlos Lopez to George Ellis Baker [Sam Ward to William H. Seward], July 15, 1861, William H. Seward Papers, University of Rochester, New York; William Henry Hurlbert to James Lyons, Dec. 16, 1861, in *The War of the Rebellion: A Compilation of the Official Records of the Union and Confederate Armies,* 70 volumes in 128 (Washington, D.C.: U.S. Government Printing Office, 1880–1901), Series II, vol. 2, pp. 1499–1500. Hurlbert's subsequent vindication of his trip appeared in the *New York Times,* Sept. 11, 1862, also discussed in the previous chapter.

26. Allan Nevins and Milton Halsey Thomas, eds., *The Diary of George Templeton Strong* (4 vols.; New York: Macmillan, 1952), 2:350–51. See chapter 3.

Rice knew the truth about the Diary, he had no choice but to conceal the name of the alleged diarist.

"The Diary of a Public Man" was not the only anonymous production of Hurlbert's published by Rice. Six years later, in January 1886, the *NAR* presented the first installment of an intermittent series entitled "Letters to Prominent Persons," written by one Arthur Richmond. In fact, no such person existed. A number of writers contributed articles under the same nom de plume, but the first installment was written by Hurlbert. It was a pompous assault on former Delaware senator Thomas F. Bayard, who was by then President Grover Cleveland's secretary of state. Apparently stung by his failure to receive a coveted diplomatic appointment, Hurlbert erupted in rage. "Arthur Richmond" sneered that Bayard lacked even "elementary preparation" to manage foreign affairs; to make matters worse, he was pro-British. He had impulsively accepted the State Department post "in a spasm of personal mortification" after failing "to gain the Treasury," that "great engine of patronage and influence." As in the Public Man project, Hurlbert assumed a convenient (and fictitious) geographical identity— as someone who lived in the Philadelphia area.[27]

Immediately after the *NAR* published the first Arthur Richmond missive, Bayard received a letter from S. L. M. Barlow. The latter had a long-standing friendship with Bayard as well as with Hurlbert. Little more than a year before, Barlow still received chatty letters from Hurlbert.[28] For reasons that likely relate to Hurlbert's anger at his Democratic Party friends, the correspondence between Barlow and Hurlbert lapsed entirely after the presidential election of 1884. Here is what Barlow wrote to Bayard on January 4, 1886:

Rice's Review contains an article by a Mr. Richmond, which you will see. It is as bitter and mean an article as was ever written and it is well done too, in a literary sense, but after re-reading it I do not see that it can do you any harm, or that any special reply to it is necessary.

27. Arthur Richmond, "Letters to Prominent Persons. No. I.—To the Secretary of State," *North American Review* 142 (Jan. 1886): 83–103; see esp. 84, 90, 91–92, 95, 101. Frank Maloy Anderson did most of the heavy lifting in tracking down the Arthur Richmond story. His notes are in Box 39 of the Frank Maloy Anderson Papers, Library of Congress.

28. Hurlbert to Barlow, Jan. 9, 10, 31, Feb. 1, 8, Nov. 1, 1884, Barlow Papers.

If there be any such person as "Richmond" which I doubt then there are two Richmonds in the field and one of them is called Hurlbert.

To my mind it is plain that he is the author. No one else could have written it. His artful attempt to injure you with the Pres[iden]t and with [August] Belmont shows this[,] and no one but he could have said so many bright things, with so much anecdote and classical lore—yet after all it is the sting of a mosquito rather than the wound of a snake and I hope you will laugh at it.[29]

Barlow's message was private. Not until July 1889, two months after Rice's unexpected death and six months after the appearance of the final Arthur Richmond letter, did the identities of those who wrote the pieces for Rice begin to move into the public realm. The *New York Commercial Advertiser* took the initiative. A series of articles published between July 8 and July 23 attempted to pin down the details. Although some confusion remained, abundant evidence pointed to Hurlbert as the author of the first article. James Redpath, the former managing editor of the *NAR,* noted that Rice had imposed "special obligations of secrecy" regarding the identity of the first contributor, but that the printers at the *NAR* "were familiar with Hurlbert's manuscript" and revealed to Redpath "the secret of his authorship." Before Rice died, Redpath reported, "he did not attempt to deny that Mr. Hurlbert wrote the first letter, and spoke of it freely to gentlemen who were not especially in his confidence." For this reason, Redpath no longer felt bound to keep the secret.[30] It remains unclear why Rice commissioned subsequent Arthur Richmond articles. Perhaps because the initial item served his purpose of stimulating interest and sales, Rice had motive to "keep up the sensation the first article created." On the other hand, Rice did not enlist Hurlbert to write the sequels, four of which appeared within the calendar year. The *New York Commercial Advertiser* claimed that Rice kept the series going to diminish some of the stigma of the first, with its "dastardly scheme of personal slander."[31]

29. Barlow to Bayard, Jan. 4, 1886, Bayard Papers. The wealthy August Belmont was a powerful Democratic insider.

30. *New York Commercial Advertiser,* July 11, 23, 1889. On Redpath's role with the *NAR,* see John R. McKivigan, *Forgotten Firebrand: James Redpath and the Making of Nineteenth-Century America* (Ithaca: Cornell Univ. Press, 2008), 178–88. The one-time eulogist for John Brown was a journalist, reformer, and entrepreneur during the postwar era.

31. *New York Commercial Advertiser,* July 11, 16, 1889, in Anderson Papers, Box 39.

The Arthur Richmond matter bears directly on the Diary in two ways. First, it further demonstrates Hurlbert's penchant for anonymous writing. Plainly he enjoyed the challenge of concealing his identity. Second, it shows that Rice and Hurlbert had previously collaborated surreptitiously. If the *NAR*'s printers knew Hurlbert's handwriting, they must have seen it before (by the mid-1880s typing had begun to supplant handwriting, but not for Hurlbert). Both in 1879 and in 1886, Rice enabled Hurlbert to shield his identity when writing something that was bound to make a splash. Rice continued to take risks in order to stir controversy. But neither Hurlbert's readiness to compose imaginary materials nor Rice's readiness to publish them can be comprehended in purely calculating terms. Both savored the thrill of pulling off a successful ruse.

One additional feature of the Arthur Richmond saga deserves mention. Hurlbert had long been considered an eccentric genius whose behavior was unconventional, unpredictable, and tainted with scandal. During his years with the *World,* especially when he was its editor, these self-destructive tendencies appear to have been held in check. Hurlbert was anchored securely within a circle of friends. He was closest to Sam Ward and a theater owner, William Stuart. When vacation travel allowed it, Rosebery enlivened his American pals. Hurlbert's ties to Barlow were still genial. The prominent Bayard and William M. Evarts may not have been part of his inner circle, but both were more than casual acquaintances. Additionally, Hurlbert always affected a high regard for Manton Marble, though that may have cooled after Marble had to relinquish the *World* to him in 1876.

In 1883, however, Jay Gould sold the *World* to Joseph Pulitzer, who launched a new era in the history of American journalism. The newly unemployed Hurlbert, briefly incapacitated by an attack of gout (too much sumptuous dining!), initially went to a western ranch to recuperate. Soon thereafter he sailed to England. No longer responsible for editing a major newspaper, he became a loose cannon. His instability probably increased following Ward's death in May 1884—the older man's sunnier temperament had somehow reinforced Hurlbert's better side. But when Bayard ignored Hurlbert's claims and appointed someone else as American minister to Italy—only to suffer the embarrassment of having the Italian government refuse to receive the appointee—Hurlbert lost his moorings.[32] His bitter, anonymous assault on Bayard, a former friend, marked the start of a downward spiral. Shortly afterwards, as will be discussed in chap-

32. *New York Herald,* Sept. 7, 1895; William Henry Hurlbert, "Catholic Italy and the Temporal Power," *Fortnightly Review,* Sept. 1, 1885, p. 311n.

ter 12, Hurlbert stumbled into an ill-fated relationship with a British actress. Her breach-of-promise suit against him proved worse than embarrassing. His resultant legal difficulties had a calamitous sequel, with Hurlbert exiled both from Britain and the United States.

One must not connect "The Diary of a Public Man" to Hurlbert's sad decline. When the Diary was published in 1879 he was at the top of his game. In 1881 Sam Ward reminded his sister, Julia Ward Howe, that "as late as five years ago Mr. Hurlbert was a *persifler* and a bohemian."[33] By editing a major newspaper, however, Hurlbert gained stature. In the next chapter, we shall examine his work for the *World* and the prominence he enjoyed in New York City by the late 1870s.

What motive did Hurlbert have for undertaking such a risky project as "The Diary of a Public Man"? It seems unlikely that he had anything consequential to gain from it, and there was much to lose if the project misfired and his role was exposed. His inadvertent bungle in the *Times* twenty years before still was remembered—newspaper cognoscenti all knew who had written "The Elbows of the Mincio." Had Hurlbert been revealed as the author of a faked diary, his career could have ended abruptly. To be sure, he probably collected a decent if surreptitious sum from Rice. But he already was amply paid as editor of the *World,* which was owned by the railroad magnate Tom Scott. For that matter, Sam Ward also was enjoying a prosperous phase in 1879, although he recently had lived under pinched circumstances.[34] His friend James Robert Keene netted a princely windfall in the stock market and generously shared his winnings with Ward. The latter closed up shop as a lobbyist, found himself a more commodious New York apartment, and showered his kinfolk with handsome presents, most notably a house on Beacon Street in Boston for his widowed sister, Julia Ward Howe.[35] Neither Hurlbert nor Ward needed money in 1879.

The Diary was all about the winter of 1860–61, and it is hard to connect it to the politics of 1879–80. None of the would-be presidential candidates, Republican or Democratic, obviously stood to gain or lose because of anything the Public Man wrote. The principals in the Diary were dead—Lincoln, Seward, Douglas, Sumner, and others. One possible political angle must, however, be

33. Ward to Julia Ward Howe, June 10, 1881, Samuel Ward Papers, Houghton Library.

34. Perhaps Hurlbert had decided—before Ward's finances improved—to bail out his pal by writing the Diary? This scenario is possible but hardly probable.

35. Thomas, *Sam Ward,* 398–408.

entertained. The *World* did have a favorite among the Democratic aspirants for 1880. This was Thomas F. Bayard, among the front-runners for the nomination. Both Hurlbert and Ward had long been on friendly terms with the Delaware senator.[36] Bayard's boosters contended that the talented border-state conservative with a fine political pedigree might best unite the fractious party, which still suffered from North-South strains. But his detractors complained that young Bayard had hesitated to choose sides in the spring of 1861. They demanded that Democrats nominate instead a candidate with undoubted pro-Union credentials.[37] Might "The Diary of a Public Man" have been some kind of preemptive strike, designed to show that patriotism and caution were compatible amid the crisis of the Union?

Bayard's 1861 record invited scrutiny. Both he and his father, James A. Bayard, who then occupied the Senate seat, believed privately in early 1861 that Delaware, Maryland, and Virginia belonged in the Southern Confederacy. Their views were at odds with majority opinion in the state, which became decisively antisecession. In public, both Bayards bewailed the effort to hold the Union together by force. As late as June 27, 1861, more than two months after the fall of Fort Sumter, young Bayard spoke out against coercion and insisted that the seceding states should be allowed to depart in peace.[38] These indiscreet comments did indeed become a political lightning rod in early 1880. Anti-Bayard newspapers, led by the *New York Sun,* took the Delaware senator to task for opposing the use of force two decades before. The issue buffeted the Bayard campaign for several weeks in late February and early March.[39] The same thing hap-

---

36. William Henry Hurlbert to Thomas F. Bayard, Nov. 8, 10, 1879, Sam Ward to Bayard, June 20, Aug. 27, 1879, Mar. 5, 1880, Bayard Papers.

37. H. Wayne Morgan, in *From Hayes to McKinley: National Party Politics, 1877–1896* (Syracuse: Syracuse University Press, 1969), nicely frames the presidential campaign of 1880 in his second and third chapters, 57–121. On Bayard, see esp. 79–80.

38. James A. Bayard to Thomas F. Bayard, Jan. 22, 28, Apr. 17, 22, 26, May 1, 1861, Bayard Papers; Charles Callan Tansill, *The Congressional Career of Thomas Francis Bayard, 1869–1885* (Washington: Georgetown University Press, 1946), 13–14; Harold Bell Hancock, *Delaware during the Civil War: A Political History* (Wilmington, DE: Historical Society of Delaware, 1961), 49, 54, 67–69.

39. Tansill, *Congressional Career,* 251–53. When Bayard finally was bested for the Democratic nomination in June 1880 by the former Union general Winfield Scott Hancock, the late-winter tiff had faded. The delegates rallied behind the candidacy of an apolitical military leader who appeared to have the best chance to win. This was neither the first nor the last time that a national party convention bypassed an experienced insider when selecting a presidential candidate. Morgan, *From Hayes to McKinley,* 82–83, 98–101.

pened again in 1884—Bayard's critics insisted that he had failed to stand by the Union at its moment of greatest need.[40]

When the storm first hit in February 1880, the *World* aggressively defended Bayard against accusations that his "ugly Southern record" would lose every state in the North. It dismissed the controversy as a sham that had been manufactured to distract voters from the real questions of the campaign. In June 1861 Bayard had hoped, Hurlbert explained, that North and South might yet resolve their differences. His views were widely shared by "all honest Democrats." Here Hurlbert skated on thin ice. The most prominent Democrat of all, Stephen A. Douglas, had played a huge role in trying to avert the conflict, but immediately after April 15 he insisted that "there can be no neutrals in this war, *only patriots—or traitors.*" Hurlbert instead validated his own outlook by claiming that Northern Democrats continued to seek an amicable settlement until Congress declared war in July. They had deprecated "mob law" and pleaded with Lincoln "for concession, for compromise, for peace and for Union!"[41]

At no point, however, as it tried to fend off Bayard's critics, did the *World* call attention to the sensational series that had appeared in the *North American Review* only months before. Had Hurlbert's real purpose in writing "The Diary of a Public Man" been to assist Bayard, surely he would have pointed out the connection for readers of the *World*. On the whole, therefore, it seems far-fetched to think that Hurlbert went to the trouble of writing the Diary for the primary purpose of enhancing Bayard's presidential prospects. If, however, the Diary was indeed a complicated favor intended to help Bayard, that might help to explain why Hurlbert came unhinged several years later when Bayard passed over his claims for a diplomatic post.

The best answer to the key question of motive may surprise many readers— but I think Hurlbert aspired to reshape historical memory. More regarding his role as an historian will be presented in chapters 10 and 11, but a few key points may be mentioned here. Rice pointed out the Diary's historical value in his introduction. The Public Man emphasized that sensible people in early 1861 were eager to prevent hostilities. He showed that their efforts came closer to fruition than was generally realized. Lincoln's decision to resupply Fort Sumter, the diarist implied, had more to do with partisanship than with national necessity.

40. Robert K. Ackerman, *Wade Hampton III* (Columbia: Univ. of South Carolina Press, 2007), 254; Morgan, *From Hayes to McKinley,* 189–90.

41. *New York World,* Feb. 17, 26, 28, Mar. 1, 2, 1880; Robert W. Johannsen, *Stephen A. Douglas* (New York: Oxford Univ. Press, 1973), 868.

Relinquishing the fort might have fractured the Republican party, but it might also have preserved the Union through peaceful means. The Diary thus swam against the dominant tide of postwar Northern public opinion. It contended that Northern Democrats, conservative Republicans, and Southern Unionists had acted more responsibly in early 1861 than extreme men on either side, who blindly stumbled into the abyss. Its laudatory treatment of Douglas anticipated the so-called "revisionist" historians of the 1930s, who commended the Little Giant for his efforts to prevent a "needless war." George Fort Milton's spirited biography of Douglas, the best short revisionist history of the secession crisis, enthusiastically embraced the Public Man. The diarist's "immense sources of information," Milton wrote, made his notations "an invaluable intimate record of Washington at this time."[42]

Whether Hurlbert wished to correct the historical record, or just possibly to assist Bayard, that still does not explain why he decided to take on the daunting and dangerous task of fabricating a diary. Perhaps he decided that it would stir more comment than a conventional historical tome. Perhaps he figured that writing it offered more challenge, or that it would be more fun. Ultimately we must come back to Hurlbert's daring streak, combined with a powerful personality that persuaded two accomplices to assist in his brazen conniving. Thomas Wentworth Higginson observed that his old chum Hurlbert never found a "lawful passion" to be "so bewildering or ecstatic as an unlawful one." But "The Diary of a Public Man" demanded far more energy and attention than any seduction. Hurlbert attempted something that no conventional person would dare to contemplate—and he got away with it. For the rest of their lives, he, Ward, and Rice could share the thrill of having perpetrated an astonishing literary deception, one that would still be remembered a century later for presenting the "most gigantic" problem of uncertain authorship in American historical writing.[43]

42. George Fort Milton, *The Eve of Conflict: Stephen A. Douglas and the Needless War* (Boston: Houghton Mifflin, 1934), 510n28 (quotation), 511n34, 512n36–37, 513n40, 514n42, 515n46, 520n2, 520n4, 535n44, 536n49, 543n23, 544n26, 546nn33–34, 537n36, 547n39, 548n40, 549n43, 550n46, 550nn48–49, 551n51.

43. Thomas Wentworth Higginson, *Malbone: An Oldport Romance* (Boston: Fields, Osgood, & Co., 1869), 151; Jacques Barzun and Henry F. Graff, *The Modern Researcher* (4th ed., San Diego: Harcourt Brace Jovanovich, 1985), 135.

William Henry Hurlbert, editor of
the *New York World,* late 1870s
By permission of the New-York
Historical Society

Sam Ward, 1874
Reproduced from Maud Howe Elliott,
Uncle Sam Ward and His Circle (New
York: Macmillan, 1938)

Samuel L. M. Barlow

The crowd assembling to witness Abraham Lincoln's inauguration,
east front of the U.S. Capitol, March 4, 1861
By permission of the Library of Congress

The obelisk, as erected in Central Park in 1881
Reproduced from Henry Honeychurch Gorringe, *Egyptian Obelisks*
(New York: Henry H. Gorringe, 1882)

10

HURLBERT AND THE *WORLD*

Political differences that came to a head during the 1860 presidential campaign forced Hurlbert to part ways with Henry J. Raymond and the *New York Times*. Raymond remained a moderate Republican who supported Abraham Lincoln. Hurlbert favored Stephen A. Douglas, Lincoln's Democratic rival. In 1862, as noted in chapter 8, Hurlbert joined the *New York World*, working directly under Manton Marble, the paper's young owner and soon a fast friend. For the next two decades, the most productive years of his career, Hurlbert wrote for the *World*. He, Marble, and two other talented journalists, Ivory Chamberlain and David Goodman Croly, made the *World* the most influential Democratic newspaper in the city and a kingmaker in national politics.[1]

Hurlbert's rambunctious prose did much to make the *World* successful. In 1869 Eugene Benson published an incisive assessment of Hurlbert's writing. In Benson's view, Hurlbert had a gift for capturing the cadences of the spoken word. His style had "sweep and dash." His "alliterative phrases" and "rich fund of expression" enabled him to make "the gravest and heaviest" political subjects come instantly alive. "No man's articles are more invariably recognized," Benson noted; Hurlbert's "*sang froid,* audacity, playfulness, and fluency" stood out. Benson admitted that he disliked Hurlbert's politics:

> The historian of the American press will have to say that while the slave was lifting his shackled hands to the North, and the land was agitated with a great moral and political question; while the men of justice and benevolence were sweating with the task of emancipation, and our armies were in the bleeding shock of battle, the most brilliant talent of the New York press was used to *persifle* the liberators of the slave and the chief saviours of the Republic.

1. George T. McJimsey, *Genteel Partisan: Manton Marble, 1834–1917* (Ames, Iowa: Iowa State Univ. Press, 1971), 95–96, 178–81; William H. Hurlbert to Manton Marble, Oct. 23, 1862, Manton Marble Papers, Library of Congress.

With "cold irony and princely disdain" but always in "the best of humor," Hurlbert satirized the "moral element" that occupied a central position in American and English culture. He directed his "superb scorn" at "what he would call moral mush or moral twaddle." Yet Benson confessed that he was hypnotized by Hurlbert's "bold touch" and by the spectacle of a "polished and adroit mind" in "full play." His writing was "always graphic" and "never prosaic." His skill with the pen was matched by "the elegant fluency of his conversation." Benson judged him "the only artist among American journalists."[2]

In 1876 Hurlbert became the *World*'s editor-in-chief. He answered to Thomas A. Scott, who hoped that owning a newspaper might improve his chances of getting a federal subsidy for the Texas & Pacific Railroad. Subsequently Scott sold the *World* to Jay Gould, who also acquired Scott's interest in the Texas & Pacific.[3] However talented, Hurlbert was ill suited to edit a newspaper. His circle of elite friendships and his rarefied aesthetic sensibilities distanced him from the mass public. He did little to make the paper popular. Instead, its circulation dwindled and it began to lose money. In early 1883, Gould threatened to sell the *World*, but Hurlbert asked for a reprieve while attempting to put it "on a paying basis." He fired many editors and reporters, but did not succeed for long in staving off the inevitable. A few months later, Joseph Pulitzer bought the *World* from Gould. Unlike Hurlbert, Pulitzer knew how to attract readers.[4]

During his two decades with the *World*, Hurlbert wrote thousands of editorials, reviews, and features. From this vast horde, we may find out what he was thinking about when he secretly crafted the enigmatic Diary. He pretended that he was writing in 1861, not 1879—but much had happened during the intervening eighteen years.

Hurlbert's job at the *World* obliged him to comment on the unfolding events of the 1860s and 1870s. The pieces he cranked out on a daily basis will help us to

2. Eugene Benson, "W. H. Hurlbut," *The Galaxy* (Jan. 1869): 30–34. Benson's essay led me to imagine how a broad-minded liberal in our own time might assess George Will's writings.

3. McJimsey, *Genteel Partisan*, 180–81, 200–1; C. Vann Woodward, *Reunion and Reaction: The Compromise of 1877 and the End of Reconstruction* (Boston: Little, Brown, 1951), 69–70, 237; *New York World*, Sept. 7, 1895.

4. W. A. Swanberg, *Pulitzer* (New York: Charles Scribner's Sons, 1967), 66–70; Croswell Bowen, *The Elegant Oakey* (New York: Oxford Univ. Press, 1956), 236; James Melvin Lee, *History of American Journalism* (Boston: Houghton Mifflin, 1923), 370–71; *Harper's Weekly*, May 19, 1883, pp. 307–8; Jan. 18, 1890, p. 47.

frame the most important thing he ever wrote. In this chapter we shall consider his writings on Reconstruction and his coverage of international affairs, primarily U.S. relations with Europe and Latin America. We also shall look at some of his other hobbies—commenting on literature and history through reviews of new books, satirizing the women's rights movement, wading into the midst of the sensational Beecher-Tilton scandal, and spearheading a drive to bring to New York City's Central Park a 3,500-year-old Egyptian obelisk, "Cleopatra's Needle." "The Diary of a Public Man" lurks offstage here, but this chapter will give readers a clearer sense for the context within which it originated.

Long after the war's end, North-South issues remained prominent in the pages of the *World,* as in other major newspapers. The battles over Reconstruction were fiercely partisan. In 1866 Republicans prevented the seceding states from rejoining the Union unless they ratified the Fourteenth Amendment, which promised equal citizen rights and threatened to trim Southern representation in Congress unless former slaves were given the ballot. Only a single ex-Confederate state, Tennessee, acquiesced. Democrats both north and south denounced Republicans for usurping the Constitution and depriving the South of representation in Congress. The *World* initially hoped that white Southern opposition might stop the Republican juggernaut, on grounds that "negro suffrage can no more be forced on the South, than the Fugitive Slave law could have been executed in Massachusetts, ten years ago." Several months later, in early 1867, when Republicans voted to abolish the old state governments in the South and to establish new ones in which all adult males could vote, the *World* reconsidered. Perhaps it made more sense to accept black voting and attempt to control it, in hopes of getting the Southern states readmitted to the Union in time for the next presidential election.[5]

By the summer and fall of 1867, however, it became apparent that precious few former slaves were receptive to Democratic blandishments. Black voters enabled Republicans to win most elections in the South. Hurlbert, who had been out of the country the previous winter, leaped into the fray. He denounced the Republican Party for failing to address the two "paramount" postwar issues— the "early restoration of national harmony" and the "establishment of kindly relations between the two races." Instead, "the South is less reconciled to the

5. *New York World,* Sept. 5, 1866, Feb. 23, 1867; McJimsey, *Genteel Partisan,* 109–15.

North, and the negroes infinitely more jealous of the whites than at the close of the war." With state governments dependent on black votes about to take power in the South, Hurlbert predicted a wave of "plunder and agrarianism under the name of reclamations for past robbery": "The reasoning is this: property is the creation of labor, and belongs of right to those who produce it. The negroes, as slaves, toiled without compensation to create the property which existed in the South at the beginning of the late war. If any part of it justly belonged to the white race, they squandered more than their share upon their armies and the negroes may fairly claim the residue as the accumulated wages of uncompensated toil."[6]

The New York editorialist therefore predicted heavy property taxes in the South. Blacks, most of whom owned no property, would neither share the burden nor have any "motives to economy." Wholesale confiscation would follow "if the white people of the South should submit." But that would not happen—the "negro suffrage experiment" would never "reach its natural termination without uprisings to resist it." The South was destined to become "a wide theatre of violence and blood," where "the negroes will be slaughtered with as little compunction or remorse as if they were herds of wolves." Only a "federal army" in the South could avert armed outbreaks, but the North would have no stomach for such harsh tactics.[7]

Hurlbert's complaints about Reconstruction were primarily abstract and theoretical. Governments that ignored "intelligent public opinion," and that alienated those with property and capital, were destined to fail.[8] If the geese that lay golden eggs were put at risk—or if they simply thought they were at risk—then an impasse existed. A decade before, Hurlbert said that slaveowners would not tolerate a president they perceived as threatening to their interests. Of course the war ultimately liquidated their right to own slaves. All the more reason, he contended, that the losers in the war would cling tenaciously to what property they had left—and would resist by fair means or foul any additional circumscribing of their power.

Hurlbert accompanied his grim predictions with a ferocious indictment of leading Southern white Republicans. "There is high authority for testing the goodness of a tree by the quality of its fruit," he observed. "Men do not gather

6. *New York World*, Oct. 30, 1867.

7. Ibid.

8. *New York World*, Sept. 9, 1868.

grapes of thorns, figs of a bramble-bush, nor statesmen from a constituency in which negroes fresh from brutalizing servitude hold the balance of power." In Tennessee, Republicans were led by William G. ("Parson") Brownlow, "an empty ribald old bruiser" best known for his "venomous tongue" and for editing "a scurrilous weekly newspaper" that routinely spouted "gutter-water." His Virginia counterpart, James W. Hunnicutt, showed that "men of the like stamp will probably be elected from the other Southern States." Always quick to detect "*sans-culottism*," Hurlbert shrieked, "The mob of Paris in the craziest days of the Revolution was not a more unfit depository of political power than are the Southern negroes. A crop of Brownlows and Hunnicutts is no better than a crop of Robespierres; with Robespierre's power they would rival his atrocities." When North Carolina's Republican governor, William W. Holden, attempted to use the state militia to counter exactly the sort of white terror tactics that Hurlbert had predicted, the New Yorker indignantly condemned "the outrageous and intolerable tyranny of this petty Radical prince." His "brutal despotism" recalled "the darkest days of the prostration of English freedom at the feet of the Stuarts."[9]

The basic flaw in Reconstruction, Hurlbert insisted, was the "stupid and infamous" policy of "setting the pyramid on its peak." A base of "negro ignorance and incapacity" delivered power into the hands of "rogues and thieves." These governments could not preserve order and thus were "worthless for fulfilling the chief function for which governments are initiated." Lacking any moral authority, Southern Republicans could not discharge "the ordinary duties of civil rulers." So what should be done? It would be "a wild and crazy quixotism" to try to end black voting: "It could not be accomplished without plunging the country into another civil war." But it also would be outrageous to use federal force against the Ku Klux Klan. The *World* howled about the "startling and revolutionary" Enforcement Acts of 1871 that threatened to topple those state governments in the South over which conservatives had regained control. Instead, Hurlbert judged, "the only practicable way of restoring good government in the South" was to accept black voting while cultivating "friendly relations with the better part of the colored population." The "best citizens of both races" knew that "their interests are really identical." Together they might yet thwart continued Radical efforts "to stir up jealousies and animosities between the two

9. Ibid., Oct. 29, 1867, July 22, 1870.

races." Three years later, in 1874, Hurlbert decided that a literacy test, applied to voters of both races, would shrink the black electorate. Even as he editorialized, white assassins in Coushatta, Louisiana, took matters into their own hands and murdered half a dozen black and white Republicans.[10]

Hurlbert confidently prognosticated even though he knew little about the postwar South. In part he was the victim of his own training. He had not apprenticed as a newspaper reporter, responsible for ferreting out facts. From the start, he was paid to write editorials and other works of opinion. (Of course, actual reporters sent south, especially those who worked for Democratic newspapers, often did no better.) Eugene Benson's strictures were true—Hurlbert was blind to the struggle for equal rights.[11] He never understood that the freedpeople, too, embraced the American dream and its values, and that they wanted simply, as families and individuals, to enjoy opportunities for advancement that whites took for granted. Worst of all, Hurlbert studiously ignored the thuggish counterinsurgency that targeted Southern Republicans. White America did badly by black America in the postwar years. Hurlbert was a flagrant case in point, but he had plenty of company.

It may seem that Hurlbert was an eager partisan, but that conclusion would be misleading. Most American newspapers in the mid- to late nineteenth century, the *World* included, had a pronounced partisan stance. As elections approached, editorial writers did their best to rouse the faithful. Shrill and repetitious blasts at the opposition echoed daily. Hurlbert did not enjoy this sort of writing. He preferred to engage the intellects of his readers. He was not on hand during the hotly contested 1866 elections when big Republican gains set the stage for Radical Reconstruction. Two years later, in mid-October 1868 during the last frantic weeks before the first postwar presidential election, Hurlbert repaired to the Union Club in Portland, Maine. From that vantage point he dispatched several chatty letters to Manton Marble, who edited the *World*. Hurlbert noted fatalistically that Democrats had been "badly whipped" in the October state elections and he appeared resigned to "the *possible* (shall I make it stronger?) fiasco in November." During the month before the pivotal 1874 elections, when Democrats rebounded strongly from their postwar doldrums, Hurl-

10. Ibid., July 13, 1870, Mar. 26, 30, 1871, Aug. 4, Sept. 1, 2, 1874. See Ted Tunnell, *Edge of the Sword: The Ordeal of Carpetbagger Marshall H. Twitchell in the Civil War and Reconstruction* (Baton Rouge: Louisiana State Univ. Press, 2001), 188–210.

11. Benson, "W. H. Hurlbut," 30–34.

bert took time to write four substantial book reviews. In October 1880, the by-then editor did bestir himself to go to Indiana, where a key state election took place a month before the presidential contest. There he demonstrated his tin ear for political detail by telegraphing back to New York on election night the good—but entirely erroneous—news of a narrow Democratic victory. The *New York Tribune* got hold of this choice morsel. It advised the "former Unitarian clergyman" to console fellow Democrats with "some of his own old hymns," for example, number 494 of the "Boston Collection":

> We will not faint; if heavy burdens bind us,
> They press no harder than our souls can bear,
> The thorniest way is lying still behind us,
> We shall be braver for the past despair.[12]

Let us shift to international relations, a subject that Hurlbert found more engaging than the tiresome partisan rituals used to woo the American electorate. To his mind, the big story of the age was the advance of industry and commerce, which created an unprecedented new basis for "human progress." While parts of the world such as Latin America remained stagnant and paralyzed, Europe and the United States successfully applied the "useful arts." Creature comforts that "half a century ago were the privileges of dukes and earls" were now enjoyed by "thousands of prosperous, though untitled men in every European country." Shadowing these achievements, however, were unstable European power rivalries that stunted democratic institutions. Constitutional government remained a "delusive sham" wherever "the mere fiat of the head of state" could plunge a country into war. Large standing armies, which remained the norm across continental Europe, undermined the "constitutional *forms*" of Germany and France.[13]

Only the United States and Britain, each blessed by favorable geography, had dispensed with large standing armies and required the executive to secure legislative sanction before going to war. Protected from "the dangers of sudden invasion" by her "insular position" and her navy, Britain reaped great political bene-

---

12. Hurlbert to Manton Marble, Oct. 15, 1868, Marble Papers; *New York World,* Oct. 12, 19, 26, Nov. 2, 1874; *New York Tribune,* Oct. 14, 1880; *New York Times,* Oct. 13, 1880.

13. *New York World,* June 4, 1867, July 20, 1870.

fits. Her political freedoms were assured because "a naval force cannot be used to overawe and subjugate the people." The United States enjoyed even greater security. Lacking powerful neighbors and "separated by a wide ocean from the great powers of the world," it was the "freest nation on the globe." It required only a few regiments to patrol the western frontier. Hurlbert rejoiced that the Civil War resulted as it did, because it "saved us from the necessities that render constitutional freedom impossible on the Continent of Europe." Confederate independence would have pitted "two jealous powers" against each other, each feeling constrained "to keep up great military establishments." Such a situation would have undermined "the liberties of both the Northern and the Southern nation," exactly what happened—or so he saw it—during wartime.[14]

The big story in continental Europe during this period was the rivalry between France and Germany. Under Emperor Napoleon III, France became the premier power on the continent as its industry and wealth tripled. While that was happening, however, a militarized Prussian state expanded to consolidate a new German nation. Suddenly in the summer of 1870, the two great powers collided in war. Hurlbert cautioned that both political parties in the United States should favor "strict and impartial neutrality." His own sympathies, however, were apparent. In his view, "Prussia and the states annexed to Prussia have been ruled by the sword as insolently as were these United States during the civil war." For four years it had been "the almost openly avowed purpose" of Prussia's rulers to provoke a war with France. To this end, they had nurtured a surge of popular nationalistic passion. In France, however, Otto von Bismarck and Helmuth von Moltke, architects of the new German nation, confronted an adversary that was well prepared and formidable.[15]

The German cause therefore enjoyed no support in the *World*. Manton Marble was ill during the summer of 1870, so Hurlbert had the last word on editorial policy. He gave the *World* a pro-French stance and reminded his readers that France had provided indispensable military support for American independence. To his surprise, however, the war resulted in a German victory. In retrospect, Hurlbert faulted Napoleon III for having fallen into the same trap as Jefferson Davis. Each stumbled into a war that spiraled out of control and that brought about calamities nobody expected. Each thus ultimately destroyed his own power. The *World* also condemned Germany's "ruthless severity" for im-

14. Ibid., July 20, 1870.
15. Ibid., June 4, 1867, July 13, 20, 22, 1870.

posing harsh peace terms on France. By seizing Alsace and marching troops ostentatiously through the streets of Paris, Germany displayed a "triumphant insolence" that would poison relations between the two countries for decades to come. Even if prescient, all of this was hardly politic. German Americans far outnumbered French Americans—not least in New York City—and Hurlbert knew that "our German fellow-citizens" took pride in their fatherland. The *World* offended many of its readers by failing to provide pro-German coverage.[16]

Although initially hopeful about the new French republic following the abdication of Napoleon III, the *World* soon found much to criticize. In March 1871 a popularly supported revolt broke out in Paris. Because he thought the Commune "commanded the support of the working population of Paris," Hurlbert refused at first to echo the "unreasoning vituperation" it roused elsewhere. His views changed. When the Communards took up arms, civil war ensued. Conservative Republican forces invaded Paris and triggered desperate street fighting. Hurlbert arraigned the Communards for suicidal "passion, extravagance, and folly." Their "monstrous blunders" proved their "incapacity." During the Commune's last days in May, the archbishop of Paris was murdered along with sixty priests. Hurlbert condemned the "venomous vermin" who, like "the Jacobins of 1792," had perpetrated that bloody deed. He was at least equally contemptuous, however, of the Republican leadership. After the French army finally fought its way into the capital in May 1871 to end the Commune, the Republicans inaugurated a repressive reign of terror that claimed tens of thousands of victims. Republican "atrocities" overshadowed all that had happened in Paris during the German siege and the Commune, Hurlbert charged. French political institutions thus were saddled with a "legacy of despair and doubt." Many in France's "great middle class," Hurlbert predicted, would look to a restored monarchy to rescue the country from "the mire in which she grovels now bruised and bleeding." Even the seemingly improbable restoration of a Bourbon king had become a possibility.[17]

While the Franco-Prussian War and its turbulent aftermath were taking place, a different international disagreement was being resolved in more decorous fashion. During the Civil War the British government proclaimed its neutrality, thereby acknowledging the belligerent status of the Confederacy. Even worse, it tolerated the construction in its shipyards of several Confederate cruis-

16. Ibid., July 22, Sept. 1, 7, 1870, Mar. 1, June 1, 1871; McJimsey, *Genteel Partisan*, 142–46.

17. *New York World*, Sept. 7, 10, 1870, May 22, 29, June 1, 5, 1871.

ers, most notably the *Alabama*. Accordingly, the United States demanded compensation for the damage inflicted by these warships, along with a British apology. An initial effort to resolve the matter failed in 1869, when the U.S. Senate rejected a treaty negotiated in the final months of Andrew Johnson's presidency. Charles Sumner, head of the Senate Foreign Relations Committee, insisted on greater British penitence. A suitable British recompense, he suggested, would be the transfer of Canada to the United States.[18]

At this juncture, the *World* launched a spirited campaign to persuade the incoming president, Ulysses S. Grant, and his secretary of state, Hamilton Fish, to reopen negotiations. It was "nonsense to insist that England shall apologize and atone for her proclamation of neutrality," Hurlbert insisted. The point at issue was that "England did not maintain and keep the neutrality she declared and professed." For that breach, the United States deserved reparations and an expression of regret. The Treaty of Washington, ratified in May 1871, secured the apology and established an international commission, based in Geneva, that subsequently awarded the United States $15.5 million in damages. Because it had published 250 editorials on the subject between 1869 and 1871, Hurlbert noted, the *World* deserved to share the credit for the outcome. By persistently advocating a negotiated compromise and denying Democrats the temptation to make political capital from "the national irritation against England," the *World* had "made the settlement safe for the administration as a party venture." One suspects that Hurlbert's readiness to rise above partisanship may have had a personal dimension. His lifelong friend J. C. Bancroft Davis was assistant secretary of state during Grant's first term. Davis helped negotiate the Treaty of Washington and subsequently served as the American secretary for the arbitration panel that met in Geneva. Hurlbert may well have persuaded the owner of the *World*, Manton Marble, to favor settlement of the *Alabama* claims.[19]

Hurlbert also was deeply involved with the other major foreign policy issue of Grant's first term, the effort to annex Santo Domingo, the eastern half of the Caribbean island of Hispaniola. Grant saw Santo Domingo as a power vacuum that invited meddling by the European powers. Like the *Alabama* negotiations, Santo Domingo placed Grant and Sumner at loggerheads. But whereas the Massachusetts senator ultimately proved amenable to accepting a revised treaty with

18. David Donald, *Charles Sumner and the Rights of Man* (New York: Alfred A. Knopf, 1970), 364–67, 374–77.

19. *New York World*, May 4, 17, 1869, May 29, 1871.

Britain, nothing could deter his opposition to acquiring Santo Domingo. Sumner decided that Grant wanted the Caribbean outpost to provide the freedmen with a refuge from the postwar South. Convinced that the federal government should not give an inch in its support for equal rights, Sumner looked askance at Grant's "latter-day colonizationist scheme." Had Grant invested a fraction of the "time, money, zeal, will, personal attention, personal effort, and personal intercession" on behalf of "Southern Unionists, white and black" that he had given "to obtain half an island in the Caribbean Sea," Sumner charged, he could have exterminated the Ku Klux Klan and established "tranquility" across the South. Sumner also gathered evidence that Grant misused his executive powers to twist arms in Santo Domingo and to steamroll the U.S. Senate. An epic confrontation resulted. The Senate rejected annexation in June 1870 when the administration failed to obtain the necessary two-thirds majority, but Grant countered in December with a plan to secure Santo Domingo through joint resolution—in other words, with simple majorities of both houses of Congress, for which Texas provided a precedent.[20] Grant also appointed a blue-ribbon commission to go to Santo Domingo and report on its findings. Hurlbert gained entry as a journalist to cover the work of the commission, which sailed south on the Navy ship *Tennessee* in January 1871.[21]

On the merits, Hurlbert leaned Grant's way. The New Yorker had made it plain during the 1850s, when writing for the *Times,* that he favored an expansive role for the United States in Latin America. In 1871 he sent upbeat descriptions of Santo Domingo to the *World* and dismissed as "simply absurd" any opposition to annexation based on "doubt of its intrinsic value as a possession." He also found that pro-annexation sentiment was nearly universal in Santo Domingo—the country's landowners and common people wanted to join the United States. The *World,* however, did not approach the Santo Domingo issue with the same bipartisan spirit that it brought to the *Alabama* negotiations. Instead, Manton Marble spurned the "notorious Santo Domingo job" and echoed Sumner, who had accused Grant of using bribery and military force to prop up Dominican

20. Donald, *Sumner and the Rights of Man,* 435–515, quotation on 513; William R. McFeely, *Grant: A Biography* (New York: W.W. Norton, 1981), 333, 337, 340, 350–51, 444; *New York World,* Dec. 9, 1870.

21. An erroneous report created fears in early February that the *Tennessee,* which carried six hundred passengers, had been lost at sea. *New York World,* Mar. 17, 1871 (Hurlbert dispatch dated Mar. 7, 1871).

president Buenaventura Baez. Democrats loved to depict Grant as a would-be dictator who stood ready to trample the Constitution. Santo Domingo was both an apparent case in point and an issue on which the president enjoyed scant public support.[22]

Hurlbert thus found himself in the awkward position of reporting on the visit of the U.S. commissioners to Santo Domingo while knowing that his newspaper would editorialize against the entire project. The *World* respectfully called attention to Hurlbert's "careful, candid, intelligent, and sprightly dispatches," but scoffed that "the commissioners will render almost precisely the rose-colored report which they were sent out to render." The *World* continued to complain that Grant had "prostituted" the U.S. Navy to support Baez and intimidate his opponents. This "unrighteous and unseemly display of insolence, arrogance, and force" was a "national disgrace." Grant used bayonets to count ballots and to consummate treaties. He deserved impeachment for having trampled the Constitution, usurped the power of Congress, and violated international law. Opposed by an oddly heterogeneous coalition that included most Democrats and the nascent Liberal Republican insurgency within Grant's own party, Santo Domingo annexation failed.[23]

Hurlbert did much more than cover political and diplomatic realms. For years he reviewed new literary and historical works. Typically the *World* featured one of his reviews each week, but occasionally he wrote two, three, or even four. These pieces, more polished than the workaday editorials he routinely dashed off, were the basis for his reputation as a *littérateur*. His reviews were characterized by a seemingly photographic recall of everything that he had ever read, combined with a happy ability to discern broad trends and draw apt comparisons.

In a single 1871 piece, for example, Hurlbert ranged far beyond the three specimens of vernacular poems and ballads under review. He placed them within a long tradition that drew upon spoken dialects and captured "the ordinary talk of unlettered men." Vernacular speaking communicated a "freshness and vigor" and a "quaint picturesqueness" often absent in more "crystallized" classical languages. Notably, James Russell Lowell's *Biglow Papers* had

22. *New York World,* Dec. 9, 1870, Mar. 17, 1871 (Hurlbert dispatch dated Mar. 7, 1871), 28 Mar. 1871.

23. Ibid., Mar. 17, 28, 30, 1871; McFeely, *Grant,* 336–52.

made admirable use of the "New England tongue," while Alfred Lord Tennyson's "Northern Farmer" likewise gave voice to the "Yorkshire dialect." Hurlbert quickly made a distinction, however. Tennyson's "eye and ear" penetrated "the Northern farmer's mind and soul," whereas Lowell employed rural New England dialect didactically, to package his own "political and theological" views. Lowell could not craft a work of imagination. Hurlbert judged that the reading public was eager for dialect writing, but not for the "blasphemy and indecency" of "that great barbaric yawper," Walt Whitman. "No living author in any language" could be compared with Whitman, Hurlbert recognized, but his writing had failed to achieve popularity.[24]

Hurlbert especially admired one American writer, Nathaniel Hawthorne. Whereas Lowell asserted that American life was comparatively "bleak and bare," lacking either tradition or the "solemn inspiration of antiquity," Hawthorne proved otherwise. "There never was a more unpromising field for a writer of romances than that which he was set to dig in the New England of fifty years ago," Hurlbert observed. Yet Hawthorne had crafted "the most intense and poetic English romance of our times." *The Scarlet Letter* breathed life into the distant Puritan world. His characters were "sympathetically conceivable by other human beings" two centuries later who lived under greatly different circumstances. By contrast, Sir Walter Scott's *Old Mortality* vividly used "the costume and upholstery of Puritanism," but the principals in Scott's novel were lifeless caricatures on whom he hung "his antiquarian drapery." The "spirit of Puritanism was invisible to him."[25]

Hurlbert brought these same aesthetic values to his reviews of poetry. A work of imagination demanded moral complexity. The "mere description of nature" would not suffice. Poetry, like all literature, needed to speak both to human hopes and fears. The poet ought not impose a message on his writing. Instead, he must create characters who embody universal truths and struggles, and who elicit "human sympathy." Poetry was shaped by its times. Eighteenth- century poetry, which could produce "nothing more striking than [Mark] Akenside's didactics, and [James] Thomson's pastorals," was "in danger of growing dull." At that point, however, the chaos of the French Revolution had left a deep mark on poetry. A vast "stirring of the waters" at the end of the eighteenth century un-

24. *New York World*, June 3, 1871.
25. Ibid., June 3, Aug. 5, 1871.

leashed new creative energies. "Germany's literary revival" and "the rise of the new English masters of song" produced a poetry that far transcended its times. Compared to the high standard of Goethe, Schiller, Wordsworth, Keats, and Byron, Hurlbert found the poetry of the 1870s lacking. "Too many of the heroes of modern song," he wrote, were "moping" and irresolute. He presciently anticipated the rise of new sensibilities. As he wrote, Matthew Arnold was about to publish "Dover Beach," an emphatically downbeat meditation, but one that previewed the modern temper.[26]

A mixture of humor and indignation informed Hurlbert's devastating critique of an 1871 novel, *The Heart of the West,* by "an Illinoian," which depicts the journey of a lumber raft down the Mississippi River in 1860. The two principal characters on the raft are "deeply distressed" by the North-South sectional conflict, then careening toward a violent outcome. They decide that a national constitutional convention might solve the difficulty. Their deliberations include long dialogues regarding the Kansas-Nebraska bill and other such matters "which one loves to have discussed in a novel." Downriver the raftsmen heroically rescue the passengers from a burning steamboat. Among them is a lovely Southern belle, accompanied by her father. Of course she immediately falls in love with the captain of the raft. The captain sells his lumber in Memphis, whereupon he and his new bride head back north to live happily ever after. "This book is one of the most preposterously absurd productions which it has ever been our fate to see," Hurlbert fumed. It might possibly have succeeded as a "burlesque" of a novel composed for the wrong reasons, yet it had been written "in sober earnest." Its author had "unblushingly" announced that he cared less about "literary merit" than about "political ideas." With such a "wicked motive as the author's," Hurlbert concluded, it was "impossible that good should result." People who were not novelists should "stop writing novels."[27]

Several years later a writer of infinitely superior ability likewise decided to place two characters on a downriver raft shortly before the war. Mark Twain withheld his masterpiece for a decade because he could not imagine a suitable way to conclude the tale of Huck Finn and Nigger Jim. But Hurlbert already was alive to Twain's gifts. Colonel Mulberry Sellers, the audacious wheeler-dealer in *The Gilded Age,* was a "most distinctively and unqualifiedly American character." The "dreams and delusions" Twain imagined for Sellers revealed much

26. Ibid., Apr. 1, 1871.
27. Ibid., Aug. 19, 1871.

about postwar American society. Hurlbert was delighted that New York crowds thronged to see the stage version of Twain's *Gilded Age*.[28]

Hurlbert also had a passion for history. To explicate the past, he noted, one needed keen political sensibilities and "erudition." One also needed persistence and ample time to do research, because the source materials were "incessantly multiplying." Hurlbert regretted that most American-born historians resided in "one small and fertile locality," the city of Boston. The "contributions from the rest of our land," he gravely noted, "practically amount to nothing." An element of "local exaggeration" resulted. Bunker Hill was "made to seem a great deal higher than it is," and one year of "paltry skirmishing" in New England became the *"annus mirabilis"* of the long seven-year struggle to secure independence. Such especially was the case for George Bancroft, whose ten-volume *History of the United States,* written between the 1830s and the 1870s, finally concluded with the American Revolution. Hurlbert, who carped that Bancroft had "taken more than twice as long to write a simple story as did Gibbon to build his magnificent temple in honor of a fallen empire," accused Bancroft of bias. Bancroft "habitually disparaged the South" and suppressed evidence to gratify his prejudices. Other Bostonians also had limitations. Jared Sparks mutilated George Washington's correspondence. William H. Prescott, who wrote about the Spanish conquests of Mexico and Peru, was "admirable in most respects," but his later books on Philip II were "occasionally prosy and dull."[29]

Then, however, there was Francis Parkman! Hurlbert confessed in 1871 that his distaste for the "school of Boston historiography" had earlier kept him from reading Parkman's epic accounts of the collision between French and English imperial drives in mid-eighteenth-century North America. Hurlbert reported with delight that Parkman had "nothing in common" with other Bostonians. Unlike John Lothrop Motley, Parkman "never dogmatizes as to present, or future." Nor did Parkman idealize the "aboriginal race" of native peoples, whom the French turned into "murderous and effective allies." Parkman was "singularly free from the cant of philanthropy, such as Indian narratives are so apt to engender," Hurlbert wrote, "and never more so than now." Parkman's renowned account of the clash in September 1759 between Montcalm and Wolfe on the Plains of Abraham above Quebec—the beginning of the end for the French em-

28. Ibid., Oct. 26, 1874. *The Gilded Age,* coauthored by Charles Dudley Warner, had been published in 1873.

29. *New York World,* Mar. 27, 1871, Oct. 12, 26, 1874.

pire in North America—struck Hurlbert as overwrought. But Parkman's un-
adorned, spare prose style was at its best when he ventured into the "forests and
overshadowing trees" of the American interior. Hurlbert singled out for praise
the taut suspense evoked by Parkman's account of an imperiled English contingent at Detroit in 1768:

> The day closed and the hues of sunset faded. Only a dusky redness lin-
> gered in the west, and the darkening earth seemed her dull self again.
> Then night descended, heavy and black, on the fierce Indians and the
> sleepless English. From sunset until dawn an anxious watch was kept
> from the slender palisades of Detroit. The soldiers were still ignorant
> of the danger, and the sentinels did not know why their numbers were
> doubled, or why, with such unwonted vigilance, their officers repeatedly
> visited their posts. Again and again Gladwyn mounted his wooden ram-
> parts and looked forth into the gloom.

The terrain covered in Parkman's books was "close by," but his grand themes
were anything but "perilously local." In Hurlbert's view, no American historian
had comparable stature.[30]

Hurlbert, who displayed an almost encyclopedic knowledge of the American
Revolution, complained in 1871 that the recent Civil War had "superseded by
its unnatural glare" the "mild radiance" of the struggle for independence. The
"petty warfare of that day," with armies composed of hundreds or perhaps a
few thousand, and the killed or wounded counted only "by the score," was "dull
work" overshadowed by the "gigantic bloodiness" the nation had just witnessed.
What was Brandywine compared to Gettysburg, or Princeton to Chancellors-
ville? Another factor worked to eclipse "the ancient story," Hurlbert thought—
the just-defeated South "stood in the shoes, or thought they did, of the rebels
of 1776." Washington "was not only a rebel, but a Virginian and a slave-owner."
Consequently, books about the Revolution had almost trickled to a halt. But
most books on the Civil War were second rate, at best, Hurlbert judged. He dis-

---

30. Ibid., Mar. 27, 1871, Oct. 12, 1874. The quoted passage is from Francis Parkman, *The Conspiracy of Pontiac, and the Indian War After the Conquest of Canada*, 6th ed. (2 vols.; Boston: Little
Brown, 1870), 1:221. For a brilliant short appreciation of Parkman, who has been unjustly denigrated
by historians such as Wilbur Jacobs, see Simon Schama, *Dead Certainties (Unwarranted Speculations)* (New York: Knopf, 1991), 40–65.

missed Horace Greeley's *American Conflict* along with Alexander Stephens's "inordinate" two-volume defense of the South, *A Constitutional View of the Late War Between the States.* He likewise panned what he considered vapid, one-dimensional biographies of Union generals. As yet there seemed little public appetite for such books. "A nation emerging from four years of incessant uproar and conflicts is in some respects like a man escaped from a shipwreck or a railway collision," Hurlbert decided; "while the shock and the struggle for life are fresh in his consciousness he naturally turns to other themes for refreshment."[31] That would change. Hurlbert would be amazed that modern bookstores often give more shelf space to the Civil War than almost any other historical topic.

Hurlbert considered it more important to understand why that "colossal conflict" had taken place than to dissect the fighting of it. From time to time he sketched his own ideas about the path that had led to civil war. He knew that efforts to codify or enlarge Southern rights had generated a backlash. Northern public opinion in the 1850s opposed the Fugitive Slave Law; the repeal of the Missouri Compromise, which previously had barred slavery from western territories north of 36° 30'; and the Supreme Court's Dred Scott decision, which validated the right of slaveholders to take their slaves to the West. Lincoln's election in 1860 effectively negated the South's controversial advantages. It showed that slavery could not expand and that fugitive slaves might become more difficult to recover. But slaveholders remained strong and had little to fear. Rather than maintain their many advantages in the Union, however, they decided most unwisely to "attempt to break out of the Union," for which they paid a high price. Hurlbert faulted the North for failing to offer concessions that might have punctured the radical insurgency in the South following Lincoln's election. Had the Republicans agreed simply to restore the Missouri Compromise line, he surmised, a "hideous and unnecessary" war might have been averted.[32] An element of wishful thinking was involved here. Republicans failed to offer the concessions that Hurlbert favored, but they acted as they did in part because the Deep South's leaders insisted that no concessions would be acceptable, and that disunion was permanent. These were themes to which he would return in 1879.

Hurlbert frequently wrote about women, whose proper roles became the focus for spirited postwar discussion. He often seemed to go out of his way to pro-

---

31. *New York World,* Apr. 15, 1871, Mar. 16, Nov. 2, 1874.
32. Ibid., Sept. 9, Nov. 27, 1868, Mar. 13, Nov. 2, 1874.

voke. Satirical, whimsical, and patronizing, he ridiculed the champions of women's rights. From Susan B. Anthony's "grim girlhood" to the present, she had devoted herself to "preaching celibacy and reconciling male humanity to its practice." Her standard was "single bedsteads and blessedness." Campaigns to elevate women struck Hurlbert as pointless. "Certainly nothing can be more monstrous," he pontificated, than the assumption that women suffered "peculiar and exclusive wrongs in any leading country of modern Christendom." The "condition of women in general," like the "condition of men in general," was undergoing steady improvement. He went further. Spurning the outcry about "the tyranny of men," Hurlbert judged that "the general influence of women in every country of Christendom" was "more powerful, politically as well as socially, than the general influence of men." This influence had nothing to do with the narrow sphere of political rights. Millions of women "despise the ballot because they know they do not need it." The "enduring despotism of women" was rooted in their power to fascinate and attract men, and to use this power for worthy ends. And most women understood as much. They remained "cruelly indifferent" to their sisters who campaigned for female emancipation. He much preferred women who did not need "boost and betterment."[33]

Hurlbert's attacks on feminists ignited a blaze of indignant rebuttal. Those who had counted on the *World* to demonstrate "an elevated spirit of respect" for women's "educational and political aspirations" cried foul. "Men prefer weak minded wives and have an instinctive dread of well-informed women," announced Mrs. J. W. Thompson of Lock Haven, Pennsylvania. "Frivolity and vacuity are the keys to man's heart, and all girls understand this," she continued. Their ability to "flatter, giggle, and chatter" won them admirers. A "finished coquette" added to her "powers of fascination" by "rolling her eyes" in a senseless manner.

> Now, in striking contrast to the encouragement that men give to imbecility in our sex, notice the impediments which they have always thrown in the way of woman's advancement. Derision has been one of the most powerful weapons employed in retarding her intellectual progress. Does she wield the pen, she is denominated a "blue-stocking." Does she ex-

33. Ibid., Oct. 17, 1874, Apr. 12, 19, 28, 1869.

press her own opinions, she is sneeringly called "strong-minded"; does she earn her own living, she is "masculine"; and does she choose to remain single, heaven help her! She is an "old maid" and subject to neverending insult. It is to save herself from this fate that she panders to the vanity of man.[34]

As part of his campaign against Republican Reconstruction policies, Hurlbert did cheer on those feminist leaders who opposed the prospective Fifteenth Amendment, which forbade curtailment of voting rights based on "race, color, or previous condition of servitude" but made no mention of suffrage restrictions based on sex. Elizabeth Cady Stanton, Susan B. Anthony, and Lucy Stone Blackwell thus found themselves with an unwonted ally. "Now that slavery is no more, and the negro has the right to rob smoke-houses and hen roosts and to sit in the legislature," Hurlbert announced, the time had come "to let the colored man and brother stand aside in favor of the white woman and sister." Contradicting other things on the subject that he had written, Hurlbert decided that voting rights for women had "long passed the stage of mere ridicule" and had "become respectable." Because women had a particular interest in matters such as schools and town improvements that most directly affected themselves and their children, he suggested a limited female franchise confined to local elections. After seeing that "women are in earnest," men might become more amenable to having women participate in all elections. He also claimed, however, that protecting the right of women to their own property was more consequential than voting rights.[35]

Hurlbert complained that much of what women wrote was "futile and forlorn." For example, he poked fun at Louisa May Alcott's *Little Men: Life at Plumfield with Jo's Boys.* "Miss Alcott, having been herself a girl, is capable of painting little girls with a charming fidelity to nature," he acknowledged, but her imagined boys were totally unlike boys. Most boys younger than fourteen were "noisy and rude." They loved dirt "for the sake of its own dirtiness" and expressed themselves with "profanity and extreme vulgarity." A few boys exhibited "abnormal piety and unnatural quiet" and showed "traces of the nobility of character which they develop with later years," Hurlbert allowed, but they were

34. Ibid., Mar. 24, Apr. 1, 4, 12, 1869, quotations on Apr. 4, 12, 1869.
35. Ibid., Nov. 21, 23, 1868.

the exceptions that proved the rule. Alcott appeared neither to have had "intimate contact with genuine boys" nor to have observed them on "the wilds of the play-ground." Instead, she chose to "develop boys for literary purposes out of her own inner consciousness." The results were "purely imaginary," so that "the real boys who read her book will laugh at her, and revile her as a maiden lady who knows nothing of the grim facts of juvenile depravity."[36]

Some allowance might be made, however, for what he saw as exceptions to the general pattern. While eviscerating Charles Reade's popular novel *Griffith Gaunt*, Hurlbert wondered how Charlotte Brontë might have handled its explosive topic of sexual infidelity—"if indeed it is possible to conceive of a woman treating such a subject." Unlike Reade, he surmised, Brontë would have "crowded the intensity of her nature" into any such novel. She would have "looked into her heart and written." Much as he admired Brontë, Hurlbert considered the French novelist George Sand "the most vigorous and richly-gifted woman of the age." Her work stood apart because "the monstrous phantom of the Revolution" was "ever present" on the "horizon of her consciousness." The values she cherished—simplicity, fortitude, and a "brotherly kindness of class for class"—were under assault from a "Titanic force" that individuals could not withstand. It is not surprising, as we shall learn in the next chapter, that Hurlbert was drawn to a novelist who depicted the French Revolution as a terrible crucible that forced individuals to make harsh moral choices.[37]

As the *World*'s chief editorialist, Hurlbert was ideally positioned to comment on the most sensational drama of the 1870s, the Beecher-Tilton affair. Abstract discussions about the respective rights and roles of men and women never proved half as engrossing as a sexual scandal. When journalist Theodore Tilton accused Henry Ward Beecher of having seduced his wife, Elizabeth Tilton, the public could not get enough of the story.

Beecher was the most admired religious leader of the era. From his pulpit at the Plymouth Church in Brooklyn, he preached an optimistic Christianity that promised God's love to all. For Beecher, nature was filled with spiritual significance, and he celebrated human intimacy as a manifestation of the divine. The Tiltons, longtime members of his congregation, once had regarded Beecher as

36. Ibid., June 24, 1871.
37. Ibid., Apr. 29, Aug. 12, 1871.

a valued friend. When the scandal exploded into the public realm in July 1874, its impact and media attention proved comparable to the firestorm that President Bill Clinton ignited during his second term in office.[38]

Beecher solemnly denied having done anything to "impugn the honor and purity" of Elizabeth Tilton, while she affirmed "before God" that she had never "been guilty of adultery with Henry Ward Beecher in thought or deed, nor has he ever offered to me an indecorous or improper proposal." Theodore Tilton, however, submitted for public perusal six letters written by Beecher between 1871 and 1873, one addressed to his wife and five to Frank D. Moulton, who had attempted to mediate the unhappy entanglement. Beecher's letters made for painful reading. Deeply troubled by some unspecified guilt, Beecher sought Theodore Tilton's forgiveness. The letters showed also, however, that Beecher pronounced Elizabeth Tilton guiltless. She was "sinned against." The minister hoped desperately that Theodore Tilton would condone "his wife's fault" and keep the matter in the private realm. The principals tried to suppress the news of their difficulties, but the arrangement came unhinged after the avant-garde feminist Victoria Woodhull publicized the gossip and accused Beecher of living by a double standard.[39]

The Protestant gentry of New York City and Brooklyn, anguished by the Beecher-Tilton fiasco, must have been further distressed to find the dubious adventurer Hurlbert adjudicating the evidence on the editorial page of the *World*. On July 27, 1874, he wrote a long and explosive analysis that stretched over four columns and focused on Beecher's insistence that Elizabeth Tilton did not share his own guilt. Her relationship with the minister could not have been physical, Hurlbert surmised. He also noted that Theodore Tilton had written in 1871 that

38. The most original effort to make sense of the story is Richard Wightman Fox, *Trials of Intimacy: Love and Loss in the Beecher-Tilton Scandal* (Chicago: Univ. of Chicago Press, 1999). For Beecher's theology, see pp. 175, 181–82, 218, 239–40, 244–45, 299. See also Debby Applegate, *The Most Famous Man in America: The Biography of Henry Ward Beecher* (New York: Doubleday, 2006).

39. *New York World*, July 27, 1874. Richard Wightman Fox documents "a deep emotional and spiritual attachment between Henry and Elizabeth." She regarded "her impassioned knowing of Beecher" a "path to personal awakening," a sentiment that the minister plainly reciprocated. In retrospect, Beecher blamed himself for allowing her to become so attached to him. Both believed that they had sinned, but both denied that the relationship was adulterous. Fox thinks the question of a physical relationship cannot be resolved (Fox, *Trials of Intimacy*, 59–61, 106–7, 130, 298, 370n5, quotations on 106, 130).

he bore no malice toward Beecher "for the great suffering which he has caused to Elizabeth and myself." If Theodore Tilton really believed Beecher and his wife guilty of adultery, Hurlbert reasoned, this was "the most extraordinary letter an injured husband ever wrote." Had Theodore Tilton shot Beecher on the basis of the evidence presented of an "adulterous connection," he would have been hanged.[40]

In August 1874, Theodore Tilton allowed a friendly newspaper to publish excerpts from over two hundred seemingly affectionate letters that he and his wife had exchanged before their relationship deteriorated. His object was to disprove his wife's claim that she had been attracted to Beecher because "he appreciated me as Theodore did not."[41] Hurlbert lambasted Theodore Tilton. Beecher's accuser was a "self-convicted liar and slanderer" who was "impaled on his own words." No sensible person could doubt Beecher's "substantial innocence." The row had political overtones. Theodore Tilton was a Radical Republican; he and Beecher began to fall out when they disagreed about Reconstruction. In Hurlbert's eyes, the "monstrous and outrageous injustice done to Mr. Beecher" had been abetted by partisanship and moral posturing. Hurlbert explained to Manton Marble that public opinion was moving toward Beecher, making it "just the time for us to swing the wider and more serious charge against him as I have tried to do."[42]

All that has been mentioned so far in this chapter was transitory. The politics of the Gilded Age, Santo Domingo, and the Beecher-Tilton debacle provided compelling drama in their own time, yet they are barely remembered today. One Hurlbert venture, however, lives on. Just to the west of the Metropolitan Museum in Central Park, today's pedestrian will encounter a striking Egyptian obelisk, Cleopatra's Needle, securely mounted at the crest of a modest wooded

40. *New York World,* July 27, Aug. 1, 1874.

41. Fox, *Trials of Intimacy,* 60, 251–91.

42. *New York World,* Aug. 1, 2, 13, 16, 1874; Hurlbert to Marble, Friday [July 1874], bound vol. 91, Marble Papers. A sensational trial subsequently took place between January and July of 1875, but the jury could not reach a verdict (Fox, *Trials of Intimacy,* 89–131). The ultimate result vindicated Hurlbert: the evidence presented against Beecher was too ambiguous to sustain Theodore Tilton's accusations. It could just as well be read to support the view that Beecher and Elizabeth Tilton's passionate attachment lacked a physical dimension.

knoll. The inscriptions on the obelisk have been eroded by a century of acid rain. But attached to its pedestal are brass plaques, which provide translations of the faded hieroglyphics—and which credit William H. Vanderbilt for defraying the costs of moving the 3,500-year-old relic from Egypt. Unmentioned in brass, but quickly revealed through old newspapers, is the identity of the mastermind behind the entire project, William Henry Hurlbert. Remarkably, his campaign to secure the obelisk coincided precisely with the appearance of "The Diary of a Public Man." Both the obelisk and the Diary, his two most memorable legacies, should be seen as accomplishments of someone with powerful historical sensibilities.

Hurlbert visited Egypt in 1869, shortly after the opening of the Suez Canal. In conversation with the Khedive of Egypt, Ismail Pasha, the cosmopolitan American first broached the subject. Years later, their discussion was summarized as follows:

> "A great way to open the harbor and hearts of New York would be for your highness to present America with an Egyptian obelisk. After all, both London and Paris have been so honored."
>
> "There is no insurmountable obstacle to preclude such a gift. Have you a particular obelisk in mind?"
>
> "Forgive the pun, Your Highness—but any old obelisk will do. There's one hanging over the seawall in Alexandria for instance. It could readily be moved."
>
> "Ah yes. The so-called Cleopatra's Needle. Yes—I think it might be arranged."

At work here was the wish of Ismail Pasha, an ambitious modernizer, to promote closer economic ties between Egypt and the rising colossus of the Western Hemisphere. Also at work was Hurlbert's strong sense of history. He knew that Rome, at the height of its power, had brought more than a dozen obelisks to Italy, and that Caesar Augustus had moved two others, including Cleopatra's Needle, to Alexandria, a Roman city. He knew too that France had erected an obelisk in the Place de la Concorde in 1835, and that British engineers were contemplating ways of moving the fallen twin of Cleopatra's Needle from Alexandria to London. If New York was to validate its status as a true counterpart to

Paris and London, it also needed an obelisk. It would mark this country as a fit successor to the great empires of antiquity, and it would demonstrate the "interconnection and interdependence of the whole field of human history."[43]

At the time of the initial conversation, Hurlbert was merely an editorial writer for the *World*, and the obelisk project lapsed. Eight years later, however, in 1877, the now editor-in-chief put shoulder to the wheel. By happy circumstance, an old friend of his, William M. Evarts—the unsuccessful aspirant for Seward's Senate seat in early 1861—became secretary of state that same year. Hurlbert persuaded Evarts to give the matter his attention, and Evarts instructed the American consul-general in Egypt, Elbert Farman, to secure a firm commitment from the Khedive. That did not happen immediately, because France and England wanted Egypt to remain a "European dependency" and opposed moving the obelisk to the United States. Farman continued to apply gentle persuasion, and finally in May 1879, a decade after the initial conversation between Hurlbert and Ismail Pasha, an agreement was reached to allow the United States to remove Cleopatra's Needle to New York.[44]

The summer of 1879—exactly the time the Diary appeared—brought a flurry of activity regarding the obelisk. The agreement with Egypt specified that all its moving costs would be borne by the United States. Hurlbert, unwilling to risk relying on a campaign of small donations, secured a commitment from William H. Vanderbilt, the wealthy head of the New York Central Railroad, to pay whatever was needed, which ultimately exceeded $100,000. Meanwhile Evarts discovered that an American naval officer, Lieutenant Commander Henry H. Gorringe, had closely observed the recent British transfer of the other Alexandria obelisk to London. After a full conversation with him, Evarts decided that Gorringe was the man for the job. The secretary of state then "referred him, with the strongest recommendations" to Hurlbert, who eagerly concurred. Gorringe thereupon inspected Central Park to find a suitable site for the obelisk.

43. Edmund S. Whitman, "An Obelisk for Central Park," *Saudi Aramco World* 26 (July/Aug. 1975): 4–9; Martina D'Alton, *The New York Obelisk; or, How Cleopatra's Needle Came to New York and What Happened When It Got Here* (New York: Metropolitan Museum of Art, 1993), 12–13; R. A. Hayward, *Cleopatra's Needles* (London: Moorland Publishing, 1978); Simon Schama, *Landscape and Memory* (New York: Knopf, 1995), 284–89, 376–78; *New York World*, Oct. 7, 1877, Feb. 23, 1881.

44. D'Alton, *The New York Obelisk*, 13–15; Henry H. Gorringe, *Egyptian Obelisks* (New York: G. P. Putnam's Sons, 1882), 2–5; *New York World*, Oct. 10, 1880.

He was accompanied by Hurlbert and Frederic E. Church, "the most eminent of American artists." They selected Greywecke Knoll, near the Metropolitan Museum of Art, then under construction. Henry G. Stebbins, New York's commissioner of public parks, agreed to provide this prime location for the artifact. On August 24, Gorringe departed for Egypt, having first obtained some "ingenious machinery" to facilitate lowering the obelisk for shipment to the United States. The equipment was custom made to his order by the Roebling Iron Works in Trenton, New Jersey, which supplied the steel suspension wires for the Brooklyn Bridge, also under construction.[45]

Gorringe proved an inspired choice. "No man knows so well as I do," Hurlbert later wrote, the "discouragements and difficulties" the naval officer faced. In Egypt he encountered many "intrigues and machinations." Safely moving an over 200-ton monolith presented all kinds of challenges. It had to be dismounted in Alexandria, floated ten miles to a suitable dry dock, and placed in the hold of an Egyptian ship that Gorringe purchased, the *Dessoug*. The starboard hull of the iron steamer had to be torn open to load the uniquely heavy cargo, and then reriveted for the transatlantic voyage, which started on June 12, 1880. Gorringe, who wisely brought along a spare crankshaft for the aged engine, was vindicated in midocean when the original crankshaft failed. The engine was repaired, and the voyage proceeded. When the *Dessoug* was spotted off Fire Island on July 19, Hurlbert sailed out in a tugboat to greet Gorringe.[46]

For the next seven months, the obelisk was constantly in the news. Once derided by some as a hare-brained scheme, the relocation of the Egyptian monument spurred growing metropolitan self-congratulation. It had to be unloaded at Staten Island before being ferried across the harbor to upper Manhattan. Then, from mid-September to early January, it was inched uphill from the Hudson River to its new site in Central Park. On January 22, 1881, the moment finally arrived for the obelisk to be rotated into a vertical position, again using Roebling's machinery that had lowered it to the horizontal in Alexandria. An enthusiastic crowd, estimated at 10,000, turned out on a bitter winter day. A committee of four presided—Gorringe, Evarts, Hurlbert, and the Secretary of the Navy, Nathan Goffe. The obelisk, covered with snow and ice and elevated about forty feet off the ground, was held in place by massive trunnions and perfectly bal-

45. *New York World*, Oct. 10, 1880, Jan. 23, Feb. 23, 1881; Gorringe, *Egyptian Obelisks*, 5–6, 30–31.

46. *New York World*, Oct. 10, 1880, Jan. 23, Feb. 23, 1881; D'Alton, *The New York Obelisk*, 64; Gorringe, *Egyptian Obelisks*, 6–30.

anced. Although a monument weighing over 200 tons was not turned "in mid-air every day," the *World* triumphantly reported, the "colossal stone" moved "as easily and delicately as if it were the minute-hand of a lady's watch." Its successful installation marked the greatest triumph of "American engineering skill." A month later, more formal ceremonies were held inside the Metropolitan Museum, which had opened for the first time in 1880. A crowd of over 20,000 swarmed outside, but only those with tickets could be admitted. The featured speaker was Secretary of State Evarts, who linked the obelisk's history to the events of the Old and New Testaments. A choir sung a specially commissioned hymn to the tune of Luther's "Ein Feste Burg." Hurlbert's graceful editorial, published the next day in the *World,* appropriately thanked Gorringe, Evarts, Vanderbilt, Farman, and the Khedive. It also offered the hope that "visible memorials connecting the present with the remote past" might give New Yorkers a higher level of "public spirit among its citizens," comparable to that displayed by Londoners and Parisians.[47]

Never again would Hurlbert enjoy such stature as in early 1881. Whatever his idiosyncrasies, he had accomplished something that required a rare mix of imagination and promotion. He stood among the leading men of the greatest metropolis in the country. Two years later, however, his connection to the *World* ended, and with it, his status as a consequential New York insider.

What might we learn about "The Diary of a Public Man" for having examined Hurlbert's preoccupations during the 1860s and 1870s? I would suggest three things. First, Hurlbert persistently distanced himself from any providential view of the sectional conflict and its ultimate outcome. Instead, the spectacle of war and emancipation and Reconstruction impressed him as a series of regrettable blunders for which the country paid a high price. He likewise stood aloof from other causes that attracted upright Victorians—temperance, women's rights, concern for Native Americans, and the use of law to promote moral order. Second, Hurlbert was an international cosmopolitan. His horizons were far wider than most of his fellow countrymen's, and he insisted that the American experience be viewed in broader perspective. He had an unusual ability to look at his home country from a distance. Third, Hurlbert had keen literary and historical sensibilities. Intolerant of bad writing, he had pronounced ideas as to

47. *New York World,* Oct. 10, 1880, Jan. 23, Feb. 23, 1881; D'Alton, *The New York Obelisk,* 38–63; Gorringe, *Egyptian Obelisks,* 31–58.

what the author of a work of imagination—or a work of history—owed his or her readers. His legacy consists of two imaginative historical contributions— one written, the other standing in Central Park. They could hardly have been more different, and they have never been linked until now.

11

CONNECTING PAST AND PRESENT

Freed from the day-to-day deadlines of newspaper work in 1883 when Jay Gould sold the *New York World* to Joseph Pulitzer, Hurlbert soon sailed to England. From there he dispatched a regular column for the *New York Sun*, under the title "An American Traveller." He also contributed to several magazines, including the *Fortnightly Review* and the *Nineteenth Century*. He even printed an article in the *North American Review* under his own name (for variety!). Most notably, Hurlbert wrote two books, one about Ireland, the other about France.

Between January and June 1888, Hurlbert paid a series of visits to Ireland. He professed to have come without preconception, with "no case to make for or against any political party or any theory of government in Ireland." He recounted meeting a cross section of people, both "high and low." By autumn, he published a sprawling two-volume diary, entitled *Ireland under Coercion*. It set down "as nearly as possible" what he "actually saw and heard," based on stenographic notes taken "each day as occasion served, and always at night."[1]

Hurlbert's book on Ireland has important implications for this study. As a diary, it invites comparison with "The Diary of a Public Man," published less than a decade before. It will be recalled that the two employed many of Hurlbert's same signature words, and they had almost identical stylometric features. In matters of substance as well as style, the two had points of overlap. Hurlbert often ruminated about the recent history of the United States as he traveled around the Emerald Isle. *Ireland under Coercion* thus offers a marvelous window into the way he understood the events of his lifetime. It offers evidence that he was indeed the author of the Diary published in the *North American Review*, and it sheds light on the reasons why he created that perplexing document.

In writing about Ireland, Hurlbert displayed his artistic bent, his historical consciousness, and his gifts as a writer. Amid the "desolate majesty" of the rugged northwest coast, he encountered "driving mists and blinding rain," along with "great stone-strewn wastes of land" where "huge boulders lay tossed and

1. William Henry Hurlbert, *Ireland under Coercion: The Diary of an American*, 2nd ed. (2 vols.; Edinburgh: David Douglas, 1888), 1:xxxi–xxxii.

tumbled about as if they had been whirled through the air by the cyclones of some prehistoric age, and dropped at random when the wild winds wearied of the fun." This harsh landscape and punishing weather made him appreciate the contrast several days later when he reached a fertile wooded valley on a sunlit day. There "the sky was the sky of Constable—silvery-white clouds, floating athwart a dome of clear Italian blue." The commanding green vistas above the Nore River in the southeast featured landscapes "to which Turner alone or Claude could have done justice." The tint of Lough Rea in the Shannon Valley could not be duplicated at any lake in Lombardy or Piedmont; from an overlook in the area "the distant hills were touched with a soft purple light such as transfigures the Apennines at sunset." Hurlbert commended Dublin's Irish National Gallery, which displayed more high-quality art than museums in Lyons or Marseilles, both of which were "much larger and wealthier cities." In a single sentence he deftly called attention to the work of nine different painters. Again and again, he framed his narrative with apt historical and geographical cues—an aged veteran who remembered that recruits had assembled there before going over to the Continent to fight the battle of Waterloo; ancient records that bore witness to bitter Catholic opposition to Queen Elizabeth; and Sir Walter Raleigh's "quaintly gabled" house, "within which, according to a local legend, Sir Walter sat enjoying the first pipe of tobacco ever lighted in Ireland, when his terrified serving-maid espying the smoke that curled around her master's head hastily ran up and emptied a pail of water over him." The American visitor also was sensitive to new cultural stirrings. A "small and beautifully printed" volume of nationalistic poems, just published, included an "exquisite ballad" written by one W. B. Yeats—who was, at that time, a quite unknown twenty-three-year-old.[2]

Irish national sentiment reached new levels of intensity in the 1870s and 1880s. The nationalist cause was fueled by tenant resentments. Sagging worldwide agricultural prices coincided with blighted potato yields in parts of western Ireland. A noncooperation campaign spread rapidly; it demanded rent reductions and struck back at landlords who evicted tenants. Charles Stewart Parnell, the uniquely talented Irish political leader, positioned himself at the head of the insurgency. He used tenant unrest to promote Irish home rule.[3]

In choosing to write about Ireland, Hurlbert deliberately interjected himself

2. Ibid., 1:72–73, 147, 149, 188–91, 2:7, 50, 72, 154, 163, 197, 296–97.
3. Joseph Lee, *The Modernisation of Irish Society, 1848–1918* (Dublin: Gill and Macmillan, 1973), 65–88.

into a political minefield. Never before had the relationship between the British government and that troubled island been so politically consequential. In 1885, Irish MP's gained the balance of power in the House of Commons. So positioned, they toppled a Liberal government. When elections restored the Liberals to power, Prime Minister William E. Gladstone decided to support Irish home rule, which would have established quasi-independence. He was unable, however, to win parliamentary approval, as Liberal Unionists who feared the breakup of the British empire voted with Conservatives, thereby narrowly defeating home rule. The Liberal government once again fell, triggering another round of elections in the summer of 1886. This time a Conservative majority that opposed home rule gained power, and would hold it for the next six years.[4]

The backdrop for Hurlbert's analysis was the Irish "Plan of Campaign," launched in 1886. As seen by nationalists, the Plan of Campaign was a kind of tenant trade union, through which tenants collectively attempted to pressure landlords to accept lower rents. All the tenants on a piece of property agreed to deposit reduced rental fees with a spokesman for the National League, who would attempt to negotiate with the landlord for lower rates. Falling agricultural prices in the 1880s made fixed rentals increasingly burdensome. As seen by Hurlbert, however, the actual operation of the Plan of Campaign meant that "well-to-do and well-disposed tenants" were "coerced by the thriftless and shiftless" and by "the village despots"—hence the use of the word "coercion" in the title of the book. Tenants who refused to cooperate with the campaign were shunned, their hay could be burned, their cattle could be stolen or mutilated, and occasionally they even were murdered. If someone rented property from which a tenant had been evicted, he risked reprisals. Tenants were instructed "to club their rents"—that is, to pool their reduced payments—so as to prevent "traitors" from agreeing independently with landlords. Hurlbert interviewed several landlords who agreed to accept reduced rents, "recognizing the fall in prices of stock and produce." For the most part, however, he found landlords and tenants locked in a bitter impasse.[5]

Hurlbert deplored the sudden intersection of "Agrarian Revolution" in

4. Peter Stansky, *Gladstone: A Progress in Politics* (Boston: Little Brown, 1979), 153–66. On the politics of home rule, see J. L. Hammond, *Gladstone and the Irish Nation* (London: Longmans, Green, 1938), and Michael Hurst, *Parnell and Irish Nationalism* (Toronto: Univ. of Toronto Press, 1968).

5. Hurlbert, *Ireland under Coercion*, 2:167–68, 176, 182, 209–10, 231, 280–81.

Ireland—a denial of the right to private property in land—with what he considered the related movement in the United States, led by Henry George, the author of *Progress and Poverty*. In 1886 these two strands came together in a way that shocked conservatives on both sides of the Atlantic. Neither quite succeeded, but both came close. In Britain, as we have just briefly sketched, the abortive Liberal bid to secure home rule took place in 1886. Many British traditionalists condemned Gladstone for the effort. In their view, he had caved in to Irish nationalists, who relied on boycotts and intimidation. Shortly after the summertime elections in Britain, which swept the Liberals from power, New York City became the arena for a political campaign like no other, as Henry George campaigned to become mayor. His famed call for a "single tax" struck Hurlbert as a confiscatory assault on landed property, and the opening salvo of "social revolution." George, who enjoyed strong support from Irish Americans and from nationalist leaders in Ireland, notably Michael Davitt, enthusiastically supported Irish home rule. George polled 68,000 votes, not enough to defeat Democrat Abram Hewitt, but close enough to cause a huge commotion. The Republican candidate for mayor, young Theodore Roosevelt, never forgot that he finished third behind Henry George—an experience that persuaded the future president to support prudent reform rather than risk heaven knows what.[6]

Hurlbert's home country and its history never were far from mind as he explored the Emerald Isle. He recalled that "bleeding Kansas" had "brought the great American Union to the verge of disruption" in 1856, and he feared that "agitated Ireland" could do "as much, or worse for the British Empire" in 1888.

Not once, but a hundred times, during the visits to Ireland recorded in this book, I have been reminded of the state of feeling and opinion which existed in the Border States, as they were called, of the American Union, after the invasion of Virginia by a piratical band under John Brown, and before the long-pending issues between the South, insisting on its constitutional rights, and the North, restive under its constitutional obligations, were brought to a head by the election of President Lincoln.

Hurlbert recognized that analogies were deceptive, but he suspected that "Ireland stands today between Great Britain and the millions of the Irish race in

6. Ibid., 1:ix, xxxiv, xxxvii, xl–xli, xlv, l–lx, 2:339–44; John Morton Blum, *The Republican Roosevelt* (Cambridge: Harvard Univ. Press, 1954), 13.

America and Australia very much as the Border States of the American Union stood in 1861 between the North and the South." The overseas Irish, especially those living in the United States, provided enthusiastic support for the Irish national cause, with little thought as to whether the funds they raised were used in behalf of parliamentary nationalists, led by Parnell, or extremist groups such as the Fenians, which carried out assassinations. Britain complained that the United States afforded Irish extremists a base outside the jurisdiction of British law. Thirty years before, Hurlbert recalled, the border states of the Upper South felt secure in the Union. The controversies that pitted the cotton states of the Deep South against New England and the states of the Upper North could never have shaken "the foundations of law and order in the Border States, could they have been left to themselves." But the impact of "conflicting passions and interests beyond their own borders" was so powerful that the border states "lost control of their own affairs, and were swept helplessly into a terrific conflict, which they had the greatest imaginable interest in avoiding, and no interest whatever in promoting." Hurlbert offered the somber thought that optimists in Maryland, Virginia, Kentucky, Missouri, and Tennessee "had greater apparent odds in their favor in 1861 than the optimists of Ireland seem to me to have in 1888."[7]

Hurlbert rejected "the very common impression" that Ireland was "either misgoverned or ungovernable." Like all agricultural countries and regions, it had suffered from a worldwide fall of prices. Its most salient problems, however, were ideological and political rather than economic. Irish nationalists had convinced themselves that owning land in Ireland was "what the ownership of a slave was in the eyes of the earlier Abolitionists—a crime so monstrous as to be beyond pardon or endurance." They attempted to make it impossible for England to govern Ireland. But even if Ireland were "turned over to-morrow to their control," they would have no way to transform their "essentially revolutionary" program into a government that could secure "social stability." Moreover, Irish independence would be resisted in Ulster, the northeastern corner of Ireland, where Protestant majorities clung to Britain. Hurlbert interviewed a Presbyterian leader in Belfast who warned that "an Irish parliament in Dublin would mean civil war in Ireland."[8]

As Hurlbert wrote about Ireland in 1888, he repeatedly employed techniques and revealed opinions that had served him well in 1879. He had an ear for dialogue (easier, of course, if recorded soon after the conversation, rather than re-

7. Hurlbert, *Ireland under Coercion*, 2:333–35.
8. Ibid., 1:ix, 2:325, 335–39.

created years later!). He effortlessly supplied historical context and perspective. He distanced himself from visionaries, such as the radical abolitionist "Comeouters" in New England "during my college days at Harvard," or those who had initiated "the fatuous and featherheaded French Revolution of 1789," out of a belief that "methods of government" could be transformed painlessly.[9] And while purporting simply to record things that he had heard from others, he mixed in generous portions of his own ideas.

As mentioned in chapter 2, *Ireland under Coercion* and "The Diary of a Public Man" have almost identical stylometric signatures, as measured by statistical analysis. This parallelism is also apparent when comparing word usage and style. Each of these 1879 staples reappeared in 1888—"absurd," "vexatious," "vexed," "seething," "careworn," "agog," "wretched," "wild," "wildest," "quaint," "mischief," "ascertained," "peremptorily," "earnest," "madness"—and many others. Both the Public Man and the visitor to Ireland used the phrase "positively refused."[10] Someone who knew Judah Benjamin and Pierre Soulé "told me a story," the Public Man noted, about the intrigues of prominent Louisiana officials in Mexico. The diarist considered the tale "so characteristic of all the persons so concerned in it that I must jot it down." Using almost identical language, Hurlbert reported in his book on Ireland that someone who knew Ulysses S. Grant "told me a story so illustrative of the simplicity and modesty which were a keynote in his character that I must note it," while another person "told me a story" about a visit to Ireland by Gladstone that was "too good to be lost."[11] Hurlbert, the visitor to Ireland, remained an inveterate alliterator—"wildly waving," "perambulating policemen," "stewed seaweed," "truculent talk," "malignant misrepresentations," a "really remarkable resemblance," "abundantly able."

The Public Man favorably compared the beautiful and graceful Adele Cutts Douglas, the young second wife of the Illinois senator, to Mary Todd Lincoln, a "dowdy and to me most unprepossessing little woman." Had "the wives been voted for," he quipped, Douglas "would be President-elect to-day" (240). The visitor to Ireland also had an eye for attractive women. He wrote an admiring description of a sixteen-year-old Irish maiden—the "beauty of Gweedore":

Her lithe graceful figure, her fine, small, chiseled features, her shapely little head rather defiantly set on her sloping shoulders, her fair com-

9. Ibid., 1:xxi, 18.
10. P. 223 herein; Hurlbert, *Ireland under Coercion,* 2:205.
11. P. 236 herein; Hurlbert, *Ireland under Coercion,* 1:171, 2:34.

plexion and clear hazel eyes, her brown golden hair gathered up behind into a kind of tress, all of these were Saxon rather than Celtic. Her
trim neat ankles were bare, after the mountain fashion, but she was pret-
tily dressed in a well-fitting dark blue gown, wore a smartly trimmed
muslim apron, with lace about her throat, and carried over her arm a
new woolen shawl, very tasteful and quiet in color. She greeted us with
a self-possessed smile.[12]

A comely woman could be counted upon to stimulate Hurlbert's observant
powers.

Hurlbert wrote as an omniscient political economist. Even if British mis-
rule had long doomed Ireland to impoverished underdevelopment, he assumed
that the necessary capital and investment to change matters also must come
from Britain, and he pointed out instances of undoubted material improvement. From such a perspective, anything that might alarm investors was bad
for Ireland—exactly as he had assessed the Reconstruction South. He repeatedly complained that "political agitation" had "checked any flow of capital" into
affected districts and thereby resulted in economic doldrums. The long-run effect of the nationalist campaign would be to reduce Ireland once again to a land
of "poverty and potatoes."[13]

Hurlbert gave short shrift to intangibles. The rise of national consciousness
in Ireland—and in many other parts of Europe by the late nineteenth century—
fanned embers of estrangement into a powerful flame. He should have recognized that the issues at stake could not have been resolved purely on the basis
of cost effectiveness. Parnell's power resulted from his recognition that long-
standing economic grievances had generated a degree of discontent that could
not be addressed simply by economic amelioration. Hurlbert failed to recognize
the astuteness of the great Irish leader or to recognize Parnell's claim on the
Irish heart.[14]

In other respects, however, the book was discerning. Some Irish nationalists, intent on independence, did spurn any lesser reforms. The resultant ideological polarization did have similarities to the North-South sectional conflict
in the United States during the 1850s. Hurlbert understood, better than many of

12. Hurlbert, *Ireland under Coercion*, 1:109.
13. Ibid., 1:197, 213, 2:299.
14. Hurst, *Parnell and Irish Nationalism*, 35.

his contemporaries, the absolutist mentality among some who identified with the cause of popular nationalism. He sensed that a few extreme men—such as John Brown in 1859 or those who later led the Easter Rising in 1916—could transform themselves into martyrs for a sacred cause. His dour warnings about how the Irish situation might trigger a civil war were not fulfilled during his own lifetime, but he was correct to predict that the struggles of the 1880s could have a violent sequel. Between 1919 and 1922, immediately after World War I, Irish nationalists mounted a guerrilla campaign that effectively extinguished British authority in most of Ireland. Ultimately, Ireland was partitioned. The Protestant-majority northeast around Belfast remained part of Britain, but the rest of Ireland became independent. The conflict that led to partition was mercifully less bloody than the American Civil War, but it was bad enough. And a nasty low-level insurgency persisted for the rest of the twentieth century.[15]

Several unmistakable strands thus link "The Diary of a Public Man" with *Ireland under Coercion*. They share a point of view, a style of writing, and, above all, a fear of civil war. Hurlbert believed that progress required political stability and the wise investment of capital. He distrusted true believers of all sorts. In his view, the hopeful world of the late nineteenth century was endangered by ideological absolutism. Rival nationalisms had the potential to engulf Europe in war, just as had happened to the United States in 1861. Moderate majorities could be whipsawed by fanatical minorities. This was both a defensible explanation of what had happened in his home country and a timely warning that Europe had something to learn from the American experience.

Hurlbert promptly followed *Ireland under Coercion* with *France and the Republic,* an indictment of the Third French Republic.[16] The two books, published only a year and half apart, shared common qualities. Each took the form of a travelogue, based on recent visits to outlying towns. In each the author posed as an objective American who wanted better to understand the politics of a foreign country. In each, too, the author interspersed his interviews and visual impressions with editorial commentary that reflected deeply conservative sensibilities. *France and the Republic* plainly attempted to piggyback on the modest

15. Lawrence James, *The Rise and Fall of the British Empire* (New York: St. Martin's Press, 1994), 375–85.

16. William Henry Hurlbert, *France and the Republic: A Record of Things Seen and Learned in the French Provinces during the "Centennial" Year 1889* (London: Longmans, Green & Co., 1890).

success enjoyed by *Ireland under Coercion.* It was studded with characteristic Hurlbert prose—"absurd," "certainly," "quaint," "mischievous," "wretched," and "folly." It also included some graceful visual descriptions—the "richly wooded" panorama from the Château de Coucy, interspersed with "fertile fields and smiling towns," and the "verdant valley of the Marne."

The appearance of *France and the Republic* coincided with the centennial of the French Revolution. For Hurlbert there was nothing to celebrate and much to mourn. He indicted the First Republic as "the deadly enemy both of liberty and of law." Its masterminds were "ambitious criminals" who masqueraded "in the guise of philanthropists and philosophers" even while inaugurating a carnival of "pillage and destruction." Perceptive Americans in Revolutionary France such as Gouverneur Morris had been "appalled by the lawlessness" they witnessed. Scorning efforts to glorify the events of a century before, Hurlbert insisted that the "follies and crimes" of the French Revolution had "checked and thwarted" the progress of "modern civilization."

Hurlbert insisted that the Third Republic had similarly ominous qualities. It was led by a "parliamentary oligarchy" such as tried to seize power in the United States during "the evil days of Reconstruction at the South." French Republicans remained in office only because of "political corruption and intimidation." Hurlbert insisted that "the masses of the French people" preferred the "stability and order" of a monarchy to the "instability and anarchy" of a republic. *France and the Republic* also assailed the French government for its anticlericalism. It called attention to the dismal history of religious persecution experienced by Catholics during the Revolution, and it predicted that the strident secularism of the Third Republic was a prelude of worse to come. Speciously claiming to defend "the moral unity of France," the Third Republic had clamped down hard on religiously supported schools.[17]

Hurlbert correctly asserted that France was a culturally divided battleground. Struggles between Catholics and secularists provided the central pivot for late-nineteenth-century French politics, historian J. P. Daughton has noted. Creating primary schools that were "compulsory, secular, and universal became *the* republican priority." In other respects, however, *France and the Republic* made for strange reading. More overtly polemical than *Ireland under Coercion,* its main message was not an easy sell. Few Americans since 1776 had extolled the virtues

17. Ibid., xxi, xxxv, lvii–iii, lxxxviii, xcvii, 52, 180, 194, 196, 200, 230, 344, 408–13, 415, 446, 454.

of monarchy. And Hurlbert, the long-lapsed Unitarian, made an odd champion of Catholic piety. One suspects the Hurlbert who reviewed many books for the *World* during the 1860s and 1870s would have dealt harshly with his own hasty potboiler on France. The *Saturday Review,* for example, dismissed his enthusiasm for a French monarch. The votes monarchists polled in the 1880s were better seen as a protest against "the misgovernment of others" than as a mandate for a new king. In effect, monarchists had become the party out of power. They too contended for popular favor, and they had no more claim to permanent authority than any other electoral competitor. By adopting "the spirit and style of a rather exceptionally bitter French Royalist," the *Saturday Review* concluded, Hurlbert prevented his message from being taken seriously.[18]

France and the Republic deserves our attention here because it offers important insights into Hurlbert's outlook. For him, the French Revolution of 1789–94 was not a dimly remembered episode from long ago. He saw it, instead, as the most important cautionary tale in modern history—how even the most sophisticated social order might fall into fanatic hands and lapse into barbarism. Had he lived to see what happened in Germany during the 1930s and 1940s, he would have identified the Nazis as the true heirs to the Revolutionists of 1789. Above all, Hurlbert always saw the American Civil War as a conflict that had the potential to replicate what had happened in France seventy years before. Majorities of Northerners, of course, would have disagreed with him, especially after war forcibly secured reunion, but he continued to see the war's outbreak both as a catastrophic failure of statesmanship and as a leap into the dark that could well have destroyed everything it was supposedly waged to save. The last significant thing Hurlbert ever wrote, *France and the Republic* sheds additional light on his motives for creating "The Diary of a Public Man," and it touches many of his life's key strands.

North-South disagreements during the 1840s and 1850s challenged Americans to take sides. Ardent minorities in each region did so first, thereby intensifying the sectional crisis; larger numbers held back until obliged to affirm wartime allegiances. Hurlbert, who was both Southern and Northern, faced an impossible choice. He was sufficiently Southern to be inoculated in advance against the perfectionist mentality he encountered in Boston and Cambridge. He could not follow the militantly assertive Northernism of his college chum,

18. J. P. Daughton, *An Empire Divided: Religion, Republicanism, and the Making of French Colonialism, 1880–1914* (New York: Oxford Univ. Press, 2006), 8–9; *Saturday Review,* Apr. 12, 1890.

Thomas Wentworth Higginson, who eventually supported John Brown and commanded a black regiment in the war. For several years during the mid-1850s, Hurlbert did echo Josiah Quincy's complaint that slaveholders exercised too much power in Washington. Soon, however, he distanced himself from all North-South sectional recrimination.

Yet Hurlbert was far too cosmopolitan to become narrowly Southern. Both in Massachusetts and abroad, he encountered liberal influences that never could be reconciled with the defensive ideology of the slave South. Few Americans of his generation were so at home in Europe. Hurlbert traveled there extensively when young, and he lived abroad for the last decade-plus of his life. He was fluent in French, Spanish, German, and Italian, and he read widely in each. Several of his closest friends, such as Rosebery and the journalist Sala, were British. And many of his American friends led transatlantic lives, including William Wetmore Story, the American sculptor, who lived in Rome from 1856 until his death in 1895; and J.C. Bancroft Davis, who held American diplomatic posts in England in the 1850s and Germany in the 1870s.[19] As a young visitor to Europe, Hurlbert encountered many who faulted American slavery. Charles Kingsley's novel depicts how the slightly fictionalized Hurlbert demonstrated to his friends and hosts in 1856 that his heart was in the right place. That marked the peak of his limited affinity for the Anglo-American reformist outlook.

After he returned to the United States, Hurlbert decided that the reform agenda threatened both national unity and political stability. By 1859 he had abandoned the Republican Party and instead embraced Stephen A. Douglas, the one remaining national political leader whose base of support crossed North-South sectional lines. When Douglas failed to assemble majorities either north or south, Lincoln was elected president and disunion followed. "The Diary of a Public Man" shows how intently Hurlbert observed the spiral of political disintegration during the winter of 1860–61, and how predisposed he was to hope that some kind of Union-saving compromise might yet be effected. In his view, unrealistic Northern antislavery utopianism had combined with heedless Southern defiance to produce an outcome that few understood or expected.

Civil war had the potential to unhinge the high level of political stability and social peace that most white Americans took for granted. At first, few people north or south appreciated the potential danger that lurked. Northern Repub-

19. All four attended Hurlbert's wedding in 1884.

licans insisted that the South never would break up the Union. When the unexpected happened, many Northerners convinced themselves that the Southern
Confederacy was a house of cards. One military defeat would shatter the secessionist conspiracy and allow the true Unionists in the South to regain control of
affairs there. Many Southerners likewise lost touch with reality. A blaze of patriotism swept the Confederacy when the war started. Its citizens confidently expected that cowardly Yankees would cut and run when they saw what they were
up against. Even Southern leaders such as Robert Toombs and Judah Benjamin
shared the widespread popular delusions, as Hurlbert was amazed to discover
when he visited Richmond in June 1861.

Far sooner than most Americans, Hurlbert learned firsthand that both sides
misunderstood what was happening. They blindly sacrificed the precious legacy
of stable governance, and opened the door both to civil war and to extralegal
fanaticism. Hurlbert narrowly escaped mob vengeance in South Carolina and
Georgia when his quixotic peacemaking role boomeranged. That brush with disaster in June 1861—followed by more than a year of Confederate captivity in
Richmond—hardened him. For the rest of his life, Hurlbert gave highest priority to order and stability. The use of political power to accomplish what might
now be called social engineering struck him as intrinsically dangerous, a way to
raise expectations that never could be fulfilled. Repeatedly his columns in the
New York World during the next two decades reflected these conservative sensibilities. The great problems facing the defeated South, he wrote in November
1865, were "social disorder" and "anarchy." Nothing could be accomplished in
the South without "civic order and local self-government." Only if "the foundations of social order" were rebuilt and property securely protected by law could
the South attract outside investment to revive its shattered economy. Seeing
Radical Reconstruction as an assault on Southern property, he turned a blind
eye to the outrageous tactics used against the new state governments in the
South. He lauded Andrew Johnson for standing firm against "the revolutionary
measures of the Radicals" and condemned the effort to impeach the beleaguered
president.[20] Later, as has just been noted, Hurlbert saw both Charles Stewart Parnell and Henry George as dangerous subversives who stood ready to undermine
both property and political order.

If read from the perspective of Hurlbert's entire adult life, *France and the Re-*

20. *New York World,* Nov. 16, 1865, Nov. 2, 1867, Feb. 24, 26, 1868.

public helps us to understand why the author saw the world as he did. His copious historical memory and his affinity with European conservatism assured that France's enormous convulsion between 1789 and 1794 would remain central to his outlook. The fumbling efforts of late-nineteenth-century French Republicans to come to terms with the Revolution and to celebrate its centennial infuriated Hurlbert. He castigated the "nonsense" perpetrated by those who saw a bright side to the Revolution—nothing could be "wider of the truth" than their efforts to glorify a perverted legacy.[21]

Hurlbert echoed Edmund Burke's indictment of the French Revolution. In an 1867 editorial, he lauded Burke as "the greatest philosophical statesman of modern times"—"or of any time"—and assigned special value to his "most celebrated production," *Reflections on the Revolution in France.*[22] Burke lamented that France had rebelled against "a mild and lawful monarch" as if he were "the most illegal usurper or the most sanguinary tyrant." Rather than building on existing foundations so as to both preserve and reform, France had chosen a path of total destruction and mob rule, characterized by "assassination, massacre, and confiscation." The Revolution's "monstrous fiction" of perfect equality served only to "aggravate and embitter," because "real inequality" never could be removed. The assault on property rights ruined large proprietors, who were "ballast in the vessel of the commonwealth." So, too, Burke condemned destruction of the church. Under the guise of rooting out "superstition and error," anticlerical fanatics were undermining society's most important stabilizing institution.[23]

The most robust modern treatment of the subject, historian Simon Schama's bicentennial epic, *Citizens: A Chronicle of the French Revolution,* largely vindicates Hurlbert's horror at the course of events between 1789 and 1794. Schama's powerful narrative indicts his fellow professionals for tending "to avert their eyes" from the wholesale violence unleashed by the Revolution. In the Vendée, for example, a rural region of western France south of the Loire, the Revolution killed one-third of the pre-1789 population, approximately one-quarter

---

21. Hurlbert, *France and the Republic,* 180.

22. *New York World,* Dec. 20, 1867.

23. Edmund Burke, *Reflections on the Revolution in France* (New York: The Liberal Arts Press, 1955), 40, 42, 44, 58, 78, 120–23, 131–35, 195–98. It may be more than just coincidence that Hurlbert's rhetorical arsenal included some Burkean elements—"folly," "wild," "absurd," and an array of words that begin with "dis-."

million people. Schama challenges those who describe the operation of "impersonal historical forces" but do not assign responsibility to human perpetrators. In his view, "intellectual cowardice and moral self-delusion" have blinded historians to "hideous atrocities." They fail to see how the Revolution dehumanized its victims and fueled the thirst for summary convictions and executions—anticipating precisely the way twentieth-century totalitarians rode to power on a comparably "militarized nationalism."[24]

Schama punctures the key tenets of Revolutionary hagiography. Did ordinary folk under the old regime suffer more severe oppression than their counterparts elsewhere in Europe, or in the wider world? No. Instead, a series of contingencies and "unforeseen consequences" loosed a "politics of paranoia" that destroyed the existing structure of authority without being able to substitute any coherent alternative. Did the Revolution open the door to a new era of material well-being? Again, no; "many trades went into steep decline" while "the rural poor gained very little at all from the Revolution." Perhaps most heretically, Schama strips the Revolution of its modern veneer. Enlightened liberal elites did have a progressive agenda, but the "mighty passions" stirred by the Revolution came primarily from those who feared or resented the chrysalid bourgeois society. The Revolution suddenly validated types of behavior that subverted all law and social order.[25]

It must be emphasized that the American Civil War rarely degenerated into anything comparable to the French Revolution. Both Union and Confederate governments enjoyed strong popular foundations. Each preserved a high degree of order within its respective sphere, once the Confederacy brought under control the epidemic of mob violence that surged in early and mid-1861. Soldiers suffered terrible casualties, because of both enemy bullets and invisible microbes. But only in areas where neither government exercised control—principally in parts of West Virginia, East Tennessee, and Missouri—were civilian lives ever in continuing peril. Overly provincial American historians too often assume that William Tecumseh Sherman's march through Georgia or Philip Sheridan's campaign in Virginia's Shenandoah Valley—assaults on property rather than persons—exposed civilians to the full horror of modern warfare. The residents of the Vendée would gladly have changed places with Georgians and Virgin-

24. Simon Schama, *Citizens: A Chronicle of the French Revolution* (New York: Knopf, 1989), 631, 791–92, 858–60.

25. Ibid., 183–99, 310–22, quotations on xiv, 853, 855.

ians. So, too, would the many civilians trapped by partisan warfare during World War II in Yugoslavia, Vietnamese peasants caught in the middle during the American war, or the victims of genocide in Armenia, Nazi Europe, Cambodia, Kurdistan, Rwanda, and Darfur.

Plainly Hurlbert exaggerated. The American Civil War was a terrible ordeal, but neither contending government was totalitarian, and each waged war with restraints that have sadly eroded in the twentieth century. The Third French Republic never imitated the First, notwithstanding Hurlbert's shrill warnings. More generally, he imagined that governments on both sides of the Atlantic contained dangerous seeds of self-destruction as the age of industry advanced. Perhaps his fears were vindicated posthumously by the ghastly spectacles of World Wars I and II, but he shared the transatlantic conservative mindset that persuaded itself social upheaval and political breakdown were imminent in the 1880s.

Hurlbert's anxieties were shaped by his own life. In the summer of 1861 he discovered firsthand what it meant to become the target of rampaging popular suspicion. He spent three days at a hotel in Atlanta

> receiving the visits of not a few intelligent persons, who deplored the madness of the mob they dared not gainsay, and whose admissions, unconsciously made, convinced me that the worst stories we have heard at the North of violence perpetrated on the poor and friendless Northern men in the early stages of this conflict, can hardly have been exaggerated. I cannot doubt what my own fate would have been, had I been an entire stranger in the land, without the means or the temper of self-defence.

Even when taken to the Confederate capital at Richmond, he remained in danger. One observer reported that "the outside feeling in this city against Hurlbert is very strong, and if turned loose here he would no doubt be summarily dealt with."[26] The Old South had become increasingly intolerant of dissenters in the late antebellum era, and the hysteria was never worse than during the first months after the war started. Then, especially, every stranger was considered an enemy unless he could somehow prove himself a friend. This small peek into the

26. *New York Times,* Sept. 11, 1862; William S. Bassford to J. I. Whitaker, June 25, 1861, in *Charleston Daily Courier,* July 3, 1861, in Box 39 of the Frank Maloy Anderson Papers, Library of Congress.

depths of hell branded Hurlbert forever. His near disaster impelled him to re-examine the political crisis of 1860–61 that had loosed such terrifying and un-predictable forces. When he wrote about Ireland and France, his outlook was grounded in his own—and his country's—experiences.

12

SCANDAL AND SUMMATION

Hurlbert's good looks deteriorated as he aged. Most of his hair disappeared. The remaining fringe above his ears and neck turned white, as did his drooping mustache. Too much good food left him "pudgy and out of shape," with wrinkled hands, baggy eyes, and a lined face "that told of the life he led." Nonetheless, he retained "the charm of manner" and the "marvelous flow of wit, anecdote and information as in olden times."[1] He also retained sufficient appeal to attract a wife.

In August 1884, not long after he had been forced out at the *World* and moved to England, Hurlbert married Katharine Parker Tracy (1840–1922), the daughter of a noted New York jurist, William Tracy. She was a cousin by marriage of the financier J. Pierpont Morgan, and was reported to have brought to the marriage "a fortune in her own right of some $6,000 a year." Both Hurlbert and his bride had reached a "mature age." Several years later a reporter described "Kittie" Hurlbert as "a stately, portly woman, with brown hair and eyes" who scrutinized the world through a "tortoise shell lorgnette."[2] The ceremonies took place at a picturesque "little parish church" in Yorkshire, with a "brilliant assemblage" of English aristocracy in attendance. Hulbert's chum Rosebery had become one of the fast-rising political leaders of the realm. As noted previously, also present were the diplomat and lawyer J. C. Bancroft Davis; the American sculptor William Wetmore Story, long expatriated to Rome; and the English journalist George Augustus Sala, all with their spouses. Hurlbert was reported "full of gloomy forebodings" before the event.[3] His motive for marrying remains unclear. He may have been attracted by the relative financial security his wife

---

1. *New York World,* Sept. 8, 1895. Here, as explained in chapter 4, note 6, I continue to use three unusually detailed biographical sketches of Hurlbert that appeared in the *New York World* on September 7, 8, and 9, 1895, at the time of his death.

2. *New York Times,* Aug. 10, 1884, May 23, Sept. 17, 1922; *New York World,* Sept. 8, 1895; *Boston Herald,* Sept. 7, 1895; Croswell Bowen, *The Elegant Oakey* (New York: Oxford Univ. Press, 1956), 256.

3. *New York Times,* Aug. 10, 1884.

brought to the marriage. But the longtime bachelor may not have been wise to give up his single status. He remained temperamentally unsuited for married life.

Not long afterwards—and just as his books on Ireland and France enjoyed modest success—Hurlbert became enmeshed in a sordid scandal. His efforts to conceal his identity from a new mistress led to a sensational court case and ultimately to his exile from both Britain and the United States. This strange turn of events was startling and yet perfectly in character. In April 1887 he and a twenty-eight-year-old British actress, Gertrude Ellis, who had adopted the *nom de théâtre* of Gladys Evelyn, chanced to travel on the same London omnibus. Apparently he was immediately attracted to her. When she alighted from the bus, he did so too, whereupon he introduced himself as "Wilfrid Murray." The next day he paid her a visit. "Wilfrid Murray" claimed to live with an aged aunt, from whom he wished to shield his private life. By her account, he soon proposed to her. When she accepted, he gave her an engagement ring. During the summer that followed, Gladys Evelyn "was on intimate terms of relationship" with the man she knew as Wilfrid Murray. After suffering a miscarriage in October 1887, Evelyn testified, she went to southern France to recuperate. She expected that Murray soon would arrive to marry her. With his approval, she picked out a dark blue dress for the ceremonies.[4]

The evidence suggests that Hurlbert either tired of Gladys Evelyn's affections by the winter of 1887–88, or that he developed second thoughts about his double life. He stopped answering letters that she directed to him (as Wilfrid Murray) and quit seeing her. He even may have had some connection with an alleged burglary at her apartment, in which some letters that he had sent to her were removed. It was his ill fortune that she encountered him by chance the better part of a year later, whereupon he was again attracted to her, as a moth to a flame.[5]

Not until January 1890, or so she explained, did Gladys Evelyn learn that Hurlbert already was married. At this juncture she apparently began to blackmail him. His old friend Oakey Hall advised him to ignore her demands.[6] Hurlbert, however, tried to buy his way out. These negotiations appear to have foundered because of a disagreement about the price. Meeting in Paris in April 1890, three years after they first had met, Hurlbert offered Evelyn $4,000 plus $650

4. *London Times,* Apr., 15, 20, 1891; *New York World,* Sept. 7, 1895.
5. *London Times,* Apr. 15, 1891.
6. Ibid., Apr. 17, 1891; *New York Herald,* Apr. 17, 1891.

per year "as balm for her wounded heart and reputation."[7] Instead of accepting the proffered settlement, she decided to sue him for £10,000 ($50,000), alleging breach of promise.

Newspapers on both sides of the Atlantic avidly covered the resulting trial, which took place in London in April 1891. Evelyn testified she had pawned her engagement ring to cover gambling losses after a spree at Monte Carlo. She did, however, produce 150 love letters signed by "Wilfrid Murray." Newspapers reported that the letters, some including photographs, were "of the most indecent and revolting character," a sure way to increase salacious public interest. The first highlight of the trial came when Hurlbert was asked to stand, whereupon Evelyn identified him—"I swear that is Wilfrid Murray. I have never known any other Wilfrid Murray."[8]

At the trial, Hurlbert testified that he had never made any promise of marriage to Gladys Evelyn, and that only twice in his life had he so much as met her. Both encounters had been of an "entirely innocent character," in the company of his private secretary, Wilfrid Murray. Since 1881 Murray had worked for him from time to time and had assisted him in the research for his books on Ireland and France. Murray sometimes used aliases, including "Rolland," because he feared Irish terrorists. Hurlbert contended that the incriminating letters must have been written by Murray, who had learned how to imitate Hurlbert's handwriting. Moreover, Murray must have been the person who conducted the relationship with Evelyn. The second highlight of the trial came when Hurlbert was shown a "bundle" of the "improper" letters. "I believe they are in Murray's writing," Hurlbert decided. "I think the writing resembles mine," but "most certainly I never wrote any of them." His lawyers insisted that "no breath of scandal" had ever touched Hurlbert. They denounced the "gross and wicked attempt to extort blackmail from a gentleman of blameless life." And they regretted being unable to produce the elusive Murray, who had disappeared.[9]

Reporters were baffled. "I find scarcely anybody who believes the woman's story" about the promise of marriage, a writer for the New York Herald observed. Her "impure life, her indecent entries in her own diary, her numerous lies and deceptions" deprived Evelyn of "all claim to credence." There was a "general be-

7. New York World, Sept. 7, 1895. Hurlbert and his wife insisted that the unwarranted blackmail threats had begun in 1889 (London Times, Apr. 20, 1891; New York Times, June 26, 1891).

8. London Times, Apr. 15, 20, 1891; New York World, Sept. 7, 1895.

9. London Times, Apr. 16, 17, 20, 1891; New York World, Sept. 7, 1895.

lief" that she had "made a living by this sort of business for years past." Yet however dubious the testimony of the "outcast woman," Hurlbert's explanation of the "vile" letters defied common sense. He "stood the cross-examination without flinching and never varied in his statements," the *Herald* reported, but his "narrative of the ubiquitous and invisible private secretary who was his *alter ego*" was regarded with as much "doubt and suspicion" as the tale of his accuser.[10]

The week of testimony from Hurlbert, Evelyn, and several of her corroborative witnesses left the presiding judge in the case, Lewis W. Cave, in a foul mood. The burly jurist, who "seized points very rapidly, and frequently cut short argument with sharp questions of counsel," described the case as a "very grave" one, "far beyond that in an ordinary breach of promise action." In his summation for the jury, Cave stated that if the defendant had written the "abominable letters," then "his character was utterly blasted." If, however, the defendant was the victim of a conspiracy to extort blackmail, then its perpetrators deserved "prosecution and penal servitude." Purely on the basis of previous reputation, he would be inclined to believe the defendant. The judge found it "almost incredible," however, that a purported forger had composed such a mass of letters that so perfectly "counterfeited the defendant's writing." Cave noted that a number of letters were sent from Ireland and Paris at times the defendant was known to have been in those places, and that the letters included "many French expressions." (The letters posted from Ireland in early 1888, for example, recapitulated Hurlbert's movements as he did his research for *Ireland under Coercion*—Dublin on February 7, Bantry on February 24, Galway on February 29, and so on.) Cave complained that no evidence had been presented to establish the existence of any such person as Wilfrid Murray. He also faulted Hurlbert for failing to produce "Mrs. Hurlbert or some servant" to corroborate instances when Evelyn claimed to have been with Hurlbert but when he claimed to have been out of town. As the judge finished his summation, a "daintily attired lady" who peered through a "gold lorgnette"—Katharine Hurlbert—burst into the chambers and announced, "My Lord, I claim a hearing. I cannot stand here and listen to a parcel of lies." However dramatic her entry, she only appeared after court testimony had ended.[11]

10. *New York Herald*, Apr. 19, 1891; *New York Sun*, Apr. 19, 1891.

11. *London Times*, Apr. 20, 1891; *New York Times*, Apr. 21, 1891; *New York Sun*, Apr. 21, 1891; *New York Herald*, Apr. 21, 1891. Cave has an entry in the *Oxford Dictionary of National Biography*, 10:601.

The jury took just an hour and a half to decide that no promise of marriage had been proven. Evelyn therefore failed to gain any compensation whatsoever. But Hurlbert's technical victory proved hollow. "I do not suppose there is a sane adult in London who is not convinced that he committed flat perjury," one reporter commented. The acquittal could not avert his "melancholy downfall." Hurlbert had been ensnared by his own recklessness. He thought of women as playthings created for his pleasure, not as potential adversaries. Never before had he encountered such a dangerous quarry as Gladys Evelyn. In the fiasco that resulted, it is far from clear which was the hunter and which the prey. Hurlbert assumed that he could enjoy the actress's favors while shielding his real identity. There is little reason, however, to think that she had any commitment to the aging gentleman or that his promises of marriage, such as they may have been, had emotional consequences for her. Testimony at the trial showed that she cohabited with a shadowy paramour named Betham Jackson during much of the time she dallied with Hurlbert.[12]

Gladys Evelyn had judged that she could command a more handsome settlement by threatening legal action, while Hurlbert calculated that she would not press the matter because the letters contained no promise of marriage. So, too, he may have assumed that a male jury would not likely find that her reputation was of a quality that could be compromised—and that she would have the good judgment to recognize the weakness of her position. At that point, however, she launched her equivalent of a nuclear weapon, the Wilfrid Murray letters. Once these devastating documents were introduced into the legal process, Hurlbert vainly attempted to salvage *his* reputation. It is likely that Hurlbert did employ a secretary, and just possible that the secretary learned to imitate his handwriting plausibly, but it entirely strains credulity to claim that the secretary conducted the sleazy affair with Gladys Evelyn. Judge Cave indignantly cast aspersions on this outrageous fiction. The damning letters could not enable Evelyn to win her case, but they ruined Hurlbert. In contemporary jargon, the tawdry business might be called a lose-lose.

In May 1891, a month after the end of the trial, Hurlbert returned to New York City. Newspapers poked fun at his promise to locate the elusive Wilfrid Murray. The *Brooklyn Eagle,* for example, deadpanned tongue-in-cheek that "William Henry Hurlbert arrived from Europe yesterday and Wilfrid Murray

12. *London Times,* Apr. 20, 21, 1891; *New York Times,* Apr. 21, 26, 1891; *New York World,* Sept. 7, 1895.

came over in the same steamer." The once-admired editor had become a public laughingstock. But Hurlbert soon faced more daunting problems. That summer the British director of public prosecutions indicted him for perjury. The new case hinged on the deposition of a handwriting expert, who compared Hurlbert's handwriting with that of "Wilfrid Murray" and pronounced the two identical.[13]

A crisis was reached in late November and early December 1891, when Hurlbert learned that British authorities soon would seek his arrest. Under terms of a new 1889 treaty, which included perjury among extraditable offenses, the United States would have no choice but to comply. A British detective arrived at the Hotel Lenox in New York City, where Hurlbert and his wife had been staying, only to find that they had vanished. Subsequent reports suggested that he might have fled to Mexico, or that he had been "received as a lay brother at the Redemptionist monastery in Rome," but his whereabouts remained a mystery. His disappearance removed him from the public realm.[14]

A few glimmers of evidence show that Hurlbert, working from behind the scenes, persuaded several friends to come to his defense. In July 1892, Sam Ward's nephew, the novelist Marion Crawford, wrote to the *Pall Mall Gazette* to explain that he and Hurlbert, who were "old acquaintances," chanced to have a conversation seven years before, in 1885, about "the peculiarities of handwriting." At that point, or so Crawford recalled, "Mr. Hurlbert then spoke of Wilfrid Murray, and mentioned the fact that he was often not able to distinguish Murray's handwriting from his own." This recollection, in Crawford's estimate, should "go far toward proving that there really was such a man." In late 1893, two additional witnesses surfaced to vouch for Hurlbert. John Gilmer Speed, a grandson of James Speed, Lincoln's attorney general in 1864–65, recalled encountering Murray in London in 1884. Murray, who identified himself as "Mr. Hurlbert's secretary," brought Speed a letter from Hurlbert and "appeared well acquainted with Mr. Hurlbert's affairs and informed as to his movements." In addition, Hurlbert's longtime friend, the sculptor William Wetmore Story, reported that he had encountered Murray in London on the morning of Jubilee Day in June 1887 when Story was visiting with "Mr. and Mrs. Hurlbert" at their Queen's Gate apartment. When Story chanced to go to the study, he "met a man who answered to the name of Wilfred Murray, and who was engaged in earnest conversation with

13. *Brooklyn Eagle*, May 26, 1891; *New York World*, Sept. 7, 1895.
14. *New York Times*, Nov. 27, Dec. 12, 1891, Apr. 7, May 26, 1892; *New York World*, Sept. 7, 1895.

Mr. Hurlbert on some business matter."[15] Notwithstanding the stature of those willing to testify on his behalf, Hurlbert's whereabouts remained unknown.

Not until 1895, over three years after his disappearance, was Hurlbert discovered in Italy.[16] He and his wife were found to be leading "a most secluded life" at an out-of-the-way inn in Nervi, a small town outside Genoa. Nobody in Nervi knew who the two Americans were, nor did they have any visitors or apparent friends. "By merest chance" a trio of New Yorkers, a mother and her two daughters, visited this inn in April 1895. There they encountered the two reclusive expatriates. Although "aged and broken," Hurlbert still loved to talk, and "his conversation was as brilliant as in former years." An audience of ladies rekindled Hurlbert's efforts to wield "his old-time power of fascination." Mrs. Hurlbert explained to the visitors that she and her husband were political refugees who had been "shockingly ill-treated in England." His views on "the Irish question" had met with disfavor in powerful quarters, and "the charge of perjury was trumped up against him."[17]

Shortly thereafter, while visiting at Cadenabbia, a small Italian town bordering Lake Como, Hurlbert suffered a bad fall. At night in a "strange house," he tumbled down "a very steep flight of stone steps." Although he claimed to be "getting on wonderfully well," he was not able "to put pen to paper." His condition deteriorated and he died on September 4, 1895.[18]

The timing of Hurlbert's death assured that the Gladys Evelyn scandal and his subsequent disappearance dominated the obituary notices. The purported

15. *New York Times,* July 10, 1892; *New York Sun,* Dec. 8, 1893.

16. Maud Howe Elliott, the daughter of Sam Ward's illustrious sister, Julia Ward Howe, later wrote that Hurlbert was "saved from a British prison" by "the combined efforts of Lord Rosebery and Mr. [Thomas F.] Bayard." He was "granted liberty on condition that he choose one country and remain an exile there for the rest of his life. He chose Italy, where I saw him often during his last years." Maud Howe Elliott, *Uncle Sam Ward and His Circle* (New York: Macmillan, 1938), 561.

17. *New York Times,* Apr. 21, 1895; *New York World,* Sept. 9, 1895. Maud Howe Elliott likewise echoed this apocryphal Hurlbert canard: "Later, while in England, he was drawn into the perpetual squabble of Irish politics and gained the enmity of one group of politicians by a book he wrote, 'Ireland Under Coercion.' He was pursued and persecuted by his political enemies, who finally brought an action against him" (Elliott, *Uncle Sam Ward and His Circle,* 560).

18. Hurlbert to T. C. Evans, June 24, 1895, in T. C. Evans, "William Henry Hurlbert," *New York Times Saturday Literary Review,* 14 June 1902, p. 408.

"shameful letters," which had been featured at his trial, had been "commented upon everywhere." Even those who had initially been "inclined to support him" rejected Hurlbert's stories about how an alleged impostor had written the letters. It seemed impossible to believe that any other person should chance to write in a manner that so exactly duplicated Hurlbert's handwriting.[19]

Pulitzer's *World*, the newspaper Hurlbert previously had edited and with which he was longest identified, struggled to sum up his puzzling contradictions. He could write "brilliant prose," generate sparkling conversation, and make friends with both men and women as fast as he met them. He had a "profound knowledge" of many different subjects, and he appeared destined, when young, for "great achievements and future fame." But he was a flawed genius whose amoral qualities ultimately undermined him. The "hopes of his friends were unfulfilled," the *World* concluded. His was a life of "wasted opportunities and dissipated brilliancy." The *New York Times*, Hurlbert's other previous newspaper, published an even frostier farewell. Although Hurlbert impressed everyone he met with his "astonishing and unique personality" and appeared capable of doing "whatever he chose," he had never chosen "to do anything in particular." Instead, he had "frittered away his extraordinary endowment" and become "the slave of his own whims and caprices."[20]

A more generous reflection on Hurlbert's life was provided by a kindred spirit, A. Oakey Hall. As we have seen in chapter 4, Hurlbert and "Elegant Oakey" first crossed paths in the 1850s. Both of these talented cosmopolitans gravitated to the Democratic Party and became regulars at its elite Manhattan Club. Ensconced there with friends, Hurlbert was in his element. He was "a talker" who was "remarkable for seldom repeating himself." He could initiate conversations on different topics each evening of the week. "Without much trouble," Hall recalled, Hurlbert could "digest more wine and spirits at one time" than almost anyone else, but he always drank "to the general joy of the whole table." Hall, who was elected mayor of New York City in 1868, boasted that he would rather hold that office than be president of the United States.[21] He fell hard from this pinnacle. The Tweed scandal broke in 1871 during his second term as mayor. Hall had signed many of the padded and fictitious authorizations, and he was

19. *New York World*, Sept. 7, 1895.

20. Ibid., Sept. 8, 1895; *New York Times*, Sept. 9, 1895.

21. *New York World*, Sept. 8, 1895; *Harper's Weekly*, Dec. 12, 1868, p. 797.

widely regarded as a key player in the massive thievery. He escaped conviction at three different trials, but his reputation was irreparably damaged.[22] Hurlbert employed him for several years as city editor for the *World*, where he became "the active editorial director of the paper." Both, however, departed for England in 1883 after the *World* was sold to Joseph Pulitzer.[23] Their intertwined lives and mutual falls from grace gave the two colorful rogues a common bond.

Hall summed up the case for his friend—Hurlbert had "elastic powers of thought," a "masterful command of language," a "marvellous memory," and he was "fascinating in address and manner." Hall also hinted cryptically at Hurlbert's use of "ingenious means" to accomplish ends that were "justified by results." Might we read between the lines that Hall had learned the tightly held secret of his old friend's role in creating "The Diary of a Public Man"? Possibly so. Finally, "after a long life of celibacy"—Hall's aside would have generated howls of amusement—Hurlbert had the "good fortune" to "take to the altar" a "gifted" lady who was suited "to be the companion of a litterateur."[24]

Should one accept the mainstream view that Hurlbert wasted his talents and failed to make his mark? Certainly a case can be made that Hurlbert sold his pen to the highest bidder. He wrote a laudatory campaign biography of George B. McClellan in 1864, even though he knew from his unique vantage point behind Confederate lines that McClellan had bungled the great test of his generalship in the Peninsula Campaign. He became editor of the *World* under circumstances that obliged him to talk up Tom Scott's Texas & Pacific Railroad. When Scott sold the *World* to Jay Gould, Hurlbert remained beholden to someone who had priorities other than high-quality journalism. It was widely rumored that wealthy conservatives paid for his books on Ireland and France. As Eugene Benson lamented, Hurlbert had no fixed principles.[25]

There is, however, another side to the story. Perhaps Hurlbert stood outside

22. Kenneth D. Ackerman, *Boss Tweed: The Rise and Fall of the Corrupt Pol Who Conceived the Soul of Modern New York* (New York: Carroll & Graf, 2005), 61–64, 158–59, 176–80, 242–46, 349–50. Ackerman also is astute on the anti-Irish and anti-Catholic undercurrent among the reformers who toppled William M. Tweed (ibid., 136–38, 183–84).

23. Phyllis Field, "A. Oakey Hall," *American National Biography*, 9:844–45; Bowen, *The Elegant Oakey*, 232–36.

24. *New York World*, Sept. 8, 1895.

25. Eugene Benson, "W. H. Hurlbut," *The Galaxy* (Jan. 1869), 30–34.

the framework of conventional genteel rectitude because he disagreed with Victorian America's prevailing ideologies. Perhaps he did have principles, but not the same ones professed by his critics. Most especially, he rejected the postwar North's celebratory, providential nationalism. He thought those who expressed "moral indignation" about the plight of the slave had unwittingly set the stage for civil war. He likewise thought that an unholy coalition of visionaries and opportunists, ostensibly anxious about the fate of the freedmen, had prolonged the war and mangled the Constitution. In his view, the war should have been prevented, abolition should not have been made a precondition for reunion, and Reconstruction needlessly kept North-South relations in turmoil for years after the end of the war. Plainly these ideas would not have been popular among educated northeastern elites in his own day, and they must appear reprehensible to most historically conscious Americans today. But to say, as Benson did, that Hurlbert was "not saddled with principles" is to miss the way in which he marched to a different drummer. He was a Burkean who lived in a nation that had little use for principled conservatism.[26] Hurlbert cared enough for his own principles in 1860 to quit his comfortable job with the *New York Times*. In other ways too, Hurlbert was his own man. The one-time Unitarian minister abandoned all theistic belief. He disdained what he saw as the empty ritual of conventional churchgoing. He distanced himself most especially from accepted norms of marriage and sexual fidelity, but some women must have welcomed his overtures and shared his radically libertarian code of intimate behavior.

Even if Hurlbert failed to accomplish as much as he could have or should have, one thing he did do was absolutely masterful. His responsibility for "The Diary of a Public Man" has not been established until now, but it was his premier achievement, more formidable even than the obelisk. Like the man who created it, the Diary is an astonishing pyrotechnic display. It is riveting to read, tremendously persuasive, and frustratingly mysterious. Many parts of the Diary are demonstrably valid, even though the document is a memoir rather than a diary. It could not have been composed on the dates indicated, but the after-

---

26. Volume 24 of the *Harvard Classics*, ed. Charles W. Eliot (New York: P. F. Collier & Son, 1909), is devoted to Edmund Burke. Included, of course, are his *Reflections on the Revolution in France*. The editor cautioned: "Much that was hopeful in the Revolution he failed to see." Eliot nonetheless advised that "in this country to-day, with our traditional sympathy with the great upheaval, it is in the highest degree valuable to see these momentous events through the eyes of a great contemporary conservative" (p. 150).

the-fact composer had an extraordinary ability to reconstruct what people were talking about on these dates. I think that it reflects an honest effort at truth telling—other than its fabricated hocus-pocus regarding a nonexistent diarist.

A case can be made, however, that Hurlbert was too erratic and unreliable to be accredited as a legitimate source of information. Although blessed with "a Walter Scott memory" that enabled him to "carry in his brain" the "most accurate impressions," Hurlbert apparently took liberties in reconstructing dialogue. James Gordon Bennett, the longtime editor of the *New York Herald* and one of the giants of American journalism, dubbed Hurlbert a "literary alchemist." He had the "happy faculty of transmuting base metal of style at the mouth or ink-stand of orator or scribe into gold." His writing enabled speakers to say things that they "ought to have said."[27] These skills engendered controversy. A critic once sputtered that Hurlbert employed "the raconteur's trick of putting his own sapience, his own epigrams, his own glittering historical generalizations into the mouth of somebody who can no longer deny it." Thus (with reference to one of Hurlbert's books), "Gen. Grant, for example, talks Hurlbertese with a glibness that would make his old messmates stare."[28]

I shall be the first to acknowledge that reasonable doubt about the Diary's validity persists, and that considerable mystery remains. Hurlbert was an unconventional genius. He invented a diarist who never existed. He put quotation marks around words that speakers may or may not actually have said. Most of the Diary could not have been based on conversations that he heard with his own ears. An apparent compulsion to live by his own rules clouded his last years with scandal, so that he died in exile, a fugitive from the law. One would prefer a more credible source of information. For good reason, historians disdain those who blend fact with fiction. The question, ultimately, is this—should those who are committed to finding historical truth exclude "The Diary of a Public Man" because it is not the diary it claims to be? Or should we consider it an unusual hybrid, grounded in reality but in the end neither absolutely authentic nor purely spurious?

Historians never can "reconstruct a dead world in its completeness," Simon

27. Recollection of A. Oakey Hall, *New York World*, Sept. 8, 1895. Widely admired modern memoirs—such as Russell Baker's *Growing Up* or Barack Obama's *Dreams from My Father*—likewise rely on reconstructed dialogue. But an historian could not dare to follow their example in remembering exact words spoken twenty or fifty years before.

28. *New York Times*, Apr. 27, 1890.

Schama has shrewdly noted. "However thorough or revealing their documentation," they are "doomed to be forever hailing someone who has just gone around the corner and out of earshot." The "teasing gap separating a lived event and its subsequent narration" leaves us with "nothing more than broken lines of communication to the past." Novelist John Updike reached the same conclusion after spending parts of several years trying to write history. "The passage of time takes everything with it," he decided. Any "allegedly historical account" loses "most of the artifacts of our daily life, all but a few of our spoken words, and all of our precious feelings."[29] William Henry Hurlbert attempted an ingenious solution to these manifold problems. He wrote about the past, but he pretended that the past was the present—and he even placed himself at the center of the action. This conflation of past and present, accompanied by the concoction of a nonexistent diarist, scandalously violated the norms of historical scholarship. Yet Hurlbert's audacity must elicit a more complex response than mere censure. His construction technique was unorthodox—indeed, deceitful—but the materials with which he built appear to meet the historical test. It was a virtuoso performance that nobody else would have dared to attempt.

29. Simon Schama, *Dead Certainties (Unwarranted Speculations)* (New York: Knopf, 1991), 320, 325; John Updike, *Buchanan Dying: A Play* (New York, 1974; rpr. Mechanicsburg, PA: Stackpole Books, 2000), x.

EPILOGUE
"The Diary of a Public Man" and the Lincoln Legend

Let us conclude by assessing the broader significance of "The Diary of a Public Man." It long was regarded as valid by historians of the first rank—Frederic Bancroft, Roy Franklin Nichols, Allan Nevins, and David Potter—each of whom had a fine command of archival materials pertaining to the secession winter. Why did they find it compelling? They recognized that it contains information known only to those who have invested deeply in the sources. The Diary's basic architecture reflected the crisis as it unfolded, not as it appeared through hindsight. Its "tone, accuracy, and scope" rang true.[1] Although Hurlbert could not have been party to most of the private discussions recorded in the Diary, he provided unforgettable glimpses of what was being said behind closed doors. The Diary captured the "tense atmosphere just preceding the Civil War with a vividness that makes it seem as yesterday," noted Lincoln's biographer, James G. Randall. Its author "showed remarkable skill and accurate knowledge of events and incidents unavailable to the wider public."[2]

David Potter came closest to understanding the true nature of the Diary. He saw that it abounded with details that could never have been imagined—and that its contents repeatedly had been verified by subsequent disclosures. But he realized too that its "taint of anonymity" raised questions that could not be resolved. If Potter did not quite grasp the nettle, he nonetheless defined it. Here were "astonishing" revelations made by someone "who possessed an authori-

1. Frederic Bancroft, *The Life of William H. Seward* (2 vols.; New York: Harper & Brothers, 1899–1900), 2:43n. Bancroft, who had more basis for so judging than anyone else, thought the diarist must have been "an intimate friend of Seward" (ibid.).

2. James G. Randall, "Has the Lincoln Theme Been Exhausted?" *American Historical Review* 41 (1936): 277–79; James G. Randall, *Lincoln the Liberal Statesman* (New York: Dodd, Mead & Co., 1947), 31. We saw in chapter 1 that Randall tried and failed to identify the diarist. This frustrating experience made him less willing than his elite contemporaries to accept the Diary's authenticity.

tative personal knowledge of affairs at the time of secession"—together with a diarist who vanished into the ether like Alice's Cheshire cat.[3]

Potter showed that when Lincoln became president he still hoped to secure voluntary reunion. Only during his first weeks in office was he driven to choose between peace and Union. The Diary anticipates Potter's Lincoln—whipsawed by conflicting advice and uncertain whether to risk war. Potter originally had used the Diary as a source for *Lincoln and His Party in the Secession Crisis.* He subsequently admitted that he would not do so again because the Diary was "if not a forgery, at least not what it purported to be." But Potter's account of decision making in early 1861 remained consistent with the Diary.[4]

The diarist knew things that must be included in any serious history of the secession winter. He knew that few either north or south in early 1861 realized that the most violent convulsion in the Western world since the Napoleonic Wars lay just ahead. He knew that Lincoln hoped to preserve the Union without war when he took office on March 4. He knew that William H. Seward and Stephen A. Douglas were the two most formidable advocates of a peace policy. Not least, the diarist knew that conventional wisdom by mid-March expected the federal government to relinquish Fort Sumter. Crack reporters working for top newspapers zeroed in on the story, and it was promptly telegraphed across the country. Some Republicans were chagrined that Lincoln had backed down. But moderates north and south breathed a sigh of relief, hopeful that war had been averted and that cooler heads would prevail. Even when the expected withdrawal from Sumter did not happen, hopes persisted for a peaceful resolution to the crisis. Until the moment when fighting started in mid-April, it was widely assumed that the situation somehow could be stabilized without resort to armed force. For those who considered war unthinkable, it was possible to lose sight of the terrible impasse—the Deep South claimed to have become a separate nation, whereas Lincoln insisted that it could not do so.

In all these respects, the Diary sticks closer to the evidence than some of Lincoln's modern admirers. They depict, instead, a farsighted Lincoln who always understood the situation better than anyone else, and who had an un-

3. David M. Potter, review of *The Diary of a Public Man, and a Page of Political Correspondence, Stanton to Buchanan,* ed. F. Lauriston Bullard, in *Journal of Southern History* 13 (Feb. 1947): 118–19.

4. David M. Potter, *Lincoln and His Party in the Secession Crisis* (New Haven: Yale University Press, 1942, 1962), preface to the 1962 edition, xxxvi.

canny sense of how the future would unfold. They promote what might be called the "Lincoln Legend." Doris Kearns Goodwin's acclaimed composite biography, *Team of Rivals,* celebrates Lincoln's management during the winter before the war started. He allowed the would-be compromiser Seward to make conciliatory overtures toward the disaffected South, and he even incorporated many of Seward's words in his inaugural address. But Lincoln also "retained an astonishing degree of control over an increasingly chaotic and potentially devastating situation." While Seward aged ten years in just a few months, Lincoln alone had the composure and inner strength to make the right decisions. Goodwin's massive tome—880 pages of text and notes—never touches Lincoln's famous disavowal, "I claim not to have controlled events, but confess plainly that events have controlled me."[5]

The purpose of the Lincoln Legend is to square Lincoln's prewar stance with what were to become his supreme accomplishments—the preservation of the Union and the destruction of slavery. Lincoln's enthusiasts cannot accept that he experienced any uncertainty on the eve of war. They downplay or ignore his repeated assurances that he had no intention of interfering with slavery in the states where it already existed. Lincoln offered to support a constitutional amendment to this effect in his inaugural address—but this is not something Harold Holzer chooses to mention in his recent *Lincoln President-Elect.* Instead, Holzer depicts Lincoln as someone who, in contrast to Seward, refused to countenance the permanence of slavery. James Oakes also finds Lincoln a radical at heart, as eager to abolish slavery as to restore the Union. He and like-minded Republicans "knowingly accepted the possibility of war."[6] Goodwin and Holzer and Oakes stand apart from Potter, who contended that Lincoln never expected to become a war president or to preside over the forcible destruction of the slave system.

In Potter's view, Lincoln "grossly underestimated the extent of the crisis."

5. Doris Kearns Goodwin, *Team of Rivals: The Political Genius of Abraham Lincoln* (New York: Simon & Schuster, 2005), 303–4; Lincoln to Albert G. Hodges, Apr. 4, 1864, in Roy P. Basler, ed., *The Collected Works of Abraham Lincoln* (9 vols.; New Brunswick: Rutgers Univ. Press, 1953–55), 7:281–83. Lincoln's observation was no offhand comment. It occurred in a carefully crafted statement on the war effort that directly anticipated his second inaugural address.

6. Harold Holzer, *Lincoln President-Elect: Abraham Lincoln and the Great Secession Winter 1860–1861* (New York: Simon & Schuster, 2008), 213–14; James Oakes, "A Different Lincoln," *New York Review of Books,* April 9, 2009, pp. 43–45.

When he took office, he remained hopeful that he could secure reunion without war. But he was confronted immediately with Major Anderson's warning that he could not maintain himself much longer at Sumter. Lincoln then faced a dilemma worse than anything his predecessors ever had confronted—worse even than James Madison's plight in the late summer and autumn of 1814 after the British had burned Washington. If Lincoln abandoned Sumter, he could limit secession to the seven Deep South states. But this would appear to acquiesce in Confederate independence. Should Lincoln attempt to hold Sumter, however, the crisis likely would turn violent—he had plenty of reason to suspect that Confederates would fight. Then the secession contagion might spread to the Upper South—to Virginia, North Carolina, and Tennessee—each more populous and formidable than any seceding state. There was good reason why the Public Man reported a "haggard, worn look" on the president's face (262). Lincoln himself subsequently disavowed any clairvoyance and confessed that "all the troubles and anxieties of his life" had not matched what he encountered in March and early April. The unexpected challenges during his first weeks in office were "so great that could I have anticipated them, I would not have believed it possible to have survived them."[7]

The most astute modern Lincoln scholars distance themselves from the Lincoln Legend. David Donald places Lincoln's 1864 disclaimer—"events have controlled me"—as the frontispiece to his biography. In Donald's view, Lincoln was reluctant "to take the initiative and make bold plans; he preferred to respond to the actions of others." During the Sumter crisis, he wrestled with the conflicting principles propounded in his inaugural address—a pledge to avoid "bloodshed or violence . . . unless it be forced on the national authority," while also maintaining possession of "the property, and places belonging to the government."[8] Richard Carwardine and Michael Burlingame celebrate Lincoln's ability to hold on to his principles and keep his party together. But they also recognize that the new president found it difficult to judge the situation in the South. Although Lincoln "showed an impressive and instinctive grasp of strategic essentials," Car-

---

7. Potter, *Lincoln and His Party*, 315–16; Theodore C. Pease and James G. Randall, eds., *The Diary of Orville Hickman Browning* (2 vols.; Springfield: Illinois State Historical Library, 1925, 1933) 1:475–76; Michael Burlingame, ed., *With Lincoln in the White House: Letters, Memoranda, and Other Writings of John G. Nicolay, 1860–1865* (Carbondale: Southern Illinois Univ. Press, 2000), 46.

8. David Herbert Donald, *Lincoln* (New York: Simon & Schuster, 1995), frontispiece, 15, 283–84; Basler, *Collected Works of Lincoln*, 4:266.

wardine writes, he misread "the southern surge toward secession" and over-estimated the tenacity of Southern Unionism.[9] Burlingame depicts the new president as a tower of strength, forced by circumstance to collaborate with an intrusive busybody—Seward—who thought he understood the South better than "naïve stiff-back Republicans like Lincoln." However, Burlingame also unearthed additional evidence that Lincoln, like Seward, saw Southern Unionists as key allies in overcoming secession. He sent them private assurances of his conservative intentions: "Tell them that I will execute the fugitive slave law better than it has ever been. I can do that. Tell them I will protect slavery in the States where it exists. I can do that. Tell them that they shall have all the offices south of the Mason & Dixon line if they will take them. I will send nobody down there as long as they will execute the offices themselves." That overture was made in February. Two months later, on April 15, Lincoln demanded that states in the Upper South either "make war against fellow Southerners" or "join them in secession"—and Burlingame faults his "questionable judgment" in doing so.[10]

Four important new histories of the political crisis that led to war have appeared in recent years. Especially when read together, these volumes provide fuller context for understanding Lincoln and fresh reminders of the excruciating uncertainties that hung over everything in early 1861. Edward L. Ayers looks at Pennsylvanians and Virginians who, "if left to themselves," would never have gone to war—but who, when forced to choose sides, did so "with a startling passion." No book better depicts the rival nationalisms that suddenly took shape in April 1861, recasting identities and transforming "deep structures of interest

9. Richard Carwardine, *Lincoln: A Life of Purpose and Power* (New York: Knopf, 2006), 140, 164. The Upper South is offstage for Carwardine. He does not know why Montgomery Blair's appointment to the cabinet appalled Southern Unionists, or why they reacted so adversely to Lincoln's April 15 proclamation for 75,000 troops (ibid., 155, 171).

10. Michael Burlingame, *Abraham Lincoln: A Life* (2 vols.; Baltimore: Johns Hopkins Univ. Press, 2008), 1:707–8, 723; 2:120, 135–36. Burlingame pays more attention to the South than other Lincoln scholars, but he mistakenly slams John A. Gilmer, Seward's key Upper South ally and would-be cabinet appointee, for writing a defiant letter on April 17 that revealed his true colors (ibid., 1:723). The letter actually was written by an inconsequential Douglas Democrat who happened to share the same last name. Gilmer's heartbroken response to the outbreak of war was communicated to Seward on April 21 (William H. Seward Papers, University of Rochester, New York). See Daniel W. Crofts, *Reluctant Confederates: Upper South Unionists in the Secession Crisis* (Chapel Hill: Univ. of North Carolina Press, 1989), 340.

and belief." Nelson Lankford describes how a fault line "zigzagged" across Virginia and Maryland with "lightning speed," in ways that were "by no means decided or preordained." He contends that "the story did not have to turn out the way it did"—and that nobody in early 1861 could have known what the future held. William W. Freehling rejects the idea of a Southern monolith and downplays the role of "impersonal drives" and "detached forces." He explains how a militant secessionist minority was able to impose its will on larger numbers of white Southerners to create an outcome that few expected. Russell McClintock revisits Northern decision making during the secession winter. He respectfully rehabilitates the efforts by Seward and Douglas to preserve the peace. Lincoln too "leaned as far toward conciliation as he could without sacrificing federal authority," McClintock writes, but ultimately the new president concluded that it would be worse to abandon Sumter than to risk war.[11] Neither Ayers nor Lankford nor Freehling nor McClintock displays any ill will toward Lincoln—and McClintock has written the most persuasive defense of Lincoln's secession-crisis role ever published. Yet they refuse to credit Lincoln with clairvoyance, and their work transcends the limitations of the Lincoln Legend.

"The Diary of a Public Man" centers on Sumter. The fort suddenly blazed to public attention when Major Anderson moved his forces there on December 26. It remained in the headlines in early January, culminating on January 9 with the unsuccessful federal resupply effort, when Confederate cannons prevented *The Star of the West* from landing and war appeared imminent. What Potter calls a "tacit understanding" between Union and Confederate authorities allowed the crisis to pass, however, so that Sumter was much less in the news between mid-January and early March.[12] The Diary accurately captured both the late December and early January spotlight on Sumter, and the subsequent hiatus. But as soon as Lincoln took office, the Sumter issue once again reared its troublesome head. The final segment of the Diary focuses on the danger that Sumter posed

11. Edward L. Ayers, *In the Presence of Mine Enemies: War in the Heart of America, 1859–1863* (New York: Norton, 2003), 187, 415; Nelson D. Lankford, *Cry Havoc! The Crooked Road to Civil War, 1861* (New York: Viking Penguin, 2007), 6–7, 235; William W. Freehling, *The Road to Disunion*, Vol. 2: *Secessionists Triumphant, 1854–1861* (New York: Oxford Univ. Press, 2007), xiv; Russell McClintock, *Lincoln and the Decision for War: The Northern Response to Secession* (Chapel Hill: Univ. of North Carolina Press, 2008), 248.

12. Potter, *Lincoln and His Party*, 271.

for Lincoln's new administration. The Diary concludes, on March 15, when a decision to relinquish the outpost apparently had been made. In all of these particulars, the Diary synchronizes perfectly with the way events occurred.

During the first two weeks of Lincoln's presidency, would-be peacemakers and conciliators, led by Seward and Douglas, saw the catastrophic potential of the Sumter situation. The Diary precisely pinpoints the multiple dilemmas it created. The Confederate commissioners insisted that Sumter be abandoned. Seward, who could neither recognize nor rebuff them, stalled for time by leading them to believe that Lincoln soon would surrender the beleaguered fort. It was far better, Seward thought, to remove federal forces from Sumter than to risk war by trying to retain it. He believed that secession could be reversed if war could be averted. Seward conveyed the same news about Sumter to leading Unionists in the Upper South. They kept telling him that giving up the fort would preserve the peace and allow them to retain and solidify their control in Virginia, North Carolina, and Tennessee. Seward agreed. As noted in chapter 6, only someone with exceptionally fine inside contacts would have known that Seward had established a secret line of communication to George W. Summers, the Union leader at the Virginia Convention.[13] Not least, the diarist also understood that Sumter threatened the structure of Northern party lines. The Republican Party stood on the verge of rupture, just having assumed power. As the Diary ends, Douglas appeared to have become the spokesman for the administration in the Senate, and members of the president's own party were chafing with discontent.

Concocting all of this purely from memory long after the fact would have been impossible. The diarist needed an exceptional memory combined with access to high-quality written records—quite possibly including his own notes or a diary from the time. Even with these, Hurlbert also had to do a remarkable job of suppressing all awareness of what happened after mid-March 1861. The vast convulsion of civil war and its continuing aftershocks during Reconstruction must have made it a huge challenge to recapture the mental world of the immediate prewar period. Take, for example, Seward's hope (which the diarist largely shared) that abandoning Sumter might avert war and lead to peaceable reunion (266). Seward assumed that prosecession allegiances in the Deep South still could be reversed. By the end of March, however, some of his would-

13. Crofts, *Reluctant Confederates*, 275–76, 301; *Nation* 29 (1879): 383–84.

be allies in the Upper South began to see that the Deep South was irrevocably estranged, so that a policy ostensibly aimed at peaceful reunion might in fact be leading toward peaceful separation. For this reason especially, Lincoln ultimately decided to try to hold Sumter.[14]

Briefly in mid-March, however, it appeared that the peace policy provided a delicate bridge to link the conciliators in Washington with the Unionists in the Upper South. As we have seen, the diarist knew all about these contacts. On March 11 and 12, based on alleged conversations with Douglas and Seward, the diarist noted that sentiment was building for a national convention "at which all the existing differences could be radically treated" (269). The Upper South's refusal to support secession was an essential precondition for peaceable reunion. The diarist understood the situation there. When a visitor just in from Montgomery and Charleston predicted that Virginia soon would secede, the diarist "gave him my reasons for believing that nothing of the sort was to be expected" (262). He was confident that the Upper South would stand firm so long as peace was preserved, with assurances arriving from Summers "that the prospect of defeating the secessionists in the [Virginia] Convention brightens all the time" (270). During March, Virginia's Unionists maintained the two-to-one majority they had gained at the polls in early February. But the diarist's guarded confidence in a peaceful outcome to the crisis soon became wishful thinking. When forced to choose sides in a war, immense numbers of Virginians who hated secession sided with the South. After mid-April, Virginia effectively was out of the Union, and for the next four years the state became the most intensely scrutinized military theater of the war.[15]

Modern slang would call it a "stretch" to get "The Diary of a Public Man" back into the historical lexicon. But that is where it belongs. It was not a diary. Instead, it was both a work of imagination and a contribution to history. It belongs in the same category that historian C. Vann Woodward defined for Mary Chesnut, the observant South Carolinian who transformed skeletal notations made during wartime into something far more polished long after the fact.[16] The two productions were comparable but not identical. Unlike Chesnut, Hurlbert only infrequently could have been direct witness to the discussions he portrays. And

14. Crofts, *Reluctant Confederates*, 283–95.
15. Ibid., 276–79, 334–52; Ayers, *In the Presence of Mine Enemies*, 95–187.
16. C. Vann Woodward, ed., *Mary Chesnut's Civil War* (New Haven: Yale Univ. Press, 1981).

only he had the audacity to fabricate the persona of a diarist who never existed. But both tried to tell the truth as they remembered it. And he may well have had access to more robust documentary underpinnings than she.

Both Chesnut's epic and the alleged extracts printed in the *North American Review* in 1879 appear "to embody the cherished characteristics peculiar to a true diary"—that is, "the freshness and shock of experience immediately recorded" and the "denial of knowledge of the future." Neither, however, is an actual diary. Like Hurlbert, Chesnut composed her apparent diary "twenty years after the events presumed to have been recorded as they happened." Although both exhibited "a keen awareness of history in the making," each had the advantage of hindsight. They knew when they wrote how the future had in fact unfolded. Chesnut "took many liberties," Woodward recognized. She expanded on actual notes taken at the time, and she often introduced "new matters entirely." Her diary was not a diary, Woodward concluded, but "the facts bear her out" and her work has "enduring value."[17] The same must be said for "The Diary of a Public Man."

17. Ibid., xvi–xvii, xxv, xxvii.

APPENDIX

The Text of "The Diary of a Public Man"

Author's Note: The Diary is reprinted as it originally appeared in the *North American Review,* vol. 129. The first installment was printed in August 1879, pp. 125–40.

UNPUBLISHED PASSAGES OF THE SECRET HISTORY OF THE AMERICAN CIVIL WAR

(As a contribution to what may be called the interior history of the American Civil War, the editor of the "North American Review" takes great pleasure in laying before his readers a series of extracts from the diary of a public man intimately connected with the political movement of those dark and troubled times. He is not permitted to make public the whole of this diary, and he has confined his own editorial supervision of it to formulating under proper and expressive headings the incidents and events referred to in the extracts which have been put at his service. When men still living, but not now in the arena of politics, are referred to, it has been thought best to omit their names, save in two or three cases which will explain themselves; and, in regard to all that is set down in the diary, the editor has a firm conviction that the author of it was actuated by a single desire to state things as they were, or at least as he had reason at the time to believe that they were. Those who are most familiar with the true and intimate history of the exciting times covered by this diary will be the most competent judges of the general fidelity and accuracy of this picture of them; nor can it be without profit for the young men of the present generation to be thus brought face to face, as it were, with the doubts, the fears, the hopes, the passions, and the intrigues through which the great crisis of 1861 was reached. It is always a matter of extreme delicacy to decide upon the proper moment at which private memorials of great political epochs should see the light. If there is danger by a premature publicity of wounding feelings which should be sacred, there is danger also in delaying such publications until all those who figured on the stage of political affairs have passed away, and no voice can be lifted to correct or to complete the tales told in their pages. In this instance it is hoped that both of these perils have been avoided. While many of the leading personages whose individual tendencies, ideas, or interest, gravely and decisively affected the cause of American history just before and throughout the Civil War are now no more, many others survive to criticise with intelligence and to elucidate with authority the views and the judgments recorded in this diary from day to day under the stress of each day's crowding story—EDITOR.)

PRESIDENT BUCHANAN AND SOUTH CAROLINA

Washington, December 28, 1860.—A long conversation this evening with Mr. Orr, who called on me, which leaves me more than anxious about the situation. He assures me that he and his colleagues received the most positive assurances to-day from President Buchanan that he would receive them and confer with them, and that these assurances were given them by Mr. B——, who certainly holds the most confidential relations with the President, not only as an editor of the official paper but personally. He declared to Mr. Orr that Anderson's movement from Moultrie to Sumter was entirely without orders from Washington, and offered to bring him into communication with Mr. Floyd on that point, which offer Mr. Orr very properly declined, on the ground that he represented a "foreign state," and could not assume to get at the actions and purposes of the United States Government through any public officer in a private way, but must be first regularly recognized by the head of the United States Government. He said this so seriously that I repressed the inclination to smile which involuntarily rose in me. I have known Mr. Orr so long and like him so much that I am almost equally loath to think him capable of playing a comedy part in such a matter as this, and of really believing in the possibility of the wild scheme upon which the secession of South Carolina seems to have been projected and carried out. He absolutely insists that he sees no constitutional reason why the Federal Government should refuse to recognize the withdrawal of South Carolina from the Union, since the recognition of the Federal Government by South Carolina is conceded to have been essential to the establishment of that Government. He brought up the old cases of North Carolina and Rhode Island, and put at me, with an air of expected triumph, the question, "If Massachusetts had acted on the express language of Josiah Quincy at the time of the acquisition of

Louisiana, declaring the Constitution abolished by that acquisition, what legal authority would there have been in the Executive of the United States to declare Massachusetts in rebellion and march troops to reduce her?" I tried to make him see that the cases were not analogous, but without effect, nor could I bring him to admit my point that the provision made in the Constitution for the regulation of Congressional elections in the several States by Congress itself, in case any State should refuse or neglect to ordain regulations for such elections, carried with it the concession to the Federal Government of an implied power to prevent any particular State from invalidating the general compact by a failure to fulfill its particular obligations. He intimated to me that for his own part he would be perfectly willing to let the claim of the United States over the Federal property in South Carolina be adjudicated by the Supreme Court, under a special convention to that effect between South Carolina and the United States, after the President had recognized the action by which South Carolina withdrew her "delegations of sovereignty" to the Federal Government. He was careful to impress on me, however, that this was simply his own personal disposition, and not his disposition as a Commissioner.

All this was but incidental to his main object in calling on me, which was to urge my coöperation with Mr. Seward to strengthen the hands of the President in ordering Major Anderson back at once to Fort Moultrie. He explained to me that, by this unauthorized transfer of his small force to Fort Sumter, Anderson had immensely strengthened the war secessionists, not only in South Carolina but in other States, who were loudly proclaiming it as unanswerable evidence of an intention on the part of the United States to coerce South Carolina, and to take the initiative in plunging the country into a horrible civil strife, which would be sure to divide the North, and in which the West would eventually find itself on the side of the South. He had seen Mr. Seward during the day, who had fully agreed with him that Anderson's movement was a most unfortunate one, and had suggested that the matter might be arranged if South Carolina would evacuate Fort Moultrie and allow Anderson to reoccupy that post, both parties agreeing that Fort Sumter should not be occupied at all by either. This would, in fact, Mr. Orr said, be conceding almost everything to the United States, as Sumter could not be held against a sea force, and Moultrie commands the town. His explanation of Anderson's movement is that he lost his head over the excitement of two or three of his younger officers, who were not very sensible, and who had got themselves into hot water on shore with some of the brawling and silly young Sea Island bloods of Charleston. As to the willingness of South Carolina to come into such an arrangement of course he could not speak, though he did not believe that Moultrie would have been occupied to-day excepting to afford a basis for it. I agreed with him that anything which could properly be done to avert an armed collision between the forces of the United States and those of any State, in the present troubled and alarmed condition of the public mind, ought to be done; but I frankly told him I did not believe Mr. Buchanan would take the responsibility of ordering Anderson to evacuate Fort Sumter and return to Fort Moultrie, and asked him what reason, if any, he had to think otherwise. He hesitated a little, and finally told me that Mr. Seward had given him reason to think the decision could be brought about through the influence of Senator ———, whose term expires in March, but who has great personal weight with the President, and, as a Southern man by birth and a pronounced Breckenridge Democrat, no inconsiderable hold upon the more extreme Southern men, particularly of the Gulf States. Mr. Seward, in fact, told him that the subject had been discussed by him with this gentleman last night pretty fully, and that he thought Mr. Buchanan could be led to see that the crisis was an imminent one, and must be dealt with decisively at once.

SOUTH CAROLINA NOT IN FAVOR OF A CONFEDERACY

For his own part, Mr. Orr admitted that he deprecated above all things any course of action which would strengthen the Confederate party in South Carolina. He did not wish to see a Confederate States government formed, because he regarded it—and there I agreed with him—as sure to put new obstacles in the way of the final adjustment so imperatively necessary to the well-being of all sections of the country. He thought that if the United States Government would at once adjust the Fort Sumter difficulty, and recognize the secession of South Carolina as an accomplished fact within the purview of the Constitution, the Independent party, as he called it, in South Carolina would at once come forward and check the now growing drift toward a new Confederacy. The most earnest and best heads in South Carolina, he said, had no wish to see the State linked too closely with the great cotton-growing Gulf States, which had already "sucked so much of her blood." They looked to the central West and the upper Mississippi and Ohio region as the railway history of the State indicated, and would not be displeased if the State could be let entirely alone, as Rhode Island tried to be at the time when the Constitution was formed. In short, he pretty plainly admitted that South Carolina was more annoyed than gratified by the eagerness of Georgia and the Gulf States to follow her lead, and that nothing but the threatening attitude given to the United States by such acts as the occupation of Fort Sumter could determine the victory in that State of the Confederate over the Independent movement.

I could not listen to Mr. Orr without a feeling of sympathy, for it was plain to me that he was honestly trying to make the best of what he felt to be a wretched business, and that at heart he was as good a Union man as anybody in Connecticut or New York. But when I asked him whether South Carolina, in case her absolute independence could be established, would not at once proceed to make herself a free State, and whether, wedged into the Gulf and the middle West as she is, she would not make any protective system adopted by the rest of the country a failure, he could not answer in the negative. He got away from the point pretty smartly though, by asking me whether a free-trade policy adopted from South Carolina to the Mexican border would not be a harder blow at our Whig system than a free-trade policy confined to South Carolina. I asked him whether Governor Pickens, who seems, from what Mr. Orr told me—there is absolutely nothing trustworthy in the papers about it—to have ordered the occupation of Moultrie and Fort Pinckney, is really in sympathy with the secession movement. He smiled, and asked me if I knew Mrs. Pickens. "Mrs. Pickens, you may be sure," he said, "would not be well pleased to represent a petty republic abroad. But I suppose you know," he went on, "that Pickens is the man who was born insensible to fear. I don't think he is likely to oppose any reasonable settlement, but he will never originate one." One of Mr. Orr's colleagues, whom I did not think it necessary or desirable to see, came for him and took him away in a carriage. Almost his last words were, "You may be perfectly sure that we shall be received and treated with."

SENATOR DOUGLAS ON BUCHANAN AND LINCOLN

He had hardly gone before Mr. Douglas called, in a state of some excitement. He had a story, the origin of which he would not give me, but which, he said, he believed: that Anderson's movement was preconcerted through one Doubleday, an officer, as I understood him, of the garrison, with "Ben Wade," and was intended to make a pacific settlement of the questions at issue impossible. I tried to reason him out of this idea, but he clung to and dwelt on it till he suddenly and unconsciously gave me the cue to his object in bringing it to me by saying: "Mind, I don't for a moment suspect Lincoln of any part in this. Nobody knows Abe Lincoln better than I do, and he is not capable of such an act. Besides, it is quite incompatible with what I have heard from him"—he had said, when he checked himself with a little embarrassment, I thought, and went on—"what I have heard of his programme. A collision and civil war will be fatal to his Administration and to him, and he knows it—he knows it," Mr. Douglas repeated with much emphasis. "But Wade and that gang are infuriated at Seward's coming into the Cabinet, and their object is to make it impossible for Lincoln to bring him into it. I think, as a friend of Seward's, you ought to understand this."

I thanked him, but put the matter off with some slight remark, and, without giving him my authority, asked him if he thought it likely Mr. Buchanan would receive the South Carolina Commissioners. "Never, sir! never," he exclaimed, his eyes flashing as he spoke. "He will never dare to do that, sir!" "What, not if he has given them to understand that he will?" I replied. "Most certainly not, if he has given them to understand that he will. That would make it perfectly certain, sir, perfectly certain!" He then launched out into a kind of tirade on Mr. Buchanan's duplicity and cowardice. I tried to check the torrent by dropping a remark that I had merely heard a rumor of the President's intentions, but that was only pouring oil on the flames. "If there is such a rumor afoot," he said, "it was put afoot by him, sir; by his own express proceeding, you may be sure. He likes to have people deceived in him—he enjoys treachery, sir, enjoys it as other men do a good cigar—he likes to sniff it up, sir, to relish it!" He finally cooled off with a story of his having got a political secret out about the Kansas-Nebraska business, which he wished propagated without caring to propagate it himself, or have his friends do so, by the simple expedient of sending a person to tell it to the President, after first getting his word on no account to mention it to anyone. "Within six hours, sir, within six hours," he exclaimed, "it was all over Washington, as I knew it would be!"

SECRETARY FLOYD AND THE PLOT TO ABDUCT BUCHANAN

Washington, December 29th.—This resignation of Floyd is of ill-omen for the speedy pacification of matters, as he would hardly have deprived Virginia of a seat in the Cabinet at this moment if he thought the corner could be turned. He is not a man of much account personally, and is, I believe, of desperate fortunes, at least such is the current rumor here; but it was of considerable importance that the post he held should be held by a Southern man at this juncture, if only to satisfy the country that South Carolina does not at all represent the South as a body in her movement, and his withdrawal at this moment, taken in conjunction with the lawless proceedings at Pittsburg the other day, will be sure to be interpreted by the mischief-makers as signifying exactly the contrary. The effects of all this upon our trade at this season of the year are already more disastrous than I can bear to think of. My letters from home grow worse and worse every week. No sort of progress is making in Congress meanwhile. B—— has just left me after half an hour of interesting talk. He shares my views as to the effect of Floyd's withdrawal; but a little to my surprise, I own, has no doubt that Floyd is a strong secessionist, though not of the wilder sort, and founds this opinion of him on a most extraordinary story, for the truth of which he vouches. Certainly Wigfall has the eye of a man capable of anything—"The eye of an old sea-rover," as Mary G—— describes it, but it staggers me to think of his contriving such a scheme as B—— sets forth to me. On Mr. Cushing's return from Columbia the other day, *re infecta,* Wigfall (who, by the way, as I had forgotten till B—— reminded me of it, is a South Carolinian by birth) called together a few "choice spirits," and proposed that President Buchanan should be kidnapped at once, and carried off to a secure place, which had been indicated to him by some persons in his confidence. This would call Mr. Breckenridge at once into the Executive chair, and, under the acting-Presidency of Mr. Breckenridge, Wigfall's theory was, the whole South would feel secure against being "trapped into a war." He was entirely in earnest, according to B——'s informant—whose name B—— did not give me, though he did tell me that he could not have put more faith in the story had it come to him from Wigfall himself—and had fully prepared his plans. All that he needed was to be sure of certain details as to the opportunity of getting safely out of Washington with his prisoner, and so on, and for these he needed the coöperation of Floyd.

He went to Floyd's house—on Christmas night, I think B—— said—with one companion to make this strange proposal, which takes one back to the "good old days" of the Scottish Stuarts, and there, in the basement room, Floyd's usual cozy corner, set it forth and contended for it earnestly, quite losing his temper at last when Floyd positively refused to connive in any way at the performance. "Upon my word," said B——, when he had got through with the strange story,

"I am not sure, do you know, that Wigfall's solution wouldn't have been a good one, for then we should have known where we are; and now where are we?" He agrees with Mr. Douglas in thinking that President Buchanan probably has given the South Carolina Commissioners to understand that he will receive them, and also that he as certainly will not receive them. That mission of Cushing's was a most mischievously foolish performance, and he was the last man in the whole world to whom such a piece of work ought to have been confided, if it was to have been undertaken at all. After sending Cushing to her Convention to treat and make terms, it will be difficult for the President to make South Carolina or anybody else understand why he should not at least receive her Commissioners. It is this perpetual putting of each side in a false light toward the other which has brought us where we are, and, I much fear, may carry us on to worse things. B—— has seen Cushing since he got back, and tells me he never saw a man who showed clearer traces of having been broken down by sheer fright. "He is the boldest man within four walls, and the greatest coward out of doors," said B——, "that I ever knew in my life!" His description, from Cushing's account, of the people of Charleston, and the state of mind they are in, was at once comical and alarming in the highest degree. Certainly, nothing approaching to it can exist anywhere else in the country, or, I suspect, out of pandemonium.

WERE THE CAROLINIANS CHEATED?

January 1st.— I took the liberty of sending to-day to Mr. Orr, who brought me the story about President Buchanan's intentions toward the South Carolina Commissioners, to ask him what he thought now of his informant. To my surprise, he tells me that Mr. B——, whom I had supposed to be entirely devoted to the personal interests of the President, persists in his original story, and either is or affects to be excessively irritated at the position in which he has now been placed. Mr. Orr wishes the Commissioners to go home and make their report, but his colleagues insist upon sending in a letter to the President, which I fear will not mend matters at all; and which certainly must add to the difficulty about that wretched Fort Sumter, notwithstanding the singular confidence which Mr. Seward seems to feel in his own ability ultimately to secure a satisfactory arrangement of that affair by means quite outside of the operations of the present Government, whatever those means may be. The South Carolina Commissioners profess to have positive information from New York that the President has ordered reënforcements to be sent to Sumter, and they are convinced, accordingly, that he has been trifling with them simply to gain time for perfecting what they describe as a policy of aggression.

WAS THE CONFEDERACY MEANT TO BE PERMANENT?

January 13th.—A very long and interesting conversation with Senator Benjamin on the right of Louisiana to seize Federal posts within her territory without even going through the formality of a secession. He is too able and clear-headed a man not to feel how monstrous and indefensible such action is, but he evidently feels the ground giving way under him, and is but a child in the grasp of his colleague, who, though not to be compared with him intellectually, has all that he lacks in the way of consistency of purpose and strength of will. Virginia, he is convinced, will not join the secession movement on any terms, but will play the chief part in bringing about the final readjustment.

My own letters from Richmond are to the same tenor. After a while I told him what I had heard yesterday from Mr. Aspinwall, whom it seems he knows very well, and offered to read him the remarkable letter from Mr. Aspinwall's lawyer, a copy of which Mr. Aspinwall, at my request, was so good as to leave with me. It illustrates Benjamin's alertness and accuracy of mind that before he had heard six sentences of the letter read he interrupted me with a smile, saying: "You need not tell me who wrote that letter, Mr. ———. I recognize the style of my excellent friend Mr. B——, of New York, and I can tell you what he goes on to say." Which he accordingly proceeded to do, to my great surprise, with most extraordinary correctness and precision. In fact, I inferred necessarily that the views expressed by Mr. Aspinwall's counsel must have been largely drawn from Mr. Benjamin himself, so completely do they tally with his own diagnosis of the position, which is, curiously enough, that the leaders of the inchoate Confederacy are no more at one in their ultimate plans and purposes than, according to my best information, are the leaders in South Carolina. Mr. Benjamin thinks that the ablest of them really regard the experiment of a new Confederation as an effectual means of bringing the conservative masses of the Northern people to realize the necessity of revising radically the instrument of union. In his judgment, the Constitution of 1789 has outlived its usefulness. Not only must new and definite barriers be erected to check the play of the passions and opinions of one great section upon the interests and the rights of another great section, but the conditions under which the Presidency is created and held must be changed. The Presidential term must be longer, the President must cease to be reëligible, and a class of Government functionaries, to hold their places during good behavior, must be called into being. I could detect, I thought, in his views on these points, a distinctly French turn of thought, but much that he said struck me as eminently sound and sagacious. He thinks not otherwise nor any better of President Buchanan than Mr. Douglas, though his opinion of Mr. Douglas is anything but flattering.

He agrees with me that, by permitting the South Carolina forces to drive off by force the Star of the West, the Government have practically conceded to South Carolina all that she claims in the way of sovereignty, though he is not surprised, as I own I am, at the indifference, not to say apathy, with which this overt defiance to the Federal authority and this positive insult to the Federal flag have been received by the people of the North and West. Certainly, since we are not at this moment in the blaze of civil war, there would seem to be little reason to fear that we shall be overtaken by it at all. The chief peril seems to me now to lie in the long period of business prostration with which we are threatened, especially if Mr. Benjamin's views are correct. I do not believe that his Confederate Government will lose the opportunity of establishing its free-trade system wherever its authority can extend while conducting negotiations for a new organization of the Union, and irreparable damage may in this way be done our great manufacturing interests before any adjustment can be reached.

SEWARD AND VIRGINIA

February 8, 1861.—I can anticipate nothing from the Peace Convention. The Virginians are driving things, as I told Mr. Seddon to-day, much too vehemently; and the whole affair already assumes the aspect rather of an attempt to keep Virginia from seceding than of a settled effort to form a bridge for the return of the already seceded States. Nor am I at all reassured by his singular confidence in Mr. Seward, and his mysterious allusions to the skillful plans which Mr. Seward is maturing for an adjustment of our difficulties. He obviously has no respect for Mr. Seward's character, and in fact admitted to me to-day as much, telling me a story of Mr. Seward's visit to Richmond, and of a dinner there given him by a gentleman of distinction whose name he mentioned, but it has escaped me. At this dinner, according to Mr. Seddon, a number of gentlemen were invited to meet Governor Seward expressly because of their greater or less known sympathy with what were regarded as his strong views on the subject of slavery. Among these was Mr. Benjamin Watkins Leigh, a man conspicuous for the courageous way in which he maintained the ground that gradual emancipation was the policy which Virginia ought to adopt. I noted this name particularly, because, in mentioning it, Mr. Seddon said: "Leigh couldn't come, and it was well he couldn't, for he was such an old Trojan that, if Governor Seward had made the avowal before him which he made before the rest of the company, I believe Leigh would have been hardly restrained from insulting him on the spot."

This avowal was in effect as follows: After dinner, in the general conversation, some one venturing to ask Governor Seward how he could utter officially what the Virginians regarded as such truculent language in regard to the way in which New York should treat Southern reclamations for runaway slaves, Governor Seward threw himself back in his chair, burst out laughing violently, and said: "Is it possible you gentlemen suppose I believe any such ——— nonsense as that? It's all very well, and in fact it's necessary, to be said officially up there in New York for the benefit of the voters, but surely we ought to be able to understand each other better over a dinner-table!" Now, it doesn't matter in the least whether Mr. Seward did or did not say just this in Richmond. Something he must have said which makes it possible for such a story to be told and believed of him by men like Mr. Seddon; and it is a serious public misfortune at such a time as this that such stories are told and believed by such men of the man who apparently is to control the first Republican Administration in the face of the greatest difficulties any American Administration has ever been called upon to encounter. From what Mr. Seward tells me, it is plain that he has more weight with Mr. Lincoln than any other public man, or than all other public men put together; and I confess I grow hourly more anxious as to the use that will be made of it.

THE NEW YORK SENATORIAL CONTEST
BETWEEN GREELEY AND EVARTS

I had a long conversation this evening with ———, of New York, on the issue of this senatorial election at Albany, which also puzzles me considerably, and is far from throwing any cheerful light on the outlook. He could tell me nothing of Judge Harris, the newly elected Senator, excepting that there is apparently nothing to tell of him beyond a good story of Mr. Thurlow Weed, who, being asked by some member of the Legislature, when Harris began to run up in the balloting, whether he knew Harris personally and thought him safe, replied: "Do I know him personally? I should rather think I do. I invented him!" Mr. ——— says there is more truth than poetry in this. He is a warm personal friend of Mr. Evarts who was generally designated as the successor of Mr. Seward, and he does not hesitate to say that he believes Mr. Evarts was deliberately slaughtered by Mr. Weed at the instigation of Mr. Seward. They are the most incomprehensible people, these New York politicians; one seems never to get at the true inside of the really driving-wheel. In his indignation against Mr. Weed my friend ——— was almost fair to Mr. Greeley. He says that Mr. Weed did not hesitate to say in all companies during the contest at Albany that he believed Mr. Greeley wishes to see secession admitted as of the essence of the Constitution, not only because he sympathizes with the Massachusetts abolitionists who proclaim the Union to be a covenant with hell, but because he thinks he might himself be elected President of a strictly Northern Confederacy. In respect to Mr. Evarts he tells me that he has reason to believe Mr. Seward does not wish to be succeeded in the Senate by a man of such signal ability as a debater, who is at the same time so strong with the conservative classes. As the chief of Mr. Lincoln's Administration, Mr. Seward will have to deal with the reëstablishment of the Union by diplomatic concessions and compromises; and, while much of his work must necessarily be done in the dark and through agencies not appreciable by the public at all, he fears lest the whole credit of it should be monopolized with the public by such a skillful and eloquent champion as Mr. Evarts in the Senate. "In other words," said Mr. ———, "he would much prefer a voting Senator from New York to a talking Senator from New York while he is in the Cabinet." On this theory it is, my friend most positively asserts, that Mr. Evarts was "led to the slaughter." Unquestionably, as the ballots show, the Harris movement must have been preconcerted, and, if Harris is the kind of man my friend Mr. ——— makes him out to be, Mr. Seward will have nobody to interfere between him and the public recognition of whatever he may have it in his mind to do or to attempt. Whether a strong man in the Senate would not have been of more use to the country than a "voting Senator" under the present and prospective circumstances of the case, it is of little consequence now to inquire.

Hayne I am told is going home to-morrow, and this Sumter business gets no better. It is beginning to be clear to me that the President means to leave it, if he can, as a stumbling-block at the threshold of the new Administration. And, in the atmosphere of duplicity and self-seeking which seems to be closing in upon us from every side, I do not feel at all sure that these South Carolinians are not playing into his hands. If they could drive away the Star of the West, there is nothing to prevent their driving out Major Anderson, I should suppose.

MR. LINCOLN'S RELATIONS TO MR. SEWARD

New York, February 20th.—A most depressing day. Mr. Barney came to see me this morning at the hotel, from breakfasting with Mr. Lincoln at Mr. Grinnell's, to see if I could fix a time for meeting Mr. Lincoln during the day or evening. I explained to him why I had come to New York, and showed him what I thought best of Mr. Rives's letter from Washington of last Sunday. He was a little startled, but insisted that he had very different information which he relied upon, and, finding I could not be sure of any particular hour before dinner, he went pretty fully with me into the question about Mr. Welles, and gave me what struck me as his over-discouraging ideas about Mr. Seward. He assured me in the most positive terms that Mr. Lincoln has never written one line to Mr. Seward since his first letter from Springfield inviting Seward to take the Department of State. This is certainly quite inconsistent with what I have understood from Mr. Draper, and still more with the very explicit declarations made to me by Reverdy Johnson; nor can I at all comprehend Mr. Johnson's views in regard to the importance of Judge Robertson's mission to the South, if Mr. Barney's statement is correct. Of course, I did not intimate to him that I had any doubts on that head, still less my reasons and grounds for entertaining such doubts; but, after making due allowance for his intense personal dislike and distrust of Mr. Seward, about which I thought he was more than sufficiently explicit in his conversation with me, I can not feel satisfied that he is incorrect. If he is correct, matters are in no comfortable shape. He admitted, though I did not mention to him that I knew anything on that point, that Seward has written repeatedly and very fully to Mr. Lincoln since the election, but he is absolutely positive that Mr. Lincoln has not in any way replied to or even acknowledged these communications. I really do not see how he can possibly be mistaken about this, and, if he is not, I am not only at a loss to reconcile Mr. Seward's statements with what I should wish to think of him, but much more concerned as to the consequences of all this. . . .

Mr. Barney said that Mr. Lincoln asked after me particularly this morning, and was good enough to say that he recollected meeting me in 1848, which may have been the case; but I certainly recall none of the circumstances, and can not place him, even with the help of all the pictures I have seen of such an extraordinary-looking mortal, as I confess I ought to be ashamed of myself once to have seen face to face, and to have then forgotten. Mr. Barney says the breakfast was a failure, nobody at his ease, and Mr. Lincoln least of all, and Mr. Weed, in particular, very vexatious. Mr. Aspinwall, who came in just as Mr. Barney went out, confirms this. He says that Mr. Lincoln made a bad impression, and he seemed more provoked than I thought necessary or reasonable at a remark which Mr. Lincoln made to him on somebody's saying, not in very good taste, to Mr. Lincoln, that he would not meet so many millionaires together at any other table in New York. "Oh, indeed, is that so? Well, that's quite right. I'm a millionaire myself. I got a minority of a million in the votes last November." Perhaps this was rather a light and frivolous thing for the President-elect to say in such a company, or even to one of the number; but, after all, it shows that he appreciates the real difficulties of the position, and is thinking of the people more than of the "millionaires," and I hope more than of the politicians. I tried to make Mr. Aspinwall see this as I did, but he is too much depressed by the mercantile situation, and was too much annoyed by Mr. Lincoln's evident failure to show any adequate sense of the gravity of the position.

THE BUSINESS ASPECT OF SECESSION

He had hardly gone, when in came S——, with a face as long as his legs, to show me a note, from Senator Benjamin, to whom, he had written inquiring as to the effect, if any, which the farce at Montgomery would be likely to have upon patent rights. Benjamin writes that of course he can only speak by inference, and under reserve, but that, in his present judgment, every patent right granted by the United States will need to be validated by the Government of the Confederate States before it can be held to be of binding force within the territory of the new republic. No wonder S—— is disquieted! If the thing only lasts six months or a year, as it easily may unless great and I must say at present not-to-be-looked-for political judgment is shown in dealing with it, what confusion and distress will thus be created throughout our manufacturing regions! I have no doubt myself, though I could not get Mr. Draper to see it as I do to-day, that these Confederate contrivers will at once set negotiations afoot in England and in France for free-trade agreements in some such form as will inevitably hamper us badly in readjusting matters for the national tariff, even after we effect a basis of political accommodation with them. . . .

MR. LINCOLN ON NEW YORK, MAYOR WOOD, AND
THE IMPORTANCE OF DEMOCRATIC SUPPORT

My conversation with Mr. Lincoln was brief and hurried, but not entirely unsatisfactory—indeed, on the main point quite the reverse. He is entirely clear and sensible on the vital importance of holding the Democrats close to the Administration on the naked Union issue. "They are," he said to me, "just where we Whigs were in '48 about the Mexican war. We had to take the Locofoco preamble when Taylor wanted help, or else vote against helping Taylor; and the Democrats must vote to hold the Union now, without bothering whether we or the Southern men got things where they are, and we must make it easy for them to do this, because we can't live through the case without them," which is certainly the simple truth. He reminded me of our meeting at Washington, but I really couldn't recall the circumstances with any degree of clearness. He is not a great man certainly, and, but for something almost woman-like in the look of his eyes, I should say the most ill-favored son of Adam I ever saw; but he is crafty and sensible, and owned to me that he was more troubled by the outlook than he thought it discreet to show. He asked me a number of questions about New York, from which I gathered for myself that he is not so much in the hands of Mr. Seward as I had been led to think, and I incline to believe that Mr. Barney is nearer the truth than I liked this morning to think. He was amusing about Mayor Wood and his speech, and seems to have a singularly correct notion of that worthy. He asked me what I had heard of the project said to be brewing here for detaching New York City not only from the Union but from the State of New York as well, and making it a kind of free city like Hamburg. I told him I had only heard of such visionary plans, and that the only importance I attributed to them was, that they illustrated the necessity of getting our commercial affairs back into a healthy condition as early as possible. "That is true," he replied; "and nobody feels it more than I do. And as to the free city business—well,

I reckon it will be some time before the front door sets up housekeeping on its own account," which struck me as a quaint and rather forcible way of putting the case.

I made an appointment for Washington, where he will be at Willard's within a few days, and agreed to write to ———. My cousin V—— came to me with a most amusing account of the President-elect at the opera in Mr. C——'s box, wearing a pair of huge *black* kid gloves, which attracted the attention of the whole house, hanging as they did over the red velvet box-front. V—— was in the box opposite, where some one, pointing out the strange, dark-looking giant opposite as the new President, a lady first told a story of Major Magruder of the army, a Southern man, who took off his hat when a procession of Wide-awakes passed his Broadway hotel last year and said, "I salute the pallbearers of the Constitution"; and then rather cleverly added, "I think we ought to send some flowers over the way to the undertaker of the Union."

During one of the *entr'actes,* V—— went down into what they call the "directors' room" of the Academy, where shortly after appeared Mr. C—— with Mr. Lincoln, and a troop of gentlemen all eager to be presented to the new President. V—— said Mr. Lincoln looked terribly bored, and sat on the sofa at the end of the room with his hat pushed back on his head, the most deplorable figure that can be imagined, putting his hand out to be shaken in a queer, mechanical way. I am afraid V—— has a streak of his sarcastic grandmamma's temper in him.

Author's Note: The second installment, beginning here, appeared in the *North American Review* 129 (September 1879): 259–73.

THE IGNOMINIOUS NIGHT-RIDE FROM HARRISBURG

Washington, February 24th.—Since I sat and listened to the silvery but truly satanic speech of Senator Benjamin, on his taking leave of the Senate three weeks ago, nothing has affected me so painfully as this most unfortunate night-trip of Mr. Lincoln's from Harrisburg here. It is in every imaginable way a most distressing and ill-advised thing, and I can scarcely trust myself to think of it, even here alone in my room. Mr. Seward feels about it as I do, though he affects, with his usual and rather exasperating assumption of levity, to laugh it off. But it has shaken my confidence, and it will shake the confidence of a good many more people in the reality of his influence over this strange new man from the West. It gives a weight and importance of the most dangerous sort, too, to the stories which the opponents of a peaceful and satisfactory adjustment have been so sedulously putting about in regard to the disposition of the border States, and particularly of Maryland; and it can not fail to excite a most mischievous feeling of contempt for the personal character of Mr. Lincoln himself throughout the country, especially at the South, where it is most important that people should at this moment have been made to understand that the new Administration comes into power in the ordinary legitimate way, and will be presided over by a man of law and order, who has confidence in himself, in the people of the country, and in the innate loyalty of Americans to the law. I do not believe one word of the cock-and-bull story of the Italian assassins, which Mr. Seward told me to-day had been communicated to Mr. Lincoln as coming from General Scott; and it was clear to me that Mr. Seward himself did not believe one word of it. Even with the brief glimpse I got in New York of Mr. Lincoln, I am slow to believe in his being so weak and vulgar a man as this performance indicates, and I am satisfied that some extraordinary pressure must have been exerted upon him to make him do a thing which, at any time, would have been deplorable and scandalous, and which appears to me, happening at this moment, to be nothing less than calamitous. I can think of nothing else. It really throws the whole machinery of our system off its center. Are we really drifting into the wake of Spanish America? This can not be; and yet, when we have reached a point at which an elected President of the United States consents to be smuggled through by night to the capital of the country, lest he should be murdered in one of the chief cities of the Union, who can blame the rest of the world for believing that we are a failure, or quarrel with desperadoes, like Wigfall, for taking it for granted? It is sickening.

THE BLAIRS AS MR. LINCOLN'S EVIL GENIUS

Washington, February 25th.—A visit this morning from Senator Douglas, and who is as much concerned as I am at the turn affairs are taking. He feels exactly as I do over this wretched smuggling business; and both startles and shocks me by what he tells me of Mr. Seward's share in it, asserting positively, as of his own knowledge, that, at the urgent request of General Scott, Mr. Seward sent his son to Mr. Lincoln at Philadelphia, to impress upon him and his friends the imminent peril they would be in at Baltimore. I expressed my utter surprise, and asked him if he had spoken with Mr. Seward on the subject since Saturday. He had not. "But you must remember," he said, "that in all this business General Scott does with Seward as he pleases; and General Scott is an old woman in the hands of those born conspirators and makers of mischief—the Blairs." He went on from this to give me his reasons for believing that the Blairs were moving heaven and earth to get control of Mr. Lincoln's Administration; and that they have made more progress that way than is at all suspected, even by Mr. Seward. I do not like any of the Blairs, and indeed I know nobody who does. But of them all I like Montgomery least; and I can imagine nothing less to be desired than his entrance into the Cabinet, which Senator Douglas regards as inevitable. He goes further than I can in his views as to the policy which he thinks the Blairs are bent on cajoling or compelling Mr. Lincoln to adopt. They are coöperating now for the moment, he thinks, with the extreme anti-Seward men both here and in New York. "What they really want," said Senator Douglas, "is a civil war. They are determined, first, on seeing slavery abolished by force, and then on expelling the whole negro race from the continent. That was old Blair's doctrine, sir, long ago; and that is Montgomery's doctrine, sir," he said, with even more than his usual emphasis; "and, if they can get and keep their grip on Lincoln, this country will never see peace or prosperity again, in your time, or in mine, or in our children's children's time. They will be the evil genius, sir, of the republic. They, and nobody else, you may depend upon it, will be found at the bottom of this abominable smuggling scheme." I asked Senator Douglas how it could have been possible for anybody to persuade Mr. Lincoln into such a suicidal act, unless he is a lamentably weak and pliable character. "No, he is not that, sir," was his reply; "but he is eminently a man of the atmosphere which surrounds him. He has not yet got out of Springfield, sir. He has Springfield people with him. He has his wife with him. He does not know that he is President-elect of the United States, sir. He does not see that the shadow he casts is any bigger now than it was last year. It will not take him long to find it out when he has got established in the White House. But he has not found it out yet. Besides, he knows that he is a minority President, and that breaks him down." Mr. Douglas then went on to give me some painful details as to Mr. Lincoln's domestic life and habitual associations in Illinois, which were very discouraging. He wound up by saying that he had made up his mind to see Mr. Lincoln at once and tell him the truth.

MR. STANTON'S ESTIMATE OF LINCOLN

I called at Willard's Hotel, and left my card for Mr. Lincoln, who had gone out. But, as I was crossing Fourteenth Street, I met the Attorney-General, who stopped me to ask if I had seen the President-elect since he "crept into Washington." It is impossible to be more bitter or malignant than he is; every word was a suppressed and a very ill-suppressed sneer, and it cost me something to keep my temper in talking with him even for a few moments. When he found that I had only met Mr. Lincoln once, to my recollection, he launched out into a downright tirade about him, saying he "had met him at the bar, and found him a low, cunning clown." I could not resist telling him as we parted, that I hoped the President would take an *official* and not a *personal* view of his successor in any relations he might have with him. I think he felt the thrust, for he bowed more civilly than he is apt to do, when he left me. But Mr. Stanton's insolence shows how very mischievous the effect of this wretched blunder has already been; and, while it appalls me even to suppose that Mr. Seward can have had any hand in it, it is not much more satisfactory to believe that he really has so little influence with Mr. Lincoln as would be implied in his not having been consulted as to such a step at such a juncture.

DID FLOYD ORDER ANDERSON TO FORT SUMTER?

Washington, February 26th.—At dinner to-day I sat next to Mr. ———, who told me positively, as of his own knowledge, that Anderson's movement to Fort Sumter was made directly in pursuance of a discretion communicated to him as from the President himself, and he added an extraordinary assertion that he knew it to have been recommended by Floyd, and as he believed for the purpose, which of course Floyd was very careful not to betray to Mr. Buchanan, of creating a situation which should make an armed explosion inevitable, and should so force Virginia and the border States into secession. The withdrawal of Secretary Cass, he said to me (and his personal relations at the White House certainly ought to make him an authority, especially when speaking confidentially as he knew he was to-day), roused the President to a sense of the dangerous position in which he is placed by reason of his well-known political and personal good will toward the South and leading Southern men. "He has never been the same man that he was, since that day," said ———. He was positive about the instructions sent to Anderson; and reiterated his assertion two or three times with an emphasis which I thought well to moderate, though, as Mr. Flores, a lively little South American Minister, sat next him on the other hand, there is no great danger, I think, of his having been understood by anybody but myself.

THE CONFUSION OVER MR. LINCOLN'S CABINET

Later on in the evening ——— came over and sat by me to urge me to go with him to-morrow to see Mr. Lincoln in regard to the Cabinet appointments. He was much agitated and concerned about them, having gotten into his head, for reasons which he gave me, that Mr. Lincoln, in his despair of harmonizing the Seward men with the Chase men, has concocted or had concocted for him a plan of putting Corwin into the State Department, sending Seward to England, and giving the Treasury to New York. I listened to him patiently, and I own I was startled by some of the facts he told me; but I have pointed out to him that, however close might be the ties between Mr. Corwin and Mr. Lincoln, Mr. Chase could not be counted out in this way unless with his own consent, which I did not believe could be got, and that I am beginning to think that Mr. Chase holds the new President a good deal more tightly in his hand than Mr. Seward does. I declined peremptorily to call upon Mr. Lincoln in the business; though I said I should certainly call upon him as a matter of respect, and that, if he gave me any reason or opportunity to speak of his Cabinet, I should tell him frankly what I thought. I found ——— quite as strongly impressed as Mr. Douglas by the machinations of the Blairs, and quite as fearful of their success. He showed me a letter he had received a fortnight ago from Mr. Draper, in New York, expressing great anxiety as to Mr. Seward's position in the Cabinet in case of the nomination of Mr. Chase, and intimating an intention of visiting Washington with several other gentlemen for the purpose of making Mr. Lincoln understand that he must absolutely drop the idea of putting Mr. Chase into the Treasury. I told him that Mr. Weed had to-day expressed the same ideas to me, and I asked him if he did not know that a counter-pressure was putting on Mr. Lincoln to exclude Mr. Seward. "Suppose," I said, "they should both be excluded?"

We were very late, and while the whist was going on I had a very interesting talk with ——— about Mr. Benjamin, in the course of which he told me a story so characteristic of all the persons so concerned in it that I must jot it down.

We happened to speak of Soulé and the curious letter which he published the other day. "I dined with Benjamin," said ——, "in January, a day or two after that letter appeared, and calling his attention to what seemed to me the nut of it, being the passage in which Soulé eloquently calls upon Louisiana, if she must leave the Union, not to follow the leadership of men who, with the Federal power at their back, had not been able to protect her rights within the Union, I said to him, '*C'est de vous et de Slidell qu'il a voulu parler'?*" Benjamin laughed, as did St. Martin and Hocmelle of the French Legation, who were also of the company, and replied: "Of course" (he was speaking of us), "that is the ruin of poor Soulé, that he can not conceal his morbid hatred of both of us—that, and his congenital incapacity of telling the truth; he loves lying, loves it more than anything else; loves it *jusqu'à la folie!*" Then Benjamin went on to tell a story of an encounter between himself and Soulé, on the way to Mexico, whither Soulé was going to prevent, if possible, the carrying out of the Tehuantepec scheme. When he found Benjamin on board of the boat, which he had not expected, he volunteered the absurd statement to Benjamin that he was only going to Vera Cruz *en route pour Tampico*! Of course he did not go to Tampico, but to the capital; and, when he got to the capital, he opened his batteries on Tehuantepec, by informing the Mexican President that he had been specially deputed by President Buchanan to advise with him on the international relations of the two countries; though he might have ascertained, with tact and a very little trouble, that Mr. Forsyth had already cautioned the Mexican Government, by direction of President Buchanan, against having any dealings with Soulé at all! I did not say to ——, though I was on the point of saying it, that I was not at all sure whether this curious story best illustrated the innate mendacity of Soulé, or the innate duplicity of a more exalted personage. —— is very bitter now against Benjamin, though still under the glamour, as I must confess myself to be in a measure, of his charming personal ways, and his rare and lucid intelligence. At this very dinner to which he referred early in January, —— tells me Benjamin spoke of the arrangements and projects of the Confederate organizers, with an apparent intimate knowledge of them all; saying that the Confederate Congress would assemble at Montgomery before February 15th, and choose a President, so that Lincoln should find himself confronted, when he took the oath in March, by a complete government, extending at least over eight States, and offering peace or war to his choice. —— does not believe the story about Yancey from Montgomery to-day. He thinks Benjamin will be sent as Confederate Commissioner to Europe, to seek recognition; and certainly a more dangerous one could not be selected. He would hurt us abroad as much as Yancey would help us. On reaching home, I found a note from ———, full of hopes for to-morrow, which I can see no reason for sharing, and another from Mr. Weed to the same effect, telling me that Mr. Douglas would see Mr. Lincoln to-night. I do not see that the Peace Conference have advanced us one step from the point where we were in January, when Mr. Ledyard came to see me, telling me that General Cass had been electrified into better spirits, ill as he then was, by the absolute certainty that Mr. Seward and Mr. Crittenden had so got their heads together as to insure a satisfactory settlement "the very next day." How many days have since gone by with no such result; and what is before us now but imbecility if not worse, in the government we have, and utter distraction in the councils of a government we are to have? Poor General Cass! I bade him good-by yesterday, and I suspect for ever. I should not be surprised if the journey brings him to the end, and I hope he has not been allowed to carry out his purpose of seeking an interview with Mr. Lincoln. He is not strong enough to bear the excitement, and it can do no good, I fear.

WITH MR. LINCOLN IN WASHINGTON

Washington, February 28th.—Half an hour with Mr. Lincoln to-day, which confirms all my worst fears. I should say he is at his wits' ends, if he did not seem to me to be so thoroughly aware of the fact that some other people are in that condition. I told him frankly, on his own provocation to the subject, what I thought would be the advantages to his Administration, and to the country, of putting ——— into the Cabinet, and gave him to understand, as plainly as I thought becoming, that he must not look on me as acting in concert with any set of men to urge that nomination, or any other nomination, upon him. I think he saw that I was in earnest; and, at all events, he advised me to write to ——— in the terms in which I wished to write to him.

I was sorry to find him anxious about the safety of Washington, and he asked me some questions about Captain Stone, which surprised me a little, and annoyed me more. I told him what I knew of Stone personally, and what had been said to me about him, by the most competent men in the army, at the time when he first came here, by General Scott's wish, to reorganize the militia of the District. He seemed very glad to hear of this, and was very much taken with a story which I told him, and for the accuracy of which I could vouch, that when Captain Stone, upon an urgent recommendation of General Scott, was appointed to the command of the District militia, in January, Governor Floyd was excessively enraged, and tried to get his own nephew, "Charley Jones," who had been previously nominated for the post, and who is a desperate fellow, to insult Stone, pick a quarrel with him, and shoot him. Mr. Lincoln's melancholy countenance lighted up with a twinkle in his eye. "That was not such a bad idea of Floyd's," he said, in a slow, meditative sort of way. "Of course, I'm glad Stone wasn't shot, and that there wasn't any breach of the peace; but—if the custom could be generally introduced, it might lubricate matters in the way of making political appointments!" After a little, he recurred to the dangerous condition of Washington. I then spoke very earnestly, for it was clear to me that he must be still under the pressure of the same evil counsels which had led him into that dreadful business of the night-ride from Harrisburg; and I urged him to put absolute confidence in the assurances of Captain Stone. I told him, what I believe to be perfectly true, that the worst stories about the intended incursions into Washington, and the like, all originate with men like George Saunders, of New York, and Arnold Harris, of Tennessee, once a particular follower of President Buchanan, but now a loud and noisy secessionist—men who came into my mind because I had passed them in the hall of the very hotel in which we were talking, and in which they have been telling wonderful stories of conspiracy and assassination, from the hotel porches, to anybody who will listen to them for weeks past. He listened to me very attentively, and, suddenly stretching out his hand, picked up and handed me a note to look at. I recognized Senator Sumner's handwriting as I took it, and was not, therefore, particularly surprised to find it alarmish and mysterious in tone, bidding Mr. Lincoln, for particular reasons, to be very careful how he went out alone at night. I saw that Mr. Lincoln watched me while I read the note, and I perhaps may have expressed in my countenance an opinion of the communication which I did not think it civil to put into words, merely reiterating, as I laid it back on the table, my own conviction that there was nothing to fear in Washington, and no occasion for measures likely to influence the public mind unfavorably in other parts of the country. As I arose to go, Mr. Lincoln pulled himself together up out of the rocking-chair, into which he had packed himself, and, scanning me good-naturedly for a moment, said, very abruptly, "You never put backs with Sumner, did you?" I suppose I looked as much surprised as I felt; but I laughed and said that I did not think I ever had done so. "Well, I supposed not," he said; and then, hesitating a moment, went on: "When he was in here I asked him to measure with me, and do you know he made a little speech about it." I tried to look civilly curious, and Mr. Lincoln, with an indescribable glimmer all over his face, continued: "Yes," he said, "he told me he thought 'this was a time for uniting our fronts and not our backs before the enemies of the country,' or something like that. It was very fine. But I reckon the truth was"—and at this point I was compelled against my will to laugh aloud—"I reckon the truth was, he was—afraid to measure!" And with this he looked down with some complacency on his own really indescribable length of limb. "He is a good piece of a man, though—Sumner," he added, half quizzically, half apologetically, "and a good man. I have never had much to do with bishops down where we live; but do you know, Sumner is just my idea of a bishop." At that moment a door opened, and a lady came in, in not a very ceremonious way, I thought, dressed as if either just about to go into the street, or having just come in. Mr. Lincoln presented me to her as his wife, and I exchanged a few words with her. Perhaps I looked at her through the mist of what Senator Douglas had intimated to me; but certainly she made a disagreeable impression on me. She is not ill-looking, and, though her manners are not those of a well-bred woman of the world, there would be nothing particularly repulsive about them, were it not for the hard, almost coarse tone of her voice, and for something very like cunning in the expression of her face. With the recollection of Mr. Douglas's account of her relations with her husband, the thought involuntarily occurred to me of the contrast between his own beautiful and most graceful wife and this certainly dowdy and to me most unprepossessing little woman. I think if the wives had been voted for, even by the women, Mr. Douglas would be President-elect to-day.

The passages were thronged as I came out. On the stairs I met Mr. Bell who stepped aside with me for a moment to tell me how much he was impressed with the conservative tone of Mr. Lincoln's mind, and to go over the story I had yesterday heard of the interview of Tuesday night. I did not think it worth while to dampen his feelings by hinting what judgments I had formed of it all from Senator Douglas's account of it, nor to ask him what hope there could be from these propositions of the Peace Congress after what took place yesterday in the New York delegation. But the truth is, I am losing all heart and hope; there has been more Cabinet-making than peace-making in the Peace Congress; and I am beginning to be afraid that the Virginia secessionists are trifling designedly with Mr. Seward and all our friends.

THE RELATIONS OF MR. SEWARD WITH MR. LINCOLN

Mr. Douglas came to see me late this evening. He has been some time with Mr. Lincoln it seems—last night again, not of course at the jam and "reception," but in a private earnest talk about the Peace Congress and the efforts of the extreme men in Congress to make it abortive. He was more agitated and distressed than I have ever seen him; and it is impossible not to feel that he really and truly loves his country in a way not too common, I fear now, in Washington; but I really can not make out what he expected Mr. Lincoln to do. He told me he had urged Mr. Lincoln to recommend the instant calling of a national convention, upon which point Mr. Seward agrees with him, as his motion in the Senate shows to-day. But he admitted that he had no success in getting Mr. Lincoln to a point on the subject, and this led us to a question of what Mr. Lincoln really means to say in his inaugural. I found that Senator Douglas knew just as well as I knew that Mr. Lincoln has not confided this yet, even to Mr. Seward; but I could not get him to feel as I do how strangely compromising this is to all our hopes of a settlement through the influence of Mr. Seward. How is it possible that Mr. Lincoln can intend to put Mr. Seward at the head of his Administration, if he leaves him thus in the dark as to the purport of the first great act of his official life, now only four days off! I can not even reconcile Mr. Seward's acquiescence in such a course with the respect I would like to feel for him as a man; and it seems to me absolutely discouraging as to the outlook for the country.

MR. LINCOLN HIS OWN PRIVY COUNCIL

Senator Douglas could not or would not see this, even though he admitted that he knew the inaugural address to have been prepared by Mr. Lincoln himself, without consulting anybody, so far as it appears, at Springfield; and though he could give me no good reason for believing that Mr. Lincoln has so much as shown it to Mr. Seward or anybody else since he reached Washington. Everything seems to me to be at sixes and sevens among the very men who ought to be consulting and acting together with united efforts to force the conservative will of the country on all the desperate intriguers of both sections. Senator Douglas tells me to-night that an effort is making now to get, not Corwin, but Sumner, into the State Department, but that Mr. Adams has refused to have anything to do with it. It is only what was to have been expected of a man of Mr. Adams's good sense; it only illustrates the desperation of the rule or ruin faction in the

Republican party; and that, I can not help but feeling, is a very formidable force to deal with, especially when brought to bear upon such a man as Mr. Lincoln, with his executive inexperience, and in the presence of the unprecedented difficulties with which he is to deal.

Still I can not think he will let go his hold on Mr. Seward and the great body of strong, sound opinion which Mr. Seward now undoubtedly represents. My chief fear, and as to this Senator Douglas agrees with me, is from Mr. Seward's own friends and representatives here. These New-Yorkers are the most singular combinations of arrogance and timidity in politics I have ever heard or read of. I do not wonder that the Western men dislike them; they are almost as much of a mystery to their nearest neighbors. Before going, Senator Douglas had a word to say about President Buchanan and the South Carolina Commissioners. He tells me that it has now been ascertained that the President nominated his Pennsylvania Collector at Charleston on the very day, almost at the very moment, when he was assuring Colonel Orr, through one of his retainers, that he was disposed to accede to the demands of South Carolina if they were courteously and with proper respect presented to him. They rewrote their letter accordingly, submitted it to the President's agents, who approved it and sent it to the White House. This, Senator Douglas says, was on January 3d, in the morning. The Commissioners spent the afternoon in various places, and dined out early. On coming in, they found their letter to the President awaiting them. It had been returned to them by a messenger from the White House, about three o'clock P.M.; and on the back was an endorsement, not signed by anyone, and in a clerkly handwriting, to the effect that the President declined to receive the communication! They ordered their trunks packed at once, and left for home by way of Richmond on the four-o'clock morning train, feeling, not unreasonably, that they had been both duped and insulted.

LORD LYONS ON THE SITUATION

Washington, Friday, March 1st.—I had a most interesting but gloomy conversation with Lord Lyons this morning, having to call on him in relation to ———'s business with those vexatious people in Barbadoes and Antigua. We fell into conversation after getting through with this; and, though he is the most discreet of men, he pretty plainly intimated to me that he was more concerned as to the outlook than most of our own people here seemed to be. He has old American blood in his veins, which does not perhaps count for much; but his family have had trouble enough with the emancipation business to make him grave, he says, when he contemplates the possible complications of the negro question to arise out of the conflict here, and he put the prospect as to that in quite a new light to me, I am ashamed to say, when he said that, to him, the question of peace or war did not appear to be in the least contingent upon anything that might or might not be said or enacted here in Washington. "How are you going to dispose of the actual occupation, unlawfully, or by force, of United States premises in these seceded States?" he said. "How can the new President acquiesce in that occupation? And, if he does not acquiesce in it, how will he put an end to it?" I really could make no answer to these questions, and they haunt me now as they have not before. How can any negotiations with Virginia affect the situation actually created for us in South Carolina, and Georgia, and Texas, and Florida? Can Mr. Lincoln pass over this difficulty in his inaugural? And yet how can he deal with it as things now stand without bringing the shadow of war over the land? Another thing that Lord Lyons said struck me, which was that, while England could not possibly have anything to gain by a real rupture of the Union, the case was clearly different with France, under her present policy and engagements on this side of the water.

I left the British Minister, feeling as if I had just landed at Washington, and come in contact with the seething peril of the day for the first time. I can not but think that his opinion of the situation is affected by his European training and ideas, and that he under-estimates the force here of that sober second thought of the people which has saved us so often, and I must hope will save us again now.

INCREASING BUSINESS TROUBLES AND COMPLICATIONS

Washington, March 2d.—The distress at home grows hourly worse and worse. And this preposterous tariff which they have assumed to establish at Montgomery points to a still worse state of things. If there are many at Montgomery bent, like some of the worst men we have here, on really driving the two sections into war, they are taking the direct way to their horrible purpose. I can get no positive light as to the actual state of things in regard to Fort Sumter; though —— writes to me from New York that he is positive Mr. Holt has taken measures to secure reënforcements for the fort, and that it will not be evacuated certainly before Mr. Buchanan retires. The news that the Confederates have made Mr. Toombs their Secretary of State is very ominous. There is no wilder or more unsafe man alive; and his last speech in the Senate was as detestable in point of spirit as the maiden speech, on the other side, of that noisy and vulgar cockney Orator Puff, Senator Baker, who came here heralded as such a wonder of eloquence, and who went to pieces so completely in his first effort under the close and withering fire of Benjamin. I met the man again to-day as I passed into the National, and I really could hardly speak to him civilly. It is such men as he who play into the hands of the worst enemies of the country and of common sense at the South.

MR. LINCOLN MAKES HIS OWN CABINET

There can be no doubt about it any longer. This man from Illinois is not in the hands of Mr. Seward. Heaven grant that he may not be in other hands—not to be thought of with patience! These New York men have done just what they have been saying they would do, and with just the result which I have from the first expected; though I own there are points in the upshot which puzzle me. I can not feel even sure now that Mr. Seward will be nominated at all on Tuesday: and certainly he neither is nor after this can be the real head of the Administration, even if his name is on the list of the Cabinet. Such folly on the part of those who assume to be the especial friends of the one man in whose ability and moderation the conservative people at the North have most confidence; and such folly at this moment might almost indeed make one despair of the republic!

—— has just left me. He was one of the party who called on Mr. Lincoln to-day to bring matters to a head, and prevent the nomination of Chase at all hazards. A nice mess they have made of it! Mr. Lincoln received them civilly enough, and listened to all they had to say. Speaking one after another, they all urged the absolutely essential importance of the presence of Mr. Seward in the Cabinet, to secure for it either the support of the North or any hearing at the South; and they all set forth the downright danger to the cause of the Union of putting into the Cabinet a man like Mr. Chase, identified with and supported by men who did not desire to see the Union maintained on its existing and original basis at all, and who would rather take their chances with a Northern republic, extending itself to Canada, than see the Union of our fathers kept up on the principles of our fathers. After they had all said their say in this vein, Mr. Lincoln, who had sat watching them one after another, and just dropping in a word here and there, waited a moment, and then asked what they wanted him to do, or to forbear. They all replied that they wished him to forbear from nominating Mr. Chase as a member of his Cabinet, because it would not be possible for Mr. Seward to sit in the same Administration with Mr. Chase. He wouldn't wish it, and his friends and his State would not tolerate it—couldn't tolerate it—it must not be.

Then Mr. Lincoln sat looking very much distressed for a few moments, after which he began speaking in a low voice, like a man quite oppressed and worn down, saying, it was very hard to reconcile conflicting claims and interests; that he only desired to form an Administration that would command the confidence of the country and the party; that he had the deepest respect for Mr. Seward, his services, his genius, and all that sort of thing; that Mr. Chase has great claims also, which no one could contest—perhaps not so great as Mr. Seward; but what the party and country wanted was the hearty coöperation of all good men and of all sections, and so on, and so on, for some time. They all thought he was weakening, and they were sure of it, when after a pause he opened a table-drawer and took out a paper, saying: "I had written out my choice here of Secretaries in the Cabinet after a great deal of pains and trouble; and now you tell me I must break the slate and begin all over!"

He went on then to admit, which still more encouraged them, that he had sometimes feared that it would be as they said it was—that he might be forced to reconsider his matured and he thought judicious conclusions. In view of that possibility, he said he had constructed an alternative list of his Cabinet. He did not like it half as well as the one of his own deliberate preference, in which he would frankly say he had hoped to see Mr. Seward sitting as Secretary of State, and Mr. Chase sitting as Secretary of the Treasury—not half as well; but he could not expect to have things exactly as he liked them; and much more to the same effect, which set the listeners quite agog with suppressed expectations of carrying their great point.

"This being the case, gentlemen," he said, finally, after giving the company time to drink in all he had said—"this being the case, gentlemen, how would it do for us to agree upon a change like this?" Everybody, of course, was all attention. "How would it do to ask Mr. Chase to take the Treasury, and to offer the State Department to Mr. William F. Dayton, of New Jersey?"

——— told me you could have knocked him or any man in the room down with a feather. Not one of them could speak. Mr. Lincoln went on in a moment, expatiating on his thoughtfulness about Mr. Seward. Mr. Dayton, he said, was an old Whig, like himself and like Mr. Seward. He was from New Jersey, which "is next door to New York." He had been the Vice-Presidential candidate with General Fremont, and was a most conservative, able, and sensible man. Mr. Seward could go as Minister to England, where his genius would find great scope in keeping Europe straight as to the troubles here, and so on, and so forth, for twenty minutes.

When he got through, one of the company spoke, and said he thought they had better thank him for his kindness in listening to them, and retire for consultation, which they did. But I fear from the tone and the language of ——— that there is more cursing than consultation going on just now. I must own that I heard him with something like consternation. Whether this prefigures an exclusion of Mr. Seward from the Cabinet, who can tell? Nor does that possibility alone make it alarming. It does not prefigure—it proves that the new Administration will be pitched on a dangerous and not on a safe key. It makes what was dark enough before, midnight black. What is to come of it all?

Author's Note: The third installment, beginning here, appeared in the *North American Review* 129 (October 1879): 376–88.

MR. SUMNER AND MR. CAMERON

Washington, March 3d.—I received this morning a note from ———, asking me to come at once, if possible, to his house, and going there instantly, as I chanced to be free to do, I found to my surprise that he had sent for me to meet Senator Sumner, whom I found engaged in close conversation with him, and who greeted me with a warmth a little out of proportion, as I thought, to the relations between us, for I have never affected an admiration which I certainly have never felt for Mr. Sumner.

It was soon explained when I found that Senator Sumner had asked ——— to send for me in order that he might urge me to call at once upon Mr. Lincoln and represent to him "in the strongest language which you can command—for no language can be too strong"—the dreadful consequences to the influence and success of the new Administration which must follow his nomination of Mr. Simon Cameron to a seat in the Cabinet. Mr. Sumner's conviction was absolute that Mr. Lincoln had bound himself by a political bargain in this case, which would itself suffice to blast his reputation as an honest man were it made known, as it would surely be; but he treated this as a small evil in comparison with the mischief sure to be done by the presence in the Cabinet of such a person as Mr. Cameron, "reeking with the stench of a thousand political bargains worse than this."

When he had abated a little of the vehemence of his language, I took occasion to ask why I should have been requested to intervene in such a matter, and on what grounds Mr. Sumner and ——— had reached what seemed to me the extraordinary conclusion that I could be induced to meddle with it. Senator Sumner interrupted me by asking, somewhat more peremptorily than I quite liked, whether I needed to be informed of the true nature of this "political Judas from Pennsylvania, whom Providence had marked with the capillary sign of his character, and who might have sat to Leonardo da Vinci for the picture in the Milanese refectory." All this made me but the more indisposed to listen to him, but I finally succeeded in ascertaining that he had sent for me on the strength of ———'s assurances as to the way in which Mr. Lincoln had been kind enough to speak of me to himself. I hastened to assure them both that any good opinion which Mr. Lincoln might have of me must have been based upon my careful abstinence from precisely such interferences—"impertinent interferences," I quietly called them—with his affairs, as the intervention to which they desired to urge me would certainly be. I told them how extremely slight my acquaintance was with the President-elect, to which ——— replied that Mr. Lincoln himself had cited my representations in favor of one gentleman whom he hoped to include among his advisers as having been "the most decisive endorsement" with him of that choice. I could only reiterate my surprise; and Mr. Sumner insisting upon his theme, began again with more fervor, if possible. He very soon gave me the true secret of his extreme anxiety on this point. He asked me what interest I or my friends could have in such a preponderance as the Middle States seemed destined to have in the Cabinet if Mr. Seward and Mr. Cameron were to enter it together, and in what way it could advance our wishes or purposes to allow the New England States—"the cradle and the spinal life of the Republican party," to be "humiliated and thrust below the salt at the board which, but for them, would never have been spread"—with much more to the same general effect, but all this with an intensity and bitterness quite indescribable. ——— was more temperate in his expressions, but almost equally urgent with me to do what I was compelled again and again in the clearest terms to let them under-

stand that nothing under heaven could make me do, even if I had the fullest belief that my action could in any way affect the matter, which I certainly had not.
It astonished me to see how hard it was apparently for Mr. Sumner to understand that my objections to coöperating with —— and himself did not in some
way arise out of some relations of my own with Senator Cameron—out of some
doubt on my part as to the measure of mischief to be apprehended from Senator
Cameron's political reputation, and from the nature of the appointments sure to
be made and favored by him.

It was idle for me to assure him again and again that I knew perhaps as much
of Pennsylvania politicians in general, and of Senator Cameron in particular,
as other people, and should regret as much as he possibly could any "predomi-
nance" of Pennsylvania politicians in the new Administration. Nothing could
stop him; and he insisted on telling me a succession of stories to illustrate the
unscrupulousness of Mr. Cameron, one of which he declared had been told in
his own presence and in a company of gentlemen by a chief agent in the transaction, who seemed to regard it, said Mr. Sumner, as a brilliant triumph of political skill, a thing to be proud of, and a decisive proof of the fitness of Senator
Cameron for any office in the country.

A CURIOUS CHAPTER IN PENNSYLVANIA POLITICS

It was to the effect that, when Mr. Cameron found his election to the Senate
in grave doubt, he turned the day in his own favor by taking a pecuniary risk
which eventually resulted in his making a considerable sum of money. According to Mr. Sumner's version of the affair, the person who gave the history of it
in his presence, and who is certainly a prominent man in the financial circles of
Philadelphia, stated that a leading member of the Legislature (I think he said a
State Senator) offered to vote for Mr. Cameron, and to induce two or more of
his friends to do the same thing, if he could be relieved of some local indebtedness in the place where he resided and put in the way of a livelihood elsewhere,
his constituents being so hostile to Mr. Cameron that it probably would not be
agreeable for him to continue among them after Mr. Cameron's election through
his help to the Senate. No bribe passed; but the local legislator was appointed
to a remunerative position in the way of his calling (as a lawyer, I think) in one
of the great Philadelphia corporations, and removed to that city, having previously paid off his local indebtedness with a loan from Mr. Cameron on the se-

curity of some stock which he happened to hold in a small railway, at that time of no appreciable value.

The loan was never called for, but through some subsequent legislation the small railway in question was brought into a more extensive railway system, and the collateral in Mr. Cameron's hands advanced to a value far exceeding the amount for which it had been ostensibly hypothecated. After listening to Mr. Sumner for a considerable time, I finally asked him why he did not go himself to Mr. Lincoln and depict the Senator from Pennsylvania in the dark colors in which he had represented him to us. He intimated that he had already done so, and after a little the conversation took a turn which confronted me with the painful conviction that all this indignation about Senator Cameron had its origin not so much in any real horror of the Pennsylvania element in politics as in the belief, which I hope is well grounded, that the presence of Mr. Cameron and Mr. Seward in the Cabinet will confirm Mr. Lincoln in his disposition to pursue a conservative conciliatory policy which may bring the seceded States back into the Union, rather than a policy aimed at a complete separation of the slaveholding from the non-slaveholding region.

NO WAR FOR THE UNION, AND NO UNION

It did not surprise me, of course, to find Mr. Sumner aiming at such a result, but the acquiescence in his views of —— does both surprise and pain me. I asked them if they did not think it better, from the point of view of the negroes, for whom they seem to be so deeply concerned, that slavery should be held for eventual execution within the Union—now that events had so clearly demonstrated the incompatibility of the institution as a permanent feature of Southern society with that general peace and order which must be as essential to the South as to the North—than that slavery should be excluded from the influences of freedom in a new confederacy, organized to uphold and develop it; but I could bring neither of them to reason on the subject. Mr. Sumner grew very warm again. He was as much horrified as I could be or any man at the idea of an armed conflict between the sections. "Nothing could possibly be so horrible or so wicked or so senseless as a war"; but between a war for the Union which was not to be thought of, and "a corrupt conspiracy to preserve the Union," he saw, he said, little choice, and he desired to see the new Administration formed "supremely in the interests of freedom." As for the slaveholding

States, let them take their curse with them if they were judicially blinded so to do. He quoted some lines, I think of Whittier, about their right to make themselves the scandal and the shame of "God's fair universe," as embodying his conceptions of what we ought now to recognize as the policy of freedom, and then he recurred finally to the original theme, and once more in concert with —— began about the visit they wished me to make to Mr. Lincoln. I was forced at last to tell them both explicitly that, while I fully agreed with them as to the supreme necessity of avoiding any collision or conflict between the States, and had no fear of any such catastrophe, my hope of averting it rested mainly upon my hope that Mr. Lincoln was of one mind with Mr. Seward on the subject, and would direct his efforts to a conciliatory preservation of the Union; and that neither Mr. Seward nor Mr. Cameron could possibly have less faith than myself in any "policy of freedom" which contemplated the possibility of a severed Union, or less disposition to favor such a policy. It was not at all a pleasant conversation, but it was a necessary conversation, as I am sorry to find, and it is painfully evident that the new Administration will have to contend with a Northern as well as with a Southern current of disaffection and disunion much stronger than I had allowed myself to suspect.

In the evening I saw Mr. Douglas, and, without telling him whom I had seen to bring me to such a conviction, I expressed to him my conviction that unless Mr. Seward entered the Cabinet, and entered it with some colleague upon whom he could rely for support in a conservative policy, Mr. Lincoln would be drifted out to sea, and the country with him.

I found that the incidents of Saturday had been communicated to him, and, as I inferred, though he did not say so, by Mr. Lincoln himself; and I was much relieved to find that he entertains no doubt of Mr. Seward's nomination, and of his confirmation. He told me that Mr. Seward yesterday received assurances to that effect from Senator Hunter, of Virginia, through ——, and he agreed with me that, whatever our private opinions of the political habits and ideas of Mr. Cameron might be, it was most important that no effort should be made to displace him at this hour from the Cabinet, at the risk of seeing a man, either of the type of the Blairs, put in who will press things to a bloody contest, or of the opinion which I fear Mr. Chase represents, that the South and slavery had better be gotten rid of once for all and together. Mr. Douglas used the strongest language as to his own determination to stand by Mr. Lincoln in a temperate, resolute Union policy, and I must own that I never saw him to such good advantage. He was perfectly frank in admitting that he would regard such a policy adopted by Mr. Lincoln as a virtual vindication of his own policy during and before the Presidential election, and that he believed it would eventually destroy, if successful, the organization of the Republican party as a political power; but a man who received a million and a half of votes in a Presidential contest has a right to feel, and Mr. Douglas evidently does feel, that he speaks for a great popular force in the country. But, as I have often felt before, so I felt again this evening, that Mr. Douglas really is a patriotic American in the strong, popular sense of that phrase. He had seen Mr. Lincoln to-day, and he intimated to me that he had heard that part of the message read which touches the assertion of the invalidity of the acts of secession, and that he was entirely satisfied with it. To use his own expression, it will do for all constitutional Democrats to "brace themselves against." I repeated to him what Lord Lyons had said to me the other day, and asked him what ground Mr. Lincoln has taken on the questions raised by the seizure of Southern forts, and by the fortifications put up in Charleston against Fort Sumter. He says that since Mr. Lincoln reached Washington he has inserted in the message a distinct declaration that, while he regards it as in his duty to "hold, occupy, and possess" the property and places belonging to the Government and to collect the duties, he will not attempt to enforce the strict rights of the Government where hostility to the United States is great and universal. I then told him that Mr. Seward, some days ago, had assured me that he believed he would be able to induce Mr. Lincoln to take such a position as this, and that it would suffice, he thought, as a basis of negotiation with the seceded States, and give the people breathing-time to recover their senses at the South; and we came to the conclusion, which I was very glad to reach, that Mr. Seward's counsels must have brought Mr. Lincoln to this stand, in which I have no sort of doubt, and Mr. Douglas has none, that the great majority of the Northern people of both parties will support him.

TELEGRAPHING TO PRESIDENT DAVIS AT MONTGOMERY

It was late when I left Mr. Douglas, but when I reached home I found —— waiting for me with a most anxious face. He opened his business to me at once, which was to ask my advice as to what he should do with a message brought to him by ——, one of Mr. Seward's New York men here, who desired him, in Mr. Seward's name, to have it sent to-night by telegraph to Mr. Davis at Montgomery, Alabama. ——— had assured him that it was expected, arrangements having been made that such a message should be sent, and that he would do a public service by sending it. I asked if he had the message, which he produced. It bore a signature not known to me, and was a simple statement to the effect that the tone of Mr. Lincoln's inaugural message would be conciliatory. I asked ——— what his objection was to sending such a message, which certainly could do no one any harm and which was probably enough true, when he called my attention to the fact that it was addressed to Mr. Davis as President of the Confederate States. I laughed, and told him that I saw no harm in that any more than in addressing Mr. Davis as Pope of Rome, and that I thought he might safely do as he preferred about it, especially as he had apparently agreed with Mr. Seward's friend to send it. I asked him then why this mysterious friend came to him with such a request, upon which he said that he had known the man very well in Wall Street, and had had occasion to avail himself of his services at various times. I finally advised him to send the message, rather than make any further confidences or communication about it, and to be a little more careful hereafter as to his associates and allies. He was in a curiously perturbed state of mind, and I am afraid, has been going into stock speculations again.

As to ———, from whom he got his message, he told me a curious story, which helps to explain the sort of irritation which Mr. Seward's particular followers so often show about him, as well as to confirm my own not very high opinion of some of these New York men in whom he takes such an interest apparently. It appears that before the message was handed to him, he had a long conversation with ——— on the subject of the President's message, and that, after trying in vain to get a definite statement about it from his New York friend, he had twitted the latter until he lost his temper so far as to admit that, when he had pressed Mr. Seward for light as to the President's message this very morning, Mr. Seward had finally put him off with the extraordinary statement that "all he had to do to insure a peaceful settlement of the whole business was to be sure and buy a lot of tickets to the inauguration ball and make it a grand success; that would satisfy the country, and lead to peace."

I really could not stand this, but burst into a fit of laughter, which seemed to annoy ——— more than it amused him. He grew quite hot as to Mr. Seward's levity and indifference to the interests of his "friends," protesting that it was nothing less than an outrage on the part of Mr. Seward to put off in this way a man of wealth and influence who was devoted to him, and who had a great material interest at stake in learning whether we were to have war with the seceded States or not, as he was a large owner of steamers which the Government would need to charter if there was to be a war or even a large warlike demonstration. I lost my patience a little with this, and told —— promptly that, if these were the motives of his New York friend, Mr. Seward deserved credit for putting him off with a recommendation to buy ball-tickets, but he came back at me triumphantly with the dispatch to Montgomery which his New York friend had secured at the end of a second visit to Mr. Seward, as a decisive sign of the peaceful prospect before us, and which he finally took away, saying that he would send it.

THE MILITARY INAUGURATION OF MR. LINCOLN

Washington, March 4th.—I am sure we must attribute to the mischievous influence of the Blairs the deplorable display of perfectly unnecessary, and worse than unnecessary, military force which marred the inauguration to-day, and jarred so scandalously upon the tone of the inaugural. Nothing could have been more ill-advised or more ostentatious than the way in which the troops were thrust everywhere upon the public attention, even to the roofs of the houses on Pennsylvania Avenue, on which little squads of sharpshooters were absurdly stationed. I never expected to experience such a sense of mortification and shame in my own country as I felt to-day, in entering the Capitol through hedges of marines armed to the teeth. ——, of Massachusetts, who felt as I did—indeed, I have yet to find a man who did not—recalled to me, as we sat in the Senate-chamber, the story of old Josiah Quincy, the President of Harvard College, who, having occasion to visit the Boston court-house during one of the fugitive-slave excitements in that city, found the way barred by an iron chain. The sentinels on duty recognized him, and stooped to raise the chain, that he might pass in, but the old man indignantly refused, and turned away, declaring that he would never pass into a Massachusetts court-house by the favor of armed men or under a chain. It is really amazing that General Scott should have consented to preside over such a pestilent and foolish parade of force at this time, and I can only attribute his doing so to the agitation in which he is kept by the constant pressure upon him from Virginia, of which I heard only too much to-day from ——, who returned yesterday from Richmond. Fortunately, all passed off well, but it is appalling to think of the mischief which might have been done by a single evil-disposed person to-day. A blank cartridge fired from a window on Pennsylvania Avenue might have disconcerted all our hopes, and thrown the whole country into inextricable confusion.

That nothing of the sort was done, or even so much as attempted, is the most conclusive evidence that could be asked of the groundlessness of the rumors and old women's tales on the strength of which General Scott has been led into this great mistake. Even without this the atmosphere of the day would have been depressing enough. It has been one of our disagreeable, clear, windy, Washington spring days. The arrangements within the Capitol were awkward, and very ill attended to. No one was at his ease. Neither Mr. Buchanan nor Mr. Lincoln appeared to advantage. Poor Chief-Justice Taney could hardly speak plainly, in his uncontrollable agitation.

HOW MR. DOUGLAS STOOD BY THE NEW PRESIDENT

I must, however, except Senator Douglas, whose conduct can not be overpraised. I saw him for a moment in the morning, when he told me that he meant to put himself as prominently forward in the ceremonies as he properly could, and to leave no doubt on anyone's mind of his determination to stand by the new Administration in the performance of its first great duty to maintain the Union. I watched him carefully. He made his way not without difficulty—for there was literally no sort of order in the arrangements—to the front of the throng directly beside Mr. Lincoln, when he prepared to read the address. A miserable little rickety table had been provided for the President, on which he could hardly find room for his hat, and Senator Douglas, reaching forward, took it with a smile and held it during the delivery of the address. It was a trifling act, but a symbolical one, and not to be forgotten, and it attracted much attention all around me.

THE BEARING OF MR. LINCOLN HIMSELF

Mr. Lincoln was pale and very nervous, and did not read his address very well, which is not much to be wondered at under all the circumstances. His spectacles troubled him, his position was crowded and uncomfortable, and, in short, nothing had been done which ought to have been done to render the performance of this great duty either dignified in its effect or, physically speaking, easy for the President.

The great crowd in the grounds behaved very well, but manifested little or no enthusiasm, and at one point in the speech Mr. Lincoln was thrown completely off his balance for a moment by a crash not far in front of him among the people, followed by something which for an instant looked like a struggle. I was not undisturbed myself, nor were those who were immediately about me; but it appeared directly that nothing more serious had happened than the fall from a breaking bough of a spectator who had clambered up into one of the trees.

Mr. Lincoln's agitation was remarked, and I have no doubt must have been caused by the impressions which the alarmists have been trying so sedulously to make on his mind, and which the exaggerated preparations of General Scott to-day are but too likely to have deepened.

THE INAUGURAL ADDRESS, AND THE EFFECT OF IT

The address has disappointed everyone, I think. There was too much argumentative discussion of the question at issue, as was to have been expected from a man whose whole career has been that of an advocate in his private affairs, and of a candidate in public affairs, and who has had absolutely no experience of an executive kind, but this in the actual state of the country is perhaps an advantage. The more we reason and argue over the situation, the better chance there will be of our emerging from it without a collision.

I listened attentively for the passages about which Mr. Douglas had spoken to me, and I observed that, when he uttered what I suppose to be the language referred to by Mr. Douglas, Mr. Lincoln raised his voice and distinctly emphasized the declaration that he must take, hold, possess, and occupy the property and places belonging to the United States. This was unmistakable, and he paused for a moment after closing the sentence as if to allow it to be fully taken in and comprehended by his audience.

In spite of myself, my conversation with Lord Lyons and his remarks on this point would recur to my mind, and, notwithstanding the encouraging account given me by Mr. Douglas of the spirit and intent of Mr. Lincoln himself, this passage of his speech made an uncomfortable impression upon me, which

I find it difficult even now to shake off. There is probably no good reason for this, as no one else with whom I have spoken to-day seems to have been affected by the passage of the speech as I myself was, and I am conscious to-night that I have been in a morbid and uneasy mood during the whole day. Mr. Lincoln was visibly affected at the close of his speech, and threw a tone of strange but genuine pathos into a quaint, queerly constructed but not unpoetical passage with which he concluded it, not calculated to reassure those who, like myself, rely more upon common sense and cool statesmanship than upon sentiment for the safe conduct of public affairs.

Upon the public here generally the speech seems to have produced little effect, but the general impression evidently is that it prefigures a conciliatory and patient policy; and, so far, the day has been a gain for the country. I anticipate little from it at the far South, but much in the border States, and especially in Virginia, which just now undoubtedly holds the key of the situation.

AN INTERESTING MARYLAND VIEW OF THE SITUATION

On my way back from the Capitol, I met ——, of Maryland, who walked with me as far as Willard's. He spoke of the inaugural very contemptuously, and with evident irritation, I thought, and what he said strengthened my own feeling that it will be of use in allaying the excitement which his friends are trying so hard to foment, not only in Virginia, but in his own State. He makes no secret of his own desire to see Maryland and Virginia carry Washington out of the Union with them. When I suggested that other States had spent a good deal of money in Washington, and that there was a good deal of public property here which had been called into existence and value by the United States, and not by Maryland or Virginia, he advanced the singular doctrine that the soil belonged to these States, and that everything put upon it must go to them when they resumed their dominion over the soil. "The public buildings and the navy-yard here," he said, "belong to Virginia and Maryland just as much as the public buildings and the forts at Charleston belong to South Carolina." He did not relish my reply, I thought, which was to the effect that I agreed with him entirely as to the parity of the claims in both cases, and saw no more reason why the property of the United States at Washington should belong to Maryland and Virginia than why the property of the United States at Charleston should belong to South Carolina. He was very bitter about the presence of Senator Douglas at the side of

Mr. Lincoln, and generally seemed to think that the day had not been a good one for the disruptionists. I hope he is right, and, in spite of my own forebodings, I think he is. The Blairs were alluded to in our conversation, and he thundered at them as traitors to their own people. He said they were execrated in Maryland, and that no man of them would dare to enter the doors of the Maryland Club, and assured me that, only a few weeks ago, the neighbors of old Mr. Blair had sent him word that "a tree had been picked out for him in the woods." Much as I dislike the Blairs, and dread their influence on the new Administration, I felt constrained to tell ——— that, in my judgment, the amiable neighbors of Mr. Blair could do nothing more likely to make his son the next President of the United States than to execute the atrocious threat implied in such a message; and so we parted. This effervescence of local sympathy, in and about Washington, with the secessionist plans and leaders, is most unfortunate, for it gives color to the inflammatory representations of men like Mr. Montgomery Blair, and supplies them with excuses for persuading General Scott into a course of military displays and demonstrations, to which his own unparalleled vanity alone would sufficiently incline him without such help.

THE CONFEDERATE COMMISSIONERS COMING

On reaching home I found a letter from Mr. Forsyth, telling me that he will be in Washington shortly, as a Commissioner from the Confederate States with others, and intimating his own earnest wish to secure an amicable adjustment of the separation, which he insists upon as irreparable at least for the present. I shall be very glad to see him, for he is a man of unusual sense, and I do not believe he can have persuaded himself into the practicability of the fantastic schemes represented in this wild confederacy. I hope his colleagues may be as able men as himself, for, though I do not see how they are to be in any way officially recognized, their presence here, if they will hear and talk reason, may be very beneficial just now.

ONE OF THE PRACTICAL CONSEQUENCES OF SECESSION

Just after dinner I was called out by a card from Mr. Guthrie, introducing to me a man from his own State, who wished to see me on "business important, not to himself only." I found him a tall, quiet, intelligent-looking Kentuckian, who had an interest in a mail-route in the Southwest and in the Northern connections with it, and who was very anxious to get at some way of saving his interest, by inducing the "Confederate Government" at Montgomery to make terms with him such as the Government had made. The man seemed an honest, worthy fellow; very much in earnest. He had copied out, on a slip of paper, Mr. Lincoln's allusion to his intended purpose of maintaining the mails, and I found that what he wished me to do was, to tell him whether I thought Mr. Seward or Mr. Lincoln would give him a kind of authority to take a contract for carrying the mails for the Government at Montgomery, on the same terms on which he held a contract with the Government here, so that there might be no interruption in the mail service. I assured him that I could not give him any light as to what Mr. Seward or Mr. Lincoln would or would not do, but that I would with pleasure give him a note to Mr. Seward, stating who had sent him to me, and what he wanted. This I did, and he went away expressing much gratitude. The incident struck me as but a beginning and inkling of the infinite vexations, annoyances, and calamities which this senseless and insufferable explosion of political passions and follies is destined to inflict upon the industrious people of this country and of all sections. What is most to be feared is the exasperating effect on the people generally of these things, and my own letters from home bear witness daily to the working of this dangerous leaven among classes not commonly too attentive to political affairs.

THE INAUGURATION BALL

I walked around for half an hour this evening to the inauguration ball, thinking as I went of poor ———'s amazement and wrath at Mr. Seward's extraordinary proposition that the success of this entertainment would settle the question in favor of peace. It was a rash assertion on Mr. Seward's part, for never was there a more pitiable failure. The military nonsense of the day has doubtless had something to do with it; for ———, whom I met just after entering the great tawdry ballroom, assured me that the town was full of stories about a company of Virginia horsemen assembled beyond the Long Bridge with intent to dash into Washington, surround the ballroom, and carry off the new President a captive by the blaze of the burning edifice! The place was not half full; and such an assemblage of strange costumes, male and female, was never before seen, I am sure, in this city. Very few people of any consideration were there. The President looked exhausted and uncomfortable, and most ungainly in his dress, and Mrs. Lincoln, all in blue, with a feather in her hair, and a highly-flushed face, was anything but an ornamental figure in the scene. Mr. Douglas was there, very civil and attentive to Mrs. Lincoln, with whom, as a matter of politeness, I exchanged a few observations of a commonplace sort. I had no opportunity of more than half a dozen words with Mr. Douglas, but I was glad to find that he was satisfied with the address and with the general outlook, though he agreed with me that the military part of the business had been shockingly and stupidly overdone. He was concerned too, I was surprised to find, about the nomination of Mr. Seward to-morrow, and gave me to understand that both the Blairs and Mr. Sumner have been at work to-day against it still. I promised to see —— in the morning, before the meeting of the Senate, on the subject. ——, of New York, who walked out of the absurd place with me, and accompanied me part of the way home, tells me that the real reason of Mr. Seward's anxiety for the success of this entertainment is, that the whole affair is a speculation gotten up by some followers of his in New York, and that he has been personally entreated by a New York politician who is very faithful to him, a Mr. Wakeman, to interest himself in its success!

Certainly Mr. Seward is one of the most perplexing men alive. I can not doubt his personal integrity or his patriotism, but he does certainly contrive to surround himself with the most objectionable people, and to countenance the strangest and the most questionable operations imaginable.

Author's Note: The last installment, beginning here, appeared in the *North American Review* 129 (November 1879): 483–96.

MAJOR ANDERSON AND FORT SUMTER

Washington, March 6th.—To-day —— came to see me, having come directly through from Montgomery, stopping only a day in Charleston on the way, where he saw and had a long conversation with Major Anderson, who is a connection by marriage of his wife, and with whom he has long been on terms of particular good will. He astonishes me by his statements, which I can not doubt, as to the real status of things at Fort Sumter. That Major Anderson transferred his garrison to Fort Sumter from Fort Moultrie of his own motion, on discretionary instructions received last winter from the War Department, he has no sort of question; and indeed his very particular account given to me of the circumstances attending the act of transfer is most interesting—so interesting that I have asked him and he has promised to write it out for me, as it is too long for me to set down here. He tells me Major Anderson has no expectation whatever of the reëstablishment of the Government over the seceded States, and that he intends to be governed in his own future course (military considerations and the question of subsistence of course apart) by the course of his own State of Kentucky. He does not sympathize at all with the States which have now seceded, but he thinks the provocation given them in the action and attitude of the Northern abolitionists an adequate provocation; and —— assures me that in his opinion Major Anderson would unhesitatingly obey the orders of a Confederate Secretary of War were Kentucky to withdraw from the Union and join this new and menacing organization. Fortunately, there seems no immediate likelihood of this, but it shows how much more perilous the situation is than I own I had allowed myself to think, and how mischievous in its effects has been the leaving open through all these years of the question of States rights, their exact limitations, and their relations to the Federal Government. —— is convinced that Major Anderson would never have abandoned Fort Moultrie had he not thought wise to remove himself from a position in which he was liable to be commanded by the authorities of South Carolina, his determination being to retain the control of the position primarily in the interest of his own Commonwealth of Kentucky, so that Kentucky might in no way be committed by his action either for or against the retention of the forts in Charleston Harbor. I asked —— to go with me and state these facts to Mr. Lincoln, pointing out to him their grave importance, and the decisive influence which an accurate knowledge of the feelings and disposition of Major Anderson might have upon the President's judgment of what may be expedient to be done in this most dangerous matter. His own conviction as to the quiet and positive character of Major Anderson, of whom he tells me that, though not a man of unusual abilities in any way, he is a very resolute and conscientious man, holding stubbornly to his own ideas of duty, I told him I was sure would weigh much more with the President than any representations on the subject coming through a third party possibly could. He was quite averse to doing this at first, but finally consented, on my urgent representations, to do so, and I have written a note this afternoon to the President, asking his permission to call on him about a public matter at some hour which may suit him to-morrow.

THE SECESSIONISTS AT MONTGOMERY

Of the proceedings at Montgomery —— gives me an account at once grotesque and saddening. He tells me that a sharp division is already showing itself in the councils of the secession leaders. Mr. Toombs has the wildest ideas of the immediate recognition by England and France of the new government, and insists that no concession shall be made to public opinion in those countries or in the North on the question of slavery. "Cotton is king" is in his mouth all the time. Mr. Memminger, the South Carolinian Secretary of the Treasury, —— thinks much the ablest man they have there, and he takes a more business-like view of the situation, being of the opinion that, unless something is done to secure the seceded States under their new nationality a solid basis of credit abroad, they will not be able to carry on the ordinary operations of a government for any great length of time. None of them anticipate hostilities, and I am glad to learn from —— that the number of persons of any weight and credit among them, who are disposed so to press matters in any direction as to make hostilities probable, is very small. Even in Charleston —— assures me there is a perfect good temper shown in all intercourse between the United States authorities and those who have the present direction of affairs there. At Montgomery —— found the women much more violent and disposed to mischief than the men, many ladies almost openly expressing their wish to see the "Confederate flag" planted at Washington. It appears too, that of this same Confederate flag a number of models have been furnished by ladies. Copies of some of these —— had brought on, and he exhibited them to me. Nothing can be imagined more childish and grotesque than most of them were. The abler men at Montgomery he tells me are urgent that the seceded States should claim the flag of the United States as their own, a proposition which I should suppose would be quite agreeable to Mr. Sumner and others who have not yet got over their disposition to denounce the Union as a "covenant with death and an agreement with hell." I asked —— what these people really mean to do or to attempt to do about patents, showing him some of my letters from home, which clearly indicate the trouble brewing in our part of the country on that very important subject. He could give me no reassuring views of the matter, but, on the contrary, led me to think that the seceded States will try to raise a revenue by exacting heavy sums of patentees for a recognition of their rights within the territory of those States. Such measures, like the adoption last week by their Congress of an act throwing open the coasting trade of all the seceded States to the flags of all nations on equal terms, are too clearly aimed at the material interests and prosperity of the country not to arouse extreme and legitimate irritation. They are a sort of legislative war against the rest of the Union, which may lead, before we are well aware of it, into reprisals and warfare of a more sanguinary kind.

MR. SEWARD'S NEGOTIATIONS WITH VIRGINIA

I asked —— what information he brought as to the relations between the people at Montgomery and the border States, especially Virginia. He had no doubt, from what he heard there, that Virginia will secede, and was apparently very much surprised when I gave him my reasons for believing that nothing of the sort was to be expected. When I told him, as, in view of his position relatively to the well-disposed people of the South and of his intention to see the President to-morrow, I thought it right to tell him, that a messenger—and a messenger enjoying the direct personal confidence of Mr. Seward—left Washington this morning for Richmond with positive assurances as to the intention of the new Administration that no attempt should be made either to reënforce or to hold Fort Sumter, he was greatly surprised, but was forced to admit that such a communication might greatly alter the aspect of things and strengthen the hands of the Union men in Virginia. He thought it would, if made known, produce a great effect even at Montgomery.

AN INTERVIEW WITH MR. LINCOLN

March 7th.—Early this morning I received a message from the President, making an appointment for this afternoon. I called for —— at his hotel and we drove to the White House. I could not help observing the disorderly appearance of the place, and the slovenly way in which the service was done. We were kept waiting but a few moments, however, and found Mr. Lincoln quite alone. He received us very kindly, but I was struck and pained by the haggard, worn look of his face, which scarcely left it during the whole time of our visit. I told the President, in a few words, why we had asked for this interview, and —— then fully explained to him, as he had to me yesterday, the situation at Fort Sumter. It seemed to me that the information did not take the President entirely by surprise, though he asked two or three times over whether he was quite sure about Major Anderson's ideas as to his duty, in case of any action by Kentucky; and, when —— had repeated to him exactly what he had told me as to the language used to himself by Major Anderson, Mr. Lincoln sat quite silent for a little while in a sort of brooding way, and then, looking up, suddenly said: "Well, you say Major Anderson is a good man, and I have no doubt he is; but if he is right it will be a bad job for me if Kentucky secedes. When he goes out of Fort Sumter, I shall have to go out of the White House." We could not resist a laugh at this quaint way of putting the case, but the gloomy, care-worn look settled back very soon on the President's face, and he said little more except to ask —— some questions about Montgomery, not I thought of a very relevant or important kind, and we soon took our leave. He walked into the corridor with us; and, as he bade us good-by, and thanked —— for what he had told him, he again brightened up for a moment and asked him in an abrupt kind of way, laying his hand as he spoke with a queer but not uncivil familiarity on his shoulder, "You haven't such a thing as a postmaster in your pocket, have you?" —— stared at him in astonishment, and I thought a little in alarm, as if he suspected a sudden attack of insanity, when Mr. Lincoln went on: "You see it seems to me kind of unnatural that you shouldn't have at least a postmaster in your pocket. Everybody I've seen for days past has had foreign ministers, and collectors, and all kinds, and I thought you couldn't have got in here without having at least a postmaster get into your pocket!" We assured him he need have no concern on that point, and left the house, both of us, I think, feeling, as I certainly felt, more anxious and disturbed than when we entered it. Not one word had Mr. Lincoln said to throw any real light either on his own views of the situation or on the effect of ——'s communication upon those views. But it was plain that he is deeply disturbed and puzzled by the problem of this wretched fort, to which circumstances are giving an importance so entirely disproportionate to its real significance, either political or military.

THE INVASION OF THE OFFICE-SEEKERS

We sent away the carriage and walked home. —— called my attention as we passed along to the strange and uncouth appearance of a great proportion of the people whom we encountered on our way or passed lounging about the steps of the Treasury Department and the lobbies of the hotels. I had not noticed it before, but certainly in all my long experience of Washington I have never

seen such a swarm of uncouth beings. The clamor for offices is already quite extraordinary, and these poor people undoubtedly belong to the horde which has
pressed in here to seek places under the new Administration, which neither has
nor can hope to have places enough to satisfy one twentieth part of the number.
After dinner I went in to see Mr. Seward, determined, if possible, to get some
satisfactory statement as to the outlook of the immediate future from his point
of view, and anxious also to ascertain what he knows, if he knows anything,
either to confirm or to contradict the story of —— as to Major Anderson and
Fort Sumter.

MR. SEWARD'S EXPECTATIONS OF A SETTLEMENT

I found Mr. Seward in a lively, almost in a boisterous mood, but I soon induced him to take a more quiet and reasonable tone. I told him what —— had
told me of Major Anderson, and that I had taken —— to see Mr. Lincoln. At
this his countenance lighted up and he exclaimed, "I am so glad you did!" He
then went on to assure me in the most positive and earnest terms that he had
no doubt whatever that Fort Sumter would be evacuated at a very early day, that
there were no military reasons whatever for keeping it, and no more or better
reasons for holding it than there had been for holding Fort Brown, which certainly would not be and could not be held. He spoke very severely of what he
called Major Anderson's folly in going into Fort Sumter at all—a folly the secret
of which, as he said, I had now explained to him, but which was only the greater
folly by reason of the motives which led to it, assuming the story of —— to
be true, as he added with a great deal of emphasis, "As I have no sort of doubt
it is." I asked him how the surrender of Fort Sumter could be effected otherwise than by violence if ——'s story was true, since Major Anderson certainly
would not give up the place on an express order from Washington if he cherished the notion of waiting for the action of his own State of Kentucky. That, he
replied evasively, would be a matter for the negotiators, and he then gave me
to understand that negotiations were, in fact, at this moment going on, which,
in his judgment, would very soon relieve the Government of all anxiety on the
score of Charleston Harbor and its forts. I then told him what account ——
had brought of the state of things at Montgomery, about which, however, he
seemed to be himself very fully informed. He could give me no good reason for
supposing it, but he seemed to be quite convinced that, as soon as the States of

Virginia, Kentucky, and Missouri rejected the appeals of the secessionists, as he has positive information they will reject them, the disintegration of the new-born Confederacy will begin. I asked him how, admitting these expectations to be well founded, we were, in the interval during the process, to get on with our postal and business relations, mentioning to him what —— had told me, that Mr. Toombs and others were strongly in favor of establishing a passport system by sea and land against all citizens of the United States. This apparently made little or no impression upon him, and I must say that I have come home quite discouraged and depressed. In the Senate no one of the Republicans seems to be just now thinking seriously of anything but the new appointments. I have been besieged for a week past with letters and applications asking me every day to see a score of persons whom I hardly know, in order to oblige a score of other persons whom, in many cases, I know only too well. It is a shameful and humiliating state of things, none the more tolerable that it was to have been expected. Mr. Seward was very anxious to get my views as to the proper treatment of Mr. Forsyth and the other commissioners. He seemed inclined to think that a mode might be found of receiving them and negotiating with them, without in any way committing the Government to a recognition of the Government which they assume to represent.

I found it difficult, indeed I may say impossible, to make him admit the hopelessness of looking for such a thing, but I told him frankly that I saw no earthly reason why he should not informally and in a private way obtain from these gentlemen—all of them, as we knew, honorable and very intelligent men—some practical light on the way out of all this gathering perplexity, if indeed they have any such practical light to give. He then gave me to understand that this was exactly what he had done and meant to do, and he repeated his conviction that the evacuation of Fort Sumter would clear the way for a practical understanding out of which an immediate tranquillization of the country must come, and in the not distant future a return of all the seceding States to their allegiance. I can only hope he is right.

THE PROGRESS OF EVENTS AT RICHMOND

Washington, March 9th.— —— came in to breakfast with me, having just returned from Richmond. He confirmed the story that an agent has been sent thither by Mr. Seward, with a most positive assurance that on no account shall

Fort Sumter be reënforced, either with men or with supplies. He says this assurance reached Richmond the day after the confirmation by the Senate of the new Cabinet appointments, and he was told by ———— at Richmond, who certainly ought to know the facts in the case, that Senator Hunter agreed to press for the immediate confirmation of Mr. Seward in conformity with the precedents, on the express understanding that such a message should be forthwith dispatched to Richmond. Certainly, but for the attitude of Senator Hunter, and one or two other gentlemen of like views, the Chase and Sumner men in the Senate would have pretty surely, I think, given Mr. Seward some trouble before that body. As things are, ———— thinks the Union men will control the action of Virginia, and that we shall consequently have no war. Heaven grant it! But in all this I do not see what the Government of the Union is negotiating for, or what we are to get for the Union by all these concessions, beyond the boon—priceless indeed, no doubt—of a peace which has not yet been seriously disturbed, and which the seceded States have at least as great an interest as we ourselves in seeing preserved. The whole thing seems to me much too onesided a piece of business, and I told ———— so plumply. Mr. Seward stopped to see me a moment, not long after breakfast, to say, with some appearance of fear, that the President's friends were "pestering" him about sending Mr. Corwin to England, and to intimate that he had put his foot down pretty forcibly in refusing to do anything of the kind. He showed me a note from a common friend of his and of Mr. Forsyth, asking him to receive and give audience to a certain Colonel ————, who had a matter to lay before him of great national importance, and asked me if I would object to seeing Colonel ———— myself, as he did not wish to do so, and yet was anxious to ascertain what Colonel ———— might have to say. I expressed some perplexity as to how such a thing could be arranged, but he laughed, and said that if I would name an hour there would be no trouble about it at all. I thought this odd, but named an hour for to-morrow morning.

A GLIMPSE OF SENSE FROM THE SOUTH

A letter from ————, at Augusta. She writes in good spirits, but is evidently much impressed with the awkward situation, and with the feverish state of feeling all about her in Georgia. Certainly there is nothing bellicose or savage in her mood, but she tells me that her husband is disturbed and disquieted by what he thinks the imminent peril of great business disasters at the South, and especially in Georgia. He may well feel in this way, with the investments which he has made in factories sure to be ruined by the policy of his "Confederated" brethren at Montgomery.

CERTAIN PLANS OF SOUTHERN LEADERS

March 10th.—While Mr. Douglas was talking with me this morning on some propositions which he means to offer in the Senate in a day or two, Mr. Seward's Colonel —— sent his name in to me. I wished to excuse myself, but Mr. Douglas insisted I should not do so, and went away, promising to come back in the evening. I found Colonel —— a very keen, bright, intelligent person, who was full of a great scheme in which he said that Mr. Davis and Mr. Forsyth both were very deeply interested, and in which he believed the eventual solution of the whole trouble, in this country would be found. This was neither more nor less than a plan for the building of a great railway to the Pacific through the southwestern portions of the country, on the surveys made under the direction of Mr. Davis while he was Secretary of War. This, he said, the Confederate States Government would at once undertake. It would unite the Confederacy with California, and make it the interest of the whole North to seek a reunion on proper terms at the earliest possible moment with the Confederate States, which would then stretch from the Atlantic to the Pacific, "enveloping Mexico and the Gulf." I listened to the man in silent amazement for some time, for certainly I never heard such wild and fantastic propositions advanced with so much seriousness and apparent good faith, and, finally interrupting him, ventured to ask him what he wished or expected me to do in the premises, and why he should have been referred to me. He seemed not at all embarrassed, but said quietly that he had wished to see me as being a conservative man and a lover of peace, in order to show me that all we needed at the North was to have a little patience, and we should see the way opened out of all our difficulties by this notable project. Is it possible there can be truth in the old notion that, in times of great national trial and excitement, so many men do go mad, so to speak, in a quiet and private way, that madness becomes a sort of epidemic?

Washington, March 11th.—The debate on the expulsion of Wigfall has gone off to-day into abstractions, which vex and irritate one in the presence of the practical questions now pressing upon us. I could scarcely listen with patience to Mr. Foster's discussion of the point whether a Senator of the United States ought or ought not to consider his seat vacated upon the passage of an ordinance of secession by his State. Nothing will come of it all, and it only gives occasion to men like Mr. Mason to add fuel to the flame all over the country, by discussing and debating the circumstances in which it will be necessary for them to swell the list of seceders and for their States to go out of the Union.

As for Wigfall himself, his bearing for the last day or two has been rather better than it was on the day of his collision with Mr. Douglas, when he really looked like a tiger, and acted not unlike one. He and all the extreme men seem to be a great deal depressed, I am glad to say, by the intelligence which has crept out of the general agreement of the Cabinet to adopt the course recommended by General Scott on plain military grounds, and order Major Anderson to abandon Fort Sumter.

THE ORDER TO EVACUATE FORT SUMTER

I had a long conversation on the subject with Senator Douglas to-day. He is entirely of my mind that the fort ought to have been abandoned already, and that much valuable prestige has been lost by the new Administration, which might have been secured had orders been sent at once to Major Anderson to that effect. The delay is attributable, no doubt, in part to the dilatoriness of Mr. Cameron in taking up the reins of the War Department; but I am sure Mr. Douglas is right when he lays a part of the responsibility on the influence of the Blairs, who keep pressing for a war policy. Even from their point of view, nothing can be more childish than to make an issue on the holding of Fort Sumter, which has already been abandoned in regard to Fort Brown, and to make that issue on the holding of an entirely untenable place. Mr. Douglas tells me, too, that a further difficulty has been raised by the friends of Major Anderson here from Kentucky, who insist that he shall not be ordered to leave Fort Sumter unless the order is accompanied by a promotion to one of the vacant brigadierships in the army, certainly under the circumstances a most scandalous and even foolish demand to make.

THE PRESIDENT WISHES THE FORT EVACUATED

Mr. Lincoln has assured Mr. Douglas positively, he tells me, that he means the fort shall be evacuated as soon as possible, and that all his Cabinet whom he has consulted are of the same mind excepting Mr. Blair, which is precisely what

I had expected. Mr. Douglas says that the President sent for him after his speech of Wednesday to assure him that he entirely agreed with all its views, and sympathized with its spirit. All he desired was to get the points of present irritation removed, so that the people might grow cool, and reflect on the general position all over the country, when he felt confident there would be a general demand for a National Convention at which all the existing differences could be radically treated. Meanwhile he did not see why the Executive should attempt to dispossess the seceded States of the forts occupied by them unless Congress insisted that he should, and gave him the means necessary for the work. "I am just as ready," he said to Mr. Douglas, "to reënforce the garrisons at Sumter and Pickens or to withdraw them as I am to see an amendment adopted protecting slavery in the Territories or prohibiting slavery in the Territories. What I want is to get done what the people desire to have done, and the question for me is how to find that out exactly."

Meanwhile, as I suggested to Mr. Douglas, no one is taking any steps that I can see to find out exactly or inexactly what the people desire to have done, and the secessionists are doing a good many things which for one I do not believe the people at all desire to have done.

BREAKING UP THE UNION BY LEGISLATION

I called Mr. Douglas's attention to a letter received by me from Mobile yesterday, in which the opinion is expressed that, if the mission of Mr. Forsyth and his colleagues turns out a failure, the Confederate Congress will certainly adopt a sort of legal non-intercourse bill already in the hands of their Judiciary Committee, dismissing all cases from the courts to which citizens of other than the seceding States are parties. Mr. Douglas agreed with me, of course, that such legislation as this would be equivalent in some degree to a war, so far as its effects alike upon the country and upon individuals are concerned; and he was not less painfully struck by another bill, a copy of which I have just received from Montgomery, prohibiting absolutely the importation of slaves from the United States unless accompanied by their owners, and with an eye to settlement within the Confederate States. The object of this, of course, is to coerce Kentucky and Virginia, and particularly Virginia, into joining the new government. How long will it be possible for us to sit still and see all the conditions of our prosperity and importance thus nibbled at and taken away piecemeal?

It may be true, as Mr. Douglas suggests, that the introduction of such legislation at Montgomery indicates the obstinacy of the Union feeling in the border States, and may so far be taken as a sign rather of hope than of imminent danger. But the spirit and the intent of it all, so far as concerns the rest of the Union, are not the less hostile and mischievous. Certainly such steps can do little to promote the objects had in view by the Southern Commissioners.

THE DIPLOMATIC PERPLEXITIES OF MR. SEWARD

March 12th.—Mr. Seward is much better to-day, and in unusually good spirits even for him; mainly, I think, because he has succeeded in getting Mr. Corwin to agree to take the mission to Mexico instead of the mission to England. He has news from Richmond, and I understood him from Mr. Summers, that the prospect of defeating the secessionists in the Convention brightens all the time, and that Virginia, after disposing finally of the importunities of the Southern States, will take the initiative for a great National Convention. Of this he feels as confident as of the complete overthrow of the schemes of the fire-eaters by the quiet evacuation of Fort Sumter, which can not now be long delayed. He is very much pleased with the tone and bearing of the Southern Commissioners, he says, "as reported to him," and certainly nothing can be more reasonable or pacific than the disposition shown by these gentlemen so far. But I do not see that they offer any practicable solution—and I told Mr. Seward so—of the situation; nor, indeed, do I see why it should be expected they could do so. The difficulties are not difficulties of sentiment, but of fact. Mr. Seward intimates to me pretty clearly that he already finds Mr. Sumner making trouble for him in the Senate, and pressing him disagreeably in his own department.

He is annoyed too, I thought, at having to send Mr. Cassius M. Clay to Spain, and said with a good deal of sagacity that if he must give a mission to Kentucky he thought it a pity to "waste it on a Kentuckian he was sure of already."

MR. SEWARD AND THE CONFEDERATES

He is hopeful of the success of the Convention plan if we can but get the better of our own mischief-makers here, who are much more dangerous to us, he thinks—and I agree with him—than the people at Montgomery. Without precisely saying as much, he gave me very distinctly the impression that the intentions of the Administration to Fort Sumter have been made known at Montgomery, and have there produced a most beneficial effect. When I called his attention to the hostile and mischievous legislation going on there, he reminded me that the direction of the practical action of the seceded States just now rests with the Executive and not with the Legislature at Montgomery, and repeated several times his conviction that no one in the government there desired a collision more than he or I, which indeed I can readily believe.

I thought Mr. Seward seemed a little annoyed at the present attitude of Mr. Douglas; at all events, he showed an evident anxiety to lead me into expressing an opinion, which I positively declined to express, as to the efforts which Mr. Douglas has been persistently making to drive the Republican Senators into showing their hands, and which of course are not made in the interests of the Republican party. But he had nothing to say when I asked him why none of the Administration Senators were willing to speak for the Administration either one way or the other.

THE SILENCE OF THE REPUBLICAN LEADERS

March 15th.—The declaration made yesterday in the Senate, that the seats of Davis, Mallory, Clay, Toombs, and Benjamin are vacant, has envenomed matters a good deal, and the debate of to-day will make them worse. It is a pity Mr. Douglas should have lost his temper, but certainly nothing could have been more irritating than Mr. Fessenden. It was perfectly obvious that the two Republicans who did most of the speaking after Mr. Fessenden—Hale and Wilson— knew Mr. Douglas to be really uttering the sentiments and sketching the policy of the President, and were pretty nearly half willing to admit as much and attack the White House, but they had discretion and self-command enough to forbear, so that Mr. Douglas really threw away his time for the moment. When the news of the evacuation of Fort Sumter comes, though, it will be his turn, and we shall then see collisions which will bring out the innermost truth as to the political chart of the new Administration, and which must pretty certainly lead to the complete reorganization of our political parties, if indeed it stops there.

ACKNOWLEDGMENTS

As mentioned in chapter 1, I first read "The Diary of a Public Man" long ago, just as I was discovering how emphatically the voters in Virginia, North Carolina, and Tennessee had rejected secession in early 1861. Guided by the late David M. Potter's classic account, *Lincoln and His Party in the Secession Crisis,* I knew that the diarist understood important matters that had eluded most historians. But for me as for Potter, the diarist and his Diary remained a mystery. The pieces of the puzzle didn't fit together. You will find no reference to the Diary in my book *Reluctant Confederates: Upper South Unionists in the Secession Crisis.*

Several years ago, however, Ryan Christiansen, then an undergraduate at The College of New Jersey, enrolled in my seminar on the North-South sectional conflict and the coming of the Civil War. He wanted to wrestle with primary sources independently—and he decided to reassess "The Diary of a Public Man." His enthusiasm provided me with a memorable reminder of why teaching can be so much fun.

Christiansen worked both with me and with David Holmes, who teaches in the Mathematics and Statistics Department at The College of New Jersey. Holmes is an expert practitioner of "stylometry," the statistical analysis of literary style, a technique that has identified authors for a number of documents of previously doubtful provenance. Christiansen tracked down writing samples from all the possible candidates who might have written the Diary. He also was first to suspect that William Henry Hurlbert—someone whom we initially knew nothing about—would prove to be the diarist. Holmes and his statistically savvy assistants eventually delivered the verdict discussed in chapter 2. Hurlbert was indeed the most likely diarist—and Holmes has since performed additional stylometric calculations that provide even more decisive results. By the time this news reached us, Christiansen and I already had come to see Hurlbert as the key to the whole puzzle. We welcomed the stylometric findings and set out to learn more about the Diary.

Because parts of the Diary so clearly ring true, both Christiansen and I resisted the verdict arrived at over half a century ago by Frank Maloy Anderson—

in *The Mystery of "A Public Man": A Historical Detective Story*—that the Diary must have been in some respects manufactured. Dazzled by parts that seem authentic—indeed, that *are* authentic—we imagined that Hurlbert somehow had written a genuine diary. Christiansen moved on with his life, as undergraduates are wont to do. Not until I had the chance to get down to the Library of Congress and rummage through Anderson's voluminous papers did his basic frame of interpretation demand acceptance—the Diary was not a diary.

Anderson's pioneering scholarship offered a solid point of departure, but he didn't get it quite right. Having come to recognize that the document was not the actual diary that he long thought it was, he tended to view all its information with suspicion. He underestimated the extent to which the diarist knew what he was writing about. Anderson also selected the wrong diarist, albeit the closest friend of the real diarist. My goal here has been to provide an up-to-date review of the entire matter, taking care to weigh the Diary against what we now know about the secession crisis. But Anderson deserves a posthumous salute. His carefully preserved notes, assembled during decades of research, made it possible for me to develop my own understanding of the Diary.

Always hoping to find a smoking gun, I spent a couple of weeks in October 2005 convinced that Hurlbert and Ward had used the term "obelisk" as a code word for the Public Man project. To my surprise, the obelisk turned out to be— an obelisk. Several times since then I have walked through Central Park to admire this monument to the gods of ancient Egypt and to Hurlbert's historical sensibilities. It still startles me that one man could juggle both the obelisk and the Diary at precisely the same moment in his life—and while editing a major newspaper.

Had it not been for the insights and inspiration of Ryan Christiansen and the statistical expertise of David Holmes, this book would not likely have been written. I also owe a debt of gratitude to each of the following: Jeffrey M. Flannery, Manuscript Reference Specialist in the Manuscript Division at the Library of Congress, a true professional; Kathryn Jacob, Curator of Manuscripts at the Schlesinger Library, Radcliffe Institute, Harvard University, whose study of Sam Ward's career as a lobbyist has just been published; Jeffrey Lash, the biographer of Hurlbert's half-brother, Stephen Augustus Hurlbut (Lash was the bulldog who demanded that I give up my wrongheaded view about a genuine diary unless I could place Hurlbert in Washington, D.C., during the secession winter); John Rhodehamel and Olga Tsapina of the Huntington Library, who helped me obtain copies of important letters; Holly Kent, formerly my student at The College of New Jersey and now in the doctoral program in history at Lehigh University, whose command of many aspects of nineteenth-century American history already exceeds my own; and Elizabeth Maziarz, the interlibrary loan specialist at The College of New Jersey, who has enabled me to read many otherwise inaccessible sources. Five fellow historians have gone far beyond the call of duty to wade through and comment on drafts of this work-in-progress—Steven V. Ash, William W. Freehling, Nelson D. Lankford, Michael F. Holt, and most especially Russell McClintock. Again and again, they have challenged me to sharpen my argument, a task for which their own exemplary scholarship sets a high standard indeed. Students in three separate classes of my seminar at The College of New Jersey in 2007 and 2008 read versions of the manuscript and offered me many constructive suggestions. A professional writer, Ellen Goldstein, applied her talents to a penultimate draft. My editor at the Louisiana State University Press, Catherine L. Kadair, is the best in the business. Anne Bowly Maxfield, my remarkable mother-in-law, caught several glitches in the page proof.

Two sabbatical semesters at the old family farmhouse in Maine provided me with the ideal locale for writing an initial draft of this book. A spartan bachelor regimen has creative advantages, but life is more fun at Quaker Ridge when Betsy Crofts can join me there. Sometimes we are treated to visits from Anita Verna Crofts and Sarah Crofts—and Sarah's pussycat. Nobody, however, wants to hear more stories about William Henry Hurlbert.

The dedication honors two giants, John Karras and Tom Allsen, who have made the History Department at The College of New Jersey such a rewarding place to work and teach. Everyone who writes about the United States should share my good fortune in having colleagues with world-historical perspective.

Daniel W. Crofts
Southampton, Pennsylvania
June 28, 2009

INDEX